The Neoconservatives

The
Neocon

THE MEN WHO ARE

servatives

CHANGING AMERICA'S POLITICS

Peter Steinfels

A TOUCHSTONE BOOK
PUBLISHED BY SIMON AND SCHUSTER
NEW YORK

First Touchstone Edition, 1980
Published by Simon and Schuster
A Division of Gulf & Western Corporation
Simon & Schuster Building
Rockefeller Center
1230 Avenue of the Americas
New York, New York 10020

TOUCHSTONE and colophon are trademarks of Simon & Schuster

Manufactured in the United States of America

2 3 4 5 6 7 8 9 10
1 2 3 4 5 6 7 8 9 10 Pbk.

Library of Congress Cataloging in Publication Data

Steinfels, Peter.
   The neoconservatives.
   (A Touchstone book)

   Includes bibliographical references and index.
   1. Conservatism—United States.   I. Title.
[JA84.U5S74   1980]   320.5′2′0973   80-15672

ISBN 0-671-22665-7
ISBN 0-671-41384-8 Pbk.

Contents

For my parents

in admiration and gratitude

CHAPTER ONE

Introduction: The Significance of Neoconservatism

THE PREMISES OF THIS BOOK are simple. First, that a distinct and powerful political outlook has recently emerged in the United States. Second, that this outlook, preoccupied with certain aspects of American life and blind or complacent toward others, justifies a politics which, should it prevail, threatens to attenuate and diminish the promise of American democracy. Third, that this outlook has nonetheless produced telling critiques of contending political views and provocative analyses of specific political proposals; it has devoted its attention to fundamental questions its rivals have frequently overlooked; and it deserves, accordingly, a thoughtful, extensive, and careful evaluation.

Hundreds of books have been written on the political developments of the sixties, the civil rights movement, student radicalism, and the counterculture. Yet, oddly enough, that decade's most enduring legacy to American politics may be the outlook forged in reaction to sixties turbulence, an outlook fierce in its attachment to political and cultural moderation, committed to stability as the prerequisite for justice rather than the other way around, pessimistic about the possibilities for long-range, or even short-range, change in America, and imbued with a foreboding sense of our civilization's decline.

From Liberalism to Neoconservatism

It has not even been easy to settle upon a label for this outlook, in itself a sign of the unfamiliar constellation of attitudes it displays. By the beginning of 1976, the terms "neoconservative" or "new conservative" had gained a certain degree of currency; they were accepted good-humoredly by some adherents of the viewpoint, though not without protests that they still thought of themselves as traditional liberals. The very fact that they were good-humored in this protest was revealing. A few years ago they would have clung adamantly to their identification as liberals (as in fact other recipients of the neoconservative label continued to do). Now, "conservative" had lost its sting for them; they merely remarked that none of these nametags mattered very much. Neoconservative or not, they did protest that it was *they* who had held their political viewpoint constant while others had gone astray. "All about us canvas tore and cables parted," wrote Daniel Patrick Moynihan in nautical style—though, still the old sea dog, he admitted in another place that this constancy might also have involved a certain degree of change: "Correcting course in a storm is a way of staying the course."

The question of what is "new," if anything, about neoconservatism is not trivial. It bears on the manner in which this phenomenon is studied and discussed. By emphasizing their continuity with traditional liberalism, by suggesting that they are only being faithful to old struggles and eternal verities, the neoconservatives displace the burden of examination from their own ideas to those of the supposed innovators, their adversaries. On the other hand, many of the neoconservatives' critics are no more disposed to grant the newness of this outlook. For them it is just the same old conservatism; what is new is its advocacy by *these* spokesmen, most of them former liberals and even former socialists. Again the burden of examination is removed from the ideas, this time to be placed on the men themselves, on their renegade status, on their motivation for sliding to the Right.

It is my contention that the neoconservatives deserve both parts of their label. In the American context their distinctive role, both for good and for ill, is to be a conservative force. I say this in full awareness of their repeated proclamations of fidelity to liberalism. It is by now a commonplace that America is the liberal society *par excellence,* that we have worked out our history almost entirely within the framework of this one tradition, and that it is now so ingrained we hardly know how to think and talk, at least about public matters, outside of it. Peter Berger has recently added to these observations the corollary that "the contemporary American ideology of conservatism is deeply and unmistakably liberal in inspiration"; Berger predicts that in America "the politically practical options will all be within the ideological ambience of the liberal 'family.' " With all this I largely agree. Yet it should not be forgotten that liberalism itself contains important conservative elements. This is true not only in the United States, where liberalism had no feudal aristocracy to combat but was itself the ethos to be conserved. It was also true of the original liberal theorists and of their view of humanity.

Classical seventeenth- and eighteenth-century liberalism, Sheldon Wolin has reminded us,

> was a philosophy of sobriety, born in fear, nourished by disenchantment, and prone to believe that the human condition was and was likely to remain one of pain and anxiety. . . . We have become so accustomed to picturing liberalism as a fighting creed, outfitted for storming the ramparts of privilege, that we find it difficult to entertain the hypothesis that Lockian liberalism was fully as much a defense against radical democracy as an attack on traditionalism. In France and the United States as well, liberalism emerged as a post-revolutionary reaction.

It is this side of liberalism which the neoconservatives reemphasize. But that is not all they do. In some instances they go beyond the boundaries of liberalism, certainly to Burkean conservatism and sometimes even to socialism, in their critique of current reality—and of current liberalism. To be faithful to certain liberal values, they have discovered that liberalism itself does not suffice. It is the resulting admixture of themes, from liberal, conservative, and socialist traditions, that qualifies their view as both "conservative" and "new." Indeed one should not be surprised to see an American conservatism emerging from a liberal background; given our singularly liberal tradition, it is precisely that which vouches for the significance and rootedness of the new outlook.

Since neoconservatism is in many ways a product of the sixties, it might be useful to compare it with the other political metamorphoses of that decade. Sixties radicalism, at least among its wider following in the civil rights and antiwar movements, was an outgrowth of activity that was simply aimed at making a liberal society cease acting illiberally. It was only as the questions pressed—*why* does a liberal society act so illiberally? why is it so resistant to efforts to make it conform to its own principles?—that many people sought answers beyond the liberal framework. In parallel fashion, the neoconservatives, for their part, set out to defend liberalism from the radicals' attack. As they did so, however, they were faced with the question, why had a liberal society produced a wave of political criticism which they perceived (in many cases quite accurately) as so illiberal and destructive? Having begun as defenders of liberalism, they too ended, to some degree, as critics of it. That explains why, when the specific conflicts of the sixties had largely abated, political debate did not return to the *status quo ante*. Peter Berger is surely right in saying that politics in America will continue to be an affair within the liberal "family." Those unambiguously outside of that family, like the violent revolutionary Marxists or the Dadaist anarchists of the late sixties, will have no significant role in our politics. But families change over time; different branches drift apart. Practical politics may continue to be played out on that wide field called liberalism. But political thought is moving steadily in two directions. There are those, like democratic socialists, who feel they must reach beyond contemporary liberalism in order to fulfill its promises. And there are those, like the neoconservatives, who feel they must reach beyond contemporary liberalism to preserve its heritage.

A Party of Intellectuals

It is time to be more specific. Who, exactly, are the neoconservatives? They are, to begin with, a party of intellectuals. *Newsweek* magazine reports:

> In intellectual circles, the social thinkers who were once the driving force of Democratic liberalism—men like Arthur Schlesinger, Jr. and John Kenneth Galbraith—have been upstaged by a group of "neoconservative" academics, many of them refugees from the liberal left, including Daniel Bell, Nathan Glazer, Irving Kristol, James Q. Wilson, Edward Banfield, Seymour Martin Lipset and Sen. Daniel P. Moynihan of New York.

The geography of the intellectuals' world is a geography of journals, and *Newsweek* quite rightly links the neoconservatives with two journals that have distinguished themselves as vehicles for the new outlook.

Commentary, the monthly published by the American Jewish Committee, has been one of a handful of leading intellectual forums; until the rise of *The New York Review of Books*, probably no other journal of serious and extended discussion of politics and culture had as wide a readership. *The Public Interest*, on the other hand, is a relative newcomer, founded in 1965 and oriented toward the analysis of public issues in the "nonideological" perspectives of the social sciences.

By no means should every contributor to these journals be considered a neoconservative, but a core of regulars has, as Moynihan would say, set and stayed the course. Besides an editorial by Irving Kristol and Daniel Bell, the first issue of *The Public Interest* featured articles by Daniel Moynihan, Robert Nisbet, Martin Diamond, Bell, Robert M. Solow, Nathan Glazer, and several others. Ten years later, in the Bicentennial issue, one finds articles by Irving Kristol, Daniel Moynihan, Robert Nisbet, Martin Diamond, Daniel Bell, and Nathan Glazer. Also in the Bicentennial issue, which has something of a neoconservative convention about it, are Samuel P. Huntington, Aaron Wildavsky, Seymour Martin Lipset, and James Q. Wilson, a contributor since the second issue and now on the journal's Publication Committee. Robert M. Solow is also now a member of the Publication Committee. Many of the same writers appear in *Commentary,* whose editor, Norman Podhoretz, launched a frontal assault against the New Left, the counterculture, and all their pomps and works in the late sixties. One also finds there Milton Himmelfarb, Walter Laqueur, Midge Decter, Paul Seabury, Sidney Hook, Diana Trilling, Edward Shils, Peter Berger, Michael Novak, Bayard Rustin, and a group of younger political activists who have emerged from "Social Democrats, U.S.A.," the militantly anti-Communist rump of Norman Thomas's old Socialist Party. One might continue to rattle off names: Roger Starr, Edward C. Banfield, Peter Drucker, Ithiel de Sola Pool, Daniel Boorstin, Lewis S. Feuer, Arnold Beichman, Ben J. Wattenberg, and numerous other social scientists. Three outstanding scholars, recently dead, who could be justly associated with neoconservatism were Alexander Bickel, Richard Hofstadter, and Lionel Trilling. Of the list of "The Seventy Most Prestigious Contemporary American Intellectuals (1970)" that Charles Kadushin constructed in his book on *The American Intellectual Elite,* I would count about one out of every four as a neoconservative.

To describe the neoconservatives as, first, a party of intellectuals is to run the risk that among many Americans their significance would be immediately dismissed. Exactly the contrary ought to be the reaction. Alexis de Tocqueville, after noting the way that political theorists and not princes, ministers, and great lords had been the shapers of the events leading to the French Revolution, went on to note the lesson for other times:

> What political theory did here with such brilliance, is continually done everywhere, although more secretly and slowly. Among all civilized peoples, the study of politics creates, or at least gives shape to, general ideas; and from those general ideas are formed the problems in the midst of which politicians must struggle, and also the laws which they imagine they create.

> Political theories form a sort of intellectual atmosphere breathed by both governors and governed in society, and both unwittingly derive from it the principles of their action.

Today, if anything, rather than being done "more secretly and slowly," the process is done more openly and rapidly. Intellectuals serve as advisers to officeholders and political candidates, write speeches, propose programs, draft legislation, serve on special commissions. The mass media amplify their ideas to a wider public, though not without considerable distortion. In all this the intellectuals have two functions. As experts in particular fields relevant to public policy they work out the details of political measures. But as traffickers in society's symbols and values, as keepers of its memories, as orchestrators of its spectacles and images, and, in de Tocqueville's words, as political theorists and shapers of general ideas, intellectuals are *legitimators*. What will be the agenda of public concerns? Where will one set the outer limits of the "responsible" opinion to which busy decision-makers should attend? Will the credibility of this or that set of policies, or of the schools of thought behind them, be eroded or maintained—or will they be eliminated from serious consideration altogether? The dueling in intellectual journals, the rallying of like-minded thinkers at conferences or in new organizations, the shifts of power within disciplines are all elements in this process of legitimation. So, one might add, is the quality of scholarship and the cogency and eloquence of argument.

The precise paths by which this legitimation proceeds, the concrete ways in which an intellectual atmosphere is created, are intriguing to follow. Daniel Bell writes a book, and a syndicated columnist appropriates its theses for his Bicentennial musings. Irving Kristol derides a "new class" of liberal intellectuals for its snobbish attitude toward a business civilization, and Mobil Oil incorporates this idea in its public relations advertising. Alexander Bickel, Yale Law School professor, writes an article on the failure of school integration in the North, and a White House aide refers to it twice in a 1970 memo to Nixon arguing that "the second era of Re-Construction is over; the ship of integration is going down; it is not our ship . . . and we ought not to be aboard."

On questions like school integration and busing, courts are influenced not only by the reasoning in law journals but by extrapolations from sociological findings, which in turn are subject to the shifting moods in the social sciences. The idea that Great Society programs "failed" works its way from technical evaluation studies to debunking articles by scholar-consultants to politicians' speeches and pundits' columns.

The political mood may also promote changes in intellectual life, and these flow back to consolidate the new politics. The McCarthy era, for example, saw a nearly complete change in the scholars reviewing China studies for *The New York Times* and the New York *Herald Tribune.* At these two papers, the group who had done over 80 percent of the reviewing in this field between 1945 and 1950 reviewed not a single book after 1952.

Clearly questions of legitimation and creation of an intellectual atmosphere exist at different levels. There are short-run questions of getting a politician's ear or promoting a new departure in policy, as Daniel Moynihan attempted to do with the Family Assistance Plan, the proposal for substituting a guaranteed income for welfare that Moynihan "sold" to Richard Nixon. There are medium-run questions of national mood or prevailing attitudes over a range of issues—the Cold War in the fifties or the "rediscovery" of poverty in the sixties. Finally there are long-run questions of sensibility and moral principles—the change in attitude toward weakness and suffering which marked Victorian "earnestness" or the growing attachment to equality which de Tocqueville ranked as the fundamental characteristic of modernity. To ascribe the initiative in all such changes, small and large, to intellectuals would be silly; and virtually no one, except possibly intellectuals themselves, has been tempted to do so. But when people repeat that politics is the art of the possible, the temptation is quite in the other way, to forget the crucial role that thinkers and writers and artists have in defining, for practical men, just what is possible.

Links with Power

Yet it will not do justice to the special position of the neoconservatives to describe them simply as a party of intellectuals, as though that fact alone justified their claim to our attention. The neoconservatives are a *powerful* party of intellectuals. Their reputations are solid; they speak from the elite universities—Harvard, Berkeley, MIT, Chicago, Stanford. They are prolific: in 1975 and 1976, for example, Midge Decter excoriated *Liberal Parents, Radical Children;* James Q. Wilson blessed us with his *Thinking About Crime;* Robert A. Nisbet peered through the *Twilight of Authority;* Seymour Martin Lipset and Everett Carll Ladd, Jr., studied the politics of the professoriate in *The Divided Academy;* Nathan Glazer argued that affirmative action has become *Affirmative Discrimination;* Herman Kahn challenged the limits-of-growth pessimists in *The Next 200 Years,* and Daniel Bell pondered *The Cultural Contradictions of Capitalism.* This list, though it contains books seriously received, widely discussed, and consisting altogether of a remarkable *tour d'horizon* of America's problems, can barely suggest the currency of the neoconservatives' ideas. Many of these books, in fact, bring together material which was published not only in *Commentary* and *The Public Interest,* but in *The New York Times Sunday Magazine, Atlantic Monthly, Encounter, Change, Science,* and *Daedalus.*

Neoconservatives have frequently complained of a liberal "oppositionist" bias in the media. Their own position in the media, however, has never been weak, and now grows increasingly stronger. Besides *Commentary* and *The Public Interest,* they have long-lasting ties with *Encounter, The New Leader, American Scholar,* and *Foreign Policy.* They turn up in *TV Guide* as well as *Reader's Digest, Fortune, Business Week,* and *U.S. News & World Report.* At *Time* and *Newsweek,* neoconservatism often appears as the comfortable middle ground between these magazines' traditional conservatism and their liberal flirtation of the late sixties. Even supposed citadels of liberalism are open to neoconservatives. *New Republic* shares a number of writers—and attitudes, especially on foreign affairs—with *Commentary.* Neoconservative themes are sounded regularly in *Harper's Magazine,* by its editors as well as contributors; the same is true for *The Washington Monthly.* Journals like *New York Magazine* and *Esquire,* though symbols of a cultural trendiness neoconservatives profess to detest, often favor neoconservative attitudes on welfare, crime, and other "bread-and-butter" (or in these cases, wine-and-cheese) issues. *The New York Times* itself has a good sprinkling of neoconservatives among its editors, editorial-page writers, and critics: enough to temper that paper's continuing liberalism.

Perhaps the success of the neoconservatives in reaching wide audiences with their ideas is best exemplified by Daniel Moynihan. Moynihan did *not* publish a book in 1975 or 1976, being busy with other things. He did, however, edit one, *Ethnicity,* with Nathan Glazer; write introductions to several others; and get his views into print in such varied sources as *Commentary* and *The Public Interest* (to be sure), *Harper's, American Scholar, The New Leader, New York,* and the *New York Times* Op-Ed page. (In the past, Moynihan has published in magazines ranging from the American Institute of Architects' *AIA Journal* to *Psychology Today. The New Yorker* has been stigmatized as "radical chic" by neoconservatives for such deeds as publishing Charles Reich's *Greening of America;* yet it also serialized much of Moynihan's *The Politics of a Guaranteed Income.)* He was on the cover of *Time,* was profiled in national publications—and of course reached millions through the televised coverage of his dramatic role as Ambassador to the United Nations, campaigner with Henry Jackson, and candidate for U.S. Senator from New York.

Moynihan's case illustrates the fact that the neoconservatives' power does not rest simply on their access to the reading—or even the TV-watching—public. They have direct access to officeholders and the political elite generally. They enjoy dinners at the White House, their advice is both solicited and volunteered on government programs and campaign positions; though Henry Jackson was the neoconservative candidate in 1976, at least one of them, Zbigniew Brzezinski, signed on early as a Carter adviser on foreign policy. They hold seats on national commissions of various sorts, of which Brzezinski's Trilateral Commission is one example. This should not suggest a conspiracy; indeed it is a reflection on the state of our political order, and of the thinking about it, that one must recall that familiarity between officeholders and citizens is not altogether improper in a democracy. The neoconservatives are not *éminences grises*. People of different views have similar access. But many others, of course, most intellectuals included, do not. Though the power of the neoconservatives must finally rest on their ability to muster ideas and rationales, these efforts are much magnified by their direct contacts.

When President-elect Nixon was read the summary of a meeting of neoconservatives on the condition of New York City, a summary which took New York's problems as evidence that "the liberal state will no longer do" but "must, on pain of anarchy or civil war, be replaced," one can suppose that Daniel Moynihan's presence among Nixon's lieutenants had something to do with delivering this message. When Nixon, upon taking office, recommended to his cabinet a *Public Interest* article in which Peter Drucker asserted that modern government had proved itself incapable of doing anything effectively except waging war and inflating the currency, it obviously was not the case that Nixon just happened to be perusing *The Public Interest* one day and came across this interesting tidbit.

Connections with government circles are not the only advantages the neoconservatives enjoy. As former liberals and even graduates of New York socialism with its trade-union component, as Cold War militants who share the anti-Communist opinions of George Meany, they have maintained good relations, at least until recently, with major elements of the labor movement. At the same time, they have moved closer and closer to big business. Elizabeth Drew captured the complications of such a double set of relationships when she described a political dinner honoring "Scoop" Jackson. Seated there were Daniel Moynihan, union leaders Albert Shanker, David Dubinsky, Sol Chaikin, A. Philip Randolph, and publicists Norman Podhoretz and Bayard Rustin.

This gathering is symbolic of the intellectual and political confusion currently surrounding the idea of liberalism. The people in this room are bound together by old ties and new reactions—old fights for social justice, and new reactions against the events of the sixties, culminating in the Democratic Party's nomination of George McGovern in 1972. They are reacting (in different ways) to what they see as the liberal excesses of the sixties. They are bound together by reactions against what they see (in different ways) as too much government intervention, too many demands by blacks, too little appreciation of the battles they have fought, too little militance against Communism. They are reacting against social and political changes symbolized by "the kids" and their sympathizers of the late sixties, against practitioners of the "new politics," who push, as they see it, exotic political notions and issues, and who also changed the rules, and, of all things—at least temporarily—took over the Democratic Party. And so ex-radicals, ex-Socialists, old liberals, new conservatives, exemplified by the group in this room tonight, have banded together in search of new and common ground. At times they find common ground, at times they are separated by great gulfs. They are on common ground in their anti-Communism: the intellectuals in their writing and the labor leaders in their political action are for strong defense policies and for anti-Soviet policies. . . . They are on common ground against what they see as the spoiled children and their indulgent elders of the late sixties and early seventies—against exoticism. They are on common ground in their belief that blacks have gone too far. And they are on common ground in their shared feeling of having been kicked in the teeth. But while the intellectuals set about building a body of literature about the supposed failures of the Great Society social programs and the dangers of big government, the labor unions push for more social programs and big government (as long as the programs do not help blacks and the poor at the expense of the middle class). George Meany probably favors the sort of government regulations that would drive Irving Kristol into a frenzy on the editorial page of *The Wall Street Journal.*

The link between neoconservative and big business has now gone far beyond Kristol's contributions to *The Wall Street Journal* or *Fortune* (where a former managing editor at *The Public Interest,* Paul H. Weaver, has served as associate editor). The pro-business concern of neoconservatism was originally muted; what distinguished it from existing conservatism was a positive stance toward the New Deal and a "practical" attitude toward government intervention in the economy. Yet neoconservatism's quarrel with a liberal intelligentsia persistently critical of commercial civilization and big business power has set in operation the old law "the enemy of my enemy is my friend." Neoconservatism has become outrightly protective of business interests. Needless to say, business, long unhappy about the relative lack of ideological support it receives from the academy, has welcomed the neoconservatives enthusiastically.

Much of this pro-business effort has been launched from a nonprofit "think tank"—oddly enough, since both business and neoconservatives have often been derisive of the burgeoning world of nonprofit research and government contracts. In fact neoconservatism has strong roots in this multimillion-dollar, extremely industrial segment of the "knowledge industry." The ties were often with foreign-policy and defense-related organizations, both "do-good" agencies like Freedom House and think tanks like Rand and the Hudson Institute. Leading neoconservatives like Kristol, Bellow, Shils, and Bell were also found performing at Aspen Institute conferences or doing papers for smaller outfits like the Institute for Contemporary Studies in San Francisco, the Heritage Foundation, or the Georgetown Center for Strategic and International Studies. For a short while, Aaron Wildavsky was chosen to head the prestigious Russell Sage Foundation.

More recently a major neoconservative base has emerged in the American Enterprise Institute. Originally a right-wing exponent of unreconstructed free enterprise, the AEI had little influence in wider circles until the early seventies when its leadership developed a shrewder understanding of intellectual politics in America. By involving prestigious academics of centrist to mildly liberal views in research and discussion with the AEI's more traditionally conservative spokesmen, the organization was gradually brought out of isolation. The institute's numerous productions, liberally funded and distributed to the press, gained credibility in the centrist-to-mildly-liberal academic community while the center of gravity in policy debates was, in fact, shifted to the right. For this purpose, the neoconservatives were perfect. James Q. Wilson and Robert A. Nisbet joined free-enterprise conservatives like Milton Friedman, Paul W. McCracken, and G. Warren Nutter on the AEI's Council of Academic Advisers. Irving Kristol became a Resident Scholar at AEI, as later did Michael Novak, Walter Berns, and Ronald S. Berman, along with conservative lights and Nixon appointees like Arthur A. Burns. Seymour Martin Lipset, Richard Scammon, Edward Banfield, Ben Wattenberg, Peter Berger, and Nathan Glazer were recruited for AEI projects. The AEI Bicentennial Distinguished Lecture Series featured, among others, Kristol, Martin Diamond, Nisbet, Berger, Daniel J. Boorstin, Banfield, Berman, and Lipset. The institute established a Center for the Study of Government Regulation with an advisory council including Kristol, Wilson, Paul Weaver, and Aaron Wildavsky. The center in turn publishes *Regulation,* a journal of information useful to business and government officials dealing with regulation, mixed with the AEI's ideological interpretation. AEI also publishes *Public Opinion,* another subtle mix, this time of ideology and polling results, edited by Lipset and Wattenberg.

In addition, the institute distributes a wide range of conference transcripts, audio and video cassettes of its forums, and specialized policy studies.

A Broad and Lasting Influence

Strategically installed in the marketplace of ideas, well connected with political, labor, and business leaders, the neoconservatives are clearly a group to be reckoned with. But it would be a serious underestimation to think of them as merely a successful lobby. The supposition that their influence will be both broad and lasting rests on several further facts.

First, the questions the neoconservatives have addressed are fundamental ones, and ones which do not promise to be resolved in the near future. These questions all swirl about the condition of our culture, meaning by that term both the general climate of belief and sensibility and the more conscious perceptions of writers, artists, philosophers, and scientists which so often act as weathervanes for the future. How can moral principles be grounded, and ultimately social institutions be legitimated, in the absence of a religiously based culture? What has been the impact on our beliefs and sensibilities of the huge increase of people exposed to some amount of higher education? What is the impact of the growth of the "knowledge industry"—that complex of media, government, university, and foundations which now manufactures, processes, packages, and distributes so much of what passes for information? Does affluence undermine virtue? Are inequality and self-aggrandizement essential to material or even spiritual progress? Some of these questions are old, some spring from recent developments—all of them have been acknowledged, yes, but still kept at arm's length by contemporary liberalism, partly because it senses that the answers may be either unduly conservative or unduly radical, partly because a strong current in liberalism has always regarded consideration of basic questions as a futile or unprofitable exercise.

Second, the answers the neoconservatives provide are congenial to powerful forces, probably *the* powerful forces, in American life. By and large the demands for change that the neoconservatives make of our major institutions are slight and tactical. If these institutions are losing their legitimacy, this loss, the neoconservatives assert, is largely undeserved. Responsibility lies elsewhere. It does not logically follow that these conclusions are untrue, simply because they happen to be convenient. It does follow, as a practical matter, that these conclusions are going to be appreciated by many who are capable of transforming their appreciation into material support. Talent is always a scarce resource, and neoconservatives have discovered the advantages of an old-fashioned means to deal with scarcity—money. Nelson Rockefeller's late Commission on Critical Choices provided Irving Kristol and Paul H. Weaver with $100,000 to obtain on short order fifteen essays analyzing "the ideas and values of human nature inherent in U.S. institutions." A recent collection of essays on the "new class" offered contributors up to $4,000 for thirty to forty pages of their thoughts. Most contributors in both cases were neoconservatives. As one scholar, accustomed to receiving fees of $75 to $300 from liberal journals or $300 to $800 for campus speaking engagements, remarked of this windfall, "It certainly clears one's calendar and concentrates the mind." Neoconservatism will not wither for want of well-heeled patrons.

Third, the work of the neoconservatives, taken as a whole, and measured against any other comparable body of contemporary American political analysis, is of a high quality. They are literate, for one thing. They marshal evidence as well as emotion. They make some effort to search out principles and relate specific problems to general ideas. They are also, I grant, selective in their concerns and in their facts, occasionally pompous, more than occasionally narrow; one can find among them an undeniable amount of opportunism and self-promotion. These are sins, however, hardly limited to neoconservatives. One can disagree fundamentally and vigorously with them; one cannot simply dismiss them except by applying some standard of quality that is applied nowhere else in American political discourse. To dismiss them, furthermore, without confronting their arguments in detail would be a mistake for their critics. It would be to mirror what is in fact one of the neoconservatives' own major faults, their tendency to treat their adversaries as feebleminded or dubiously motivated, or to admit into the circle of "honorable" opponents only those who share their style or pass some ideological Wassermann test of "pro-Americanism."

In our time the classic statement of the benefits to be secured in taking one's political adversaries seriously—and in having political adversaries worthy of being taken seriously in the first place—is found in Lionel Trilling's preface to *The Liberal Imagination*. Trilling begins with the observation that has since become the commonplace we already noted: "In the United States at this time liberalism is not only the dominant but even the sole intellectual tradition." Such a situation poses two dangers. First, the absence of conservative or reactionary ideas "does not mean, of course, that there is no impulse to conservatism or to reaction." It simply means that such impulses do not "express themselves in ideas but only in action or in irritable mental gestures which seek to resemble ideas." They may do worse, for "it is just when a movement despairs of having ideas that it turns to force."

Second, says Trilling, this situation "is not conducive to the real strength of liberalism," and he turns for precedent to the concluding argument of John Stuart Mill's great essay on Coleridge: "Mill, at odds with Coleridge all down the intellectual and political line, nevertheless urged all liberals to become acquainted with this powerful conservative mind." Mill had written that the prayer of every true reformer should be " 'Lord, enlighten thou our enemies . . .'; sharpen their wits, give acuteness to their perception, and consecutiveness and clearness to their reasoning powers. We are in danger from their folly, not from their wisdom: their weakness is what fills us with apprehension, not their strength." According to Trilling, what Mill welcomed was "the intellectual pressure which an opponent like Coleridge could exert," forcing reformers to "examine their position for its weaknesses and complacencies."

That is not quite complete, since it is clear from the immediate context of Mill's remarks that he is also making something resembling Trilling's previous point. There *will be* conservatives, Mill concludes ("the great mass of the owners of large property, and of all the classes intimately connected with the owners of large property"); therefore "to suppose that so mighty a body can be without immense influence in the commonwealth, or to lay plans for effecting great changes, either spiritual or temporal, in which they are left out of the question, would be the height of absurdity." That these conservatives be reasoning ones rather than unreasoning is better for the reformers, who in contending with them repair the deficiencies in their own thinking, and better for the commonwealth, in which conservatives are destined to have a large influence anyway.

It was Trilling's opinion that, lacking the intellectual abrasion an intelligent conservatism could provide, liberalism would have to supply it for itself. Since Trilling himself became one of the wellsprings for neoconservative thought, one could ask whether in the end he had not done his work so well that he became the very thing he set out to substitute for—which leads us back to the question of who changed and who remained constant. In any case, in the quarter-century since *The Liberal Imagination* appeared, Trilling's wish for an intelligent conservatism that expressed itself in ideas rather than "irritable mental gestures" has often been repeated. It has recently been recalled in regard to the neoconservatives. Joseph Epstein begins one of the most acute evaluations of the new outlook by noting that it is "a conservatism more purely intellectual, and hence more formidable, than any in recent decades. The names associated with it are reputable, belonging mostly to men of solid achievement in the social sciences or intellectual journalism, many of them having themselves once been figures of impeccable liberal or radical standing." Epstein concludes with the inevitable query: "Could this be the serious conservatism America has so long lacked?"

Epstein never does answer his question. He notes that, thanks to the excesses of the New Left, conservatism has finally achieved "a sort of serious standing . . . as an intellectual force in American life," and that this new conservatism would "loom large in the politics of the 1970s." But is this standing earned, or is it only a sorry reflection on the state of American politics and intellectual life? From Epstein's telling critique of leading neoconservatives, as well as from his title, "The New Conservatives: Intellectuals in Retreat," one might gather that the latter is the case.

A Serious American Conservatism

Let me not hedge my bet. I believe that neoconservatism *is* the serious and intelligent conservatism America has lacked, and whose absence has been roundly lamented by the American Left. Much depends, obviously, on what one means by "serious" or "intelligent"; if one conjures up Plato, Hobbes, Madison, Mill, or Marx, then the neoconservatives are going to look pale and petty. So will everyone else. A political tendency has to be judged by a lower standard: It must be allowed its range of thinkers, its inconsistencies, its occupational hazards, its distinctive failings. It will not do, for instance, to point out that neoconservatives contradict one another on some important issues, like the desirability of strong central government. This is true, to be sure, and worth exploring—worth exploring, also, why these differences are so little noticed and so little discussed among them. But such disagreements neither demonstrate that neoconservatism does not exist as an identifiable tendency, nor disqualify it as a serious one. All tendencies of any political significance will have their internal disagreements; such diversity may be evidence of strength rather than weakness. Overall, neoconservatism displays a remarkably unified thrust in its arguments. Nor will it do to point out that neoconservatives are consistently benign in their interpretation of the performance of established institutions, or that they are suspicious of all but the most gentle democratic and egalitarian impulses. What else does one expect? These are criticisms that can, and should, be brought against conservatism generally—they are its natural frailties—but they do not in themselves demonstrate that a given body of thinkers are not able representatives of the doctrine.

There are two ways of testing the proposition that the neoconservatives represent the long-awaited American conservatism. The first way looks to the nature of the ideas they espouse. One might begin, for example, with the arguments that were brought against previous thinkers laying claim to the conservative banner. In 1954 and 1962, Peter Viereck wrote two essays in an attempt to distinguish what he envisioned as a genuine American conservatism from the right-wing deformations associated with Senator Joseph McCarthy and from the aristocratic and integralist deformations appearing in the orbit of William F. Buckley's *National Review*. In contrast to the demagoguery of McCarthyism, wrote Viereck in 1954, a true American conservatism would revive established ways, seek to relax tensions, exhibit reverence for the Constitution and all its amendments, pursue an orderly gradualism, protect government officials from "outside mob pressure," and foster "respect—to the point of stuffiness—for time-honored authority and for venerable dignitaries." These qualities, Viereck admitted, "are the stodgier virtues. They are not invariably a good thing. All I am saying is that these happen to be the qualities of conservative rule. . . ." He added: "Ahead potentially lies an American synthesis of Mill with Burke, of liberal free dissent with conservative roots in historical continuity."

Viereck's second essay, written in 1962, was more sophisticated. His objection to the new conservatism of that time was "its rootless nostalgia for roots." The southern agrarians of the thirties had appealed to a past that never was; some of the newer conservatives did worse, importing from Europe ideologists totally at odds with native American liberalism. The genuine conservative, argued Viereck, "conserves the roots that are *really there*," and in America's case that meant the liberal-conservative heritage of Locke, of the Constitutional Convention of 1787, and of *The Federalist*. The American conservative may lean toward Washington, John Adams, and Calhoun, rather than Jefferson, Paine, and Andrew Jackson; but he does not deny the latter. He is anti-Communist but not opposed to many of the economic reforms of the New Deal (which Viereck saw as a Burkean bulwark against socialism). He may even hail the trade unions as a builder of Coleridgian "organic unity" and as counters to that atomization of society which links *laissez-faire* capitalism and authoritarian statism.

The need for conservative continuity with America's institutionalized liberal past does not mean identity with liberalism, least of all with optimism about human nature, or utilitarian overemphasis on material progress, or trust in the direct democracy of the masses. Instead, conservative continuity with our liberal past simply means that you cannot escape from history; history has provided America with a shared liberal-conservative base more liberal than European Continental conservatives, more conservative than European Continental liberals.

From "this shared liberal-conservative base," says Viereck, ". . . grows the core of the New Deal and of the Kennedy program, as opposed to the inorganic, mechanical abstractions of either a Karl Marx or an Adam Smith." That remark may be fair to neither Marx nor Smith; it certainly reveals the degree to which Viereck's genuine American conservatism fades into what others consider mainstream liberalism. His essays, it is worth recalling, appeared in the original and revised editions of the volume on the American Right edited by Daniel Bell and featuring articles by several later neoconservatives, Hofstadter, Glazer, Lipset, and Bell himself.

Viereck was a declared conservative. For a view of the same problem from another political perspective, we can turn to a more recent article by Sheldon Wolin, reviewing two books by neoconservatives. "Why has it been so difficult for theorists to develop a theory of American conservatism?" he asks. Wolin, like Viereck, touches base with Louis Hartz's argument that Lockian liberalism was the basis of the American consensus. "As a result," Wolin continues, "American conservatism was drawn to the defense of liberal principles and practices. While this confluence of liberals and conservatives produced a 'mainstream' of American politics, it left conservatism in something like a permanent identity crisis, without a distinctive idiom or vision." Conservatives identified with the propertied classes and, in Alexander Hamilton's disabused view, with the manufacturers. But "the natural allies of conservatism proved a perpetual source of embarrassment." The property holder became the innovator, "the tireless engineer of change, the creator of urban, technological America, the wizard who persuaded his countrymen that corporations were legal 'persons,' entitled to the same protections as individual property but not to the same liabilities." The growth of corporate power led to the growth of government power; both grew "while the old adversary relationship of the trust-busting era gradually eased into a fitful marriage."

Wolin sums up the situation in three powerful paragraphs:

> The progress of power in America has had a special piquancy for the conservative. While conservative politicians composed hymnals to individualism, localism, Sunday piety, and homespun virtues, conservative bankers, businessmen, and corporate executives were busy devitalizing many local centers of power and authority, from the small business and family farm to the towns and cities. They created the imperatives of technological change and mass production which have transformed the attitudes, skills, and values

of the worker; and erased most peculiarities of place, of settled personal and family identity; and made men and women live by an abstract time that is unrelated to personal experience or local customs.

The one living tradition nurtured by the groups and classes which form the power base of conservatism is a peculiarly modern tradition of rationality. It conceives the world as a domain to be rationalized into orderly processes which will produce desired results according to a calculus of efficiency. Its mode of action is 'rational decision-making'; its ethic is enshrined in cost-benefit analysis; its politics is administration. The romantic conservative, who yearns for Georgian manors, Gothic gardens, and Chartresque piety, has need of a special insensibility if he is to plead for a *status quo* so devoid of sentiment, tradition, and mystery or to ally himself with those whose profession requires that the world be objectified and abstracted of its human and historical idiosyncrasies before the decision-makers can make sense of it.

A traditionless society that conserves nothing; ruling groups that are committed to continuous innovation; social norms that stigmatize those who fail to improve their status; incentives that require that those who move up must move away: such a society presents a formidable challenge to the conservative imagination. Although it is possible to identify particular American writers as conservative in outlook—A. Lawrence Lowell, Randolph Bourne, Irving Babbitt, Santayana, Faulkner—no distinctively conservative idiom has appeared, no powerful theory that could analyze and explain the corporate and technological society which emerged in the twentieth century, no conception of a praxis connecting politics with the values symbolic of a conservative view of society.

In describing the difficulties faced by an American conservatism, Wolin, like Viereck, suggests the agenda such a conservatism would assign itself, though unlike Viereck he may not mean to do so. To make my point (and it is mine, I should stress, not his), I would have to emphasize certain of his words and modify others. First, it is noteworthy that he speaks of the modern concept of rationality, with its calculus of efficiency and its preoccupation with administration and modes of decision-making, as a "*living* tradition." Second, he exaggerates in speaking of "a traditionless society that conserves nothing" and "ruling groups that are committed to continuous innovation." Not quite "traditionless"; there is at least that "living tradition" of rationality; and in fact there is a good deal more. This society may conserve far less than it should, but "nothing" is surely an overstatement. Nor are the ruling groups purely and simply committed to innovation; they entertain at least some attachment to the past. Even with these modifications, Wolin is certainly right in saying that American society "presents a formidable challenge to the conservative imagination." Formidable, yes, but perhaps not, as he implies, impossible. Such a conservatism would have to embrace and defend the "living tradition" of modern rationality and argue that this tradition, possibly limited by gradualism (invoke Burke) and intermediate institutions (invoke de Tocqueville), actually promises to protect what has been conserved in America, for instance the "liberal principles and practices" Wolin mentioned earlier. Surely this would not be a conservatism of those yearning for Georgian manors and Chartresque piety but it might be a conservatism of those enamored simultaneously of Victorian cadences, cost-benefit analysis, and the *Statistical Abstract of the United States*. Several writers for *The Public Interest* come to mind.

From Viereck and Wolin, one can derive a rough notion of what a genuine American conservatism might look like. However confusing to those who would take Sir W. S. Gilbert as the final authority on political categories, an American conservatism would be devoted to liberalism—but a liberalism of the harder, more fearful sort. Pessimistic about human nature, skeptical about the outcome of political innovation, distrustful of direct democracy (the "mob"), it would defend the principles and practices of liberalism less as vehicles for betterment than as bulwarks against folly. Where even conservative liberals like the Federalists were bold about creating new institutions, defying tradition if necessary and constructing a new constitution, today's American conservatives, identifying "revolution" with 1793 or 1917 rather than 1776, would add to the limiting structures of liberalism Burke's advocacy of gradual change and historical continuity. They would not try to turn back the clock on the New Deal but welcome its stabilizing and by now thoroughly established alterations of American life. They would also accept the modern corporation-dominated economy. Functional rationality, economic efficiency, and the concomitant economic growth an American conservatism would hold as necessary to the resolution of conflicts and the maintenance of stability. Yet recognizing the destabilizing effects of these very forces, it would counter them by the restraining influence of private life—above all, the family—and intermediate institutions—labor unions, churches, neighborhoods, universities. To prevent these from being infected by the individualistic and acquisitive dynamic of the economy would require a constant surveillance and supervision. This should be the work of the culture and of the intellectuals. The very harshness of modern instrumental rationality, Weber's "disenchantment" of the world, which erodes "sentiment, tradition, and mystery," must itself be transformed into a source of respect and authority, its demands surrounded with a religious aura of tragedy and sacrifice—a secular Protestant Ethic whose reward for most citizens would be the exercise of a moderate liberty, the enjoyment of a hard-won though uncertain comfort, and the avoidance of the sad fate, kept prominently displayed, of nations which have given themselves over to utopian fevers.

Is this program, especially in its latter aspects, viable? Like Wolin, I have my doubts. Like him, I believe it is cramped, less than we are capable of, a withering of America's possibilities. But it is plausible. It corresponds, as the agrarian or aristocratic or integralist visions did not, to the realities of America's past and present. It is both serious and American. And of course it is recognizable as the general outlook of the neoconservatives.

If the nature of the ideas espoused by a group is the first test of that group's seriousness, the manner in which they are espoused is the second. Numerous radical notions of the last decade were painfully pertinent to the American scene, and yet were advanced in a manner that was slipshod, illogical, undocumented, exaggerated, even brutal—in sum, in a manner that abused both the ideas themselves and political debate generally. Judgments about these things are subjective. Clearly it is hard to separate one's opinion of the ideas themselves from one's opinion of the manner in which they are argued. By no means have all radical points been presented in the way just described, and yet it has not been unusual to hear careful work dismissed as "conspiracy theory" or "vulgar Marxism." People who should know better refer contemptuously to revisionist history of the Cold War, for example, despite the fact that revisionists have done the lion's share of solid research and original thinking. The revisionists may not be right in their interpretation of the Cold War: nothing can be more certain than the further shifts of historical evaluation. But to have derided their scholarship was, in effect, to announce the principle that any conclusions which do not agree with one's own must *ipso facto* be based on shoddy work.

The neoconservatives, too, have suffered from this attitude. Because they have been skeptical of government welfare services, because they have argued that efforts to achieve racial equality took a self-destructive turn in the mid-sixties, they have been characterized as anti-poor and anti-black; and their arguments dismissed as essentially those of the guy down the street griping about cheats on welfare and the blacks getting everything served to them on a silver platter. If nine out of ten people who admire Daniel Moynihan do so for the wrong reasons—what *Time* greeted as his "fighting Irishman" image and his "dukes-up diplomacy"—nine out of ten people who vehemently denounce Moynihan for his views on the Negro family, the poverty program, and welfare are incapable of assembling even a faint approximation of what those views actually are.

Of course, rebutting unfair disparagement is not quite the same thing as demonstrating, in a positive sense, the quality of the neoconservative *oeuvre*. It is true that *The Public Interest* is a journal of relatively narrow range: it concentrates on public-policy issues, straying afield to general cultural matters only when the political connection is direct and close; it is written almost entirely by political scientists, economists, sociologists, and individuals engaged in or teaching public administration. *Commentary* concerns itself with all that *The Public Interest* does not; it publishes fiction as well as criticism of books, drama, art, and so on. But *Commentary* suffers from a narrowness of a different sort. Ever since its editor, Norman Podhoretz, embarked on his scorched-earth campaign against the New Left and counterculture, his monthly has grown much more predictable. To establish *Commentary*'s position on any topic, went the formula, locate the New Left or counterculture position (or imagine one, these enterprises having been out of business for some years now), turn 180 degrees, and march off in the opposite direction. The operation borders on the ludicrous when Podhoretz sends out skirmishers to do in, for instance, counterculture disrespect for competitive sports or to flush out a threat to the Republic lurking unrecognized in E. L. Doctorow's *Ragtime.*

For all that, *Commentary*'s main battle pieces are often spectacular—frontal assaults, verbal rocketry, a matchless sense of the adversary's weakest points. *The Public Interest,* within its special range, is even better. Its first issue noted that "the ideological essay, as a literary form, tends to be more 'interesting'—it always *seems* to go deeper, point further, aspire higher." But since not all social problems are amenable to that kind of treatment, some being rather plodding affairs, the editors promised that while trying "to make *The Public Interest* as lively, as readable, and as controversial as possible, we nevertheless are determined to make room for the occasional 'dull' articles. . . ." In fact, they have more than occasionally transformed what had every likelihood of being a dull article into a fascinating one. The specialty of the house is the blending of personal tone, general principles (ideology, if you will, which they won't), and evidence, often quantitative and drawn from social-science research, government reports, or census data, into a literate and persuasive essay.

Neoconservatism has yet to plumb any depths; it swims just below the surface of current events, but there it swims very well indeed. As often as I find myself infuriated by a particular argument or distressed by the cumulative effect of its admonitions, I am challenged and provoked by its arguments and seldom find that I can pass through a major neoconservative essay without having learned something that transcends this month's news. That cannot be said about much political writing.

Beyond Personalities and Motives

In the past year or so, the full power, if not the full seriousness, of neoconservatism has been acknowledged. The newsweeklies have made the necessary introductions. The Right crows that "Great Society liberalism is on the run. . . . Neo-conservative ideas, nurtured in newer think tanks, and debated on editorial pages, have seized the intellectual and political momentum." The Left pays a worried attention. Why did it take so long, however, for this recognition? Why, even today, do the critics of neoconservatism often refuse to take these ideas seriously?

The first reason is that neoconservatism was long viewed in terms of personalities. When note was taken in 1970 and 1971 of the growing antagonism between *Commentary* and *The New York Review of Books,* this was translated into a personal vendetta among Manhattan literati, even into a simple falling-out between Norman Podhoretz and Jason Epstein, former friends who were leading figures on the two magazines. When Daniel Moynihan gained headlines at the United Nations, he did his best to make clear that he spoke for a new school of thought. Yet Moynihan's intriguing personality, rendered more intriguing by speculation about his political future, served as a lightning rod this time. A sharp attack by Frances FitzGerald on the neoconservatives was subtitled "a philippic against Daniel P. Moynihan and the augurs on the Right." It was still political personalities more than political ideas which captured the media's attention.

The second factor clouding most discussions of neoconservatism is related to the first, except that it continues to operate today, long after the movement's influence has been admitted. This is the emphasis on motivation. Both neoconservatives and liberals have branded each other as renegades. Neoconservatives believe that liberals have abandoned their principles for the elixir of Youth and Revolution; liberals think that neoconservatives have become apologists for their own newly acquired privileges. There is probably no emotion as destructive of political analysis as the sense of betrayal. Political opponents are honorable men; former allies are something else. Anger clouds judgment; embitterment destroys reflection. Convinced that there was previously a secret motion behind the other party's display of loyalties, one tends not to principles but to motives.

A young black writer on the Op-Ed page of *The New York Times* provides a characteristic reaction in denouncing "the retreat of the liberal sages."

> The root of their retreat from magnanimity lies, I think, in the position in which these men—the others are Daniel Bell, Samuel P. Huntington, Seymour Martin Lipset, Robert Nisbet, Norman Podhoretz [the writer has already referred to Kristol, Glazer, and Moynihan]—found themselves as the Vietnam War was ending. The young had mobilized politics, the minorities now rudely insisted on speaking for themselves and the true conservatives ignored them. It was a kind of purgatory that has silenced less resilient men. . . . Soon, however, they found the pulley to power. And not for the last time, and certainly not for the last group, they used, cynically, "the Negro question." . . . The neo-conservatives had found their cause. They hurried to pull out their quills to denounce quotas as un-American, to "prove" that busing did not help black children, to argue that extra money spent on educating the children of the poor was no guarantee of their future success . . . And as they drone on into oscitancy about the dangers of the "New Equality," they will find that the noble tradition that they readily bartered away for power and pottage was worth more than a grudging invitation to William Buckley's *pied-à-terre*.

Now this, however understandable the frustration behind it, is unfair. Most of the neoconservatives named did not, in fact, concern themselves centrally with the "Negro question"; and of those that did, there is simply no evidence to show it was a cynical ploy for power. Not fair but, more important, not helpful. Who can deny that motivation and personality are crucial in politics—perhaps more crucial than principle? Unfortunately it is very difficult to plumb the recesses of the human character. We may have to do it when we grant someone power, when we evaluate a Moynihan as a prospective officeholder, for example. All the obscure ingredients of character make a difference then; he will represent us in the future on questions which cannot now be examined. But when we judge him as a thinker, these strengths, frailties, and quirks are secondary; it seems wiser to stick closely to what the individual has actually said or written. The neoconservatives' arguments about quotas, busing, or remedial education can be examined on their own merits. They may be preposterous, even if motivated by the deepest commitment to civil rights. They may be perceptive, even if motivated by the desire to avenge some adolescent injury or, worse yet, have a drink with William Buckley.

I willingly grant the subjective element in all this. Coming across an egregious example of polemical meanness, plasterboard scholarship, or selective tough-mindedness, I wonder whether I have not been led to take the neoconservatives so seriously by the very seriousness with which they obviously take themselves. But on which side is it wiser to err? Critics, in particular, might heed some lines from *Henry V:*

> In cases of defense 'tis best to weigh
> The enemy more mighty than he seems.

I myself find fortification in Mill: "And even if we were wrong in this, and a Conservative philosophy were an absurdity, it is well calculated to drive out a hundred absurdities worse than itself."

CHAPTER TWO

The Road to Neoconservatism

NEOCONSERVATISM CANNOT be understood apart from its history. One might say that of any intellectual or political movement, but especially is it true of an outlook that insists on its fidelity to constant principles and defines itself against the flux it perceives among liberals. In the editorial statement introducing the initial issue of *The Public Interest,* Daniel Bell and Irving Kristol replied to the charge that they were publishing "a middle-aged magazine for middle-aged readers." It was not, after all, a bad description: compared to the naive young or the nostalgic old, they wrote, "middle-aged people, seasoned by life but still open to the future, do seem to us—in our middle years—to be the best of all political generations." What was the seasoning that life had given this generation?

Socialism and the Anti-Totalitarian Impulse

There is no problem in terming the neoconservatives a generation. Almost all of them were born in the 1920s or shortly before or after. It is harder to define the generation they belong to. Should it be identified with the thirties, a time when some of them, but not all, made their precocious debut in politics? Should it be identified with the fifties, when most of them came into their own as scholars or writers? The very different, even contradictory, images conjured up by those two decades, the thirties and fifties, the Red Decade and the Age of Apathy—the one of desperate radical activism, the other of satisfied quietism—suggest the problem. Yet if one is less spellbound by the labels of these decades and looks to the common concern which tied them together, the issue which defines this group as a generation stands out. The political reality that loomed over those years, and that provided the formative political experience for these men, was the rise of totalitarianism and the failure of socialism in the face of that threat. This experience was to determine their attitudes and give all their later work its moral impetus. Here is the *mystique* behind all their later *politique*. Whatever one may think of the latter—after all, Péguy invented the distinction to describe the degeneration of a moral impulse he had shared—the neoconservatives cannot be understood without an appreciation of the former.

The rise of totalitarianism and the failure of socialism—for many Americans the two events were not as inextricably linked as they were for many of the neoconservatives. Many of them were, of course, Jews, coming to age in a decade that saw fascism triumph and Nazi power swell till it exploded in world war and the Holocaust. They were also socialists, growing up in a milieu in which political hopes were assumed to be bound up with socialism. Alfred Kazin has described that milieu in *Starting Out in the Thirties:*

> "Socialism" was a way of life, since everyone else I knew in New York was a Socialist, more or less . . . I felt moral compulsions to be a Socialist, since the society in which sixteen million people were jobless that summer and a million on strike did not seem to admit saving except by a Socialist government. But my socialism, though I felt it deeply, did not require any conscious personal assent or decision on my part; I was a Socialist as so many Americans were "Christians"; I had always lived in a Socialist atmosphere.

Alas, socialism, whether in its prosaic or flamboyant varieties, not only failed to deter the triumph of fascism and Nazism (neither had middle-class liberalism or old-fashioned conservatism, for that matter), its traditional categories of analysis had to be contorted even to explain this new terror. In a vague way the socialist tradition had been exploited by the Right: Mussolini was an ex-socialist, Hitler was a National *Socialist,* and both adopted techniques of mass mobilization from the Left. But this was nothing compared to the deformation of socialism in the Soviet Union: there a socialism claiming orthodoxy and apostolic descent from Marx became not the conquered opponent of totalitarianism as in Germany but the very vehicle of it. In August 1939 Hitler and Stalin signed a non-aggression pact; the two totalitarianisms joined hands. In September the war began.

The leading neoconservatives who were socialists in those years were virtually all anti-Stalinists. They had already combated Communists in the name of various socialist factions; the brutal dogmatism, the Moscow Trials, the liquidation of anarchists and Trotskyites in Spain, the anti-democratic maneuvers of Communists in unions and left-wing organizations had fully educated them in anti-Communism long before the Stalin-Hitler pact, the postwar expansion of Soviet power, or the revelation of Stalin's concentration camps. In strict logic they did not have to abandon their beliefs; but socialism was more than logic, it was a moral "myth," it was a panoply of formulas, slogans, symbols, rituals, associations which now were rent, tattered, even bloodstained, which had proved to be obstacles to effective thought rather than aids to it, which had even turned out to be the manipulable instruments of terror. At the very least, socialism had to be reexamined. The result was an outburst of creative energy.

What occurred among socialists was in fact part of a larger mood of reexamination. What had promised to be the steady prevailing winds of the century had switched directions, whipped up maelstroms, smashed all but the mightiest vessels with unforeseen gales. The watchwords of a chastened intellectual class became irony, ambiguity, paradox, complexity. In Europe, the optimistic faith in human rationality and progress, undermined by the intellectual currents at the end of the nineteenth century, had barely survived the trenches of World War I. It lived on more sturdily in distant America, occasionally finding strength there, as in Europe, from reports that rationality and progress had been rekindled in the Soviet Union. Alfred Kazin caught the mood in his characterization of the "clear and shining liberalism" of Granville Hicks. "He wrote as if history—even literature—consisted in coherent answers to sensible questions." But faith in rationality and progress was soon counted among the many victims of Hitler and Stalin. It expired in the gas chambers of Auschwitz, was scattered with the ashes from Treblinka's furnaces. It could not revive in the fog of lies that cloaked the purge trials of Eastern Europe, nor in the Siberian wastes of Stalin's prison camps. Nor in the rubble of Hiroshima and Nagasaki.

Could any coherence and sense be rescued from these horrors? Not without a severe and painful rethinking of political premises. And though that rethinking, in turn, sometimes led into blind alleys or was absorbed into the mental regimentation of the Cold War, the necessity of undertaking it cannot be denied.

A less sanguine view of human nature, a greater respect for the recalcitrance of the world to rational schemes of betterment, the recognition that history was not a dependable current but a directionless sea, and an insistence on the rediscovery of first principles—these were themes common to liberal as well as socialist reexamination. The neoconservatives nevertheless retained some elements from their early Marxism, enough at least to provoke later critics to call them "quasi-Marxist conservatives" or the equivalent. They retained, for instance, the Marxist impatience with bourgeois "sentimentality," the Marxist impulse to unmask the group and individual interests that presumably operated behind the surface of political rhetoric. They retained a preference for analyzing political events in terms of long-run socioeconomic shifts, which were to be demonstrated with an adroit marshaling of quantitative data, those *facts* which are eminently superior to the sentimental longings or speculative impressions of the bourgeois literary intellectual. Here was a happy marriage between the positivism of academic social science, to which so many of these young intellectuals gravitated, and the polemical theorizing of socialist factions. The Marxist emphasis on class was fragmented into a concern with a variety of interest groups, with ethnic and sectional conflict, with status groups, with the intellectuals as a body in society.

The last was perhaps the most striking element in the Marxist legacy, and in its way surprising. In the old-fashioned world of vulgar Marxism—post-Marx but pre-Lenin—intellectuals were in an anomalous position. In practice socialism always had a special appeal to intellectuals, in theory their role should have been distinctly subordinate to that of the workers; intellectuals, after all, belonged to the epiphenomenal world of ideology and culture. And yet correct doctrine had always been of enormous importance—Marx himself set the example here with his fierce polemics—and this increased the significance of intellectuals in the movement's struggles. With Lenin the whole question of the intellectual's role became central, no less for his opponents than for himself. Building as much on a native tradition of the Russian intelligentsia as on Marxism, Lenin insisted on the need for a professional revolutionary vanguard to escape the grip capitalist consciousness maintained over the working class. Bolshevism put the intellectual, acting as a disciplined party operative, at the center of revolutionary theory and practice. And the success of Bolshevism, seizing power in Russia despite what were held to be the most unlikely material conditions—and then splitting the socialist movements in almost every nation—seemed only to confirm the Marxist insistence on correct doctrine. A small group of intellectuals armed with a novel theory could apparently have the most enormous impact. Lenin distrusted intellectuals; they were too apt to value their own independence over party discipline. But his opponents grew to distrust intellectuals as well—they were too apt to be tempted by the Communist lure of a place near the heart of power, a part in the secret drama of history. Both Communists and anti-Communist socialists became preoccupied with intellectuals; they were a group requiring constant scrutiny lest they stray into the wrong camp.

Perhaps this situation was exacerbated in the United States, where socialism was even more identified with intellectual circles than in Europe; outside of a few links with sectors of the labor movement—and even here the solidity of the connection varied from period to period—socialists were isolated from the masses of citizens. Socialist politics were intellectual politics, and that has remained the case with ex-socialist politics as well.

The Cold War

The neoconservatives' "seasoning" began, in many cases, with socialist beginnings; it continued, in almost all cases, with immersion in the Cold War. Well drilled in Marxist texts and socialist history, blooded in the tribal wars between Communists, democratic socialists, and fifty-seven varieties of Trotskyists, they were already trained and in motion when the Cold War put their skills at a premium and promoted them to the front lines. Daniel Bell has mapped the headwaters of this political current: "*Partisan Review, Commentary,* and *The New Leader,* the three magazines, and the writers grouped around them, that originally made up the core of the American Committee for Cultural Freedom," a body of illustrious intellectuals formed in 1951 to counteract "mendacious Communist propaganda" and oppose all forms of "thought-control." The neoorthodox realism of Reinhold Niebuhr ("the father of us all," in George Kennan's often quoted view) linked the group to the religious world; and the American Committee for Cultural Freedom was kin to the Paris-based Congress for Cultural Freedom, which in 1953 began generating, from Germany to India, a family of magazines, including the influential Anglo-American monthly *Encounter.*

To be sure, not only future neoconservatives were involved in this effort. But several of them played important, organizational roles. Irving Kristol spent the better part of a year as executive secretary of the American Committee for Cultural Freedom, then departed for London to become the founding editor of *Encounter.* Bell spent a year working for the Congress for Cultural Freedom in Paris. Others, like Sidney Hook, had a hand in planning the congress-sponsored international conferences and choosing editors for *Encounter.* The outlook held by this milieu was known as "hard anti-Communism"; according to Norman Podhoretz, it rested on two basic assumptions:

(1) the Soviet Union was a totalitarian state of the same unqualifiedly evil character as Nazi Germany, and as such could not be expected to change except for the worse . . .; (2) the Soviet Union was incorrigibly committed to the cause of world revolution, to be furthered by military means when necessary, and when possible by a strategy of internal subversion directed from Moscow; only American power stood in the way of this fanatical ambition to destroy freedom all over the world, and only American awareness of the threat could generate policies that would thwart it.

The liberal advocates of "hard anti-Communism" were generally opposed to Joseph McCarthy and at least the more raucous and visible forms of McCarthyism; but their opposition was of a very qualified kind. As many observers have noted, their complaint against McCarthy often seemed to be that he was making a hash of a job that professional and more knowledgeable anti-Communists (like themselves) could do better. McCarthy picked on the Voice of America, for instance, something no *smart* anti-Communist would have considered. McCarthy, moreover, was giving left-wing intellectuals abroad the raw material for their own unflattering visions of the United States, to the rectification of which the "hard anti-Communists" devoted even more energy than to criticism of the Wisconsin Senator.

Irving Kristol, as an editor of *Commentary,* denied in March 1952 that McCarthy was endangering civil liberties and suggested that Americans had good reason for putting their confidence in McCarthy rather than "the spokesmen for American liberalism." In September of the same year, Elliot Cohen, the senior editor, declared that McCarthy's "only support as a great national figure is from the fascinated fears of the intelligentsia." And the next March, concluding a generally acute dissection on Mc-Carthyism, Nathan Glazer announced, "It is a shame and an outrage that Senator McCarthy should remain in the Senate; yet I cannot see that it is an imminent danger to personal liberty in the United States." Podhoretz, who sided with the "hard anti-Communists" during that period, wrote in *Making It:* "The charge that they were soft on McCarthyism struck me as ridiculous and, in fact, for most of them it was. . . . On the other hand, there can be little question that the hard anti-Communists were more concerned with fighting what they took to be misconceptions of the nature of Soviet Communism than with fighting the persecution to which so many people were being subjected in the early fifties; and it shames me to say that I shared in their brutal insensitivity on this issue." *

---

* Podhoretz may have since changed his mind on this point. In the April 1976 *Commentary* ("Making the World Safe for Communism," p. 32) he writes very matter-of-factly about these persecutions, seeing in them the instrument of what he approved as a good liberal policy: "transforming what might have seemed a

The fact that a considerable part of this activity turned out to be financed by the Central Intelligence Agency should not consume all our attention—as though the deception and manipulation which this involved drained every bit of merit from the "hard anti-Communist" case. But neither should this matter be passed over too lightly. Neoconservatives have dwelt much on the problems of interaction between intellectuals and government, the necessity of preserving intellectual independence in political and cultural matters, the danger of confounding political ideals and self-promotion, and the complicated relationship between ends and means in historical action. Their Cold War efforts were waged in the name of "cultural freedom." That these efforts were organized and maintained by the espionage and covert-action arm of a Great Power appears to have distressed these intellectuals very little. Several of them may have been complicit in this arrangement all along—it is of the nature of secret operations that we have no way of knowing for sure, only circumstantial evidence and the garbled admissions of involved parties. Others greeted the eventual exposure unblinkingly: Their justifications were untroubled, their endorsement of what had occurred and those perpetrating it was virtually unqualified. "We were free," went the standard defense, "from all CIA interference"—a fact that is by no means established—"and institutions like the Congress for Cultural Freedom and *Encounter* promoted a wide spectrum of political views"—a fact that is patently false.

Whatever one may hold in principle about the proper relationship between intellectuals and a secret government agency like the CIA—and I can imagine circumstances where cooperation between them might well be justified—the studied naiveté of these responses (as though the largesse of the CIA toward one group of thinkers when others were promoting their views on shoestring budgets, or not at all, wasn't already a form of "interference"), combined with a melodramatic hardboiledness ("Americans are such virgins!" one prominent intellectual, caught out lying on behalf of *Encounter,* kept repeating in a conversation at the time), was surely inadequate to the issues involved. The neoconservatives

---

remote abstraction into a clear and present danger, so that sending money to Europe or sending troops to Korea could be represented as necessary measures of self-defense against a danger which had already moved inside the gates and even, as it were, under every bed." In *Making It,* Podhoretz wrote sardonically of the jailing of "dangerous characters like Dashiell Hammett" and the blacklisting of "enemies of freedom like Lillian Hellman." In June 1976, however, *Commentary* greeted Lillian Hellman's account of those years, *Scoundrel Time,* with a harsh review by Nathan Glazer, who complains that a new "truth" about the fifties is now being "created," in part, by "memoirs of some of those who lived in that period." Is Podhoretz, in publishing Glazer's review, now disavowing his own "memoir"?

were to urge on the Left the exercise of a skeptical self-scrutiny and a sensitivity to political and moral complexity, yet the CIA episode suggested from the start the limits to their own capacities for self-scrutiny and the selective character of their interest in complexity.

Key Words of the Postwar Liberals

We should not exaggerate how much these Cold War commitments, including those with CIA strings, tell us about the future neoconservatives; in all this, they were not distinguished from many other liberals, except perhaps by a slightly greater degree of ideological sophistication and anti-Communist militancy. Furthermore they evolved political views during these years that are not done justice by simple mental association with charged terms like "Cold War" and "CIA." To get the flavor of those views—and I make no pretense to a comprehensive analysis—one might well turn to other terms that did appear frequently in books like Seymour Martin Lipset's *Political Man,* Daniel Bell's *The End of Ideology,* or the essays by Lipset, Bell, Richard Hofstadter, Nathan Glazer, and others on McCarthyism and the "radical Right." Among the key words were:

Mass society, mass politics, mass culture. Earlier in the century, "mass" was a word with favorable connotations on the Left: *The Masses* and *The New Masses* were of course the titles of two of the Left's most significant journals. The word represented the oppressed majority whose very numbers lent every ripple of political upheaval the promise of great victories to come. On the Right, "mass" was a term of foreboding. It carried hints of the eruption of political id that the Right had usually dreaded in the image of "mob." But "masses" were almost too vast and amorphous an image to have the same brute force as "mob." Instead it suggested a loss of individuation and distinction, mediocrity and a superficial quality of life, whether marked by untutored emotion or by aimlessness and loss of vitality. "Mass production"—of men and culture as well as material goods—was the disdained reality.

In postwar America it was the latter set of connotations that predominated, on the Left as well as on the Right. At best, "mass" indicated the triumph of quantity over quality; at worst, it recalled rallies in Nuremberg and the audience for Dr. Goebbels' propaganda. Against this background, future neoconservatives like Bell, Lipset, and Edward Shils expressed an interesting mix of attitudes. On the face of it, the United States fitted the conservative model of the mass society—it was, at least relative to other nations, democratic and egalitarian; it was proud of the material wealth flowing from its industrial base; it was devoted to almost incessant change. Yet America had weathered its Depression and fought a war without giving way to a "mass politics" of crude emotional mobilization. Why?

The reply proceeded along several interrelated lines. For one thing, thoroughgoing modernization did not lead to mass politics; in fact it surmounted them—material affluence, for example, relieved the pressure of economic demands and installed a large, stabilizing middle class. It was the *process* of modernization, especially rapid industrialization, that posed the great dangers: social groups were dislocated and world views threatened, the situation was ready for explosions of irrational resentment against modernity. The United States had almost—though not quite—traversed this phase of development. The United States was also resistant to mass politics because its citizens were not atomized members of the "masses"; they were integrated into the political community by membership in numerous groups, both the voluntary ones, which de Tocqueville had long before noted as characteristic of America, and natural ones formed by ethnic and regional ties. As for the reality of mass culture, future conservatives like Bell, Lipset, Shils, Leo Rosten, and like-minded liberals did not deny the diluting of elite standards it represented, but they viewed it benignly nonetheless: *on balance,* the greater access to higher education and the mass distribution of cultural artifacts in the form of recordings and reproductions marked a gain in sensibility that elitist critics were loath to admit. In effect, this position accepted the terms of the conservative critique on one level: the possibility that modern industrial societies were inherently volatile and destructive was the problem; and the analysis was conducted in terms of a search for integrating and stabilizing factors. Yet they denied the applicability of the critique to the United States, instead insisting that it be revised in view of the American experience.

Pluralism. The alternative to mass politics was group politics. Mass movements expressed the desperate and irrational cohering of isolated and alienated individuals. In groups, however, individuals had roots and could recognize and seek their rational self-interest, including their self-interest in preferring compromise over conflict *à outrance*. Pluralism's emphasis on groups in politics was methodological, descriptive, and normative. Pluralist political analysts criticized approaches, like Marxism or populism, which subsumed the multiplicity and diversity of group interests into large categories like working class and capital, the people and the interests. Pluralists maintained that the reality of political life was most accurately described in terms of the extremely complicated interactions between numerous groups, shifting coalitions in which the various organized interests, brokered by politicians, attempt to get a "piece of the action." And finally they insisted that such a complex and shifting set of relationships *ought* to characterize politics—it dispersed power and allowed the compromises necessary for stability.

Pluralism was an admission that democracy did not work according to the textbooks—it granted the subordination of the individual citizen and formal procedures like elections to "interests" and informal bargaining among elites in the corridors. But pluralism made virtues of what, for the textbooks, had been vices. The limited jostling of group interests, tempered by the sophistication and common ties of their leaderships, was an alternative to the politics of mass movements, in which it was supposed that the individual citizen, isolated and unknowing of the realities of political give-and-take, would be inflamed by emotional and utopian appeals.

Pluralism, of course, has been criticized on as many grounds as it was advanced. Its methodological emphasis on the multiplicity of groups rather than broader divisions in society has been questioned: one can always look at the trees instead of the forest, or divide the human body into its organ systems and these into further units right down through cells to DNA; but this possibility does not resolve the question of whether one level or another is the crucial one for analyzing a given problem.

Pluralism tends to treat all groups as both equal and similar, neglecting the patterns of consistent dominance by some groups or coalitions rather than others, and neglecting the differences between and within groups— some may have more legitimate public claims than others or more democratic standards internally. While pluralism presents itself as a critique of an atomistic liberal theory of society, in which individual citizens are supposed to be identical atoms each pursuing its own self-interest and clashing or combining so as to construct some relatively satisfactory social state, the pluralist vision seems to replicate that view on a slightly different scale, with interest groups rather than individuals as the swirl of atoms. Finally, in its emphasis on bargaining among group *leaders,* usually assumed to be rational and moderate, pluralism can be said to be anti-democratic. Citizen apathy is rationalized, and any degree of mass citizen participation is perceived as a threat and a precursor of totalitarian democracy. The anti-democratic impulses of elites are consistently underestimated. Thus Michael Paul Rogin concluded his study of pluralist reaction to McCarthyism with this estimation:

Pluralism has attacked several traditional left-wing shibboleths. It has exploded myths about popular virtue and revealed the dangers in thoughtlessly democratic thinking. It has pointed out the risks to constitutionalism inherent in millennial preoccupations. Pluralism has stressed the value of groups, of diversity, and of the rule of law. . . . At the same time, because of its underlying preoccupation, the pluralist vision is a distorted one. The fear of radicalism and the concern for stability, however legitimate as values, have interfered with accurate perception. Thanks to its allegiance to modern America, pluralism analyzes efforts by masses to improve their condition as threats to stability. It turns all threats to stability into threats to constitutional democracy. This is a profoundly conservative endeavor. Torn between its half-expressed fears and its desire to face reality, pluralist theory is a peculiar mixture of analysis and prescription, insight and illusion, special pleading and dispassionate inquiry. Perhaps pluralism may best be judged not as the product of science but as a liberal American venture into conservative political theory.

Consensus. The clash of groups in the pluralist model took place within a consensus about the rules of the game and the fundamental values that sustained these rules. America had been particularly blessed in this regard. Lockian liberalism had encountered virtually no challengers as the framework for American politics. No established aristocracy provided the economic and social base for resisting the democratic and egalitarian current of the nineteenth century. Aided by the safety valves of size and wealth, and by its remarkable political institutions, including the two-party system, the new society had developed a gift for compromise and pragmatic adaptation.

Few would gainsay this picture in its main lines. But the sixties did see strong criticism of certain aspects of this "consensus history." First it was asked whether the strength of the consensus was to be judged as such an unmitigated good: had it not left Americans barren of alternative ways of seeing their way through recent political problems? Then it was argued that the emphasis on consensus and successful compromise had diverted attention from underlying conflicts in American society. The "rules of the game," for example, had been originally constructed to allow for slavery, and the great compromises presented in grade-school textbooks—counting slaves as three-fifths of a man in the Constitution, the Missouri Compromise, the Compromise of 1850, the end of Reconstruction—had all assumed racial oppression. That the rules of the game had been altered only by one of history's bloodier wars, and that violence was a constant factor in American life and social change, both as a means of enforcing the consensus and of modifying it, were consistently underplayed. Thus even dedicated liberals tended to view racism as an unsightly blot on American history rather than the fundamental flaw perceived by outsiders like de Tocqueville, graffiti disfiguring a beautiful edifice rather than structural faults in the foundation. To be sure, it is not clear that this criticism issues in any particular conclusion for political theory; of the several possibilities, one might well be a reaffirmation of the importance of consensus. But it does go some way to explain why so many thinking Americans, having contemplated the national experience through lenses tinted "consensus," were unprepared for the racial, generational, and antiwar agitation of the sixties.

Moralism. If America's great virtue was compromise and pragmatic adaptation, its great defect was moralism. Moralism was a "peculiar American inversion of Protestantism," a product of the frontier evangelicalism that, even more than Puritanism, was the matrix of the American character. Moralism, first, focused on the reform of the individual. Brought into politics, it sought out culprits rather than systemic flaws. Second, moralism dissolved the lines between public and private, between law and morality, that liberalism had established in hope of minimizing conflict over fundamental beliefs; thus Prohibition and other blue laws, as well as an insistence on personal moral rigor that first led to hypocrisy and then was scandalized by it. Third, moralism was intolerant of accommodation and ambiguity; reality was perceived in extreme terms of good and evil, and anything less than black-and-white judgments was unworthy. Different writers expressed slightly different views of the role of moralism in American history. Daniel Bell, for example, was grateful that "apart from its rhetorical use in political campaigns," moral indignation, focusing as it did on culture and personal conduct, had played a relatively small role in actual politics. Thus "the United States has been able to escape the intense ideological fanaticism— the conflicts of clericalism and class—which has been so characteristic of Europe." Seymour Martin Lipset, on the other hand, found that "Americans are more likely to view politics in moralistic terms than most Europeans." All were agreed, however, that moralism posed a serious threat to stability. Bell worried over "a peculiar change" occurring in American life: "While we are becoming more relaxed in the area of traditional morals . . . we are becoming moralistic and extreme in politics."

If there was anything exceptionable in these characterizations of the American "style," it was, perhaps, that they themselves were so unambiguous, even moralistic. That personal fervor and moral rigor, distaste for compromise and emphatic individualism, might also have made some contribution to the achievement and maintenance of liberty and equality was given little consideration. Both de Tocqueville and Burke, favorite authorities for pluralist commentators of the fifties, had remarked on the close connection between American Protestantism and American democracy. Indeed, in a later disquisition on moralism, Lipset even cites as support Burke's description of the unyielding Protestantism of the northern colonies. Lipset drops from the passage, however, Burke's basic point, that the colonists' faith was "not only favorable to liberty, but built upon it"—part of a lengthy explanation of the Americans' "love of freedom" and "fierce spirit of liberty."

Burke, to be sure, was trying to grapple intellectually with an incipient revolution, while critics of moralism had largely eliminated from consideration those sorts of political conflicts that are almost always unamenable to unimpassioned negotiation. This made moralism a somewhat easier target. Not only did the critics lack nuance and sympathy toward the evangelical roots of American moralism, there was a tendency for the term to be loosened from those roots altogether and be applied at will to whatever strongly felt political position the commentator might disagree with. It often seemed that only certain matters of style, a surface irony or cosmopolitanism, protected against charges of moralism, absolving a Dean Acheson but not a John Foster Dulles in a way their actual differences in policies hardly warranted. Since popular movements, of any sort whatsoever, are rarely marked by such style, they are almost inevitably open to charges of moralism by any unsympathetic observer. Those denouncing moralism were apt to ignore Nathaniel Hawthorne's warning that "the influential classes, and those who take upon themselves to be leaders of the people, are fully liable to all the passionate error that has ever characterized the maddest mob." And Michael Rogin has pointed out the tendency, in treatments of the Populists' moralism, to overlook precisely the same attitudes and rhetoric in their conservative opponents. Moralism remains a useful concept for interpreting and criticizing American political culture, but its very flexibility laid it open to misuse. In this respect it resembled another key term, with which it was closely linked—status politics.

Status politics. The volume on *The New American Right*—so Daniel Bell wrote in his opening essay in 1955—attempted to explain the new, prosperity-created social anxieties that "conventional political analysis, drawn largely from eighteenth- and nineteenth-century models, cannot fathom." To this end the book offered a "new framework . . . drawn from some of the more recent thought in sociology and social psychology"; it was "a new and original contribution which, we feel, extends the range of conventional political analysis." The recent concepts to which Bell referred turned out to be "the role of status groups as a major entity in American life and status resentments as a real force in politics."

The idea of status politics had been advanced by Richard Hofstadter and became, in the fifties, the key concept in his work. Along with Lipset, Hofstadter distinguished status politics from interest or class politics. Interest (Hofstadter) or class (Lipset) politics meant "the clash of material aims and needs among various groups and blocs" (Hofstadter) or "political division based on the discord between the traditional left and the right, i.e., between those who favor redistribution of income, and those favoring preservation of the *status quo*" (Lipset). Status politics, in contrast, means "the clash of various projective rationalizations arising from status aspirations and other personal motives" (Hofstadter), or "political movements whose appeal is to the not uncommon resentments of individuals or groups who desire to maintain or improve their status" (Lipset).

Hofstadter and Lipset agreed that interest or class politics flourished in times of economic hardship, status politics in times of prosperity; yet this distinction, devised to explain McCarthyism as an expression of status politics, was ignored when inconvenient. Hofstadter, for example, used the status concept to interpret the Jacksonians, the Populists, and the Progressives, as well as McCarthyism. Psychology was substituted for economics, in keeping with the mood of the decade. In the hands of a sensitive writer like Hofstadter, whose borrowing from the social sciences was transformed by imaginative and literary gifts, this psychological analysis enriched the economic and political interpretations of American culture. As a staple of political argument, however, the "new framework" that Bell hailed turned out to be another, slightly more sophisticated, reductionism. Reform movements in U.S. history were rendered as so many neurotic impulses. Populism, in particular, was redrawn as the nostalgic, conspiracy-haunted, moralistic, xenophobic, anti-industrial, anti-Semitic, and authoritarian expression of a desperate class of displaced farmers. Supposedly a movement on the Left, it led directly to the Klan and McCarthyism.

However appealing to an age eager to "lose its illusions" about disturbing radical elements in the American past, this interpretation has been steadily demolished by scholars of both Populism and McCarthyism. In the process, they also exposed the weakness of the concept of status politics.

Hofstadter's "central idea," as Bell set it forth in introducing *The New American Right,* was "that groups that are upwardly mobile . . . are often as anxious and as politically febrile as groups that have become dé-classé. . . . Groups which have lost their social position seek more violently than ever to impose on all groups the older values of a society which they once bore. . . . Groups on the rise may insist on a similar conformity in order to establish themselves." Hofstadter himself wrote, in one place, of "people who had either risen upwards or moved sideways in the social scale"; and, in another, of "persons moving downward, and even upward"—all exhibiting status anxiety. Quoting these passages, Arthur Schlesinger, Jr., by no means a hostile critic, summed up the problem:

> On close examination, the status approach appeared to adapt itself to every situation. . . . People moving up the social ladder, people moving down,

people moving sideways and people staying in the same place—all evidently suffered from status anxiety. In the same way old Yankees had status anxiety because their position was threatened, and new immigrants had it because their position was insecure. Protestants were anxious, and so were Catholics, and so were Jews; and so were the old, and so were the young. Every view everyone held, no matter how incompatible particular views might have been, could be traced to origins in some form of status insecurity.

But a theory that explains a reaction and its opposite with equal facility does not greatly help in making clear why individuals choose one rather than another. . . . The status interpretation verges on becoming a heads-I-win-tails-you-lose proposition. It begins by explaining too much and ends by explaining all too little.

The utter flexibility of the concept led to its arbitrary application—and polemical misuse. Schlesinger points out that Hofstadter, partial to the New Deal, refrained from applying the status interpretation to it, though "many leading New Dealers were from the same social classes and presumably from the same psychological predicaments which produced Progressivism."

Rogin reminds us that "those with severe personal problems are likely to turn their back on politics" and that "status anxieties may find an outlet in political moderation." Not status anxieties *per se* but the "intervening political and organizational structures and attitudes are crucial." It has even been suggested that, in attacking McCarthyism as an irrational, anti-Establishment movement, *The New American Right* itself was only expressing the status anxieties of a group of upwardly mobile professors with left-wing histories, and on the verge of acceptance by the Establishment!

The end of ideology. A phrase that served in the trenches as emblem of the prevailing political and intellectual outlook of the fifties and early sixties, the "end of ideology" has been the tattered subject of almost endless debates. Not the least reason for this was the ambiguity of the phrase itself and the different uses to which it was put by writers like Bell, Lipset, Raymond Aron, and Edward Shils. What was meant by ideology? Did it refer to any comprehensive theory or set of ideas for explaining the world and social change, possibly even to fundamental values that are no longer explicitly articulated? Or did it refer to a manner of holding such a theory—passionately or dogmatically (not the same thing, of course)—or to *some* sets of ideas that were likely to be held in *some* manners, or to what? Was "ideology" simply sociological shorthand for Marxism or socialism or, even more specifically, for Communist political practice? Was the assertion of its "end" merely descriptive—a statement of fact—or even a topic for inquiry, as when Lipset followed the phrase with a question mark? Or was the "end" a normative statement—a recommendation, a plea, a declaration of approval?

Let me cut through the complexities and contradictions of the literature with some rough-hewn assertions. I would agree, for example, with the summary made by Robert A. Haber:

> The "end of ideology" theory states that political theory and practice which aims at radical social transformation has ended, at least in the West. The reasons for this are: first, the disillusionment of the last forty years with mass movements, with revolution, and with the socialist-classless utopia projected by Marxism. Second, Marxism-Leninism which has been the main carrier of ideology has been discredited as an intellectual-political system. Third, the class conflicts and system-wide problems which give rise to ideology have generally been solved, so no longer is there an objective base for such a social analysis. Further, the problems which are pressing for the society are of high complexity, do not have clear solutions, and political methods don't appear the most fruitful means of treatment. . . . In addition to this contention about reality, the "end of ideology" theorists make a value assertion. They see the end of ideology as a desirable development. In its place they describe a different kind of politics—the politics of "civility," or . . . reformism.

To which I might add that the ambiguity about the "end of ideology" was an important element in its significance. This or that writer, when challenged, may have been willing to opt for a specific sense—a normative claim, for instance, rather than a descriptive one, or "ideology" defined in narrow terms of "apocalyptic belief" or *total* ideology." Yet even within the work of single authors, let alone the body of writings to which cross-references were repeatedly made, the term was used so loosely as to carry the usually negative connotations from its core definition over to a wide range of political views and phenomena of which the authors disapproved. Thus "ideology" and "ideological" were attached to beliefs and groups, from conservative businessmen to left-wing professors, of which the "apocalyptic" character was hardly well established. With a few exceptions, such terms were never attached to middle-of-the-road political positions and forces, no matter how passionate or dogmatic, and of course not to the "end-of-ideology" school itself.

The empirical claims involved in declaring the end of ideology led to extended dispute, much of it unprofitable. That the political and ideological temperature rose sharply in the sixties was often cited as grounds for dismissing the literature of a few years previous. Yet the end-of-ideologists insisted that their theorizing could encompass such developments, and in fact their findings on the decline of political fervor had earlier been acknowledged as widely by radicals who regretted this decline as by those centrists who welcomed it. The real issue was *why* such changes in the ideological temperature took place, and what raised hackles was the considerably less empirical claim that "the fundamental political problems of the industrial revolution have been solved" and that politics, though still expressing economic and class differences, should henceforth be limited to a consensual and managerial incrementalism guided by social science. To the degree that the celebration of an end of ideology was only a plea for an end of fanaticism, and that this proclamation voiced an affirmation of democratic procedures and a revulsion from totalitarian doctrines, there can be no quarrel with it. But its formulations (and its examples) went further, essentially to identify such democratic values with the *status quo* in the liberal democracies and to legitimate both that *status quo* and a major role for social scientists within it. In this sense, the frequently made charges that the "end of ideology" was simply another ideological position appear justified, although, especially for those who would defend ideology as inevitable, that cannot be the final word on the matter.

Triumph of Anti-Ideology

Looking back on the analysis of McCarthyism by writers like Bell, Hofstadter, Glazer, and Lipset, even a sympathetic and moderate reader like Jeane Kirkpatrick finds that they "sometimes sounded embarrassingly like embattled defenders of a threatened aristocracy." But in fact they could not entertain any traditional notion of an aristocracy, because their first commitment was to "modernity." Modernity had passed by both Left and Right. There was plenty to be embattled about—the possible resurgence of ideology and the moralistic revolt of those whose status had been shaken by modernity. Nonetheless there was an underlying confidence and optimism in these writers. They felt on the side of the future— if only they could preserve it from the desperate grasps of a dying past.

Perhaps it was less an aristocracy than the *place* of an aristocracy that these political commentators of the Cold War period wished to defend, for with the sixties they were certainly coming into their own. This is not to say that they were moving to the right on the political spectrum. Despite the conservative themes in their thought, as the Cold War damped down, some could even be said to have moved left. Nathan Glazer was among the editors of *The Correspondent*, a journal David Riesman and Erich Fromm founded to revive discussion of arms limitations and détente. Norman Podhoretz became editor of *Commentary* in

1959, provided a platform for much of Paul Goodman's *Growing Up Absurd,* and published revisionist critics of American foreign policy like Staughton Lynd. Nonetheless, the views they had espoused in defending post–New Deal stability against both Left and Right were readily adopted by the New Frontier. By 1962, the "end of ideology" was Presidential doctrine. Speaking in May of that year to the White House Economic Conference held in Washington, John F. Kennedy made his famous distinction between "myth and reality":

> Most of us are conditioned for many years to have a political viewpoint, Republican or Democrat—liberal, conservative, moderate. The fact of the matter is that most of the problems, or at least many of them that we now face, are technical problems, are administrative problems. They are very sophisticated judgments which do not lend themselves to the great sort of "passionate movements" which have stirred this country so often in the past. Now they deal with questions which are beyond the comprehension of most men.

A month later, at Yale, Kennedy reiterated the message:

> The central domestic problems of our time . . . do not relate to basic clashes of philosophy and ideology, but to ways and means . . . sophisticated solutions to complex and obstinate problems.
>
> What is at stake in our economic decisions today is not some grand warfare of rival ideologies which will sweep the country with passion but the practical management of a modern economy. What we need are not labels and clichés but more basic discussion of the sophisticated and technical questions involved in keeping a great economic machinery moving ahead. . . . Political labels and ideological approaches are irrelevant to the solutions. . . . Technical answers—not political answers—must be provided.

In *The End of Ideology* Daniel Bell complained of intellectuals' tendency to embark upon what William James had termed "the faith ladder." For some time he and Irving Kristol felt the need for a journal to explore "the ladder of practicality," a ladder that by the mid-sixties was obviously reaching into the higher offices in the land. In the fall of 1965, the first issue of *The Public Interest* appeared.

From the start the magazine assumed that the main obstacle to effective public policy was that people didn't know what they were talking about. And the reason they didn't was

> a prior commitment to an ideology, whether it be liberal, conservative, or radical. For it is in the nature of ideology to *preconceive* reality; and it is exactly such preconceptions that are the worst hindrances to knowing-what-one-is-talking-about.

The editors knew enough philosophy to admit that "human thought and action is impossible without *some kinds* of preconceptions." So why weren't one man's "preconceptions" another man's "ideology"? Bell and Kristol assumed that legitimate (and unavoidable) preconceptions somehow had only to do with the "purposes" or "ends" of thought and action whereas ideologies prefabricate "interpretations of existing social realities." This was not a distinction but a muddle, and the editors extricated themselves in the usual way, by adding the intensity of a belief as the litmus test of "ideologies"—"interpretations that bitterly resist all sensible revision." But what does it mean to *bitterly* resist, and who is the judge of *sensible* revision?

A more intriguing muddle was the editors' hemming and hawing on the new journal's title. They were unwilling to break with pluralist political scientists who disdained the notion of a discernible public interest in favor of the image of struggle among self-seeking individuals and groups for the attainment of their separate private interests. And yet, finally, the new journal did insist on some notion of an authentically public interest, as distinct from the equilibrium of conflicting private ones. The editors cited Walter Lippmann's definition: "The public interest may be presumed to be what men would choose if they saw clearly, thought rationally, acted disinterestedly and benevolently." By implication, these were to be the virtues the journal would bring to the formation of opinion: clarity, reasonableness, disinterest, and benevolence.

The Public Interest combined skepticism with a rock-bottom confidence: if not confidence in the possibility of actually "fine-tuning" public policy, then at least confidence in the power of their analyses to delineate the limits of remedy—and of the country to live within these limits. In other words, the muted confidence of the fifties minus the threat of McCarthyism. In the lead article of the first issue, Daniel Patrick Moynihan revealed that reform had become "professionalized." What with the newfound ability to manage industrial economies, the professional style of the middle class, the growth of social science, and the discovery that "fiscal drag" required the government regularly to plow large sums of revenue back into the economy, Moynihan declared that devising new programs in the public interest had become the routine and necessary charge of a new class of capable public servants. The days of mile-long petitions and mass rallies were over. Reform efforts "are less and less political decisions, more and more administrative ones. They are decisions that can be reached by consensus rather than conflict."

Not all future neoconservatives agreed with the thinking behind the magazine. Norman Podhoretz objected "to their notion that 'ideology' was dead and that all problems were therefore now technical (a notion resting ultimately on the fifties belief that the system under which we were

living in America was the best a fallible human nature was likely to be
able to build)." Podhoretz refused to "believe that intellectual discourse,
even within the realm of politics, need limit itself so masochistically. . . .
The proposed Bell–Kristol solution to the problem of the intellectuals was
assimilation into the surrounding environment of 'hard-headedness' and
'practicality.' "

The Sky Changes

This disagreement would soon be bridged. In March 1965 the first
teach-in against the war in Vietnam took place; in April the United States
sent troops to the Dominican Republic; throughout the summer the
massive buildup of American forces in Vietnam was set in motion. In
August, Watts exploded. The year 1965 was the pivot of the decade. Even
as the first issue of *The Public Interest* was prepared, the sky changed and
the wind rose. *"The Public Interest,"* wrote Moynihan, who had op-
timistically suggested the new journal be named *Consensus,* "was soon
sailing anything *but* a summer sea. . . . All about us canvas tore and
cables parted."

The sixties began with sit-ins and Camelot and the Peace Corps, went
out with student guerrillas and the Nixon–Agnew White House and Kent
State. In between, there were urban riots, marches on Washington,
occupied campuses, tanks in the streets of Chicago. There was much talk
of people being "radicalized," and in turn much talk of right-wing
"backlashes." But "backlash," as the word implies, was an angry,
reflexive action. There was no term for the slower evolution of a
significant party of liberals. They were, we might say, "conservativized."

From among those events that piled up, one on top of the next, during
the sixties, it is difficult to select the few that transformed liberals into
neoconservatives. Berkeley, 1964, was certainly one of the first. In
carrying a dispute over campus restrictions on political activity to the
point of civil disobedience, the occupation of Sproul Hall, and a
confrontation with police, the New Left effectively proposed a parallel
between the conditions of the "multiversity" and those the civil rights
movement had known in the South. Could the same analysis and tactics be
applied to the liberal Clark Kerr and the redneck Bull Connor? Many
academics were disoriented by the very idea. They may or may not have
supported the students' immediate aims, but this larger assault on
liberalism was either passing rhetorical excess, or dangerous nonsense.
Was Berkeley, they wondered, an exception, or a portent? A portent, as

it turned out—but not because the New Left made converts. The relentless expansion of the war in Vietnam and the string of exploding ghettoes accomplished that.

In 1965 and 1966 the opponents of the war launched demonstrations that failed the liberals' tests of "responsibility"; the demonstrators refused to credit Washington's good intentions and dissociate themselves from the Vietnamese enemy. At the same time the revelation of minority frustrations in the urban riots and the growth of separatist sentiment among a highly visible segment of blacks raised questions about the viability of a political approach priding itself on compromise and consensus, and viewing American history and institutions as sound and benevolent. If anything more was needed to throw numerous liberals on the defensive, it was the 1966 exposé of collusion between liberal intellectuals and the Central Intelligence Agency, collusion conducted in the name of exactly those principles that liberals were trying to defend. Finally, 1968: the McCarthy and Kennedy campaigns, the barricading of buildings and clashes with police at Columbia University (a local American production of a national event in France); the televised street battles during the Democratic convention in Chicago; and, in New York, a drawn-out teachers strike focusing on community control of schools and provoking charges of racist attitudes among organized teachers and anti-Semitism among local black activists.

Liberals could respond to these events in several ways. They could abandon their previous positions for New Left radicalism. They could accept specific objectives of the student radicals, the antiwar movement, and minority militants, even much of the criticism these groups expressed of liberalism, and yet reject major elements of the radical outlook, in particular its revolutionary and violent impulses. Or they could carry the combat to the radicals, attacking *their* principles and practices.

Naturally liberal response mixed these alternatives in complicated and not always consistent ways. There was much improvisation: What do you take seriously and what do you tolerate as rhetoric? Was there a line between the inevitable simplification of all social movements and the demagogic fanaticism of the *grands simplificateurs,* and when was it crossed? To whom do you give the benefit of doubt? On whom do you place the burden of proof? If there had been any doubt before, 1968 convinced one segment of liberal opinion to opt resolutely for the third alternative. Nathan Glazer expressed this choice in the concluding sentence of an article tracing his evolution from a "mild radical" to a "mild conservative":

I, for one, indeed, have by now come to feel that this radicalism is so beset with error and confusion that our main task, if we are ever to mount a

successful assault on our problems, must be to argue with it and to strip it
ultimately of the pretension that it understands the causes of our ills and
how to set them right.

"Our main task, if we are ever to mount a successful assault on our
problems"—this was an assignment of priorities pregnant with implications. Bombs rained more heavily than ever on Vietnam, to which
Cambodia was then to be added; the movement toward racial equality,
simmering in the juices of police and militant violence, was stymied;
Nixon and Agnew were trying to rally their "silent majority." First, crush
radicalism; and *then* attend to those other matters?* Would sweeping the
streets of radicals really open the path to those other problems? To take
the obvious example, it did seem unlikely that the annihilation of radical
dissent would weaken Kissinger and the Pentagon in their determination
not to depart Vietnam except under American terms. Still, one could
make the case. But did one have to? Whether prerequisite to other tasks
or not, reducing radicalism was indeed the "main task" that many liberals,
put on the defensive in their principles, challenged on their own pasts,
were impatient to undertake. A decade earlier, Daniel Bell had puzzled
over the uncertain identity of his "generation"—not yet self-consciously
"middle-aged" and the "best of all political generations," as the first issue
of *The Public Interest* would later have it. Bell noted "an inability to
define an 'enemy.' One can have causes and passions only when one
knows against whom to fight." At long last, the "enemy" was found.
    Oddly enough, open warfare was declared even as the "enemy" was
already in decline. Between 1965 and 1968, student radicalism had been
wandering in exile. The "beloved community" of the civil rights movement and the rejection of dogmatic theory by the early New Left had not
survived racial conflicts in the North, black nationalism, and the bitterness
of antiwar feeling. In 1967, a "New Politics" conference in Chicago tried
to bring together the fragments; instead, the conference itself exploded
over a black nationalist minority's insistence on controlling half the votes.
If radicalism revived in 1968 it was not from inner strength; it was the

*In many ways this single-mindedness was out of keeping with Glazer's usual
tone. The simple linking of all political issues—from race to Vietnam to university
polity—and their resolution by a single key he described as one of the objectionable tendencies of student extremists. Was that why this programmatic sentence
did not appear in the Introduction to *Remembering the Answers,* of which his
article "On Being Deradicalized" was a version? One recalls Glazer's 1953 analysis
of McCarthyist support and the passage minimizing the Wisconsin demagogue that
unaccountably appeared at the end of it, "almost," wrote Irving Howe at the time,
"as if from another hand." Whatever Glazer's own attitude toward the single-
minded pursuit of radicalism implied in his proposal, he certainly voiced the desire
of others.

reflex of desperation responding to outer provocation. It took the Tet offensive, the McCarthy and Kennedy candidacies (actually demonstrating the enduring attraction of liberalism, given half a chance, among the student activists), the assassinations of Martin Luther King and then Bobby Kennedy, and the Columbia occupations to set in whirligig motion the forces that jammed the parks and streets of Chicago. After that, however, exhaustion . . . and the pathetic myth of secession to Woodstock Nation. The turn to calculated violence was overwhelmingly rejected by the student population; terrorism was a testimony of weakness, not strength, a problem for police rather than ideologists. The campuses rose once again in response to the invasion of Cambodia. And given a degree of administrative ineptitude on the part of university and law-enforcement officials, specific events in specific localities—trials of Black Panthers or war resisters, dismissals of teachers, appearances by Administration spokesmen—could provoke confrontations and violence. Still, as time went on these outbreaks seemed less and less capable of catalyzing large and loyal bodies of supporters. The nation, after all, had elected Nixon, even if narrowly. The middle class, if it was moved to opposition at all, was still devoted to organizing candlelight marches, or approving the revelations of Ellsberg, or possibly supporting the avowedly nonviolent raids on Selective Service by religious pacifists like the Berrigans. Only the moral pall cast by Vietnam over the society and its governing institutions provided radicalism with its remaining force. By the 1970–71 school year, campus protests were down, *Time* magazine was hailing "The Cooling of America," and radicals themselves were denouncing Black Panther violence as the "Movement's Mylai" and the "politics of psychotic fantasy."

It was just about then, however, that the neoconservative offensive against the "enemy" gathered steam. Norman Podhoretz, for example, having spent several months away from his editor's desk reviewing the events of the sixties for a possible book, descended from the mountain as though with a checklist of transgressors on tablets of stone. *Commentary* began what looked like a systematic assault. One month's lead article would develop a parallel between New Leftists and the German Communists who helped pave the way for Hitler. Another month's would argue that talk of repression in America was merely that—so much talk—and anyway dissidents were bringing it on themselves. The next month's would attack the Black Panthers, and the next Women's Liberation. The December 1970 issue dissected "apologists for the Counter-culture"— Charles Reich, Theodore Roszak, and the report of the National Commission on Campus Unrest. In January 1971, the lead article supported the prosecution of the defendants in the Chicago Conspiracy Trial as "legally plausible." In February four articles argued the danger to

Jews posed by the "Movement." In March, a major article by Daniel Moynihan warned that "our capacity for effective democratic government" may be threatened by press hostility to the White House. And so on. A lot of mopping up was performed in the secondary articles and book reviews.

Even this short list of subjects indicates another odd element about the neoconservatives' "enemy." Not only did neoconservatism strike out at a force already on the decline, the attack widened to embrace and assimilate a number of other phenomena—the counterculture, of course, but also women's liberation, then muckraking journalism generally. *The New York Review of Books*, Ralph Nader, the ecology movement, the American Civil Liberties Union, John Gardner's Common Cause were all added to the list of villains. In 1971, Podhoretz was willing to describe not only the New Left but virtually the entire middle-class New Politics movement—Senator Eugene McCarthy excepted but not his followers— as "Stalinist" and "anti-American." This attitude was reflected a year later in *Commentary*'s reaction to the McGovern candidacy.

What was happening did not go unnoticed. As early as November 1970, *The Wall Street Journal* called Podhoretz "a most improbable conservative," improbable only because of his liberal background. *The New York Times* and *The Washington Post* were equally alert to the ideological shift. *National Review,* having sniffed suspiciously at *Commentary*'s new direction at the end of 1970, gave its imprimatur in March 1971: "Come On In, the Water's Fine," urged a headline in the spokes-journal of American conservatism.

Yet there was an understandable impulse to characterize this development in trivial terms—Podhoretz's revenge for the bad reviews of *Making It,* a personal feud with his former friend and business associate Jason Epstein, or journalistic rivalry with *The New York Review of Books*, of which Epstein was a founding spirit and major contributor. Many who recognized that something more serious was at stake nonetheless expected this "liberal schism" not to outlive the passion and confusion of the antiwar agitation. Only as the inciting conflicts of the sixties faded into the background or underground could it be seen how far these defenders of liberalism had edged from this liberalism themselves—toward a new conservatism.

CHAPTER THREE

What Neoconservatives Believe

WHAT ARE THE CHIEF TENETS of neoconservatism?

Obviously no formal answer will be forthcoming from a movement that is reluctant to identify itself, or at least reluctant to identify itself as conservative. We have no Neoconservative Manifesto, no Neoconservative Program for the Seventies and Eighties, no statements issued from the National Association of Neoconservatives. As with all political tendencies, there are inner differences, variations, and crosscurrents—as well as fringe members, fellow travelers, and vague sympathizers. All generalizations risk an injustice to this or that writer. Indeed it may be that no neoconservative is *the* neoconservative; the center of gravity of a collection of individuals may rest somewhere between them and outside of any single person. That is one of the reasons why this book includes studies of some individual neoconservatives.

There are several levels at which one can describe a political movement. Its position on specific controversies, for example. Or its basic principles. Or its development over time. Or its characteristic style.

Current Politics

Start with current issues. Neoconservatives, like most Americans, disapprove of the unequal treatment suffered by racial minorities, women, and the poor. But they have given far more attention to criticizing current strategies for remedying those inequalities than they have to the inequalities themselves. They are strongly opposed to minority separatism, disruption as a means of dramatizing conditions and forcing action, and civil disobedience except in very extreme circumstances. They have been vocal critics of affirmative action and busing, and cool to community control, many poverty programs, campaign finance reform, and schemes to redistribute income through tax changes.

New educational programs at the primary-school level as well as open admissions at the college level have been greeted skeptically by neoconservatism; so have most proposals to extend medical services, to guarantee employment, and to protect the environment. Neoconservatism has little use for liberal concerns about the rights of prisoners, thinks the beneficial effects of severe punishment deserve more consideration, and puts in a good word for censorship. Neoconservatism has been hostile to various expressions of the women's movement, indifferent to the rest. Virtually nothing linked to the "counterculture" has escaped its condemnation.

On matters international, neoconservatives divided over Vietnam, though the opponents kept their distance from militant antiwar efforts. The war was a tragic "error," not a national "crime." Neoconservatives have been strong supporters of Israel, dubious about Arab intentions and most initiatives for a negotiated settlement, including Washington's. But the United States—and its military power—remains, in their eyes, a global force for good; they suspect détente and the evolution of Communist parties in Western Europe; they assertively defend Cold War anti-Communism, the CIA, and images like the "free world"; they are unsympathetic to the economic claims of Third World nations.

A number of leading neoconservatives openly supported the reelection of Richard Nixon in 1972; others opposed McGovern both as a candidate and a nominee from within the Democratic Party. Many backed the Committee for a Democratic Majority, an anti–New Politics vehicle for Senator Jackson and the leadership of the AFL–CIO. Watergate was an embarrassment slightly relieved by equating it with the civil disobedience of war resisters or the lawlessness of violent radicals. Jackson was the neoconservative candidate in 1976.

Despite the inevitable foreshortening of complicated positions, such a summary does help locate neoconservatism. An outspoken advocate of prison reform, affirmative action, the Equal Rights Amendment, open admissions, and the McGovernite reforms within the Democratic Party is not likely to fit the type, even though he may be fervently pro-Israel and have second thoughts about campaign-financing laws and busing. The individual with a good word for censorship, capital punishment, consciously elitist higher education, backroom methods for nominating Presidential candidates, the Cold War, meritocracy, and Senator Jackson is quite likely a neoconservative even though he may favor the ERA, welfare reform, and national health insurance.

A political outlook is more than a conglomeration of positions, however. At any moment, and on any one issue, men and women may reach agreement although their political premises are vastly different. Issues change; a movement's response is determined by some more general points of agreement. Presumably a few general principles inform neoconservatism, at least loosely. Yet a massive literature offering wildly different definitions of even long-standing notions like liberalism and conservatism warns us how treacherous the identification of these principles can be.

A Neoconservative's Definition

Luckily one neoconservative has himself braved the dangers of generalization, and thereby provided others with a starting point for definition. Admitting to the existence of an influential political current "deemed" neoconservative, Irving Kristol has attempted to describe the "vague consensus" he saw underlying it.

First, "neoconservatism is not at all hostile to the idea of the welfare state, but it is critical of the Great Society version of this welfare state. In general, it approves of those social reforms that, while providing needed security and comfort to the individual in our dynamic, urbanized society, do so with a minimum of bureaucratic intrusion in the individual's affairs. . . . In short, while being for the welfare state, it is opposed to the paternalistic state."

Second, neoconservatism has considerable respect for the market as an instrument for allocating resources efficiently while preserving individual freedom. "Though willing to interfere with the market for overriding social purposes, it prefers to do so by 'rigging' the market, or even creating new markets, rather than by direct bureaucratic controls."

Third, neoconservatism is "respectful of traditional values and institutions: religion, the family, the 'high culture' of Western civilization. If there is any one thing that neoconservatives are unanimous about, it is their dislike of the 'counterculture' that has played so remarkable a role in American life over these past fifteen years."

Fourth, while neoconservatism affirms traditional notions of equality of opportunity, it rejects as dangerous to liberty an egalitarianism which insists on "everyone end[ing] up with equal shares of everything."

Fifth, "in foreign policy, neoconservatism believes that American democracy is not likely to survive for long in a world that is overwhelmingly hostile to American values. . . . So neoconservatives are critical of the post-Vietnam isolationism now so popular in Congress, and many are suspicious of 'détente' as well."

With but a small space in which to describe a large movement, Kristol has not done at all badly. Yet his description, like most that try to present a reality in as favorable a light as possible, at once says too much and too little. Most liberals, for example, would equally claim to be for "the welfare state" but against paternalism. Most would criticize the Great Society, and is there anyone who does not favor "a minimum of bureaucratic intrusion"? Such phrases are platitudinous until they are filled with specifics.

Again, how many liberals or even radicals insist on what Kristol calls "a dangerous sophistry"—"that there is no true equality of opportunity unless and until everyone ends up with equal shares of *everything*"? (My emphasis.) Perhaps a few. But this attack on a straw man is really too broad to identify the difference over egalitarianism between neoconservatives and others.

Kristol is quite right about the "great respect" neoconservatives have developed for the market. Liberals certainly don't share this admiration, although even in this case there are significant exceptions. Yet out of political necessity if not respect, liberals have generally proceeded by "rigging" the market rather than by intervening directly. That was precisely the principle behind most Great Society initiatives: Medicare and Medicaid, the most expensive Great Society innovations, were efforts to rig the market. The fact that neoconservatives were so unhappy with the Great Society may only suggest that this rigging was not done competently, in their view, or more likely it suggests that some other objections are operating.

A similar difficulty exists in regard to foreign policy. Many who are not neoconservatives would readily subscribe to the proposition that American democracy is unlikely to survive in a world hostile to American values. The problem, of course, is that American values are not a unified entity. They include our founding principles—liberty, equality, self-government—as well as economic expansion, anti-Communism, nationalism, and other impulses. Nor are these values unchanging. A southern neoconservative of the 1850s might have listed slavery among American values; a neoconservative of the 1880s might have listed Protestant Christianity. Attitudes toward what Kristol calls "the post-Vietnam isolationism now so popular" and toward détente may not derive from any general position about the influence of American values in the world, but from convictions about *which* values should be influential abroad, which should be nurtured at home, and what are the policies most likely to serve these purposes.

The Neoconservative Analysis

One could go on making distinctions, even about respect for traditional values and institutions and hostility toward the counterculture, the point where Kristol is on firmest ground. Kristol's description is insufficiently general and insufficiently specific. He does not convey the animating spirit of neoconservatism, its paramount concern, the standpoint from which it poses almost all its questions. Nor does he plunge deeply enough into the particulars of its positions. What follows is an attempt to do this.

1. *Neoconservatism holds that a crisis of authority has overtaken America and the West generally. Governing institutions have lost their legitimacy; the confidence of leading elites has been sapped. Social stability and the legacy of liberal civilization are threatened.*

In 1970, Daniel Bell published an article in *Encounter* called "Unstable America." The title sums up the preoccupation and paramount concern of neoconservatives—stability. In this, they only continue the postwar focus of pluralist liberalism. America, in contrast to most European nations, had proved stable in the face of the Depression, war, and challenges from Right and Left. The pluralists were out to unravel the secret of this success and, once having unraveled it, to make it the guiding principle of national policy. In the mid-sixties they were shocked to discover that the success story appeared to have come unplotted. It was now *in*stability that gripped their attention, and demanded diagnosis and remedy.

In the America of the late sixties, such a concern for stability was hardly implausible, but it was not inevitable. One might contrast it with a preoccupation with justice. Of course, the two are not exclusive. Those concerned, first of all, with stability would insist that it is a prerequisite for justice. Those concerned, first of all, with justice would insist that no real stability is possible, or worthy, without it.

Yet in practice the two emphases diverge. The justice seekers concentrate on specific events or conditions; they may confine their attention to these one or two issues, or they may find themselves widening their critique as they pursue the causes of injustice; they may or may not, in other words, be worried about the institutional fabric as a whole. The stability seekers, on the other hand, are *very* worried about the institutional fabric. This they believe to be generally benign and yet fragile to the point of imminent collapse. The social order is a frail child. Its temperature must be checked; its diet managed; its exertions regulated. In the course of this surveillance, specific events and conditions are apt to be reduced to symptoms and sore points rather than treated as problems in themselves.

The preoccupation of the neoconservatives with the question of stability was demonstrated again and again. It began with the challenge to the authority and legitimacy of their own favored institution, the university. It swiftly became their point of view on the entire society. Moynihan's writings are suffused with his concern for authority and his sense—he often quotes John F. Kennedy on this point—of the fragility of American society. By his own account, he entered the Nixon Administration "absorbed with the evident erosion of political authority in America, the seeming inability of liberals to comprehend and defend liberalism, the real enough prospect of a polity regressing toward protracted violence and irresolvable conflict." The 1975 Trilateral Commission "Report on the Governability of Democracies," a document expressing many neoconservative themes, spoke again and again of "the delegitimation of authority generally and the loss of trust in leadership." "In doubt today are not just the economic and military policies but also the political institutions inherited from the past." The same themes are echoed by Bell, Kristol, and Glazer. They are sounded in the very title of Robert Nisbet's *Twilight of Authority*.

Neoconservatives write in the context of "crisis." And yet they deplore "crisis-mongering" by other social critics. It is interesting to note how differently neoconservatives can describe our condition when they want to—and dismiss whoever refuses to admit to their visions. Here is Aaron Wildavsky, in *Commentary,* wondering why "we are all, in fact, doing better and feeling worse." That we are all doing better is, to Wildavsky, undeniable: "Every standard of well-being . . . shows that every sector of the population . . . has improved its lot in past decades." Even crime and drug use, "areas in which we are vividly conscious of recent deterioration, have been considerably reduced . . . since the turn of the century."

And here is James Q. Wilson describing how "crime soared" in the Sixties.

> It did not just increase a little; it rose at a faster rate and to higher levels than at any time since the 1930s and, in some categories, to higher levels than any experienced in this century. The mood of contentment and confidence . . . was shattered, not only by crime, but by riots and war . . . the prosperity of the decade was also accompanied by alarming rises in welfare rates, drug abuse, and youthful unemployment.

Wilson also describes how, in 1960, narcotics-related deaths in New York City "touched two hundred for the first time since at least 1918, and perhaps ever." By 1967, the number of such deaths "had passed seven hundred a year and was still climbing."

Such differences can partially be explained at the level of detail. Wildavsky's interpretation depends heavily on his flexible use of time. Everything has been improving for everybody "in past *decades.*" To fit drug addiction into this pattern he turns back further, to "the turn of the century." In contrast, Wilson presumes that when it comes to "feeling worse," people may not take quite such a long view. And yet such differences, apart from their place in the rhetorical strategy of the essays in question, can be resolved at a deeper level. They both operate within the second of neoconservatism's leading beliefs:

2. *The current crisis is primarily a cultural crisis, a matter of values, morals, and manners. Though this crisis has causes and consequences on the level of socioeconomic structures, neoconservatism, unlike the Left, tends to think these have performed well. The problem is that our convictions have gone slack, our morals loose, our manners corrupt.*

Thus Wildavsky's insistence that all goes well on the practical, material level is only prelude to a diagnosis of a deeper cultural malaise. On this, Wilson would probably agree. The idea of a "crisis of authority" or a "legitimation crisis" is common to other social critics, liberal or radical; but *neoconservatives part company with them by refusing to emphasize the role of capitalist institutions in producing this crisis.*

Likewise, *neoconservatives refuse to put responsibility for the present situation heavily on the shoulders of governing elites, or even to give a major place in their analysis to specific recent events like racial conflict and the war in Vietnam.* These, they argue, were not entirely novel events in American history: why had they become more explosive now than previously? Nor were they factors in Europe and Japan, where the sixties saw similar outbursts of social turmoil and youthful dissidence. Whatever part of present troubles the Trilateral Commission's report would at-

tribute to specific issues and government failures, it is always subordinate
to the unsettling role played by the "democratic spirit" itself. Two causes
are "reflexively invoked," complains Wildavsky, to explain our malaise,
the war in Vietnam and racial inequity. But the first "has come to an end"
and the second "has clearly and visibly diminished." That such an able
social scientist could dispose of these issues so fácilely—the war was
barely six months over when he wrote and the diminishment of racial
inequity was perhaps not so clear and visible to blacks and whites more
familiar with their neighborhoods than with national statistics—only
suggests how determined neoconservatives are not to be sidetracked from
what they consider the real source of today's crisis.

Some of them refer to the decline of religion, some to the lure of
hedonism, some to the march of equality. But there is almost unanimity
on one explanation. *Behind the crisis of authority looms the rising
influence of the "adversary culture."* "Adversary culture" was, of course,
Lionel Trilling's phrase. Trilling had in mind the "subversive intention"
characterizing modern writing, its opposition to bourgeois society, its
affirmation of the self against social constraint, its contempt for convention, its incessant exploration of experience, its estrangement from the
"ordinary" in life, family, the neighborhood, the routine job. Romanti-
cism had breathed life into the adversary culture; Bohemia sheltered it.
But by the mid-twentieth century, the avant-garde was no longer an
embattled minority. Mass higher education put the scriptures of the
adversary culture on everyone's list of required reading. A commercial
culture voracious for new sensations had marketed Bohemia. The result,
wrote Richard Hofstadter in 1967, did not seem to fulfill the hopes of
some that the voyage into personal exploration and social opposition
would be completed by a return journey into dissenting but responsible
social commitment.

> Perhaps we are really confronted with two cultures (not Snow's), whose
> spheres are increasingly independent and more likely to be conflicting than
> to be benignly convergent: a massive adversary culture on one side, and the
> realm of socially responsible criticism on the other.
> Is it not quite possible that the responsible society will get little or no
> nourishment from modern literature, but will have to draw mainly on
> history, journalism, economics, sociological commentary?

In fact, it soon turned out that history, journalism, and sociological
commentary (economics was a little better) behaved as irresponsibly,
from the neoconservative point of view, as had modern literature.

*The adversary culture was thus discovered to be the ruling spirit of an
entire "new class."* In neoconservative writings, references to the "new
class" make up in frequency and vehemence what they lack in precision.

Exactly who is in it? Intellectuals, to be sure. Professors and journalists, though they may or may not be intellectuals, are also part of it—the "knowledge industry" is frequently invoked in this connection, or the "university-government-media" complex. Sometimes the "new class" includes professionals in general, or technicians and "service" workers as well. Sometimes it extends to all the college-educated, or to all those undergoing college education. Sometimes it seems to refer simply to the inhabitants of affluent suburbia or affluent enclaves in the inner city. The element common to all these notions of "new class" or "new middle class" is some degree of higher education, cosmopolitanism, or theoretical training.

In fact the "new class" is half analytic concept, half polemical device. Social theorists have long been grappling with the emergence of new groups—professionals, technicians, and bureaucrats, for example—that replaced the petty bourgeoisie as a stratum between the powerful controllers of wealth and the working class. There are clearly major shifts here that deserve examination, and when neoconservatives seek explanations in the realm of socioeconomic change, it is usually in connection with the emergence of the "new class"—the growth of science-based industry, the media, and higher education. To cite but one dramatic example, in the half-century between 1920 and 1972, the number of faculty members in American colleges and universities increased from 48,000 to over 600,000, with a quarter of that growth occurring in a mere five years, between 1965 and 1970. The college student population increased more than sixfold between 1930 and 1970. Changes like these have led some to argue that "the university has become the great legitimating and certifying institution of contemporary secular societies." One can certainly assume that such developments will not be without *some* important cultural impact.

At the same time, the "new class" is often only a convenient (because vague) way to label whomever the neoconservatives don't like and to invest them with an aura of massiveness and threat. Writing about "the new class structure" that is "altering the cultural base of the Democratic party," Michael Novak begins by pointing out:

> Over 35 percent of the GNP is now supplied by the knowledge industry: federal and local government workers, researchers, lawyers, planners, consultants, educators, information systems operatives, journalists, social workers and others. Most of the workers in this industry depend for their livelihood on expanding and activist government expenditure (with its attendant corruptions). Most are Democrats.

These new elements in the Democratic Party are represented by what Novak calls the "Know-Everythings," many of whom are "affluent professionals, secular in their values and tastes and initiatives, indifferent to or hostile to the family, equipped with postgraduate degrees and economic security and cultural power." In contrast to the "cultural nihilism" of Know-Everythings, "most Americans" still believe in "the traditional values of honesty, decency, hard work, competitive advancement, religious faith, compassion for the suffering and social cooperation."

Novak does not use the term "adversary culture," but the description he offers of the Know-Everythings and their "cultural nihilism" is equivalent. Not only is it implied that they represent 35 percent of the GNP and are the main force behind government expansion, Novak says flatly that they represent "established power." Not all the neoconservatives are as primitive as Novak about these matters. Daniel Bell, who understands the technical nature of the statistics that Novak manipulates, is much more exact and modest in his description of the "knowledge class." In 1978 many neoconservatives began working on a New Class Study, a collection of papers that might give their assertions some precision and documentation. It was a rather belated effort, the "new class" notion having long been propagated through syndicated columns, newspaper editorials, and Mobil Oil ads. Until then, if there was any difference between Novak's sweeping statements about the "new class" and those of most other neoconservatives, it was only the latter's more tactically effective use of vagueness.

This does not mean that the neoconservative thesis is wrong. It does mean that at several crucial points it rests on speculation and personal judgment. To what extent do "adversary" attitudes dominate some new class? How extensive and powerful is this class? On both counts, Novak's view is representative. The cultural, if not political, power of the new class and its set of modernist anti-values is almost complete. This perception charges the neoconservatives' sense of crisis, their fears for social stability, and their militancy.

3. *Government is the victim of "overload." Attempting too much, it has naturally failed and thereby undermined its own authority.*

According to the Trilateral Commission report: "In recent years, the operations of the democratic process do indeed appear to have generated a breakdown of traditional means of social control, a delegitimation of political and other forms of authority, and an overload of demands on government exceeding its capacity to respond." The tenth-anniversary issue of *The Public Interest,* published as a separate Bicentennial volume called *The American Commonwealth—1976,* tracked the problem of "overload" through most of our governing institutions. Samuel P. Huntington (in a chapter that also forms part of the Trilateral Commission report) warns against an "excess of democracy." Aaron Wildavsky predicts that the Presidency will become so frustrating a post that

Presidents will evade leadership. James Q. Wilson laments the growth of an activist bureaucracy in response to new demands on government; and Nathan Glazer, of an activist and "imperial" judiciary. Along with other contributors, they see free society threatened by the consequences of allegedly unrestrained political pressures.

The background for the diagnosis of "overload" is what Samuel Huntington terms the "Welfare Shift." From the mid-1960s on, according to Huntington, government expenditures underwent a "Welfare Shift" corresponding to the "Defense Shift" that had marked the Cold War years. The proportion of government budgets devoted to defense dropped (from 13 percent in 1953 to 6 percent in 1974); the proportion devoted to education, health, and income transfers as well as other nondefense expenditures such as interest on public debt rose (from 15 percent in 1953 to 27 percent in 1974). As a percentage of our Gross National Product all government expenditures increased from 28 percent in 1953 to 33 percent in 1974.

The electric metaphor of "overload" is more than descriptive; it expresses a value judgment and assesses responsibility. If a fuse blows in my household—and in neoconservative opinion this is exactly what has happened in American society—there are several ways I can view the matter. Perhaps the wiring is defective, in which case I should have it repaired. Or the wiring, though not defective, may be insufficient for my needs, in which case it should be replaced or supplemented. Or finally I may simply decide that the amount of current I was using was inordinate and unnecessary, in which case I cut back on my demand for electricity. Liberals and radicals who share with neoconservatives the opinion that society has "blown a fuse" are apt to conclude that political practices or leadership have been defective or that the socio-economic-political system needs an overhaul. Neoconservatives are apt to choose the third possibility. Too much is being demanded from government and politicians.

But how do we know what, in fact, is too much? (Unless, of course, we have reached an *a priori* judgment that the system is neither defective nor due for change, and therefore any evidence of "overload" is by definition a sign of "too much.") In neoconservative opinion the demands that have been placed on government are "impossible," "incompatible," "insoluble," or "unreasonable"; and the shrewder among them realize that their case would be strengthened if they could demonstrate that these demands are *logically* impossible, incompatible, and so on, thereby eliminating the possibility that an improvement in the capacity of government or politicians could make any difference. Such attempted demonstrations depend rather heavily, however, on the precise construction that neoconservatives themselves give to popular demands.

In the instance of welfare reform, Aaron Wildavsky points out that the "same people" who ask for more money are "just as likely" to condemn welfare "in the next breath" as a "total failure" deserving to be scrapped. But drop the coloration added by *"total* failure" and there is nothing "incompatible," as Wildavsky would have it, about this set of complaints. The claim that welfare is a failure (though not a total one) and should be replaced but that, in the meantime, levels of support should be raised merely reflects everyday distinctions between short-run and long-run options, or between first-choice and second-best. Other examples of recent demands turn out to be incompatible or impossible only in the sense that society's resources are limited. Every household must divide its budget between food, clothing, and shelter; and no one thinks of these competing demands as essentially incompatible or impossible, though obviously to insist on the utmost in every sphere would be so.

To the extent that neoconservatives believe the citizenry wants the utmost of everything and all at once to boot, they are mistaken: plenty of data indicate that despite the hyperbole of our political rhetoric Americans are more reasonable than that. But there is a deeper neoconservative worry. By "impossible," "incompatible," and so on, they really seem to mean *unrelenting.* Even if demands on government are made within the usual American framework of incrementalism, are they entirely open-ended? Can the desire for better health care or greater equality be satisfied by *any* improvement in government performance or contained within *any* new set of institutions? For the conservative, change should lead toward a greater equilibrium, not away from it. Demands that do not hold out that promise are necessarily "overload."

How did this "overload" come about? It is the normal work of politicians, after all, to balance competing demands and to keep expectations in some reasonable relation to resources. Perhaps politicians and our whole complex system of political accelerators and brakes have never succeeded completely at this task; but why should they have suddenly done so much worse?

Neoconservatives have several explanations. The first points to a set of supposedly native attitudes: *Americans, and especially American liberals, suffer from naive good-heartedness and social sensitivity combined with an optimism, confidence, and ambition bordering on arrogance.* This is alleged to have been the outlook of the New Frontiersmen, the ruling elite of the early sixties. They are the actors in that long-running American drama, the Fall from Innocence. Their political and social initiatives under Kennedy and Johnson set in motion a doomed revolution of rising expectations. In domestic affairs they promised more than they could deliver; abroad, they strove mightily to pursue a limited war while avoiding full-scale ideological and economic mobilization at home. Good intentions did what good intentions, since Dr. Johnson's famous pronouncement, have always been said to do, and the country was soon on the road to perdition. Neoconservatives don't dwell on it, but some, like Moynihan, are willing to admit that they themselves were part of this folly.

The second explanation for "overload" is more socioeconomic. *America is beset with the problem of an "underclass."* Alternatively termed the lower class or the lumpenproletariat, this is a large element, especially of the urban population, whose condition is barely amenable to remedy. Whether by nature or by nurture, by constitution or by culture, the members of this group have been so seriously deprived, so deeply injured, that they are to a large degree ineducable, unemployable, and alien to middle-class norms of behavior. They are, to boil it all down, "shiftless."

The notion of an "underclass" is bound up with the complex debate about a "culture of poverty." That poverty has negative effects on the poor appears obvious; why, otherwise, would we be concerned about it? But how permanent and extensive are such effects, even when the want of money has been repaired? To what degree are they merely the common lot of human failing, which poverty renders exaggerated and catastrophic and for which affluence could greatly compensate? To what extent do such effects become, in turn, causes of continuing poverty despite opportunities for escaping it? Is it possible that there is even a biological or genetic base for the outlook and behavior characteristic of the underclass?

The neoconservatives hold no consensus on these questions, and one must be cautious in suggesting what place the underclass idea plays in their views. They do *not* equate all the poor, minority groups, or slum dwellers with the incorrigible and irresponsible underclass. Yet they appear to believe that the presence of this latter element is considerable, and that it in fact is at the root of many of the problems of poverty, integration, housing, education, and urban government that policymakers confront. In the name of facing reality they criticize those who are unduly concerned with "protecting the reputation of the poor." In the name of free discussion they are prone to defend those who have proposed "unthinkable" theories, either genetic or cultural, that suggest nearly irremediable traits accounting for people's own disadvantaged state.

Are the poor basically like the rest of us except that they have less money? At times the neoconservatives seem to say yes. They prefer an "incomes strategy" that would provide the poor with cash over a "service strategy" that would provide counseling, job training, and so on. On closer examination their preference reflects less on their confidence that the poor mainly need money and more on their detestation of the "new class," whom they associate with the providers of services, and on their belief in the advantages, political and economic, of an incomes strategy for the non-poor. It is a matter of emphasis, then, and for the neoconservatives the emphasis is on the difference between the poor and the rest of us. Between the risk that public hardheartedness might be nurtured by stressing these differences and the risk that naive or inefficient policies might be accepted by underestimating them, the neoconservatives are far more worried about the latter.

The third explanation for "overload" is again cultural. *It is the American, indeed the Western, demand for ever-increasing equality, not merely legal and political equality, not merely equality of opportunity, but equality of social and economic condition.* One might protest that Americans have lived with a great deal of inequality and seem content with a rather glacial movement toward any equality of condition. But neoconservatives have a vision that makes almost any shift toward equality destabilizing: as inequality decreases, they argue, the remaining differences between individuals grow more and more intolerable. Egalitarianism thus becomes a treadmill on which society is forced to run faster and faster.

None of these explanations of "overload" stands alone. The truly threatening dynamic is in their interaction and, above all, in the opportunity they provide for the machinations and ambitions of the "new class." The new class is ridden with guilt and *ressentiment* and a fervent anti-Americanism. It expresses this temper by seizing upon the real (but allegedly insoluble) problems of the underclass as an indictment of contemporary America. (Some neoconservatives even accuse the new class of having created or enlarged the underclass by fostering a climate of permissiveness. *New York Times* editorials calling for aid to riot-torn ghettoes in the sixties, Presidential commissions denouncing "white racism," and efforts to assure the rights of accused prisoners are held responsible for encouraging looting and idleness among black youth.) On the basis of social inequities, the new class erects a dogmatic and leveling egalitarianism, which actually cloaks its own self-interested yearning for power. The national commitment to equality, native optimism about improving the condition of the disadvantaged, and the moral prestige gained in the civil rights and antiwar movements leave established leaders defenseless against this campaign. Restless and resentful, corrosive with its adversary culture, the new class presses moral claims against the government that can neither be resisted nor met. The result is "overload" and the sapping of legitimate authority.

There is at least one other thing to be noted about the theory of "overload": *its assumption that the only excessive demands on government take the form of liberal proposals.* This is never stated explicitly, and no doubt most neoconservatives would deny such an obviously untenable notion. But in fact examples of "overload" are almost always drawn from the liberal side of the agenda. Generally ignored is one of the most debated sets of demands in the 1960s, and one of the most clearcut cases of "overload"—the Johnson Administration's insistence that America could fight a war abroad and pursue the Great Society at home, the "guns-and-butter" (and no-tax-increase) policy that proved so illusory. Equally unmentioned are other sets of demands arising from business, the military, or "middle America." The beneficiaries of increased nondefense spending included many more segments of the population than the term "Welfare Shift" might suggest. Even the distinction between the Welfare Shift and the Defense Shift blurs when one recalls how Cold War rivalry inspired new expenditures on education after *Sputnik* in 1957 and how John F. Kennedy's campaign to "get the country moving again" played on fears of lost world leadership as much as on democratic or egalitarian ideals. (Demography, too, played its part: schools were swollen with the cohorts of the postwar baby boom while the growing ranks of the elderly needed more medical care and social security. Government services expanded because certain age groups expanded.) These realities forgotten or ignored, "overload" becomes a kind of code word; a superficially neutral, mechanical metaphor that in practice operates only against a particular set of political and social programs.

The Neoconservative Strategy

4. *In the face of this crisis, neoconservatism insists that authority must be reasserted and government protected.*

In an article called "Government and the People" and written almost entirely from the point of view of government, Aaron Wildavsky neatly sums up the neoconservative concern with a few lines from the economist Alfred Marshall: "Government is the most precious of human possessions; and no care can be too great to be spent on enabling it to do its work in the best way: a chief condition to that end is that it should not be set to work for which it is not specially qualified, under the conditions of time and place."

At times the neoconservative solicitude for government verges on the attitude expressed in Brecht's *mot,* that when the people lose confidence in the government, it would "be simpler for the government to dissolve the people and elect another one." Rather than getting the government they want, the people should want the government they get; they should be retutored to fit its current capacities. One could think of other candidates for the exalted title of "most precious of human possessions"— liberty or justice, for example. But such expressions, taken comprehensively, arrive at similar points: in principle, the neoconservative is not the less worried about liberty or justice because it is government that looms largest to him as their guarantor. It is in the everyday negotiation, not of stark choices, but of smaller risks, risks of overstraining government, or of growing complacent about liberty, or of tolerating injustice, that the neoconservative preference shows itself. Marshall's elaboration that in the care and grooming of government "it should not be set to work for which it is not specially qualified" would be perfectly unexceptional, were it not that defining such qualification is always a matter of some uncertainty and hazard and even self-interest.

The neoconservative strategy for the reassertion of authority and the protection of government can be described at the levels of government, the public, and leading elites.

In principle, neoconservatives support government programs that would foresee, forestall, or relieve destabilizing social tensions. There is no consensus, however, on specific proposals. Some neoconservatives favor expanded government planning; many oppose it. Most probably favor mild extensions of the welfare state; a few are opposed in general, and more doubt than approval is apt to greet any particular idea. *In practice, the burden of proof sits heavily on any new government initiative, especially one that might fuel the fires of egalitarianism, be wasted on the intractable problems linked to the underclass, or increase the influence of the new class.*

Furthermore, if impossible demands doom a high proportion of government programs to failure, *the authority of government should be shielded by dispersing responsibility for this failure as much as possible.* That is a major argument for reversing the post–New Deal liberal belief in the federal government as the most likely agent of progressive social change and for distributing responsibility to state and local governments. *It leads, moreover, to a new ground for honoring the market.* Where conservatives, or classic liberals, had previously argued for the market on the grounds of liberty or efficiency, neoconservatives added what might be called an argument from inefficiency: when nothing works, the market has the advantage of not providing the citizen with anyone to blame. Moynihan put the argument in rather uncharacteristically heavy prose, in keeping perhaps with the somewhat devious point: "Diffusing responsibility for social outcomes tends to retard the rise of social distrust when the promised or presumed outcome does not occur." If social problems could not be entrusted to the market altogether, then government should enlist the market as much as possible in its remedial schemes, removing its own authority from the firing line.

At the level of the public, neoconservatism's message is simple: lower your expectations. Yet neoconservatism is not in any significant sense a popular movement, with the "public" for an audience. If it has influenced the policies of budget-cutting politicians, this has been at a remove. On the one hand, it offers intellectual legitimation for "hard decisions" and "tough-minded" measures. On the other hand, it refrains from any corresponding analysis of the burdens of lowered expectations and how they are being distributed.

But neoconservatism's real targets are the decision-making elites. *The new class and its adversary culture must be tamed, under threat of being purged from responsible milieus.* This effort to discredit its ideological enemy is waged on all fronts, from the arts and higher education to government agencies and political organizations. The struggle takes the form of exposing every manifestation of what could be considered an oppositionist mentality and tracing its "logic" so as to link it to various expressions of extremism: drawing the connection between modernism and nihilism, between radical criticism of the United States and "anti-Americanism," between poverty programs and looting, between government regulation and totalitarianism, between criticism of arms expenditures and subservience to Communism, between Women's Liberation or homosexual rights and the destruction of the family, between civil disobedience and Watergate, between the Left generally and terrorism, anti-Semitism, and fascism. Against the permissiveness of the new class, neoconservatism raises the banners of the work ethic, intellectual excellence, and discipline. Against equality of condition, it poses equality of opportunity.

In particular, neoconservatives have set themselves against two weapons, believed to be in the hands of the new class: sentimental humanitarianism and guilt. The chief defense against the first is *the theory of unanticipated consequences.* By insisting on the layers of complexity that divide any policy from its ultimate effect, neoconservatives warn their audience to restrain its sympathetic impulses and recognize in them all kinds of shibboleths, unproven assumptions, and self-interested motives. In one sense, this is the essence of all social theory, an awareness that common-sense explanation and the conventional wisdom will not quite do: the political economists discover "private vice, public virtue"; Hegel, the "cunning of history"; and so on. In another sense, it is a claim to special expertise; if the working out of social change has become "counter-intuitive," as computer scientist Jay W. Forrester maintains and

Moynihan and others repeat, then the laypeople should repress their intuitions and turn matters over to the instructed. And finally, applied unselfconsciously (what are the unanticipated consequences of a theory of unanticipated consequences?) and selectively against ameliorating proposals, it becomes a renovated version of the attack on ignorant "do-gooders" and "bleeding-heart liberals" familiar to *laissez-faire* capitalism and social Darwinism.

The attack on "guilt" is more complicated. It is part of the wash of psychologizing that spread over social theory in the 1940s and 1950s. "Guilt" is assumed to be bad, a sign of some unresolved inner conflict rather than a proper reaction to an external reality. More important, whatever responses the neoconservative critic judges to be self-abnegating or excessive are interpreted as "guilt." Oddly enough, such a strategy appears to aim at making people feel guilty about feeling guilty. *Its effect, in any case, is to shift the locus of the "problem," from whatever allegedly stirred these suspect feelings to the individuals afflicted by them.* This shift, I must add, is not only polemically useful to the neoconservatives; it is, given their analysis of the new class, entirely appropriate.

In launching their attack on the new class, neoconservatives can draw on their own radical backgrounds. Stalinism, Trotskyism, and other offshoots of Leninist Marxism had a deep reserve of scorn for middle-class reformers, with their sentimental belief in the power of altruism rather than self-interest, their desire to avoid conflict and unpleasant choices. Neoconservatives can also draw on the provincial and populist distrust of cosmopolitan elites. Compared to academics and their "heavy disquisitions," goes a characteristic line in *Commentary,* "three workingmen discoursing of public affairs in a bar may perhaps display more clarity, shrewdness, and common sense."

Of course, that is true. So is William Buckley's statement that it would be preferable to be governed by the first thousand names in the Boston telephone directory than by the Harvard faculty. But one does wonder how much time neoconservatives, or in that case a professor at the London School of Economics and Fellow of the British Academy, have been spending "discoursing of public affairs" in working-class bars. For neoconservatism itself is an elite current of opinion, and *the bulwark it envisions against the forces of chaos is not a widened democracy but a new establishment.* The New Deal and postwar establishment of liberal patricians, internationally minded military and business leaders, Wall Street lawyers, and academic braintrusters has broken down. Its young recruits, brought into Washington with Kennedy, lost their authority over the war in Vietnam. Neoconservatism looks forward to the reassembling of an Establishment. "I don't think a society gains strength on the basis of its people being wiser or less wise," says Daniel Bell, "though it's important to have that as a base."

> A society has vitality if it has a strong establishment. . . . Today you find no American establishment. . . . We've lost a generation. It's not that we've lost "The Great Leader." . . . What we have lost is a milieu. The Stimsons and Lovetts represented, as I said, a milieu for leadership—the Wall Street legal firms and investment companies. There was a burgeoning establishment—largely out of the academic world. But it was destroyed by the policies of the Johnson and the Nixon Administrations. We're going to take a long time recovering from the gap.

Moynihan, too, sees the nation floundering "between" Establishments, Vietnam having discredited the promising young men of Camelot. But "time heals such hurts," he consoles us, "time and the circulation of elites of which Pareto wrote."

Who will form the new Establishment? What mixture of industrial and financial leaders, of defense experts, of policy intellectuals from Harvard and Rand? What mix of "cosmopolitans" and "provincials"? Indeed, what place for a chastened new class? Or will it simply be the old Establishment refurbished? Neoconservatism appears to have no common opinion. Its technocratic wing leans toward policy intellectuals and international businessmen. Its Burkean, "philosophic" tendency leans toward more traditional business leaders and representatives of "middle America." Its New Deal loyalists would reserve a larger place for old-line trade-union leadership. What they all agree upon is that an emerging establishment must be infused with self-confidence. Its members must be vaccinated against the contagion of the adversary culture. They must wield their authority with a good conscience, free of the sentimentality or guilt that would inhibit decisive and painful measures. They must feel secure in the power and prerogatives they enjoy: if they have not been elected to their positions, they have been brought there by a legitimate inequality and concentration of wealth or by their own merits. They must be protected from excessive demands, treated gently in their failures, and honored for their successes.

5. *A precarious international order requires a stable, unified society at home; renewed emphasis on the Communist threat and on the Third World's rejection of liberal values is needed to generate the requisite national allegiance and discipline.*

By background most neoconservatives were militant anti-Communists and Cold Warriors. They were also firm believers that international relations, like the domestic economy, could be better "managed"; the

Kennedy Administration had no less a hope of "fine-tuning" the one than the other. In the early sixties, opposition to this cooler style of crisis management came not from the Left but from right-wing anti-Communist crusaders and segments of the military. By contrast, neoconservatives could see themselves as the spokesmen of restraint. The war in Vietnam divided them: they were linked both to the outlook and the governing circles that had carried on the war; yet they were distressed by the domestic disarray that had resulted from an apparent overextension. If a new center of gravity could be found in their foreign-policy views, it was one just slightly to the left of the Administrations in power, calling for a gradual withdrawal from Vietnam, uncertain but willing to take Vietnamization and Washington's negotiating posture at face value, and adamantly hostile to the systematic critiques of U.S. foreign policy emanating from radicals. Irving Kristol might write of the burden—on us—of American empire, but no credence could be lent to talk of the burden—on others—of American imperialism. For the most part, however, neoconservatives concentrated on domestic politics; when they wrote of Vietnam it was apt to be in terms of the dangers of student radicalism or right-wing patriotic backlash.

In recent years, this emphasis has changed. It may have been the threat posed to Israel by the Yom Kippur war. It may have been the fear that defeat in Vietnam would be taken as complete vindication of the radical critiques. It may have been the OPEC oil boycott. For one reason or another, neoconservatives have given more and more attention to international affairs. On the one hand, they perceive a growing threat to the West from the Soviet Union and a rising tide of anti-Western, anti-liberal forces in the developing world. On the other hand, they decry a "failure of nerve," and a "culture of appeasement," within America. The first calls for greater armaments and a refusal of the economic concessions demanded by the "Third World." (Both these positions are of course argued on technical grounds; but with neoconservatism no less than other ideological currents, a particular analysis of the arms race or international trade is apt to be preferred over another not so much on the basis of the technical details as of the political presuppositions.) The second demands a rallying of public opinion, a mobilization of elites, possibly even a purging of elites, similar to that which occurred during the Cold War.

To what extent do neoconservative concerns for national order and unity spring from a perception of international threat? To what extent does the insistence on international threat spring from a desire to shock society into national order and stability? Neoconservatives are shrewd students of social dynamics who know well the interaction of foreign and domestic politics. Their renewed emphasis on foreign affairs emerged after the New Left and the "counterculture" had dissolved as convincing foils for neoconservatism, and just after Watergate had proved an embarrassment. Their determination to find an overseas opponent, whether Idi Amin, Fabian socialism, Eurocommunism, or Soviet power, seemed constant despite the vast differences in the military and geopolitical factors. Their emphasis on the power of Communist—and then even socialist—ideology not only appeared to tout their own services as seasoned ideological firefighters; it aimed at discrediting radical social and economic criticism in the United States and rather easily shaded into a defense of the American economic establishment. On the other hand, a body like the Trilateral Commission undertook its neoconservative study of democratic "governability" out of a concern for "a stable international order and for the fashioning of more cooperative relations" between Europe, Japan, and the United States. "Imperial powers need social equilibrium at home if they are to act effectively in the world," wrote Irving Kristol in prescription for the United States.

In fact, domestic and international elements are inextricably mixed in the neoconservative vision. The United States must have a strong, confident elite willing to employ American power swiftly and decisively if the nation is to cope with international danger. But international danger exists, *ipso facto,* if the United States is lacking in a strong, confident elite willing to employ its power. The argument is not quite circular, but ultimately rests on the more or less permanent state of international rivalry that exists between great powers rather than on the specific events cited as cause for concern. With the exception of the precarious situation of Israel, developments abroad, in Angola or Afghanistan, are less important in themselves than as markers of how far America has fallen from the necessary strength of will. Thus neoconservatives are undoubtedly sincere in their anxiety over international affairs, at the same time as the essential source of that anxiety is not military or geopolitical or to be found overseas at all; it is domestic and cultural and ideological. The neoconservative vision of the strong society is one resembling the United States in the Cold War era. The existence of an ideologically armed and intact elite is the crucial ingredient, and its role in resisting external pressure is only the reverse side of its role in resisting internal disintegration.

CHAPTER FOUR

The Neoconservative Style

NEOCONSERVATISM HAS DEVELOPED a style to match its substance. It conveys its message in a distinctive manner. It strikes a distinctive attitude. The form and tone of its discourse reveal its character and account for its success.

The neoconservative style is formal, literary, learned, and serious. It is quite different from the political reportage in journals like *New Republic* or *The Nation,* from the muckraking of the old *Ramparts* or the new *Mother Jones,* from the analyses of social problems in *Society* or *Social Policy,* from the popular psychology or sociology of *Psychology Today* or *Human Behavior,* from the academic studies in most of the quarterlies. It is scholarly, and yet unlike scholarly publications; it is combative, and yet unlike the denunciatory literature of the Left and Right.

From Higher Journalism to Political Philosophy

Though today the leading neoconservatives may be comfortably fixed in the halls of research or instruction, many of them served apprenticeships on the political-literary journals of New York. They are, it should be understood, essentially essayists and practitioners of the Higher Journalism. Even their books are usually collections of essays, many of which first appear as articles in one or another of their journalistic outlets.

Irving Howe once attempted to describe the kind of essay peculiar to the "New York intellectuals." It featured "a characteristic style of exposition and polemic," far-ranging, contentious, dazzling in its taste for novelty and the "wrenching of accepted opinion." Howe may have had in mind writers like Robert Warshow, Mary McCarthy, Dwight Macdonald, Harold Rosenberg, Philip Rahv, Lionel Trilling, Paul Goodman, F. W. Dupee, Clement Greenberg, Alfred Kazin, Richard Chase, and Leslie Fiedler. From these the neoconservative style diverges, and in significant ways; but its heritage is still apparent.

That heritage can be seen most clearly by contrast with muckraking, a staple of liberal (and sometimes right-wing) journalism. (When the young left-wing monthly *Mother Jones* surveyed its readership in 1976, the subscribers, mostly college-educated, overwhelmingly chose the "exposé" as the kind of article they preferred.) The muckraker concentrates on a very particular set of conditions. He dwells on the "facts," revealing and dramatizing what his readers did not know. His is a chronicle of wrongdoing, with little moral complexity. The "facts" may be deeply obscured, the thread of iniquity may require painstaking unraveling; but the larger principles by which the matter is to be judged are not themselves under discussion. They are taken for granted—everyday norms of right and wrong. In what ways is the matter under investigation representative or systemic? What forces might have operated other than personal virtue or vice? What can be expected from the available remedies? The muckraker does not dwell on these wider questions. Theoretical issues are slighted, or dealt with by assertion. The muckraker is more concerned about the "inside story," the reality "behind the scenes"; and his language is often that of exhortation. Muckraking combines the detective story with the morality play.

Like the muckraker or any other political commentator, the neoconservative essayist is interested in discovering and displaying the *real* story, but his rhetorical strategy is entirely different. Almost never do neoconservatives investigate a single institution or episode with the muckraker's concentration on specific deeds, or with the intention of bringing to light previously unknown realities. They are interested in reflection, not reportage. They write at a remove, not up close to their topic. Rather than address an issue directly, they are likely to address other *views,* other explanations, of it. Their approach is thus theoretical from the start. They may open with a reference to a book or other document, to a conversation or anecdote that reveals some standard opinion of the matter, to a past prediction that has proved wildly mistaken. Against this background, commonly presented as the "fashionable" view or the "conventional wisdom," the neoconservative writers may wax derisive or puzzled. In either case, the problem, as conventionally defined, is seen to be largely misconstrued; a new definition is in order. This may diminish the issue, as typically occurred in neoconservatism's "cooling" phase, when it argued that public "crises" were largely the fantasies of crisis-mongering intellectuals; or the new definition may enlarge the issue, stretching it to the dimensions of civilization itself. It is in the dismissing of current explanations and the redefining of public issues that the neoconservatives delight in the paradox, the "bravura" and "dazzle" that Howe mentioned as marks of the New York essay. There really is no housing problem (except in the mind of New York intellectuals); there really is no undue inequality (except in the mind of New York intellectuals); the United States is actually a socialist country, "owned" by workers through union pension funds; Watergate was not really a Nixon assault on the Constitution but a liberal assault on anti-Communist foreign policy; the "energy crisis" is a media myth; limits on campaign spending will benefit the rich; the turmoil of the sixties was not caused by racial inequities or Vietnam but by demography.

Again in Howe's phrase for the earlier work of the "New York intellectuals," the neoconservative essay is "taut with a pressure to 'go beyond' its subject, toward some encompassing moral or social observation." Neoconservatism, it might be said, is literary criticism and social science aspiring to the rank of political philosophy. Behind muckraking stands the crusading reporter; behind much "social problems" writing stands the reforming social scientist—both figures of the Progressive era. Behind the neoconservative style stands the literary critic and the philosophical man of letters. It is an older and a richer tradition. Neoconservatism's willingness to take up general questions of culture and morality, when both academic philosophy and religion have abdicated this task and when other political currents focus on immediate issues or sectarian squabbles, fills an important place in American political discussion. Neoconservatism responds to a deeply felt need, the need for a principled or, if you will, *ideological* articulation of America's predicaments and possibilities.

Other factors add to the credibility of neoconservative writings. By contrast with a good deal of political journalism, in which qualification is a lost art, neoconservatism displays an awareness of complexity and irony. It avoids the language of simple exhortation and denunciation, or at least cloaks it with an artful elegance. It is learned and sophisticated, with a wide range of references at its disposal, drawing from literature, history, and philosophy as well as specialized studies in political science, sociology, and economics—and, of course, the "great tradition" of modern social thought, Marx, Weber, and Freud. Finally it has a moral seriousness, sometimes approaching "earnestness" in the Victorian sense, that derives from its anti-totalitarian mystique.

Cracks in the Facade

With the exception of the last, these qualities are often less substantial than they appear. There is a sharp limit to neoconservatism's awareness of complexity; at certain points it issues sudden appeals to simple truths and what everybody knows. The United States "must play the hand dealt us," Daniel Patrick Moynihan declares, and almost all neoconservatives agree: "We stand for liberty, for the expansion of liberty." Neoconservatives will acknowledge the painful facts contradicting this flat conclusion; but rather than allow that in international politics our nation has stood *both* for liberty and against it, they finally resolve the tension utterly by doughty assertion. Neoconservatism evinces little awareness of the complexity of "complexity" itself—how it, too, has become a politically charged notion, convenient for bolstering one's self-esteem in the face of ethical challenges, or rationalizing the reservation of political power to "competent" elites. Reference to historical ironies, or latent purposes, or unintended consequences can become mental tics, mechanical exhibitions of cleverness. The intellectual breadth and depth of the neoconservatives are also a good deal less imposing on close inspection. The learning of a polymath like Daniel Bell is real enough, though unfortunately displayed with all the subtlety of Mussolini's architecture. In other cases, the wide-ranging references may turn out to be facade, "got up" for the occasion (Moynihan keeps repeating the same literary allusions, quoting the same lines of poetry); or the startling "fact" turns out to be dubious. In political philosophy and history the neoconservatives may be two steps ahead of most political commentary but can be surprisingly narrow for all that. They seem to have all gone to the same school; depend on the same secondary works; and, whether the topic be Rousseau, the French Revolution, American populism, or the Cold War, possess only the most cursory awareness, if any at all, of scholarly conclusions at odds with those they rely upon.

None of this would be consequential were it not for the *knowing* attitude which is so much a part of the neoconservative style, the assertiveness that distinguishes it from much scholarship at the same time that it claims to respect scholarly values. What Irving Howe, "with some admiration and a bit of irony," called the New York intellectuals' "style of brilliance" surely accounts for much of the impression neoconservatism has made. No less an experienced observer than David Riesman recalled in awe a Harvard address in which Moynihan compared student radicals to the religious sects of seventeenth-century England and then predicted that student activism would subside along with the effects of the postwar baby boom. "There aren't many people," *Time* magazine quotes Riesman as saying, "who have enough knowledge of the Fifth Monarchy Men of the 1640s and of demographics to advance those two thoughts." That the impression may be more important than the reality is suggested by the fact that what so provoked Riesman's admiration was, in fact, two speeches, delivered six years apart, and neither of them predicted an end to student activism. (The second speech, given in 1973 and based on a memorandum by Norman B. Ryder to a Presidential commission, did offer an explanation for what had already occurred, though that explanation, unfortunately, did not fit the theories put forward in the earlier speech.)

"Facts are facts, however unpleasant," wrote Edward Banfield, an "ultra" among the neo's, "and they have to be faced unblinkingly." It is this assurance about possessing the facts, or possessing a sophisticated sense of historical complexity, that makes the neoconservatives persuasive to many who themselves have no way of knowing whether these are indeed the facts. The reader who follows Peter Drucker's dazzling and paradoxical account of "Pension Fund 'Socialism' " is unlikely to know that Drucker is not only reversing a judgment he made in 1950, with equal self-assurance, that pension funds were a "mirage" and "will not last long," but that Drucker's latest pronouncements are shot through with the most elementary and egregious misstatements of economic and demographic facts. The reader who is not himself devoted to thick tomes of academic philosophy may have little idea that the neoconservative depiction of John Rawls's *A Theory of Justice* as an expression of radical egalitarianism is wild caricature.

I am not saying that the ratio of error to accuracy is higher in neoconservative essays than in other political writing. It is probably, on the whole, lower. But while other political currents are more likely to wear their partisanship on their shirtsleeves, alerting the critical reader to bias, neoconservatism manages to modulate its exhortations, advance its ideology as anti-ideology, and express the conflict of political values as a conflict of competence and character: the knowing and sophisticated versus the ignorant and naive.

The Crusade Against Cant

The neoconservative style cannot really be understood except in this context of conflict. Where the muckraker is pitted against a mob of Interests that have hidden their malefactions, the neoconservative is pitted against a swarm of intellectual theories that have muddled, or at least failed to clarify, our thinking. Howe wrote of "a sense of *tournament*" among New York intellectuals. The phrase is hardly strong enough for, say, the *Commentary* of recent years. Howe had in mind a degree of playfulness: dialectical knives were not only wielded, they were "juggled"; the writer's aim "was not judiciousness." It is here that the neoconservatives diverge from the style Howe described. They are almost always deadly serious. They aim to be the very sword and buckler of judiciousness, of good sense against nonsense. A line from *Commentary*'s promotional literature gives the clue: "If anything unites all the different voices that speak through *Commentary*'s pages, it is shared abhorrence of cant."

Yet rolling back the sea of cant may be a more perilous enterprise than often realized. One thinks of the description, in John Gross's *The Rise and Fall of the Man of Letters*, of the mid-nineteenth-century *Saturday Review*.

> With men like Henry Maine and Fitzjames Stephen among its regular contributors, the *Saturday Review* . . . assumed an imposing degree of cultivation among their readers, and specialized in enthusiastic exposures of shoddy thinking or defective scholarship. Contemptuous of the age in which they lived as one "of vapours and smelling-bottles," their pet victims were hot-gospellers, demagogues, sentimental novelists. Undeniably they provided a bracing corrective to a great deal of nonsense which up till then had gone pretty much unchallenged. But where they deluded themselves was in supposing that "the educated class" as they defined it could somehow stand permanently aloof from party interests. . . . Contributors raged against trade unions, vied with *The Times* in their hostility to the North in the American Civil War, jeered at the campaign to bring in a secret ballot. . . . Nor was their astringent "realism" the wholly commendable policy which it may sound in the abstract. Many of the attitudes which they derided as mawkish might better be described as humane, while the fact that they took for granted the conventional taboos of the age only makes their deliberate callousness seem that much more distasteful.

Just as the *Saturday Review* of John Gross's description "provided a bracing corrective to a great deal of nonsense," so have *Commentary* and *The Public Interest*. At the same time, neoconservatism has made itself hostage to those it so relentlessly criticizes. Its victories can only be as substantial as its adversaries, and it has tended, in its crusade against cant, to choose the most insubstantial targets. Yes, there are feminists who are petulant, privileged, and unable to cope with their own freedom; yes, there are socialites fierce with revolutionary rhetoric and professors servile toward "relevance"; yes, there are arrogant government planners and middle-class liberals silly with guilt; yes, there are Scandinavian students—aren't we told so at the beginning of a *Commentary* essay?— who bemoan the restraints on freedom in their own society and declare their admiration for Albania; yes, as another *Commentary* article tells us, there are egalitarians who would determine college admissions by lottery. Yes, there was and is (somewhere) an Abbie Hoffman. It does not take much to explode such targets, but a debate conducted on these grounds is quite apt to avoid the truly difficult questions of our time.

From making "cant" the main object of one's critical energy, it is only a small step to treating whatever one criticizes as though it were cant. *The most debilitating intellectual weakness of neoconservatism is its lack of respect for its political opponents.* In this it resembles, not surprisingly, the New Left against which it first mobilized—the old tale of enemies mirroring one another. To diverge from the neoconservative position is not merely to be wrong in a complicated world; it is to exhibit some weakness of mind or character.

This attitude may account for the neoconservatives' blindness to their own double standard about discourse. On the one hand they uphold the values of "rationality, moderation, balance, tolerance"—"the enduring need for civility, tolerance, and intellectual rigor." They ridicule loose talk about repression in the United States, fascism, genocide, and the "immorality" of American foreign policy. On the other hand, they are not fastidious about parallels between American radicals and those who paved the way for Nazism; about charges of anti-Semitism and Stalinism. *The New York Review of Books* became an obsession with the neoconservatives; it represented the "totalitarian Left"—from among its authors "the next Stalin and his speechwriters will emerge." It was a sign of reasonableness to lean sparingly on moral rhetoric in discussing Vietnam, but a particular turn of Kissinger diplomacy in the Middle East is unmistakably "immoral." For a while the neoconservatives' favorite term of abuse for their adversaries was "anti-American," it being obvious that those whose criticism of the nation went beyond what the neoconservatives had established as precisely appropriate were root-and-branch detesters of this society. Various nice points were produced to demonstrate how "anti-American" had nothing in common with the discredited epithet "un-American." Later, with anti-Communism more readily associated with Soviet dissenters than an unpopular war, neoconservatives came perilously close to making old-fashioned accusations of aiding and abetting the Communist enemy. Quoting Solzhenitsyn to Harvard alumni, Moynihan warns ominously that "the liberal political tradition" is the object "of violent assault from its enemies without, and *no less treacherous* defense by its putative adherents within." (My emphasis.) In the face of Garry Wills's introduction to Lillian Hellman's *Scoundrel Time*, Nathan Glazer cannot restrain himself: "[Wills] tells us with no hint of embarrassment that he prefers Communist totalitarianism to democracy." Wills tells us nothing of the sort. He writes as though the United States initiated Cold War hostilities—and should not have. Take issue with that, if you please, or with Wills's account of the connivance between liberalism and McCarthyism; but no degree of faultfinding with Wills's facts or his historical sensitivity adds up to a preference for Communist totalitarianism. That Glazer "deduces" such a preference and writes that Wills "tells us" of it "with no hint of embarrassment" only suggests how easily neoconservatives abrogate to themselves the task of establishing other people's loyalty, how naturally they conduct controversies in terms of who shall or shall not be considered, to cite Glazer again, among "the principal enemies of freedom."

The double standard operates in another way. Explaining why the New Critics attained so much more success in the 1950s than the New York "family" of critics around his *Partisan Review,* William Phillips once observed, "All they ever do is praise and promote one another, and all we ever do is attack one another." Phillips made this remark to Norman Podhoretz; and, much later, when Podhoretz began rallying the neoconservatives, he appears to have learned the lesson. Neoconservatives disagree among themselves on major issues: the potential of federal power or the executive branch as a necessary and positive instrument of social change; international affairs and defense policy; even the degree to which society's discontents reflect the real situation of millions of people or are generated by the fantasies and misconceptions of intellectuals and culture-managers. With few exceptions these differences are repressed. There is none of the toe-to-toe slugging of an earlier period.

This is partly the result of neoconservatism's concentration on its external enemies. The believer in federal authority and Presidential initiative can make his case against the "liberal" advocates of slowed growth, "small-is-beautiful," decentralization, community control, Congressional dominance, what-have-you. The neoconservative opponent of federal authority and executive initiative can likewise make *his* case against the "liberal" advocates of regulation, planning, welfare initiatives, and so on. Deriding their enemies, they avoid confronting one another. Facts that contradict leading neoconservatives' theses are brought forward, but their relevance to those theses either goes unmentioned or is passed over lightly. A *Commentary* reviewer of John Dean's *Blind Ambition* dwells on the ease with which the White House manipulated the press to blacken Dean's reputation. This evidence is assimilated to neoconservatism's low opinion of the media, without noting its pertinence to the neoconservative theory that the media are deeply "oppositionist."

An article in *The Public Interest* presents evidence suggesting that not Moynihan but two of his favorite objects of ire, Frances Fox Piven and Richard Cloward, turned out to have the better explanation for expanding welfare rolls in the 1960s; the same article argues that the failure of the Family Assistance Plan in Congress is not to be explained by the "perfidious liberal" theory—offered, as it happens, by Moynihan. Another article in the same issue, on school desegregation, notes Nixon's "true but misleading" claim to have achieved more desegregation in one year than his predecessor ever had: in fact, "the orders which produced that result had largely been issued in the last days of the Johnson Administration." The same "true but misleading" claim was, of course, made on Nixon's behalf by Moynihan.

The interpretation of court action in this same article on school desegregation leaves a considerably different impression than Nathan Glazer's vision of "an imperial judiciary" in *The American Commonwealth* or even Glazer's depiction of court and federal aggressiveness in *Affirmative Discrimination*. There are no rules that say neoconservatives should go out of their way to attack themselves. That would be a little like the joke explaining the difference between Democrats and cannibals: cannibals only devour their enemies. But the gentlemanly, matter-of-fact manner of such differences of opinion (if attention is drawn to them at all) is in marked contrast to their treatment of others.

The neoconservatives are hypersensitive to error and foible when it is not safely tied to an approved political outlook; they are tolerant when it is. Is John Cheever too forgiving toward the criminal hero of his latest novel? This, writes a *Commentary* reviewer, "is inadequate as criminology and, more broadly, as moral statement." The point is well argued and Cheever is treated respectfully; the criticism is artistic, not political. But one feels that *Commentary,* as distinguished from the reviewer, would not be so concerned that Cheever is "artistically soft" were it not for the possibility that he is criminologically soft. In the same issue, after all, one finds another review declaring that in his writing Tom Wolfe "has done more than any other to encompass the spirit of the age." His latest essays "confirm his remarkable literary gifts" and his scathing denunciations of the intellectual Left "raise him into the ranks of those few writers whose ideas and whose opinions represent an important contribution to the overall health of the culture." At only one point does the critical scrutiny given Wolfe approach that given Cheever: Hailing Wolfe's contribution to cultural health, his reviewer prudently inserts "opinions" along with "ideas."

Settling Wolfe's true stature as a satirist and thinker is not the point. The point is merely to imagine what, if his politics had not passed muster, *Commentary* might have done with this erstwhile laureate of sixties excess and the "new sensibility"; this former prophet of the demise of pre-McLuhan journals (like *Commentary)* that "pass judgment in a learned way" on books and politics; this celebrant of stock-car drivers and go-go dancers; this pioneering voice of the *"nostalgie de la boue"* he later pinned on the wealthy donors to Black Panther bail funds; this master of a style that flaunted ego and subjectivity throughout what he now derides as "The Me Decade." Without the moat of his current politics, Wolfe would be an undefended city. How relentlessly the "cant" could be exposed and duly abhorred.

It is here that neoconservatism, as a serious strand of political thinking, is most in danger of undoing itself. If all political writing emulated the neoconservative manner at its best, we might drop beneath the burden of seriousness and skepticism; but we would be far less likely to perish from folly. On the other hand, to proclaim a high standard of discourse, to pride oneself on that standard, and to adhere to it often enough, yet finally to be ruled by party spirit and factional passion, may more gravely endanger that standard than would an initial stance that was frankly partisan and less intellectually rigorous. To acclaim civility, and yet treat one's adversaries as ignorant, neurotic, or power-driven totalitarians; to honor complexity, and yet divide the intellectual world into two camps and set out to police it on behalf of one; to profess independence of mind, and yet insist on a new conformity; to reject the tyranny of "fashion," and yet rehearse another set of shibboleths—in so doing, neoconservatism threatens to discredit the very values it aspires to serve.

Nothing sums up the effects of the neoconservatives' sense of beleaguerment better than the promotional material *Commentary* has employed for a number of years, the same material that declared its abhorrence of cant. A promotional mailing reveals both a journal's self-image and its calculated estimate of the potential audience's state of mind; it expresses, in brief, the mental world in which a journal exists.

Commentary's world is not a happy one. Blazoned across the envelope received by a potential subscriber is the single word SANITY—in two-inch letters. After quoting a harebrained bureaucratic regulation from the Polish government, the promotional letter begins: "Dear Fellow Inmate, Don't laugh. Life in this part of the world hasn't been much saner." In the midst of madness, however, *Commentary* offers "sane thinking" and "uncommon rationality." The magazine will "do our best to restore your faith in Reason and in Sanity too." The return postcard repeats the message: Subscribe to *Commentary*, "In the Interest of Sanity." (Recent postcards, with the same message, have also expressed *Commentary*'s feelings by reproducing nineteenth-century engravings of schoolteachers or headmasters harassed by unruly children.)

This is a remarkable self-revelation. Magazines are given to claiming that they are right when others are wrong, stimulating when others are dull, bold when others are timid, thoughtful when others are superficial. But "sane" when others are . . . what? Such a stance is not conducive to political dialogue.

CHAPTER FIVE

Irving Kristol,
Standard-Bearer

IRVING KRISTOL is the standard-bearer of neoconservatism. Almost alone among his colleagues he has not been reluctant to declare his conservative instincts. Where Nathan Glazer appears slightly puzzled at finding himself become a "mild conservative"—it is at least a matter deserving of explanation—Kristol asserts that his own conservatism is only what "an adult's normal political instincts should be." At the same time, having admitted his discomfort "with what passes for either liberalism or conservatism in the United States," Kristol has taken up the prefix "neo-" with pleasure: "The more I think about the term, the more I like it."

Up from Trotskyism

If Horatio Alger had written about intellectuals instead of newsboys, Kristol could have been one of his heroes. *Irving, the Editor; or, From Alcove No. 1 to the President's Dinner Table*. Alcove No. 1 was the bit of "turf" in the City College of New York cafeteria that tradition had assigned to the non-Communist socialists. The Communists and their friends exercised their territorial imperative over Alcove No. 2. Here, in the late thirties, Kristol's "real college education took place"; he passed the hours studying "a Marxist scholasticism that was as rigorous and

learned, in its way, as the Jesuit scholasticism it so strikingly paralleled,"
aspiring to understand the articles in the *Partisan Review*, and sparring
ideologically with such fellow denizens of Alcove No. 1 (and future
neoconservatives) as Seymour Martin Lipset, Nathan Glazer, Daniel Bell,
and Melvin Lasky. Kristol, of course, no longer believes in that Marxist
scholasticism; but as the Jesuits—who continued to believe in *their*
scholasticism—used to say about learning Latin, "it was good for the
mind." The fierce and endless ideological debates, the terrible concern
"with being 'right' " in everything—though not as brutal and inquisitorial
as the conformity demanded in Alcove No. 2—provided a certain type of
intellectual formation, "inclined to celebrate the analytic powers of mind
rather than the creative." The milieu also encouraged a remarkable
confidence: "It would never have occurred to us to denounce anyone or
anything as 'elitist.' The elite was us—the 'happy few' who had been
chosen by History to guide our fellow creatures toward a secular
redemption."

Kristol graduated from City College in 1940—"and the honor I most
prized was the fact that I was a member in good standing of the Young
People's Socialist League." It was not long before he put these childish
things behind him, however, turning in his membership card to the
Trotskyist YPSL.* Out of the armed forces at the end of the war, Kristol
started on the neoconservative *cursus honorum,* writing for and then
taking an editorial post at *Commentary.*

Kristol's activities during the fifties are still, almost a quarter of a
century later, capable of stirring the most heated discussions. The
controversies center on two issues: his attitude toward McCarthyism and
his involvement, as a founding editor, with the CIA-funded *Encounter*
magazine. At the end of 1976, a meeting of New York intellectuals could
explode into shouting over the frequently cited closing sentences of
Kristol's March 1952 *Commentary* article on McCarthy. ("There is one
thing that the American people know about Senator McCarthy; he, like
them, is unequivocally anti-Communist. About the spokesmen for American liberalism, they feel they know no such thing.") Kristol had also
served for the better part of a year as executive secretary of the American
Committee for Cultural Freedom (which distributed the *Commentary*
article), and recalls "issuing protests against one instance after another of
McCarthyism."

In 1955, Michael Harrington gave a different interpretation:

---

* As chance had it, the person to whom he handed the card was the critic and
essayist Irving Howe, who like Kristol would soon reject Trotskyism but, unlike
Kristol, would maintain an unflagging commitment to democratic socialism.

Under the guidance of [Sidney] Hook and the leadership of Irving Kristol, who supported Hook's general outlook, the American Committee cast its weight not so much in defense of those civil liberties which were steadily being nibbled away, but rather against those few remaining fellow-travelers who tried to exploit the civil-liberties issue.

At times this had an almost comic aspect. When Irving Kristol was executive secretary of the ACCF, one learned to expect from him silence on those issues that were agitating the whole intellectual and academic world, and enraged communiqués on the outrages performed by people like Arthur Miller and Bertrand Russell in exaggerating the dangers to civil liberties in the U.S.

And Christopher Lasch has characterized the ACCF's position as manifesting a concern not for "cultural freedom" *per se* but for establishing the ground rules for effective and professional, and not counterproductive, anti-Communism. Thus its defense of the Voice of America against McCarthy's onslaughts (two of Kristol's successors at the ACCF were former Voice of America employees); its criticism of embarrassing outbreaks of philistine anti-Communism as well as of "anti-anti-Communism"; its elaboration of tests of "sincerity" and "clean hands" for defenders of civil liberties. "Government agencies," wrote Hook, "find their work hampered by the private fevers of cultural vigilantism."

The Encounter *Affair*

The American Committee for Cultural Freedom was affiliated with the international Congress for Cultural Freedom, founded in 1950—probably with CIA support from the start and, in any case, with a CIA agent, Michael Josselson, as executive director. In 1952 both the Paris-based congress and its British offshoot separately developed proposals for an English-language journal. Stephen Spender had been the British group's choice to edit the journal it had in mind; Irving Kristol had been proposed by the indefatigable Hook to edit the congress journal. The two ideas—and the editorial direction—were merged. The first issue of *Encounter* appeared in October 1953, edited by Spender and Kristol in London. Promising "the uninhibited exploration" of differences of opinion, its initial editorial celebrated the death of Stalin and risings of workers in East Germany and Czechoslovakia. Although these marked "the destruction of the Marxist-Leninist creed," problems remained. "The dark side of the moon may no longer be mistaken for the rising sun, but it is still there and still dark. And shadows move among us; almost too many to count and sometimes even hard to name."

Encounter was one in a family of journals sponsored by the international Congress for Cultural Freedom, including *Preuves* in France, *Tempo Presente* in Italy, *Forum* in Austria, *Hiwar* in Lebanon, *Cuadernos* and *Examen* in Latin America, the *China Quarterly,* and *Survey, a Journal of Soviet and East European Affairs.*

In 1966, an article in *The New York Times* reported the CIA support of the congress and its magazines, thereby initiating a period of evasive "denials" from Spender, Kristol, Melvin J. Lasky (who had succeeded Kristol as editor of *Encounter* in 1958), John Kenneth Galbraith, George Kennan, Robert Oppenheimer, and Arthur Schlesinger, Jr. A year later, however, *Ramparts* magazine's exposé of CIA manipulation of the National Students Association reopened the whole file. In *The Saturday Evening Post,* former CIA official Thomas W. Braden, apparently deciding that the best defense was a good offense, announced his pride in the CIA's "immoral" cultural activities:

> And then there was *Encounter,* the magazine published in England and dedicated to the proposition that cultural achievement and political freedom were interdependent. Money for . . . the magazine's publication came from the CIA, and few outside the CIA knew about it. We had placed one agent in a Europe-based organization of intellectuals called the Congress for Cultural Freedom. Another agent became an editor of *Encounter.* The agents could not only propose anti-Communist programs to the official leaders of the organizations but they could also suggest ways and means to solve the inevitable budgetary problems. Why not see if the needed money could be obtained from "American foundations"?

Encounter's friends had already prepared a second line of defense: The source of the journal's funds was irrelevant; the editors had always enjoyed and exercised complete editorial independence; indeed the magazine had no particular political "line" at all.

This, however, proved a regular Swiss cheese of an argument, it was so full of holes. It was true that neither the Paris congress nor the CIA dictated editorial policy to *Encounter* in any direct way. At the most there seems to have been a discreet hint from Paris now and then, no more, Kristol later recalled, than the editors of *Commentary* received from its institutional sponsor, the American Jewish Committee. "In both cases, such gentle interventions were not entirely ignored; an independent editor need not be a prima donna."

At the same time, there is no question that *Encounter* had a distinct political mission, not only to be anti-Communist but, if one might exploit the revealing weakness of the period for piling up negatives, to be *anti-anti-American*, that is, to root out, smooth over, or absorb whatever might provoke thoroughgoing opposition to the United States. This work was accomplished with a great deal of subtlety and sophistication; even the CIA recognized that the credibility of a front had to be maintained "by not requiring it to support every aspect of official American policy." The pertinent question about *Encounter*'s independence was not whether there were instructions cabled to the editors from Washington, but who chose the editors in the first place, and who established the clear bounds of "responsible" opinion within which differences were uninhibitedly explored. One doubts whether editors—or the CIA—would have tolerated consistent and fundamental criticism of America or American foreign policy in the pages of *Encounter*.

In 1967 a special problem existed for the editors and ex-editors, one of whom had been implicated by Braden as an "agent." By everyone's account, Spender was out of the running for this designation; somehow he seemed the natural dupe. That left Kristol and Lasky. Of Lasky's complicity there was plenty of circumstantial evidence. For one thing he finally admitted that he had known about the CIA money since 1963 and had been "insufficiently frank" with his fellow editors and the public. ("Insufficiently frank" is evidently the way an independent intellectual describes lying.) Furthermore, Lasky had served in the American Information Service and started *Der Monat* with the support of the American occupation forces in Germany. Along with Josselson, he had organized the original Berlin meeting of the Congress for Cultural Freedom. In short, he was a knowledgeable frequenter of the circles where propaganda efforts, secret and otherwise, are put into operation. The problem, of course, is that the tasks Braden mentions in connection with his "agent" had to be performed long before Lasky came on the *Encounter* scene. Securing financial support, for example, is an essential job for a founding editor like Kristol. Kristol, however, has always insisted he knew nothing of the CIA presence. He announced a suit against Braden, while saying that his lawyer warned it might be difficult to prove that alleging employment in the national intelligence agency was *ipso facto* defamatory. Braden fudged his remarks a little, and in any case the suit was dropped.

According to others, the matter hardly turns on Braden's revelations. Rumors about the CIA's subsidy of *Encounter* and the Congress were rife for years, they report. Was it possible that Kristol wasn't in on the secret? Kristol grants the rumors but argues that there were good reasons not to take them seriously. First of all, they "issued from sources—left-wing, anti-American or both—that would have been happy to circulate them, true or not," and so he discounted them in advance. Second, there was the concrete fact of the foundations that supplied the funds. Third, there was the absence of any direct censorship. Kristol is not unaware of the difficulties. "Perhaps it will be said that my own frequently expressed political opinions were so clearly 'safe,' from the CIA's point of view, that censorship was superfluous. Maybe so." Even this kind of control, he contends, is challenged by the fact that Kristol, after differences with Spender, was scheduled to be replaced at *Encounter* by Dwight Macdonald. "Could the CIA really have 'endorsed' *him?* Dwight has spent a fruitful life and distinguished career purposefully being a security risk to just about everyone and everything within reach of his typewriter." Unfortunately, the incident does not support Kristol's point but indicates that *someone,* whether or not the CIA, was standing watch. Macdonald, as a matter of fact, did not get the job. The ubiquitous Hook and other ideological elders quickly scurried around and made sure that Macdonald's term was a one-year assignment only. Kristol's permanent replacement turned out to be the old trooper Melvin J. Lasky.

That the CIA should have been sponsoring *Encounter* did once seem to be an exotic and unlikely fancy to the uninvolved observer—just as today, with some good grounds, the uninvolved observer is apt to suspect CIA finagling in just about everything. But Kristol was not uninvolved. He was, after all, a founding editor of the journal, a veteran of Cold War ideological disputes with their conspiratorial maneuverings, an old college associate of Lasky's.

Diana Trilling writes:

I was a member, then an officer, of the American Committee for Cultural Freedom, an independent affiliate of the international organization. Even before I came onto the Executive Board of the American Committee, I was aware, and it was my clear impression that everyone else on the board was also in some measure aware, that the international body with which we were associated was probably funded by the government. I do not say that we had hard evidence to this effect, of a sort to which one swears in a court of law, but we strongly suspected that the Fairfield Foundation, which we were told supported the congress, was a filter for State Department or CIA money. What made the CIA appear to be the more likely source was the fact that, alone among the national committees, ours in America got no financial help. Since it was known that the CIA was not allowed to spend money within the United States, we concluded that it must be the CIA which funded the various programs of the congress throughout the free world, including its magazines in many countries. And this was often a subject of discussion between myself and my friends: the editors of *Partisan Review,* for instance, felt handicapped in terms of foreign circulation by lack of a subsidy such as was given *Encounter,* the intellectual journal which the congress supported in England. Finally our speculation that the CIA was the source of the congress funds became certainty for the members of the American Executive Board who happened to be present at a meeting when its then-chairman, Mr. Norman Thomas, many times Socialist candidate for the presidency of the United States and a man whose personal integrity and record in defense of civil liberties is not open to question, reported that, chronically insolvent, we now lacked money even for the next month's rent. Mr. Thomas could see but a single solution: he would "phone Allen"; he returned from the telephone to tell us that a check for a thousand dollars would be in the mail next morning. None of us could fail to know that the "Allen" who tided us over was Allen Dulles, head of the CIA, and that in the strictest sense it was even a breach of legality for him to give us help. But none of us, myself included, protested.

This episode doubtlessly dates from a period after Kristol's departure to London. What is most telling, however, is the casualness with which this milieu accepted such a link with "Allen." Was Kristol an exception?

There is no decisive proof one way or the other, and Kristol's problem should be appreciated: How can he prove a negative, that he was *not* in the know about the CIA? The burden of proof, obviously, must be with his critics. It seems a mite naive simply to take Kristol at his word: clearly, he has no principled objection to the CIA's arrangement with *Encounter* —his concern for his own reputation would have been perfectly well served as long as secrecy was maintained—and he later exhibited great amiability toward those who had supposedly deceived him. And yet one cannot sustain a definite conclusion that he is dissembling.

Kristol's entanglement with the CIA was a time bomb that did not explode until the mid-sixties. Meanwhile he had returned to the United States as an editor at *The Reporter,* and moved on to be editor and executive vice-president at Basic Books. With Basic Books for editorial space and Freedom House for a tax-exempt sponsor, Kristol launched *The Public Interest* in 1965. Meanwhile he kept up his political provocations; in *The New Leader* he regularly dashed cold water on the poverty program and other fond hopes of sixties liberalism. In 1968, Kristol declared himself a Hubert Humphrey supporter—early, when the salient contest was between Humphrey, Eugene McCarthy, and Robert Kennedy for the Democratic nomination. Humphrey and Nixon, he explained, "are the only two candidates who make a nationwide 'majority appeal.' "

> In these pages, I need not explain why the prospect of electing Mr. Nixon depresses me. Suffice it to say that he appeals to *the wrong majority* to govern the United States in these times—a majority whose dominant temper will be sullenly resentful of the social changes we have been experiencing and impulsively reactionary toward the crises we shall inevitably be enduring.

The actual election of Mr. Nixon proved less depressing to Kristol than the prospect. Or at any rate, perhaps in keeping with his conviction that maturity implied increasing conservatism, he soon adjusted to the "wrong majority." Within two years he was having dinner with Nixon in the White House. What brought the editor and the President together was their fear and loathing of the New Left. A month after their meeting, a front-page story in *The New York Times* announced "U.S. to Tighten Surveillance of Radicals."

> The Nixon Administration, alarmed by what it regards as a rising tide of radical extremists, is planning to step up surveillance of militant left-wing groups and individuals. . . . Preparations for expanding and improving the domestic intelligence apparatus—informers, undercover agents, wiretaps— were disclosed in a series of interviews with key officials who requested anonymity. . . .
>
> On March 12, the same day that bombs exploded in three Manhattan office buildings, Mr. Nixon met over dinner in the White House with Irving Kristol, professor of urban values at New York University.
>
> One aide who attended the dinner said the discussion included attempts to draw parallels between young, middle-class, white Americans who are resorting to violence and the Narodniki—children of the mid-19th century Russian aristocracy who murdered Czar Alexander II, and between militant black nationalists here and Algerian revolutionaries.
>
> Mr. Kristol told the President it was not unrealistic to expect the Latin American resort to political kidnappings to spread soon to Washington. Mr. Kristol confirmed the dinner meeting and commented, "Some of these kids don't know what this country is. They think it's Bolivia." *

Two days after this story in the *Times,* Vice-President Agnew was praising Kristol's no-nonsense views on higher education at a Des Moines, Iowa, Republican rally. In a 1968 article, Kristol had dealt with "a restructuring of the university" in terms such as "the basic principles of riot control." "It is clearly foolish," he wrote, "to assemble huge and

---

* The story continued: "Some, but not all, of Mr. Nixon's domestic advisors are convinced that the situation is critical. One of the more conservative aides contended, 'We are facing the most severe internal security threat this country has seen since the Depression.' . . . To keep tabs on individuals referred to by the President as 'potential murderers' will require updating an intelligence system geared to monitoring the Communists three decades ago, the aide said. . . . Administration sources would not disclose details of the changes they are preparing in the intelligence mechanism, although they said a good deal of departmental discussion about them was under way. . . . The White House is aware of the political sensitivity of domestic intelligence gathering, which one aide described as 'hangups in the question of snooping.' "

potentially riotous mobs in one place. . . . We should aim at the 'scatteration' of the student population, so as to decrease their capacity to cause significant trouble." There was much more to warm the hearts of Agnew and his audience: "Quite a few of the universities have already decided that the only way to avoid on-campus riots is to give students academic credit for off-campus rioting ('fieldwork' in the ghettos, among migrant workers, etc.)."

In 1972, Kristol was firmly and publicly in the Nixon camp, a signer of a major advertisement in which several handfuls of intellectuals declared, "Of the two major candidates we believe that Richard Nixon has demonstrated the superior capacity for prudent and responsible leadership." ("I think I'll just say nothing," Kristol replied in September 1973 when a *Times* reporter asked how he then felt about his endorsement.) After Nixon's victory there was even a report that Kristol might be appointed "a broad gauge advisor on domestic policy" in the reconstituted Administration.

Kristol's institutional affiliations followed his politics. It may have been ironic that, as the *Times* story mentioned, he had become Henry Luce Professor of Urban Values at New York University. Since Kristol's opinion of urban values was almost as negative as his opinion of student values, one critic remarked that the appointment was "for all the world like putting W. C. Fields in charge of a children's day care center." But Kristol's other assignments were more expressive of his continued trajectory into adulthood. He began writing on "Books & Ideas" for *Fortune*, and joined the "Board of Contributors" of *The Wall Street Journal*, an appointment signifying regular appearances on the newspaper's editorial page. Finally he left his chair at NYU to become a Resident Scholar at the American Enterprise Institute, the "conservative Brookings" dedicated to protecting and enlarging the private sector's role in society.

At the beginning of 1972, just after the bombing of Hanoi, Kristol was again in attendance at the White House. It was a different kind of dinner this time, a white-tie party, with a hundred guests: cabinet members William P. Rogers, John B. Connally, John N. Mitchell, and Maurice H. Stans, and Bob Hope, Norman Vincent Peale, Billy Graham, Frank Borman, and even Kristol's old mentor Sidney Hook. The occasion was the presentation of Medal of Freedom Citations to Mr. and Mrs. DeWitt Wallace, founders and directors of *Reader's Digest*. Through *Reader's Digest*, said President Nixon, the Wallaces had "made a towering contribution to that freedom of the mind from which spring all our other liberties." "We'd have a utopia in this country," commented Mr. Wallace, "if every community adopted all the advice we offered from time to time."

The evening was blemished, however, like so many evenings during the Vietnam War. As the Ray Conniff singers were about to begin the entertainment, Carol Feraci, one of the singers, suddenly waved a placard reading "Stop the Killing." "You go to church on Sunday and pray to Jesus Christ," she called out to President Nixon. "If Jesus Christ were in this room tonight you would not dare to drop another bomb." As the dinner guests shuffled, booed, and groaned, Mr. Conniff asked the young lady to leave.

Utopia had evidently not arrived. But Irving Kristol? It was a long way from Alcove No. 1.

The Crisis According to Kristol

As a journalist and author of occasional essays, Kristol has revealed his ideas everywhere and set them forth nowhere. The closest he has come to an extended statement is the eight previously published essays he chose to assemble in the slim volume *On the Democratic Idea in America* (1972) and the half-dozen major essays which, with two dozen *Wall Street Journal* columns, he collected in *Two Cheers for Capitalism* (1978). The earlier book falls into a genre well known to political philosophy: an analysis of decline. His common theme and concern is "the tendency of democratic republics to depart from . . . their original, animating principles, and as a consequence to precipitate grave crises in the moral and political order." We are approaching a "historic watershed"; "there is a vast unease about the prospects of the republic"; the problems of American society, though perhaps individually soluble, are together "creating habits of mind that threaten the civic-bourgeois culture bequeathed us by Western civilization." This culture is "being casually and almost contemptuously subverted from within," a process involving "the slow draining away of legitimacy from existing institutions and prevailing traditions."

In one essay Kristol ascribes this condition to five causes:

(1) the sense of being carried away by technology's alteration of our lives and prospects;

(2) the expectation that our every demand and desire will be fulfilled— by government if not otherwise—and the abandonment of all self-restraint under the tutoring of affluence and egalitarian democracy;

(3) the emergence not only of a separate world for the young but one that challenges the legitimacy of any adult moral authority;

(4) the takeover of popular culture by the anti-bourgeois avant-garde

with its derision of traditional bourgeois virtue and celebration of drugs, promiscuity, homosexuality, and terrorism;

(5) the inability of religion any longer to answer the fundamental question every society must settle in regard to certain behavior, "Why not?"

In another essay Kristol describes our situation as one of becoming "an urban civilization." Civilization has always maintained itself in the tension between city and province: "It is not too far-fetched to say that each was an indispensable antibody for the other's healthy existence. Life in the city could, for example, be careless of conventional morality . . . precisely because of the reassuring certainty that, throughout the rest of the nation, there prevailed a heavy dullness and conformity." In America, however, "this provincial nation has been liquidated." We may dwell in small cities and suburbs rather than in great metropolises, but in *spirit* we are an urban civilization; "the culture of the city becomes everyman's culture. . . . urban habits of mind and modes of living become the common mentality and way of life for everyone." Now this development is traced against the background of the Founding Fathers' doubts that the vices fostered in great cities were compatible with "republican morality"— doubts they shared with much political philosophy—and in particular their fear of the urban "mobs," to them "the very antithesis of a democratic citizenry." Though in fact material success transformed this mob into respectable bourgeois masses, in the past decades the process has been reversed. The citizenry "are beginning to behave like a bourgeois urban mob." They exhibit a "state of mind which lacks all those qualities that, in the opinion of the founding fathers, added up to republican morality: steadiness of character, deliberativeness of mind, and a mild predisposition to subordinate one's own special interests to the public interest." The cause? The adversary culture, incorporated into conventional schooling and popular culture, is the best answer Kristol can provide. We suffer, finally, from a "startling absence of values."

In yet another essay Kristol pushes the problem back further in time. For the Founding Fathers democracy was problematic: "They were sober and worldly men, and they were not about to hand out blank checks to anyone, even if he was common man." They were concerned about what kind of man the common man would turn out to be under whatever form of government they devised, and what uncommon men and uncommon ideals the common man would be capable of choosing for guides. Is it true, as Al Smith said, that all the ills of democracy, of our mass media, our political parties, our foreign policy, our race relations, can be solved by more democracy rather than traced to our current democracy itself? Elsewhere Kristol expresses concern not that the people have become corrupt—yet—but that "they are so blandly free from self-doubt about this possibility"; or again, that social scientists should judge the quality of democracy simply by the working of its machinery and regardless of the virtue it fostered. Such blindness he feels can be traced—and he attempts to do so in the treatment of democracy by American historians—to the replacement of "the original political *philosophy* of democracy" by "a religious *faith* of democracy"—"the Jacksonian-egalitarian-populist transcendental faith in the common man." This revolution in American thought took place within half a century of the Founding Fathers' own work—though, respect for them being what it was, much more time had to pass before the alteration was readily recognized and openly advocated.

The causes of our woes, according to almost all the essays in *On the Democratic Idea in America,* are "cultural," in the sense of existing essentially in the realm of ideas and ethos. Without tending toward any kind of materialist or economic reductionism, one can still wonder how such transformations can be described with so little reference to the economic system by which the society maintains itself and, indeed, has flourished. Kristol writes of the "technological imperative" and its vertiginous effects without any mention of capitalism. Of the "revolution of rising expectations," he writes that "to see something on television is to feel entitled to it"; and nowise hints that this is exactly the reaction that someone has intended, in fact spent considerable sums of money, to create. The "generation gap" and the "takeover" of popular culture by the anti-bourgeois avant-garde are but the same thing: the generation gap is only the leading edge among the young of the anti-bourgeois culture. The death of God is equally an intellectual fact, and the causes of the transformation of America into an urban civilization "are so obvious as to need no elaboration: one can simply refer in passing to the advent of the mass media and of mass higher education, and there isn't much more that needs to be said." Especially about the relationship of cities, masses, media, and education to our advanced economy. Kristol directs his attention to pornography, foreign policy, the organization of the university, and the inflated language which afflicts American public life, and one might conclude that the influence of intellectuals on these matters as compared to economic impulses and considerations exists in a proportion of about a hundred to one.

Yet this is not quite fair. One essay in *On the Democratic Idea in America* does take up capitalism directly, and Kristol of course returns to the topic in *Two Cheers for Capitalism.* After all, he has written that Americans who defend capitalism these days are called conservative, and "if they are willing to accept a limited degree of government intervention for social purposes, they are likely to be designated as 'neo-conservative' "—which does give him a special interest in the matter.

Capitalism, too, is caught up in the crisis of legitimacy. In its way it generates the crisis, yet in Kristol's portrayal it appears mostly as a "victim"; its sins seem to be those of omission rather than commission. In no way is capitalism's performance at issue, as it is for those who point to the massive population movement from the rural South to unprepared cities, or to national inability to achieve full employment, or to our great inequalities in wealth and power, or to the constant generation of new needs through advertising. Kristol would argue that such failings cannot be laid to capitalism's account or, as in the case of inequality, are not failings at all. As an engine of material goods, capitalism cannot be faulted. If decisive proof is needed, one can simply observe the socialist economies.

Kristol is consistent about performance, however. If he is utterly assured that capitalism's performance has nothing to do with the erosion in its legitimacy, he also warns capitalists that their appeals to performance, to efficiency, will not counteract that erosion: such notions are too hard to measure, and who can ever speak confidently about the efficiency of an institution in the long run? Legitimacy must rest on solider foundations.

No, the problem is not with the failures of a liberal-capitalist society to make good on its promises. Those who take that line are simply disguising, or are too timid to understand, their real intentions; and Kristol is ruthless in telling us what the New Left or other intellectual critics of capitalism *really* want. The problem is the liberal-capitalist ideal itself.

To begin with, "liberal society is of necessity a secular society, one in which religion is mainly a private affair." Disestablishment undermines faith in "the traditional consolations of religion—especially . . . life after death." Bereft of an infinite happiness in the afterlife and still desiring compensation for the unavoidable frustration of their existence, the masses seek an infinite happiness in the here-and-now.

Liberal capitalism also divorces freedom from any substantive notion of merit, distributive justice, or the good society. Whatever pattern of gains or losses results from the free market deserves to be respected, since no one is competent to decide for others what is fair or meritorious. "Under capitalism, whatever is, is just. . . . all the inequalities of liberal-bourgeois society must be necessary or else the free market would not have created them, and therefore they must be justified." The personal virtue of the capitalist is irrelevant. By seeking his own good, whether out of greed or dedication to hard work, whether by speculation or entrepreneurship, he benefits the public. Private vices, argued Mandeville and Hume, become public benefits.

But ordinary people, says Kristol, are unpersuaded, indeed repelled, by this argument. It looks like self-serving ideology. Moreover, artists and intellectuals opposed this world view from the start, and for several reasons. They were offended by the philistinism of bourgeois capitalism, which dispossessed them of their "traditional prerogative . . . to celebrate high nobility of purpose, selfless devotion to transcendental ends, and awe-inspiring heroism." They believed that society had to be governed not by the market but by higher ideals—"as conceived and articulated by intellectuals." Such convictions were aristocratic and elitist; the alienated intellectual "was more likely to move 'Right' than 'Left.' "

None of this was of crucial importance as long as the liberal-capitalist ethos was linked to what is now called the Protestant ethic. That ethic did "prescribe a connection between personal merit—as represented by such bourgeois virtues as honesty, sobriety, diligence, and thrift—and worldly success"; and on that basis capitalism laid claim to be not only a free but also a *just* social order.

Here, too, "bourgeois society was living off the accumulated moral capital of traditional religion and traditional moral philosophy"—which it soon began to deplete. Capitalism, says Kristol, has virtually severed its link with the Protestant ethic; but unlike other writers who make this point, he passes over the impact of the "consumer society" on public attitudes, save for an infrequent reference to "affluence"; and he describes a more roundabout, inadvertent process.

The critical development is the rise of the large corporation, or what Kristol sometimes calls the "bureaucratization of the economic order." The large corporation was not part of the earlier liberal capitalist vision. It did not represent the venture of a single individual or family; it did not exist for a specific purpose but could change its purposes to serve its own permanence. Legally it was private property, but citizens, much earlier than courts, felt that it was actually quasi-public. Legally it was a "person," but it took no personal risks and assumed no personal responsibility. Politicians were naturally concerned about such large concentrations of apparently unaccountable power. What is more, corporations seemed to be subverting capitalism itself, as then understood in individualist terms. Anti-corporation feeling, expressed in antitrust legislation, was in fact a defense of the traditional capitalist ethos.

The corporation has survived, of course, and flourished, but according to Kristol "it still needs a legitimating idea." The "faceless and nameless personages" who direct our large corporations "have no clear title to their privileges," precisely because, unlike their nineteenth-century predecessors, whose biographies were inspirational reading, they are nameless and faceless.

The corporation has produced more than invisible leaders. It has produced the "new class." "These are the people whom liberal capitalism had sent to college in order to help manage its affluent, highly technological, mildly paternalistic, 'post-industrial' society." From the intellectuals this class adopted the older anti-capitalist animus (learned, presumably, in college), but now, as befitting a movement of several millions, gave it a democratic rather than aristocratic guise. "The simple truth is that the professional classes of our modern bureaucratized societies are engaged in a class struggle with the business community for status and power. Inevitably, this class struggle is conducted under the banner of 'equality.' " The new class is persuaded it "can do a better job of running our society" than either businessmen or the people acting through the market. It has mobilized the native anti-corporation—though not anti-capitalist—spirit to its own ends; and under the cover of solving specific ills, it is expanding its own base of power, the government, so that "the structure of American society is being radically, if discreetly, altered." Before this assault, capitalism "is not merely vulnerable, it is practically defenseless." The corporation is "an utterly defenseless institution . . . literally *[sic]* up the creek without a paddle, alienated and friendless . . . the essence of flabbiness . . . picked on and bullied so easily."

In distilling these general ideas from Kristol's essays, have I denatured them at the same time? I can imagine both admirers and detractors saying yes. Reducing Kristol's arguments to a series of propositions does ignore much of what is most characteristic about them.

The Kristol Spirit

As with neoconservatism itself, Kristol's "case" is equal parts manner and matter. Before examining his response to the crisis of legitimacy it is necessary to look at these other dimensions of his writing.

To read any amount of Kristol is to discover three spirits operating in the same breast; and in this, though a greater division of labor may be practiced where less versatile writers are concerned, he is representative of neoconservatism. He is, to begin with, the philosophical essayist, on the model of a nineteenth-century "amateur," speculating thoughtfully but uninhibitedly about the largest questions of personality, ethics, and politics. He is secondly the modern counselor of governments, what Theodore White once called the "action intellectual"; though Kristol never adopts the style of the think-tankers, the economists, and the policy analysts, he is full of respect for their tough-mindedness, their attention to precisely demonstrable facts, their "anti-ideological" skepticism about popular generalizations. He is thirdly the political polemicist, less concerned with large truths or precise facts than with skewering particular political opponents; or rather concerned about wielding large truths or precise facts *in order* to skewer particular political opponents.

Obviously, the three spirits are not in perfect harmony. Kristol's high tone sits oddly with what is often low polemic. He employs a slightly antique turn of phrase—"*On the Democratic Idea in America*"—or vocabulary—"vice" and "mob" for our personal sins and public disorders—as though to insist that verities have not changed, that the realities of political life are the same now as in the eighteenth century. But the apparent achievement of a certain distance and generality is undercut by jabs and sneers:

> It is worth lingering for a moment over that word "idealism" and the significant change in meaning it has experienced in the past 200 years. In the Judeo-Christian tradition, an idealist was someone who, in a spirit of charity, gave away his own money to those less fortunate than he. Today an idealist is someone who, in a spirit of compassion, gives away other people's money.

This is merely Bob Hope without the timing. "Significant change . . . past 200 years . . . Judeo-Christian tradition" are so much intellectual scrollwork. "Idealist" has no particular standing in "the Judeo-Christian tradition," except as a technical philosophical term; certainly it had nothing to do with alms-giving, and even its pejorative use as a term for an impractical altruist is not new.

Kristol's wit is often better than that. Borrowing from Robert Nozick, he has made much of liberals' willingness to tolerate all kinds of acts between consenting adults—except capitalist ones: "In the United States today, the law insists that an 18-year-old girl has the right to public fornication in a pornographic movie—but only if she is paid the minimum wage."

In any case there is little amiability in Kristol's humor, no hint that the blemishes of his targets might be part of a larger human frailty which even the author shares. The common note is disparagement and the suggestion of bad-will and hypocrisy. Note, for example, Kristol's solicitous attitude toward businessmen. Even when he is criticizing their passivity about unethical corporate practices, he hurries to ward off any misunderstanding

("The majority of corporate executives are certainly honest and honorable men"); and his usual complaint is simply that business is a mite dull-witted about assuring a climate of opinion favorable to its survival. Compare this with his attitude, say, toward the enforcers of antitrust legislation:

> There may be a few lawyers left in the Justice Department or the Federal Trade Commission who sincerely believe that such laws, if stringently enforced, could restore capitalism to something like its pristine individualist form. But it is much more probable that the lawyers who staff such government agencies launch these intermittent crusades . . . because they prefer such activity to mere idleness, and because they anticipate that a successful prosecution will enhance their professional reputations.

(By posing the one alternative in an extreme version—a belief in restoring capitalism to "its *pristine* individualist form"—the experienced debater at work here makes the other alternative—mere entertainment and ambition—sound all the more plausible; but of course there are a whole range of more modest hopes one could hold in regard to the effect of antitrust litigation.) As in this example, Kristol usually concedes some semblance of sincerity to the objects of his disparagement but in such a way as to leave an even less favorable impression. The "new class" is "surely sincere," says Kristol, in what he considers its "contradictory commitment" to individual freedom (i.e., libertarian in all areas of life except economics), but then, he goes on to say, "these same people . . . are quite admiring of Maoist China and not in the least appalled by the total collectivization of life—and the total destruction of liberty—there." In other words, their sincerity is merely indicative of a warped mentality so basic as to escape conscious thoughts ("their deepest fantasies," he tells us).

The "new class" is never mentioned except in connection with its self-seeking and authoritarian tendencies, though Kristol may quickly grant that it is "not motivated by any *pure* power-lust"! (My emphasis.) And even this dubious compliment—he doesn't *always* beat his wife—is qualified: after all, he adds, "very few people are."

The "new class" and, behind it, the intellectuals, of whom the "new class" is only a mass-produced version, constitute Irving Kristol's King Charles's Head. Like poor Mr. Dick in *David Copperfield,* he cannot get on with his case without, at the first opportunity, dragging the "new class" or the intellectuals into it. If the intellectuals have sinned grievously, then God no doubt sent Kristol to be their scourge and chastisement; it has been the great occupation of his career. The second issue of *Encounter* editorialized on all the twentieth-century catastrophes that had led

Europe into an age of nihilism. The editorial absolved "the people" from responsibility for this development and instead pointed at the intellectuals. "But if intellectuals today have no right to accuse the people, there is a class of people whom they can and must judge—themselves."

A shadowy figure hovered menacingly over *Encounter's* mental world— the fellow traveler, the naive do-gooder, the Popular Fronter. *Encounter* flew the banner of intellectual freedom, but it had very little faith in intellectuals, an untrustworthy lot always ready to sell out society to Jean-Paul Sartre. They had to be spooned regular doses of The God That Failed, kept on a short leash, and house-trained to a deferential and "mature" realism. The first small shoots of the New Left and—ironically enough—the leftward orientation given *Commentary* by Norman Podhoretz in the early sixties were noted by *Encounter* in a disdainful "Letter from New York":

> At three successive cocktail parties I have heard various men of letters roundly proclaim that they have lapsed into socialism. . . . I call this development to your attention so that you'll know what is *chic* with us. . . . For at least some of the middle-aged (to put the matter delicately), socialism seems to be a moral equivalent for adultery—a last desperate flight from the respectability that comes with rising incomes and falling hair. . . .

Would one actually have to check the by-line to know that the author of this report was Irving Kristol? A few years later, Kristol was informing *Encounter* readers that the teach-ins and antiwar activity were attributable to the boredom and resentment of students and junior faculty. As a focal point of political agitation, Vietnam was "conveniently at hand."

These bored and resentful intellectuals were not to be confused with the experts, however. Psychologists, mathematicians, chemists, and philosophers were the figures prominent in teach-ins; the experts on Asia, Communism, and international affairs were notable by their absence. "They have too great an appreciation of the complexity of the mess we are in. . . . Besides, practically all of them have contacts in Washington and they know that, had they a new, good idea about Viet Nam, they would get a prompt and respectful hearing."

In 1967, Kristol expanded on his explanation of the antiwar agitation. "What we are witnessing," he assured his readers, "is no mere difference of opinion about foreign policy, or about Vietnam. Such differences of opinion do exist, of course." Intellectuals may talk about the events in Asia—"for credibility's sake." But the real issue was the "sociological condition and political ambitions of the intellectual class, for the intellectual, lacking in other-worldly interests, is committed to the pursuit of temporal status, temporal influence, and temporal power with a single-minded passion that used to be found only in the highest reaches of the Catholic Church." Most important, a new intellectual "mass"—as distinguished from members of "the permanent brain trust . . . who commute regularly to Washington"—has emerged, "full of grievance and resentment." The United States, Kristol explained, had become an "imperial power" and could do nothing about it; the burdened policy-maker could use intellectual and moral guidance in carrying out his imperial responsibilities, but what he was destined to get was only the irresponsible acts of a disaffected intellectual class trying "to establish a power base of its own."

This was not the first time that Kristol distinguished between the resentful and power-hungry intellectuals and presumably disinterested "men who commute regularly to Washington." Though Kristol belittles the mechanical approach of much academic political science and urges a return to classical political philosophy, against the intellectuals he also urges a respect for complex and inconvenient realities, of the sort that policy analysts and economists regularly publish in *The Public Interest*. The introductory editorial of that journal, after all, warned against the "ideological essay": "it always *seems* to go deeper, point further, aspire higher. Its bland disregard of opposing fact, its very pretentiousness, sometimes even its very smug self-assurance, can give it a readability and literary attractiveness that a more matter-of-fact and more truthful essay does not often instantly achieve." The description, unfortunately, comes close to much of Kristol's own writing. Here again, the three spirits are at war—the philosophical essayist parading grand generalizations, the polemicist offering utterly definitive remarks on details, and the middleman of policy analysis denying the same privileges to everybody else.

A Gift for Assertion

Kristol's gift for assertion is sometimes refreshing—it does put on the table large issues that a hundred volumes of social science might never broach. But it is also breathtaking.

"The unanticipated consequences of social action are always more important, and usually less agreeable, than the intended consequences."

"The history of all modern industrial societies is the story of the gradual transformation of original urban mobs into a people."

"Today drug-taking has become a mass habit—among our young masses especially—whose purpose is to secede from our society and our civilization."

"What is called 'the revolution of rising expectations' has reached such grotesque dimensions that men take it as an insult when they are asked to be reasonable in their desires and demands."

"All the codes of sexual conduct ever devised by the human race take . . . a dim view of autoerotic activities and try to discourage autoerotic fantasies."

"Religion begins and ends in orthodoxy—the whole purpose of religion is to establish a viable and vital orthodoxy."

"The Founding Fathers *intended* this nation to be capitalist and regarded it as the *only* set of economic arrangements consistent with the liberal democracy they had established."

"The Left in Europe, whether 'totalitarian' or 'democratic,' has consistently been anti-liberal. That is to say, it vigorously repudiates the intellectual traditions of liberalism. . . ."

". . . the members of this 'new class' . . . believe—as the Left has always believed—it is government's responsibility to cure all the ills of the human condition."

Leave aside the cases where such statements can be set against some record—what competent and serious history of the democratic Left, for example, informs us that it has consistently and vigorously repudiated the intellectual tradition of liberalism or looked to government to cure all human ills? What marks these statements is (a) the way they simplify complex realities; (b) their exaggerated quality; (c) the certainty with which they are advanced. Note the frequent appearance of "always," "all," "ever," "whole," "only." Joseph Epstein has nicely characterized Kristol's writing as "commanding in tone, supremely confident about subjects that are elsewhere held to be still in the flux of controversy, assuming always that anyone who thinks differently is perverse or inept." Indeed, as soon as Kristol announces something as obvious ("Obviously, socialism is an 'elitist' movement") or the plain truth ("The plain truth is that it is these [liberal, individualist] ideals themselves that are being rejected" by the dissident young) or the simple truth ("The simple truth is that the professional classes . . . are engaged in a class struggle with the business community for status and power"), one immediately suspects that the matter is not obvious or plain or simple at all. As soon as he announces something as demonstrably the case "—the proposition (de-monstrably true) that the salaries of professors compare favorably with the salaries of bank executives"; "It is a demonstrable fact that in all modern, bourgeois societies, the distribution of income is also along a bell-shaped curve"—, one suspects that the matter is either undemonstrable or demonstrably false.*

As on large social observations, so too with particular political questions: Kristol's attribution of New York's financial problems to a blind "politics of compassion" is only amusing to those familiar with the wheeling and dealing, by bankers and lawyers like John Mitchell as well as politicians, that laid the groundwork for those troubles. Kristol was confident that welfare broke up families when Moynihan was admitting that the evidence was unclear; Kristol was confident that high welfare levels drew people to New York when the evidence said it didn't. Kristol can dismiss "all of those Great Society illusions" or "the dogmatic and irrational court decisions on school busing" or the economic views of "the trade unions . . . with their typical mindlessness," although one would have to turn no further than *The Public Interest* itself to demonstrate that such cavalier pronouncements (or Kristol's recommendations for "conservative" welfare measures like tax credits for medical insurance) are not well founded.

Writing of the average American's alleged isolation or powerlessness, Kristol points out, "The few serious studies . . . indicate that we have highly romanticized notions of the past . . . and highly apocalyptic notions of the present." The skepticism thus engendered is not extended to his own observations on other topics. On pornography, for instance: "What is at stake is civilization and humanity, nothing less." No one, it seems, is allowed an apocalypse but Kristol himself. More important, because less rhetorical, is his view of the past. Kristol's reference points for characterizing the past are either intellectual history or popular images. The result is an inoffensive, sanitized, and finally nostalgic impression. The shortcomings of capitalism, as already noted, are primarily the shortcomings of its *theory*. Any suggestion that this theory has affected practice is limited to criticism of capitalism's willingness to market the subversive goods of the counterculture. The bourgeois ethos is summed up in terms of its leading ideals. He offers but one, still relatively abstract, reference to the "philistine culture . . . so smugly affirmed" by the old *Saturday Evening Post* and "the spiritual torpor that . . . was so thin in its sense of

---

*Data on bankers' incomes is not readily available; a 1972 *Forbes* magazine article spoke of many in the $200,000–$250,000 range, but then what is a "bank executive"? A junior loan manager? An executive trainee? The considerable publicity given to Bert Lance's loans and overdrafts shed an interesting light on the amount of resources commanded by even provincial bank executives as compared to tenured professors. Income in the United States and other Western societies is *not* distributed along a bell-shaped curve but along a distinctly lop-sided curve—reflecting the few rich and many poor and near-poor.

humanity." Otherwise there is little hint of the less attractive, or even the downright cruel and destructive, aspects of that liberal-bourgeois-capital-ist ethos: no *Hard Times, Vanity Fair,* or Mark Twain; no reference to a sizable body of social history. Does Kristol discard all such critical accounts as expressing the animus of adversary intellectuals? He looks to Samuel Smiles and Horatio Alger; he watches old movies on television and sees "farmers' daughters . . . happy, neighborly suburban families . . . prim schoolmarms and prissy schoolmistresses . . . absent-minded professors . . . hicks who run gas stations and cops who drop in for apple pie . . . virginal college maidens and hardly any graduate students at all . . . in short . . . a race of people who only yesterday were the average and the typical. . . ." But of course they weren't, and his own note of irony admits that they were, instead, our *ideal* of the average and the typical. He knows that there is a difference between what people paid lip service to and how they actually behaved—one thinks of Samuel Butler's description of rural parishioners who "would have been equally horrified at hearing the Christian religion doubted, and at seeing it practiced"—and he is also right to insist on the importance of the code, however much honored in the breech; but finally the two, the prescript and the practice, have to be brought together for a complete picture, and this he does not do.

Virtue and the Market

Kristol's apocalyptic view of the present and his benign view of the past are two of the points where, inevitably, style and substance intersect. There is one major rift in Kristol's intellectual position, and to it the jarring elements in his manner are directly linked. On the one hand he recognizes the necessity of what might be called a politics of virtue: it is the function of governing institutions, guided by political reflection, not only to *select* out good and worthy citizens (howsoever they came to exist) as governors, but to be so arranged as to *produce* such citizens, that is, to foster and nourish virtue, or even in a period of moral decline, to regenerate it. This has to be done with a degree of consciousness and calculation, though with a respect for the wisdom congealed in enduring institutions and practices. In this connection he looks back to "pre-modern political philosophy—Plato, Aristotle, Thomas Aquinas, Hooker, Calvin, etc."—and he takes issue with the empty belief of secular, "libertarian" capitalism that simply "to be free is to be good."

On the other hand, Kristol is a devoted defender of the politics of the market. When he challenges the belief that "the actions of self-serving men will coalesce into a common good, and that the emancipation of the individual from social restraints will result in a more perfect community," he immediately makes an exception for the marketplace, which is supposed to be "the domain of 'economic men' rather than of citizens" and where "bankruptcy does impose a kind of self-discipline." The idea that the marketplace can be isolated from the polity as a whole and "economic men" from citizens is untenable, and in fact Kristol makes no serious effort to defend it. Indeed his theoretical essays and his considerations of specific political problems reveal the interconnectedness of economics and politics at every point. Thus again and again Kristol ends up defending the capitalist liberalism (and denigrating its critics) that he elsewhere finds so wanting.

On one occasion he may dispute the capitalist justification of market outcomes ("whatever is, is just"); on another occasion he will not only argue that such a conception is inherent to liberal society, which still leaves him the possibility of being less than a wholehearted advocate of liberal society, but characterizes all those who disagree as "sincere dogmatists" and "true believers."

It is this hopping back and forth from one philosophical leg to the other that accounts for Kristol's peculiarly uncertain attitude toward the "common man." On one leg he denounces the democratic faith in the common man that inhibits the kind of cultural scrutiny and discipline which has always been the task of an intellectual elite; the common man is become an urban mob, lacking all moderation, and Middle America is deep in decadence. On the other leg he hails the common man whose "common sense" and disinterest in egalitarian demands constitute society's thin defense against the millennial enthusiasm of its intellectuals.

It is the polemic against intellectuals that patches over the difficulty here, and only verbal skill keeps the cracks from showing. For example, Kristol attacks the intellectuals' conviction that bourgeois civilization lacks any higher ideal in the service of which common men might find true happiness: "It was, and is, a highly presumptuous and self-serving argument to offer—though I am *not so certain* that it was or is *altogether false.*" (My emphasis.) The weaseling negatives allow Kristol to discredit his opponents and yet reserve the possibility that their position has substantial merit.

What Kristol is facing, or perhaps evading, is of course that basic dilemma of American conservatives. The institutions they wish to conserve are to no small extent the institutions that have made the task of conservation so necessary and so difficult. The "irony" or "paradox" of "conservatives wishing to preserve liberal institutions and liberal values" he dismisses as an eruption of "silly liberal chatter"; and of course it is, if posed on the level of labels—"conservative" and "liberal." But if those institutions and values contain tremendous energies for the dissolution and change of traditional mores—as modern capitalism does—then the problem is quite real.

It is this split in Kristol's thinking that accounts, I believe, for the striking inconclusiveness of his major statements. Typically, he poses a problem, hints at an answer, but proceeds no further. His essay on urban civilization ends with a digression on drugs and then with Pogo's "immortal words"—by now a poor imitation of profundity—about the enemy being "us." Several essays end with references to the decline of religion and the "death of God"—but there is no attempt to explore the causes of this development or ask whether it is definitive. He links capitalism and the erosion of the bourgeois ethic—but so delicately that one can get no real grasp at what might be done about it. He announces that we shall have "to start the long trek back to pre-modern political philosophy"—but in fact he never really embarks on it. *"Why,"* he asks, was "the political philosophy of the founding fathers . . . so ruthlessly unmanned by American history?" Was that philosophy inherently flawed? Or did their statesmanship fail, or external events intervene? "These questions have hardly been asked, let alone answered"—and Kristol does not proceed to try. The Founding Fathers are his veritable anchor, yet he recognizes that they reconciled their version of democracy with slavery— and does not make this an opening to further reflection. He has pinpointed the decades when the democratic idea, as he sees it, was transformed—but does not seriously consider what happened, including the burst of capitalist development, on the one hand, and of reform efforts like abolitionism, on the other, during those years. If the present subversion of our liberal institutions is to be halted, he elsewhere concludes, conservatism will have to "give its own moral and intellectual substance to its idea of liberty"; and though the country is temporarily in a moderate mood, "in the longer run, of course, American conservatism will have to face up to a far more profound problem: its cultural impotence—its inability to propose an ideal of moral and spiritual excellence that could challenge the predominance of liberal egalitarianism." These projects, like the long trek back to pre-modern philosophy, remain just over the horizon.

The problem may go to the very "validity of the original liberal idea"— the belief that the individual could "cope with the eternal dilemmas of the human condition" without the "moral authority of tradition, and some public support for this authority." How this moral authority "can be assimilated into a liberal-capitalist society"—Kristol does not ask *whether* it can be assimilated—"is perhaps the major intellectual question of our age."

Such reticence might be attributed to a seemly modesty; and though Kristol is otherwise diligent in keeping that particular light under a bushel, it is no doubt part of the explanation. Still, it seems likely that his simultaneous attraction to a politics of virtue and defense of a politics of the market inhibit both his exploration of the past and his projection of any ideal for the future. To go further would mean choosing one road or the other, or forging an entirely new path.

Stability, Liberalism, Polemic

The immediate values Kristol would like to see restored are clear enough: sobriety, moral earnestness, self-discipline. But how can our society generate and safeguard such virtues? With what institutional arrangements are they compatible? What larger "ideal of moral and spiritual excellence" would ground them, so that they are not simply a self-interested exhortation that the less advantaged be docile and contented with their lot? Kristol's replies, or lack of them, provoke two suspicions.

One is that stability itself is the fundamental principle. In place of the subversive (because unacceptable to the masses) doctrine "Whatever is, is just," does Kristol only offer the alternative "Whatever is stable, is just"? At times that appears to be the case. The task of statesmanship and political philosophy is to create a congruence of beliefs, so that the whole coheres and is persuasive; what counts is that people "feel" free or equal, whatever be their actual rights. Consider Kristol's distress over "the influence of Christianity, with its messianic promises" and his judgment that "the only *corrective* to this *shadow* of illegitimacy that has hovered *threateningly* over the politics of Western civilization for nearly two millennia now was the 'common sense' of the majority of the population, which had an intimate and enduring relation to mundane realities that was relatively immune to speculative enthusiasm." (My emphasis.) This is to hint at a radically conservative philosophy of history indeed. Western history is seen from the point of view of the Merovingian kings, the feudal lords, the medieval emperors, the absolute monarchs, as well as of the bourgeois liberal governments; and the dramatic "problem" is how legitimacy can be preserved from the threatening shadow of speculative enthusiasm. In such a perspective, the case must be strong for the maintenance of serfdom, illiteracy, and the Inquisition, lest the majority lose their "intimate and enduring relation to mundane realities."

In more immediate affairs, Kristol also seems to suggest that legitimacy and stability are the final criteria of policy. The welfare state is good when it is a conservative welfare state, bad when it is not; fiscal risk is good when Republicans take it for conservative purposes, bad when Democrats take it for purposes of change.

At other times, Kristol appears to be deeply committed to *liberal* institutions, not simply because they are the existing institutions, but because they are liberal. Unfortunately this commitment is usually expressed most vigorously in close conjunction with his defense of the market and of the very capitalism that has done so much to undermine the ethos on which he believes these liberal institutions rest. To preserve this liberal inheritance, he announces himself a "conservative reformer." But unlike the models he mentions, Herbert Croly and Matthew Arnold, he is very much conservative and very little reformer. The proposals he makes for corporate reform—that corporations legitimate themselves by exhibiting some form of "the representative principle," that they appoint public board members, and that they "look as poor as possible"—appear to be casually thought out and almost entirely cosmetic: "A few very small and maybe symbolic gestures are very important in politics."

He presents a provocative case for the censorship of pornography on the grounds that a democracy has to be concerned about its "republican morality"; but when a furor arises over corporate bribery overseas—a practice more readily connected with domestic political habits and "republican morality" than pornography—Kristol grows worldly and complains that "post-Watergate morality" has become "self-righteous" and "too good for our own good."

Kristol's inconclusiveness and inconsistencies have led some to conclude that he does not care about his larger themes at all. Wrote one reviewer of *On the Democratic Idea in America:* "Kristol, alas, rarely cares about his ostensible subject. His concern is with the emblems, practically the battle flags, of what has come to seem a conflict between 'two cultures.' " In effect, he is absorbed in the clash between the political establishment of the sixties and the "silent majority," on the one hand, and the "movement" of political and cultural dissent, on the other. The Great Issues are only stalking horses for the polemical ambushes.

As a description of intent, this is doubtful; but as a description of result, it is accurate. As a conveyor of policy analysis, Kristol occasionally makes a good argument against current assumptions; more often he is careless about facts and inattentive to complexities. As a political essayist, he is stalled at the crossroads of two very different political visions. We are left with the polemicist.

Yet Kristol is right in his insistence on certain realities. Despite his exaggerations, he is right to insist that we suffer from a *spiritual* chaos and not simply a variety of institutional shortcomings. He is right to insist that we cannot understand our condition while ignoring the central place that religion has held in past societies and no longer does in ours. He is right to insist on the importance of political ideas—to "establish and define in men's minds the categories of the politically possible and the politically impossible, the desirable and the undesirable, the tolerable and the intolerable"—against both those political managers and those political dissidents who would eschew ideas for an energetic mindlessness.

Nonetheless it is hard to envision where Kristol can go intellectually with these insights. Society, for him, must be guided by a religion or a political philosophy. He has always been interested in religion and writes regretfully of its decline; but in fact he is out of sympathy with any religious impulse that might burst the old wineskins of social control. Young people who believe in a divinity might rudely inject their belief into a Presidential party for *Reader's Digest*. "Transcendent" is a negative word in his vocabulary. Kristol would like the authority of the Decalogue without the unreliability of God. As for political philosophy, he can harken back to *The Federalist* or wistfully recall Edmund Burke shaking hands with Adam Smith; but once he must take into account that neither the religious nor economic conditions of the late eighteenth century still obtain, he has little more to say. "In the longer run, of course, American conservatism will have to face up to a far more profound problem . . . to propose an ideal of moral and spiritual excellence. . . ." But for now, it is all holding action. There is always the adversary culture. . . .

CHAPTER SIX

Daniel Patrick Moynihan, Professorial Politician

MID-NOVEMBER 1965. The opening session of a White House planning conference on civil rights and racial equality. Bert Bernhard, the executive director of the conference, announces, "I want you to know that I have been reliably informed that no such person as Daniel Patrick Moynihan exists." The assembled participants are amused. They are also relieved. For several months civil rights activists and government officials have been caught up in controversy over a document entitled "The Negro Family: The Case for National Action," more familiarly known, after its author, as the Moynihan Report. Now the director's quip signals that the report, along with its author, are officially consigned to the circular file of history.

Almost precisely a decade from that White House meeting, Moynihan was standing before the United Nations General Assembly. To what was an audience of millions he delivered the United States' reply to an Arab-sponsored resolution classifying Zionism as a form of racism. One year after that, Moynihan was elected U.S. Senator from New York. The rumors of his nonexistence had apparently been exaggerated.

Daniel Patrick Moynihan is the most widely known neoconservative. Practically no other political American political figure, excepting Presidential candidates, Kennedys, and Dr. Kissinger, has been as widely interviewed and reviewed, analyzed and characterized—above all, televised. Irish charm, Celtic wit, Gaelic eloquence, etc., etc.—Moynihan is a media *personality*, that is, a fairly extended and stable conglomerate of clichés. The commonest cliché has been "flamboyant." Once christened "flamboyant," as in "the flamboyant Ambassador to the United Nations" or "the flamboyant junior Senator from New York," what could Moynihan do to escape the label? Any behavior worth noting, including keeping his mouth closed, would only be further evidence of his flamboyance. And yet what a peculiar description this is. Moynihan does not fly airplanes like Barry Goldwater, engage in risky sports like the Kennedys, sleep on the floor like Jerry Brown. He is tall but physically unprepossessing; his speech pattern is odd; his life-style appears utterly conventional. A "combination of Oxford don and Colonel Blimp," says Garry Wills of him, hardly the lineage of flamboyance.

Yet Moynihan has created something new, a new public type, and flamboyance is only the press's uncertain effort to grasp it. Moynihan is a *professorial politician*. Not that academics who enter politics are something rare: There is Woodrow Wilson, of course, and Dr. George McGovern, though both came across more as preachers than professors. There are those who cultivate the image of the intellectual in politics— Adlai Stevenson or Eugene McCarthy—though most intellectual politicians have found it politically safer to wear their interest in ideas lightly. Moynihan has gone beyond the intellectual in politics; he is the professor in politics. He does not suppress the professorial, he flaunts it. He has made it his style, just as Sam Ervin was a "country lawyer" and various wealthy western politicians project themselves as cowpunchers. In part Moynihan's success indicates the degree to which higher education in America has "arrived" and the public has come to accept the notion of Harvard intellectuals sitting in the halls of government. When Moynihan's 1976 Senatorial opponent in New York, James Buckley, derisively referred to "Professor Moynihan," Buckley was reflecting in this, as in his politics generally, a bygone reality. There is no evidence that the supposed epithet did "Professor Moynihan" anything but good; polls show the public holding a higher opinion of college professors than of politicians, businessmen, or lawyers, the occupational groups with which Buckley was identified. At the same time, the professorial style is novel enough for the media to find it "flamboyant."

In time we may get used to the professorial politician; Moynihan and the neoconservatives may see to that. For the moment, however, the type is not only flamboyant for the press but disconcerting to some of the rest of us. It poses the problem of the intellectual in politics, and it poses the problem in spades. The professorial politician is not just *in* politics; he is, no mistaking, a *politician*. The intellectual and professorial element is not only critical in shaping his outlook; it is in the foreground, offered as qualification for holding power. Moynihan was a distinctive candidate for office not because he had favored and fought for certain policies—many others had done the same, and more effectively—but because he had exhibited the capacity to conceive and analyze those policies. Moynihan's most widely known qualification for appointment as Ambassador to the United Nations was not his previous diplomatic post, as Ambassador to India, but the fact that he had written an article in *Commentary*. Here is a man who hops between government and the university, a man "happiest," says his wife, "when he writes every day," a man who tosses off general formulations as a comedian does one-liners, who gravitates to the battleground of ideas as naturally as a Dubliner to a pub, who cannot resist the intricate or oblique example, the startling or even inflammatory phrase.

The New York Times once published a photograph of Moynihan making a point at a press conference. One arm was thrust out, flailing the air. His body teetered dangerously at the point where a lunge becomes a pratfall. He looked like an improbable ballet master or an overweight dueling instructor, but the image was well suited for Moynihan the political intellectual and professorial politician: almost thrown off balance by the momentum of his own thought, a virtuoso, dancing on an intellectual and political tightwire, occasionally with one foot in his mouth.

"Benign neglect," for example. An oxymoron in a china shop, and yet how irresistible to an intellectual for that very ring of paradox and to a professor for its historical cachet. (No matter that the phrase was not actually used by Lord Durham, the reforming nineteenth-century Governor General of Canada, to whom Moynihan attributed it—intellectuals and professors are not necessarily scholars.) Or consider the Moynihan Report, where most of the excitement began. Lee Rainwater and William L. Yancey, in their study of the controversy the report provoked, point out the stylistic features which contributed to its misinterpretation:

> In his writing, Moynihan uses the word "fundamental" quite frequently as a more emphatic way of saying "important." In his report, he used this word four times—family structure is "the fundamental problem"; the deterioration of the Negro family is "the fundamental source of weakness of the Negro community"; the reversal of roles of husbands and wives is a "fundamental fact" of Negro family life; but also, "the fundamental, overwhelming fact is that Negro unemployment . . . has continued at disaster levels for 35 years." This set of "fundamental" quotations about the family was widely quoted and appears much more accusatory in short press articles than in the report itself; the adjective could well have been avoided in a public document.

In arguing that the regime of Jim Crow had particularly humiliated Negro males, demanding a public submissiveness which "worked against the emergence of a strong father figure," Moynihan was necessarily fishing in speculative waters. Yet, even at a time before the woman's movement gathered its full force, he did not help his case by adding, "The very essence of the male animal, from the bantam rooster to the four-star general, is to strut." Newspaper reporters were as unable to resist quoting that not very relevant sentence as Moynihan had been unable to resist writing it.

What we have here is more than a cautionary tale about writing government memos—or editing them before they are released. The Moynihan Report accurately reflected the mixed impulses of the political intellectual who wrote it. It was a consciously political initiative taken in an intensely political context: Moynihan was proposing a new strategy for a faltering civil rights movement, a strategy that he believed, wrongly, would be politically attractive because it centered on the family. (Unfortunately, motherhood is not always as American as apple pie—not when it involves black mothers, welfare funds, and illegitimacy rates. Then it raises the old specters of race and sex and puts them into explosive combination.) Yet Moynihan also displayed the intellectual's impulse to face up to uncomfortable truths that liberal politicians and social workers preferred to ignore. "Discovery" and "revision" are the professor's stock in trade. To which Moynihan added the tendency, a personal one but also characteristic of the intellectual, to dramatize and generalize.

Moynihan's overuse of "fundamental" is not a quirk of prose style; it is a habit of thought. He is always announcing new eras or the passing of old ones. (The family policy he was arguing for in the Moynihan Report might have been, he wrote elsewhere, "the central event of our new era of social legislation." A few years later, comparing his book on the poverty program with Robert Graves's *Goodbye to All That*, he wrote that with the death of Robert F. Kennedy, "a political era had come to a close." On the other hand he agrees with "the judgment of Kenneth Boulding that mankind is entering a profound new era" of social self-consciousness.) His writings abound with references to eras, periods, our age, our time, and the "defining qualities" or the "essential fact" about them. He is quick to detect "firsts": radical protest movements in the sixties are "the first heresies of liberalism"; the 1967 AFDC amendments of the Social Security Act were "the first deliberate anti-civil-rights measure of the present era"; Lyndon Johnson was "the first American President to be toppled by a mob." Fearlessly Moynihan charts the rise and fall of political generations and "new classes," the turning or nonturning of various turning points, the clash of opposing ideals and theories.

Distrust and Fascination: The Blurry Image

Moynihan's novel style accounts for at least part of the strong reactions he provokes. Any public figure elicits conflicting opinions; Moynihan does something more. The public looks on with passive interest. But among those who have had closer contact with him, Moynihan creates admirers and detractors so fierce in their estimations that the man himself is nearly lost behind the clouds of praise and scorn. Among many of his critics the only point of discussion seems to be whether he is a blatant racist or a subtle one, whether he is an evil genius or an evil dullard. Among many of his admirers, the only question is whether he is the last good hope of America or of all Western civilization.

Much of the negative reaction traces back to the undeniable fact that Moynihan has been the victim of misrepresentation and abuse, above all the charge of racism arising from the 1965 Moynihan Report and his 1970 "benign neglect" memo to President Nixon. Yet these charges could have taken hold and flourished so widely only in the fertile earth of distrust, a distrust of this odd beast, half politician, half professor, and yet, unlike the mermaid or the centaur, never successfully joined.

Distrust, of course, is only the reverse side of fascination; and if Moynihan can complain about abuse from some liberals, he must admit that, even before *The New York Times*'s influential endorsement in the 1976 Democratic Senatorial primary and the November election that followed, he had been the recipient of exceptional publicity in the liberal press. *The New York Times Sunday Magazine*, for example, has profiled him no less than five times since 1965, and always sympathetically. (Reviews of his books in the *Times Book Review*, on the other hand, have been generally critical.) *Time* has had him on its cover twice.

Almost all these stories retailed Moynihan's account of a poverty-stricken boyhood in New York's Hell's Kitchen, a history which is not so unrelated to the confusion surrounding a professorial politician as it might at first seem. Although some doubts were infrequently expressed about details of this slum kid's saga—Pete Hamill pointed out that "the mothers of the poor did not run saloons, as Moynihan's mother did"—it was only in August 1976 that Timothy Crouse, author of *The Boys on the Bus*, put the story in perspective.

Until Moynihan was eleven, his "family lived a comfortable, quasi-suburban existence first in New Jersey and then in Crystal Gardens, a middle-class section of Astoria." After Moynihan's father abandoned the family, they did plunge suddenly into poverty, the life of tenements, welfare, and shining shoes in Times Square—the life Moynihan has frequently referred to. "This period," reports Crouse,

> when the family literally did not know where the next meal was coming from, lasted only three or four years. Around the time Pat entered high school, his mother married a man with some money, and the family moved to the green pastures of rural Kitchawan, in Westchester County. When that marriage fell apart, she took her children to live with relatives back in Indiana (where the boys sometimes worked as golf caddies). . . . By the time the family returned to New York, the war had started and the worst of the Depression was over. Margaret Moynihan got a good job as chief nurse in a munitions plant, and they lived once again in Astoria. When the war ended, she borrowed $10,000 from a distant relation and bought a saloon on West 42nd Street. . . . Pat and Mike tended bar off and on there while going to college. Once, when Pat was at Tufts, his mother got sick and he took three months off to run the bar. . . .
>
> Later on, Pat Moynihan would select one brief episode from his preadolescence, combine it with one brief phase from his college years and construct an American myth. It was the story of a spunky and extraordinarily bright shoeshine boy from Hell's Kitchen who grows up to become a gentleman. No mention is ever made of Astoria, Westchester, or Indiana, which would spoil the story. The tale is true insofar as it suggests that he was not a rich kid, that he suffered a number of psychological blows and that he often had to work hard as a child. It is a lie insofar as it suggests that he was born into the lower classes and was sympathetic to their plight. In reality, he passed among them as a lonely, frightened and often horrified observer.

The last sentence can be discounted as speculation, but Crouse's report contains enough hard data to revise the image Moynihan has fostered. Besides Moynihan's suburban and rural interludes—caddying on an Indiana golf course is a somewhat different image from shining shoes in Times Square—there is the fact that Moynihan's maternal grandfather was a successful attorney, his mother a nurse perfectly capable of finding a job teaching English. And though his father disappeared when Moynihan was young, we really should have given more thought to this skilled journalist and friend of humorist H. Allen Smith. These were clearly middle-class people, with middle-class talents and education and aspirations. Class involves much more than financial insecurity.

But so what? Isn't every politician born in a log cabin, up from the slums, a peanut farmer, or some such thing? Kennedy obviously wasn't— so he fostered a cult of PT-109. LBJ was known to alter his history the way other men changed their clothes, and for the same reason—to suit the circumstances. Nixon was never far from suggesting that the entire

Depression had been arranged simply so that his youthful mettle could be tested and found true. If Moynihan were a politician pure and simple, no one would much mind the ragged edges on his story, or rather the storied edges on his rags. Perhaps no one would have taken them so seriously in the first place. American naiveté endures, however, if not about our politicians, then about our professors. We imagine that they should have some special leaning toward the truth. When Moynihan recalls that he had never heard of any college but Notre Dame, and Crouse reports that his closest high school friend was entering Yale the fall after graduation, when Moynihan, honor student and first in his graduating high school class, says that he never considered going to college and only took the City College entrance exam as a lark, we are more troubled than we would be by LBJ's tall tale of a great-great-grandfather dying at the Alamo. Worse yet is the use of such "stretching," as Mark Twain would put it, as reinforcement of scholarly insight. To write, as Lee Rainwater and William Yancey do in their generally fine book on the Moynihan Report, that Moynihan's fellow shoeshine boys were blacks and that Moynihan "got to know something of their world and they something of his; and he was impressed by the fact that these seemed to be much the same world," is to purchase a first-class ticket to fantasy land. How many of those black shoeshine boys had grandfathers who were successful lawyers, fathers who were moderately gifted writers, and mothers who taught English? Could it be that Moynihan, who was undoubtedly Rainwater and Yancey's source for this observation, believes it himself? Blarney is one thing, self-deception something else.

The Moynihan of Crouse's profile is very bright, very charming, very opportunistic, and very self-important. He is a thin-skinned, mean-spirited bounder—indeed one thinks of "that remarkable man and self-made Humbug, Josiah Bounderby of Coketown," with his tales of having been born in a ditch, abandoned by his mother, and raised in the gutter. "That lady who said Americans are starving . . . Any Americans who are starving, it's because they are idiots. If they are not idiots, they deserve to be." This could be Bounderby but it's not—it's Moynihan engaged in professional tough talk, as reported by Crouse. Such a portrait presents a problem for scrupulous Moynihan watchers.*

---

* Among whom I would count myself. A natural friendliness existed between Moynihan and *Commonweal* magazine, where I was an editor for seven years. Early on, Moynihan wrote that the natural person to unite the New York Democratic party would be a "Catholic liberal . . . an Irish Catholic county leader who reads *Commonweal.*" Moynihan was among the fifty notables who formed a fund-raising committee to mark *Commonweal*'s fiftieth anniversary in 1974. *Commonweal*, for its part, welcomed the Moynihan Report, defended it against

Even Crouse, however, admits the merits of a number of Moynihan's ideas and is almost tempted to like him from time to time. "Nearly everybody who knew Pat during the fifties and early sixties," he reports, "remembers him as the jolliest, humblest, most self-effacing, wittiest, most whimsical fellow they ever met—a bouncing encyclopedia of arcane historical fact, literary reference and political lore." Is it only a coincidence that those recollections date from the period before Moynihan's break with many liberals?

Again, what to make of all this? Successful politicians often run more to ambition and arrogance—at least when you catch them off guard—than meekness and charity; and political gossip is not likely to exaggerate their virtues. Moynihan again suffers from the uncertainty of standards to apply to a professorial politician.

Yet what standards do apply? Moynihan's associate in urban studies, Edward Banfield, once insisted, "Moynihan has no politics. He belongs to a nearly extinct species in America: the *public man*. He is preoccupied neither with getting himself or someone else elected to office nor with policy as a means to that end; rather, his mind turns naturally to large public concerns as another's turns naturally to making money, or to raising the fervor of fellow ideologues." This is patently absurd today, when Moynihan has campaigned successfully for office; but it was equally absurd when written in 1973. It reveals the sentimentality which clouds the vision of such tough-minded, unsparing examiners of the lower classes as Banfield when they turn their gaze to their own kind. Moynihan had been political from the start. He worked for Averell Harriman, directed a Senatorial campaign for Robert Morgenthau, and in 1965 ran for president of the City Council in New York, a position known to have few advantages except as a springboard for other political offices. No doubt Moynihan himself would smile at Banfield's high-minded description. It is not all that different, however, from the ideal that Moynihan established for the political intellectual: the intellectual's contribution is nothing if it is not clarity; his contribution is worse than nothing if he confuses his own interest with that of the ideals he ostensibly serves, if he blinks at discomforting facts in his rush to impose a sensible pattern on a recalcitrant reality. It is measured against this standard, his own, that Moynihan can provoke such intense distrust. One does not have to turn to political gossip or reports like Crouse's. The careful reader of Moynihan's

---

hasty critics in 1965, hailed Moynihan's entry into the Nixon government in 1968, and backed the Family Assistance Plan, Moynihan's proposal to remake welfare along the lines of a guaranteed minimum income and help for the working poor. All this predisposed me to discount the many tales circulating in Washington of Moynihan's bureaucratic vendettas and exorbitant denunciations.

published essays is always stumbling across instances of deft evasion, retouched shading, and personal promotion that clash disturbingly with the image of the man of knowledge in politics he has projected for himself and others.

Let me be specific. In May 1968, then supporting Robert Kennedy for the Democratic Presidential nomination, Moynihan wrote that the New Hampshire primary and Lyndon Johnson's decision not to run again demonstrated how "reasoned and non-violent opposition to the course of American foreign policy did prevail. . . . The retirement of the President is an act without precedent, but the substantive point is that policy changed almost routinely in response to a changed public opinion. This is what is meant by the democratic process."

Eight months later, in a memo prepared for President-elect Nixon, Moynihan described the same events: "But the fact is that he [Johnson] could not win [in Vietnam], and the all-important accompanying fact is that the semi-violent protest that arose in consequence forced him to resign. In a sense he was the first American President to be toppled by a mob. No matter that it was a mob of college professors, millionaires, flower children, and Radcliffe girls."

There are facts to support each of these views, and personally I believe the truth to be somewhere in between. But Moynihan marshals the facts so as to create virtually contradictory impressions. Both views dovetailed with Moynihan's political aims of the moment: in the May article, to assimilate the anti-Johnson (and also anti-Humphrey) movement to the political center; in the January 1973 memo, to warn Nixon from committing himself to the war, a warning which would be more persuasive when garnished with a sneer at the "mob of college professors, millionaires, flower children, and Radcliffe girls." Liberals might like to think that Moynihan really held to the first interpretation, and later dissimulated his opinion before Nixon, perhaps for a good reason (to argue effectively against the war) or a bad one (to curry favor with his employer). But at two points in Moynihan's *Maximum Feasible Misunderstanding*, written either before or immediately after the May article and long before his association with Nixon, Moynihan also speaks of Johnson being "toppled" and uses imagery like that in the Nixon memo. Which of these views, then, did Moynihan *believe*? Or did he believe neither of them, tailoring his rhetoric to fit the opportunity? Or both of them, persuading himself as well as others, as his mood swung?

Or again: in September 1972, as the Nixon-McGovern race was underway, *Life* magazine published an article titled "How the President Sees His Second Term." The article did more than assume Nixon would be reelected; it was a perfectly pitched contribution to that end. It began by sounding the main theme of the President's campaign: Nixon was a man of peace successfully building a new world order. Domestic affairs were dealt with by repeating Nixon's belief that Congress was at fault for the Administration's mediocre performance. The President's strong opposition to quotas was recalled, and linked to the number of Jews among his close advisers, nicely supporting the determined Nixon effort to woo that group of voters. The *Life* Nixon was as far from the voice on the Watergate tapes as George Washington from Mark Hanna. The President was a man in search of "a coherent philosophy of what it is we hope for and how we propose to realize our hopes." He seeks "a world view . . . in terms of the next quarter-century, of the next four centuries." For this Oval Office philosopher, "the question of how we are to conduct a rational debate about the issues that divide us has become at least as important as the issues themselves."

Nixon, in short, is an apostle of "civility." Not just cloth-coat Republican civility, either. The President invited us all to nothing less than "the 'Stevensonian' concept of civility and rational discourse." Being not only an apostle of civility but "in his own way, as much an intellectual as any President in modern times," Nixon is naturally saddened by the intellectuals' retreat from government and polite dialogue. "Kennedy had meant so much to them," says the *Life* author, "that when he went, they went. Back, that is, to opposition and to ever more savage criticism that only concealed but could not ease their own hurt." And having reduced the opposition to Vietnam to psychological trauma over Kennedy's assassination, the author proceeds unflinchingly to deal with certain doubts about Nixon's past. Perhaps the man who called Stevenson "Adlai the Appeaser" and "a graduate of Dean Acheson's spineless school of diplomacy" would seem an unlikely exemplar of Stevensonian civility. But who, after all, is perfect? "Neither he for his part, nor the academics for theirs, could point to a past of flawlessly modulated and perfectly controlled behavior." That was all behind Nixon now: "A quality of the presidency is that it focuses on the future. He has changed the world, he feels. He knows that it has changed him."

And who was the author of this *tour de force*? Who else? Daniel Patrick Moynihan, soon to be Ambassador to India.

But wait. In 1973, Moynihan published *Coping*, a collection of his essays "on the practice of government." The introduction was a lament about the incompetence of governing elites, in particular liberal ones. It fitted the mood of pre-Watergate Nixonism fairly well; indeed it was written about the same time that the *Life* piece appeared. Before *Coping* went to press, however, Watergate broke; and so Moynihan tacked an addendum onto the introduction, discreetly taking his distance from the latest, sordid developments. The introduction, he tells us, was written at a time when "For the first time in my adult life a Presidential campaign was in full swing, and *I had not the least part in it*. A Democrat, I had served in the Cabinet of a Republican President, and *I judged this to impose an obligation of neutrality and silence*." (My emphasis.)

Perhaps this is a small item, but small items, like the pulled thread that unravels the garment, can be revealing. What are we to make of it? Is this Nixon, apostle of civility, a pure fiction—political hackwork of a crude but familiar sort? Or is this the Nixon Moynihan actually experienced—or created? Was Nixon so skillful a dissembler, or Moynihan so ardent a believer? In either case, what are we to think of Moynihan's judgment? And what are we to think of his claim to "neutrality and silence"? Again, is he simply deceiving his readers? Or has he persuaded himself that a four-page puff in *Life* doesn't count? Who is fooling whom? Nixon fooling Moynihan, Moynihan fooling us, Moynihan fooling himself, or all of the above?

Need examples be multiplied? In fact it is easier to multiply examples than to draw from them a precise conclusion that satisfies. There is too much evidence, including the sheer complexity of the man, that stands against the view that this is simple political hypocrisy or simple opportunism. With Moynihan, nothing is apt to be simple. The whole effect is that of a man out of synchronization with his own image; the register on the printing press is off, so that the colored masses of his figure don't quite line up with his outline; the sound track is faulty, so that the words we hear don't match the ones his lips are forming. The sheer brainpower concentrated on each of his timely shifts of opinion, the eloquence and evidence he summons so handily, are themselves disturbing. Compared with most politicians', Moynihan's shifts before the wind are minor; but most politicians mumble these things away with a few platitudes. Moynihan dresses them in the finery of high theory. His sensitivity to principle is surely a cut above that of the average politician—and his powers of rationalization four cuts above. Here is a medium-sized car with an 800-horsepower engine. One fears it may fly out of control, and in any direction.

Failing Upwards

Daniel Patrick Moynihan is a notable example of that phenomenon known as failing your way up the ladder. One after another, enterprises with which he was connected failed to achieve their immediate ends, sometimes with an assist from his own rhetoric. The Moynihan Report blew up in his face. He lost his race for president of the New York City

Council in 1965. (I recall shaking his hand at 72nd and Broadway, by "Needle Park," a then-notorious locale for heroin transactions. He had the pained air of a man who would rather be home reading a book. Since that was my view of the matter as well, I approved of his campaign style and gave him my vote. Other New Yorkers did not agree.) The Family Assistance Plan broke up on Congressional shoals. As Ambassador to India he did what any American ambassador to that country could have done during 1973 and 1974, that is, just about nothing. A case can be made that, at the United Nations, Moynihan's blunt tactics only ensured the passage of the resolution condemning Zionism, alienated a number of nations needlessly, and had no lasting effect on American foreign policy. A case can be made for the opposite conclusions. Neither case is overwhelming. Taken together they seem to imply that as a diplomat Moynihan made a fine Senatorial candidate. Indeed, as a diplomat Moynihan made a better Senatorial candidate than he did as a Senatorial candidate. But by some magic of reverse propulsion, this series of political failures boosted him, like the stages of a rocket, into a seat in the Senate.

The secret, of course, was that while Moynihan may have been failing as a politician, he was meanwhile succeeding admirably as an intellectual, often enough by acutely analyzing (and defending) his own failures. Between Washington and Cambridge he left a trail of ideas, of prickly challenges to accepted notions. He did not produce original scholarship, but he knew how to use it, how to uncover its implications for policy, how to translate it to the world of opinion and politics. *Beyond the Melting Pot*, which was four parts Nathan Glazer and one part Moynihan, had already, in 1963, reminded a wide audience that ethnicity remained a basic category for understanding American political life. *Maximum Feasible Misunderstanding* and *The Politics of a Guaranteed Income* were autopsies on the community-action programs in the War on Poverty and on the Family Assistance Plan. Few critics of these works, and there were many, could fail to grant the extraordinary intelligence and experience—and gift for language—which Moynihan brought to bear on the problems of instituting and implementing social programs. Tom Wicker, for example, took sharp issue with much of *The Politics of a Guaranteed Income* in *The New York Review of Books*, but not before granting it praise that can hardly be taken as *pro forma*:

> *The Politics of a Guaranteed Income*, it should be said at the outset, is a first-class piece of work, maybe the best we have—anyway the best written in English rather than social scientese—on the interplay of government and politics in America, on the complexities hidden in John Kennedy's frequent remark that "to govern is to choose," on the difficulties of defining social need, suiting political action to it, and persuading a bewildering con-

stellation of interests and institutions to take and sustain that action. At that high level, Moynihan succeeds brilliantly. . . . [W]ith one of the quickest intelligences in public or university life today, Moynihan writes with rare authority, with perception tempered by experience, and without much illusion.

His book is full of sage counsel and striking analyses, both of what ails and what distinguishes us. . . . Breathes there a liberal with soul so dead that he has not forced himself to consider, if not answer, these questions?

Along with these major works Moynihan produced a stream of articles, speeches, and prefaces—on education, urban policy, architecture, violent crime, student radicalism, and more recently international affairs. Some of this material was collected in the 1973 book *Coping*. The volumes he has edited included *On Understanding Poverty: Perspectives from the Social Sciences*, *On Equality of Educational Opportunity* (with Frederick Mosteller), *Toward a National Urban Policy*, and *Ethnicity* (with Nathan Glazer).

Moynihan's thought can be organized around four clusters of themes. The first is that of liberalism and the shortcomings of liberal social and economic policies. The second is that of the interlocking problems of poverty, race, and city governance. The third is that of the relationship between social science and policy, or more generally between knowledge and government and between the claims of professional expertise and those of democracy. The fourth is that of foreign affairs. Moynihan's treatment of the third cluster, exposing as it does the strains between the claims of professional expertise and those of democracy, will be taken up in the chapter on democracy. The first cluster, however, in many ways subsumes the others and deserves to be examined first.

Against Liberalism: Criticism and Alienation

As a liberal, Moynihan was from the start both orthodox and a maverick. He was orthodox insofar as he seems always to have accepted pluralist political theory, indeed never to have ventured seriously outside it in his studies (there is not a single reference in his corpus to suggest that he has paid any attention to serious Marxist thought); he seems always to have accepted the Cold War assumption of America's salutary international role; he seems always to have accepted the view of the liberal state as a flywheel regulating what is an essentially sound and benign capitalist economy. There is even a sense in which he was orthodox by being a maverick: among intellectuals, after all, if not among politicians, playing the maverick is one of the several major routes to success. Moynihan did have a special perspective, nonetheless, and it was not unrelated to his background. One of his first important essays, for example, dealt with "bosses" and "reformers" in New York politics. *Last Hurrah* nostalgia for the old political machines was nothing new, but Moynihan presented the case for the Democratic Regulars in New York with a minimum of sentimentality and a sharp eye for the failings of both factions within the party. Moynihan was himself a reformer, part of Averell Harriman's entourage; and his understanding portrait of Catholic politicians had bite partly because it came from within the largely Jewish reform camp (the essay appeared in *Commentary*) and was addressed to a reform audience. Right through 1968, Moynihan would think of himself as speaking strictly within liberalism, and his criticism thus had a tension which was lacking later. He simply had interests that were not prominent in this liberal world. One was ethnicity, another was the family. He was also free of some of this group's obsessions. If he shared the liberal view of aggressive world Communism, his writings were still unscarred by the sectarian enmities inherited from the intellectual battles of the thirties. The fact that he had been shining shoes (and caddying on a golf course) while other future neoconservatives were debating Trotsky's latest pronouncements in Alcove No. 1 may not have brought him closer to the black poor but it cemented his attachment to the rest of middle-class America.

In view of the political impulse behind almost all of his intellectual efforts, it is not surprising that Moynihan's most maverick period coincided with the years he was out of Washington—1966 to 1968. As a benchmark one might take his Phi Beta Kappa Oration at Harvard in June 1967, later published under the title "Nirvana Now," and one of his finest forays outside the specialty of urban affairs. The talk was an analysis of radical protest among American youth, and it came rather late in the decade, when the escalation of the war in Vietnam had brought on an escalation of draft resistance, direct action, and dropping out. The Berkeley demonstrations were three years in the past; hardly anyone remembered that in 1964 Students for a Democratic Society was willing to go "Part of the Way with LBJ." By 1965, unable to accept the "bad mistake" theory of the war as sufficient explanation for Washington's ever-escalating commitment, SDS was backing into a dogmatic Marxism, and other Marxist groups, old or new, were enjoying a sudden ascendancy. Black nationalism had shattered the continuity of the civil rights movement, given rise to a rhetoric of violence, and disintegrated morale among white activists. Hippiedom had left its heart, and maybe its head, in San Francisco; Timothy Leary was preaching the religion of LSD.

In these circumstances it is not surprising that Moynihan's address included a firm affirmation of the Western liberal tradition.

> To see history as an earnest evolution from the peat bogs to John Stuart Mill, or to the 1964 Democratic platform, is a simplicity that will not much commend itself to anyone any longer. . . . But neither would I reject the theme of J. H. Plumb's new series, *The History of Human Society*, "that the condition of man now is superior to what it was." Things are better, and where they are best is in the liberal industrial democracies of the North Atlantic world. I hold these regimes to be the best accommodation to the human condition yet devised, and will demand to know of those who reject it, just what they have in mind as a replacement. . . . The less than soul-stirring belief of the liberal in due process, in restraint, in the rule of law is something more than a bourgeois *apparat*: it involves, I argue, the most profound perception of the nature of human society that has yet been achieved, and, precisely in its acknowledgment of the frailty of man and the persistence of sin and failure, it is in the deepest harmony with the central tradition of Judeo-Christian theology. It is not a belief to be frittered away in deference to a mystique of youth.

What *is* surprising about this address, however, is the original and generous manner in which youthful protest is analyzed. "We have been seeing," said Moynihan, "in the flamboyance of the hippies, the bitterness of the alienated college youth, the outrageousness of the New Left, little more than mutants of the old Bohemianism, the never-ending conflict of generations, and perhaps the persistence of neo-Marxist radicalism. We may be wrong. Just possibly, something more important is abroad. We may be witnessing the first heresies of liberalism." Liberalism had become the established creed of the ruling elites, and it was now undergoing a spiritual crisis. Moynihan developed a series of colorful comparisons between youthful protest and "heresies" of the past—between the hippies of Haight-Ashbury and the Brethren of the Free Spirit, or Ranters, of Cromwell's England, and between the alienated dropouts and the followers of Sabbatai Zevi. For the New Left radicals, however, he reserved his most surprising analogy.

"Who are these outrageous young people? I suggest to you they are Christians arrived on the scene of second-century Rome." Moynihan took off from James Anthony Froude's great Victorian essay on the confrontation between the Epicurean Celsus and the Christian Origen.

> The second century was not unlike the twentieth, and . . . let there be no doubt that we are the Romans. It was a world, Froude writes, in which "Moral good and moral evil were played with as fancies in the lecture-rooms; but they were fancies merely, with no bearing on life. . . ." It was a

tolerant world that knew too much about itself to expect words and deeds invariably to conform. "Into the midst of this strange scene of imposture, profligacy, enthusiasm, and craving for light," Froude continues, "Christianity emerged. . . ."

Who were these Christians? They were first of all outrageous. They were "bad citizens, refusing public employment and avoiding service in the army; and while . . . they claimed toleration for their own creed, they had no toleration for others; every god but their own they openly called a devil. . . . Fathers and tutors, they say, are mad or blind, unable to understand or do any good thing, given over to vain imagination. The weavers and cobblers only are wise. . . ." Of learning they had little and cared less. Nor had they any great interest in respectable people who observed the rules of society and tried to keep it running. . . . They were altogether of a seditious and revolutionary character.

Such people were a bafflement to Celsus. If he spoke bitterly about them, he observed, it was because he was bitter. One can imagine him thinking, if not quite putting to paper, "Do they not see how precarious is the balance of things; how readily it might all be brought down?" He was every bit an admirable, reasonable man. "He considered," Froude writes, "that human affairs could be best ordered by attention and obedience to the teaching of observed facts, and that superstition, however accredited by honorable objects or apparent good effects, could only be mischievous in the long run. Sorcerers, charlatans, enthusiasts, were rising thick on all sides. . . . Of such men and such messages Celsus and his friends were inexorable antagonists." . . . The Christians, Celsus declared, were welcome to stay and become part of the commonwealth, but . . . they must live by its rules. Otherwise, be gone. Nothing was required that a reasonable man need find objectionable: to salute the sun, or to sing a hymn to Athene did no harm to anyone. Whatever private views one might have on the subject were one's own affair. But society had a right to allegiance.

Point by point Celsus took on Christianity. Point by point he won the intellectual argument, and lost the moral and spiritual one. For he was thinking about the world, and Christians were thinking about the soul. . . . Can there be any mistaking that the New Left speaks to the rational, tolerant, reasonable society of the present with the same irrationality, intolerance, and unreasonableness, but possibly also the same truth with which the absurd Christians spoke to Imperial Rome?

Moynihan's amazing generosity toward the New Left is the first thing that strikes us about his discourse, though perhaps it was not the best nor most informed.* What is truly astonishing about this comparison is Moynihan's insight into the *antagonists* of the New Left, those established

---

* My own report on the so-called New Politics convention, held in Chicago shortly after Moynihan made his address, flatly concluded that the movement was politically and morally in tatters.

liberals about whom he was excellently informed because he was one of them. Indeed, in his portrait of Celsus, sympathetic yet keen to the man's limitations, one could divine more than a few traits of the speaker: the sense of society's precarious position, the belief that orderly and effective government requires minute attention to observed facts, the opposition to enthusiasms and intolerance.

The Harvard Phi Beta Kappa Oration was addressed to liberals. It was spoken in the mother church of the liberal religion. And liberalism, said Moynihan, had much to do with three American problems. First, liberal optimism had "led us to an increasingly dangerous and costly effort to extend our system abroad. . . . Liberals have simply got to restrain their enthusiasm for civilizing others." Second, liberal values have not been at all secured at home, even among the liberal elites:

> During the past year we have had to begin admitting that during the height of the cold war the United States government began secretly using intelligence funds to support organizations of liberal and even left-leaning students and intellectuals. This was done out of a sincere and almost certainly sound conviction that the activities of these groups would aid in the struggle against totalitarianism. Observe the irony: the liberals running American foreign policy were forced to resort, in effect, to corrupt practices—totalitarian practices if you will—in order to advance liberal causes—*because the popularly elected Congress would never dream of doing so*.

Third, liberalism had lost touch with "the primal sense of community." It had let society become what Durkheim called "a dust of individuals." To the rational liberal, said Moynihan, "the tribal attachments of blood and soil appear somehow unseemly and primitive."

What the very style and structure of this talk demanded of liberals was that they stretch their imaginations. What Moynihan asked explicitly was that they (and he no doubt included himself) *listen*. "Young people are trying to tell us something. They are probably right in much of what they say, however wrong their prescriptions for righting matters. . . .There is altogether too much that is shoddy and derivative, and in a final sense dishonest, about American life. . . . awareness of this fact is more diffused within the American electorate than it will have suited the mildly dissenting liberal *cognoscenti* to imagine." Liberals had better limit their commitments better to their resources, and match their performance to their standards. They would have to begin by acknowledging "that what we have so far made of our opportunity is very much less than we should have."

No one could call Moynihan's argument an "orgy" of self-accusation, as the cliché of that time would have it; no one could suspect him of collapse before the "mystique of youth," against which he explicitly warned; but he did not exculpate himself or his liberal audience. If their world was being shaken, this was in large measure their own responsibility.

How differently he would sound by 1975. Explaining why Americans were hobbled in presenting their case to the world, he turned to the doubts about our national virtue found among the university-educated. American intellectuals, he explained, had fallen within the orbit of Communism in the thirties, and "when this influence began to move into the universities, as it did after World War II, resistance to it was disorganized and uncomprehending—often save only for the opposition of ex-Communists and others of the Left who had been close enough to the phenomenon to recognize it for what it was. Nonetheless, by the late 1960s the Stalinoid student newspaper was common on campuses everywhere, and remains so. And as the cohort of former communists and anticommunist socialists gradually disappears, universities seem even more uncomprehending and undefended than ever." Where are Celsus and Origen now? If they were a fanciful account of the New Left, they were openly so. Here the fanciful account is the hard anti-Communist one, verging on simple McCarthyism, of subversion—subversion staved off only by the toughened ex-Communists and anti-Communists who had been part of what Moynihan previously identified as the resort to corrupt and totalitarian practices. The liberal university is the passive victim, aggressed upon by the outside agitator. And the word "Stalinoid"! When did this harsh survivor of the left-wing sectarian diatribes enter Moynihan's vocabulary? What had happened? What brought on this descent from the self-demanding, disturbing, complex formulations of 1967 to the exculpatory, comforting, simple formulations of the seventies?

This is not a question of elevating the old orthodox liberal Moynihan at the expense of the later neoconservative one. In 1967, Moynihan was clearly not orthodox, and plenty of neoconservative themes are present in the Phi Beta Kappa Oration. His statements of the next year took a progressively more conservative position, but they were far from the sour belittling of his adversaries that would come later.

In September 1967, for example, Moynihan addressed a plea for "a politics of stability" to the National Board of Americans for Democratic Action. The tone was far more anxious than in his spring Phi Beta Kappa address, and no doubt a major reason was the over fifty American cities which had been racked by riots in the meantime. Newark and Detroit had made the country wonder whether civil war was about to break out—forty-three people died in Detroit; half a billion dollars' worth of property was destroyed. Liberals generally responded to those events by trying to temper public opinion with explanations of the black population's grievances and frustrations, and by calling for more massive and vigorous federal action. Moynihan's response, in contrast, can reasonably be called conservative. He offered three propositions for liberals to consider. First, they "must see more clearly that their essential interest is in the stability of the social order" and accordingly ought to seek alliances with political conservatives who shared that interest. Second, "liberals must divest themselves of the notion that the nation—and especially the cities of the nation—can be run from agencies in Washington." If the federal government had become the main source of social innovation, that was largely because the states and cities had been allowed to get into fiscal straits. The federal bureaucracy was clumsy and complacent. And the federal government inevitably gave priority to foreign affairs. "A system has to be developed, therefore, under which domestic programs go forward regardless of what international crisis is preoccupying Washington at a given time. This, in effect, means decentralizing the initiative and the resources for such programs." Moynihan favored revenue sharing: "The federal government is good at collecting revenues, and rather bad at disbursing services." He also favored using private business to develop domestic programs, and it didn't bother him if the lure was simply "to let enough men make enough money out of doing so."

Third, liberals had to stop "defending and explaining away anything, however outrageous, which Negroes, individually or collectively, might do." Moynihan particularly complained that liberal sensitivities about anything which might reflect badly on the black classes had paralyzed their ability to think or act decisively on the harsh realities of Negro conditions.

Along with being conservative, these propositions were highly debatable. Should liberals have made stability their first concern? Moynihan himself has more recently pointed out that past experience and contemporary evidence indicated a decrease in violence and racial conflict. The data behind the Kerner Commission's report cast doubt on the commission's own conclusion of growing racial polarization, at least to the point of violence. The riots were, in behaviorist terms, "aversive behavior," or in medical language, "autoimmunizing." Moynihan has even suggested—no, boasted—that all this was clear to him in 1968, possibly even in 1967: "This was an impression easily enough gathered in Detroit in the summer of 1967." Of course Moynihan did not mention this "easily enough gathered" impression in print until several years had passed—and it really does make hash of his plea for a politics of stability. But putting this aside as intellectual showboating and assuming things were not so certain in 1967, we still might conclude that Moynihan was taking the rhetoric of revolution more seriously than he should have been. Besides, a "politics of stability" only took on meaning when explained in terms of an alliance with conservatives. In 1967 that meant abandoning thoroughgoing opposition to the war in Vietnam and risking the residue of Great Society programs. Similar objections could be raised to Moynihan's points about decentralization, private business, and so on. Nonetheless, these were thought-provoking criticisms of liberal assumptions and priorities. Moynihan was thinking where so many others were only repeating.

The same could be said of his analyses of "The Crises of Welfare," of the Coleman Report on educational opportunity, of the issues which decentralization and quotas raised for racial peace (it seemed that giving Harlem a vote on its own school budget presented problems that Moynihan overlooked when urging revenue sharing with Mississippi). These were all forceful and thoughtful Moynihan products during this period. They had in common his skepticism about liberal assumptions and programs backed by his deft handling of data, his wit, and his skill at dramatizing and elaborating a complicated question.

What Moynihan had recognized, and what gave his work from this period its bite and its originality, was that the critique of liberal interventionism directed at the war in Vietnam might extend to domestic policy as well. A number of radicals made the same point, but their analyses were clogged with concepts of imperialism and colonialism so broad and borrowed that specific applications seemed fanciful and unpersuasive. Most liberals stuck with the traditional contrast between foreign adventures and domestic reform. They thought these rival impulses, not, as Moynihan was suggesting, one and the same. According to him, the aggressive young men who accompanied Kennedy to Washington had demanded a foreign-policy posture of flexible and graduated response in order to avoid the drift toward massive retaliation; thus brushfire wars, counterinsurgency, and so on. They had also demanded a host of domestic programs to forestall urban decay, racial conflict, and the loss of scientific and economic leadership. Neither the one variety of federal interventionism nor the other had been a success. It was time to rethink this experience, to evaluate the innovations set into motion, to reach some conclusions about what went wrong and how it might be set right.

Moynihan expressed this opinion nowhere better than in a May 1968 article exploring the issues facing Democrats in the wake of Lyndon Johnson's withdrawal from the Presidential race and the assassination of Martin Luther King, Jr. Moynihan did not call for the outright abandonment of federal interventionism. That was the position of the New Left in foreign policy and of a more diverse coalition in domestic policy; and Moynihan was worried about that as well. "We are in danger of losing not only the substantive gains that began to be made under Kennedy and then, for a while, continued under Johnson, but also the vision that gave clarity and purpose to the fight for those gains. The plain fact is that the present trend of events is leading us toward a conservative Republican President and a conservative-to-reactionary Congress: a regime marked by indifference to events abroad, save for intermittent threats to blow up the world, and by hostility to social change at home." Moynihan pleaded that interventionism be "*reappraised*, not discarded." America must recognize the limits of its power abroad. "But this is no less true in the area of domestic problems. For on any list of things that have contributed to the miscalculations of the decade, one would have to place the disposition of liberal Democrats to underestimate and misinterpret the forces in American society that are resistant to meaningful change and which limit the power of the federal government to bring such change about." Thanks in part to past liberal initiatives, there is a "conservative majority" of Americans who have been brought into the system and now identify their interests with "one or more institutions that are manifestly part of the established order." As a result, "government induced social change is not only likely to be slow, but will be slowed down even further if pressed in ways calculated to agitate and alarm that majority." It was time liberals responded to the genuine concerns of these groups, not pretending, for example, that ordinary Americans have nothing to lose from school integration. "If we acknowledged possible losses, would we not be more readily believed when we spoke of probable gains?"

As in Vietnam, liberals had a credibility problem. "The great liberal failing of this time is constantly to over-promise and to overstate, and thereby constantly to appear to under-perform." Rhetoric was related to a failure to define problems correctly. By extending the "vocabulary and moral imperatives" of the southern civil rights struggle to the social and economic problems of the North, liberals had transformed class issues into racial ones. When "the issue at hand is a recognizable problem of lower-class behavior . . . not much good and very likely some harm is done by turning directly to the subject of white guilt."

Moynihan had departed somewhat from his earlier advocacy of a massive program aimed directly at the Negro community (though in the name of a value, family stability, which he supposed acceptable to all Americans) to a strategy of "enclosing" the urban racial problem in the general problem of lower-class life-style and living conditions. It had been one of the criticisms of the Moynihan Report that he had described as characteristic of the lower-class *Negro* family what in fact tended to be marks of lower-class families generally. Thus his statistics had compared blacks and whites without breaking down the white population to focus on income levels which were much more typical of the black community. Whether or not Moynihan acknowledged this criticism, in effect he absorbed it into his later proposals, which were meant to support, say, the

Negro family in the course of supporting lower-income families across the board. This was the thinking behind both the Family Assistance Plan and the "benign neglect" memo.

Despite the appeal for rhetorical restraint and a deemphasis on race *per se*, Moynihan's notion of what was to be done, and his confidence about achieving it, remained largely unaltered: "We must create full employment, provide some form of income supplement, build houses, and devise social institutions that work. . . . We know *how* to do each of the first three things, and are beginning to get ideas about the last." The Republican-Southern coalition in Congress would not act, however. Liberal Democrats would have to win at the polls, and to this end Moynihan warmly endorsed the candidacy of Robert Kennedy.

A month after this article appeared, Kennedy was dead and Pat Moynihan, sad, shaken, but "suffused with a sense of clarity and—terrible to say—almost a sense of inevitability," sat down to write his own version of *Goodbye to All That*. It was a critique of the community-action programs which Kennedy, in words prepared by a boyhood friend, had strongly endorsed before Congress as giving the poor "a real voice in their institutions."

Turning Points

Daniel Patrick Moynihan has identified a number of turning points in his political-intellectual career. A number of these marked a growing disillusionment with his political associates, in 1958 with the New York State Democratic reformers who risked their state ascendancy rather than support Frank Hogan, a qualified Catholic regular, for the Senatorial candidacy; in 1963 with the national liberals who refused his advice to get federal custody of Lee Harvey Oswald and later to investigate President Kennedy's assassination with a remorselessness that would not leave the public in doubt; in 1965 with the activist liberals and black militants who distorted the Moynihan Report and denounced its author. Another turning point was intellectual—the publication, in 1966, of the massive Coleman Report on *Equality of Educational Opportunity*, which, in Moynihan's view, challenged virtually every assumption that had been made about the role of public education in American life, and posed difficult problems about the relationship between public policy and new findings by social science.

Yet another turning point might be described as social. In March 1967,

Nelson Rockefeller convened a meeting on new approaches to welfare at Arden House in New York. The conference, at which Moynihan gave one of his excellent papers, was largely an affair of big businessmen; and the upwardly mobile academic and New Deal Democrat was clearly impressed. "They got some very attractive, big guys to run it," he told a reporter later. "Republican guys. Joe Wilson of Xerox, Arjay Miller— millionaires. . . . What was fascinating was that the businessmen didn't know anything about welfare and they got very interested. They'd say, 'Hmmm, now there's a hell of a situation, an interesting problem. What do you do about it?' They didn't just sit there dumb, saying 'Stick with what you've got and maybe everything will be all right.' They were very open, coming up with problem-solving ideas." Moynihan admits that the Arden House experience influenced his ADA speech with its proposal of an alliance with conservatives and a greater reliance on private business.

And finally, if one can use such a word for a career of so many turning points, there was Moynihan's acceptance of a place in the Nixon Republican Administration.

Two of these episodes deserve more discussion. In regard to the Moynihan Report, it should be noted that by no means was all the liberal response critical, nor was all the critical response abusive. At times Moynihan acknowledges this. At other times, as in a 1967 *Commentary* essay, he has said, "The reaction of the liberal left to the issue of the Negro family was decisive. . . . They would have none of it. No one was going to treat their poor people that way." Simply not true. *The New York Times*, *Commonweal*, *The New Yorker*, *Newsweek*, and *America* were among liberal journals receptive to the report. *New Republic* was cool but interested. Christopher Jencks in *The New York Review of Books* was skeptical but described Moynihan's more irate critics as "somewhat paranoid" about the report. Black psychologist Kenneth Clark backed Moynihan firmly, telling *Newsweek* that "if Pat's a racist, I am." Martin Luther King, Jr., while nervous about the report's impact, spoke in parallel tones about the Negro family. So did the Black Muslims and the followers of Malcolm X. Critics like black activist Bayard Rustin and sociologist Frank Riessman insisted that Moynihan's intentions were excellent and rejected the charges that he was a racist. Socialist author Michael Harrington defended Moynihan's intentions against conservative interpretations of the report.

Furthermore, as Rainwater and Yancey point out in their study of the controversy, the report was open to quite legitimate criticism on a number of grounds. A document meant to dramatize an issue and provoke action, it was necessarily oversimplified. Moynihan had been selective in his use of evidence, and his emphasis on the pathological character of matriarchy was questionable. Much of the criticism along these lines, according to Rainwater and Yancey, showed "high technical sophistication and intimate knowledge of the issues involved."

At the same time, Moynihan was hardly without resources for defending himself. The national media—*The Washington Post*, *The New York Times*, *Newsweek*, *Life*, *Look*, and the TV networks—provided him with an ample platform, which he utilized over a six-month period with characteristic vigor. A year after the report surfaced, Moynihan was ensconced in the liberal heartland as director of the Harvard–MIT Joint Center for Urban Studies and was being profiled as a likely model "for an inspirational novel by some contemporary Horatio Alger Jr." in *The New York Times Magazine*. Though Moynihan's complaints about some of his liberal critics were surely justified, the reception of his report by no means amounts to a case against the liberal-left community.

Of Moynihan's entry into the Nixon Administration, it should be noted that this is one turning point Moynihan himself, even at the time it took place, has never stressed. On the contrary, he has always treated the event as a kind of inevitability, a matter almost beyond choice. "When the only President we have asks me to come work for him, I am pretty much disposed, on the terms he asked it, to do anything he asks. . . . I was doing what any person ought to do. You don't decline to serve the President of the United States in an advisory capacity, under almost any circumstances—that is, if you've got the internal fortitude to advise him as you really see it. On what grounds would you say, 'No, I will not advise the President'?"

The question is put as though, barring the case of Nazism, there is no reply. Yet Moynihan must know that the answer is not at all obscure, though it might require some distinctions in that easy glide from "advise" (the occasional trip to Washington, the drafting of a position paper) to "work for" (full-time identification with the Administration) to "do anything he asks" (John Dean? or merely promising not to resign over disagreements). If one estimates that an Administration, for whatever reason, is unlikely to enact the policies one favors, and is in fact apt to strengthen the policies one abhors, then one lends one's talents and energies to the opposition, one retains the privilege of criticizing freely, and one builds the foundation for the election of a different Administration more likely to enact the desired measures. Moynihan did not serve Nixon because, once asked, it was the only reasonable course to take; but because, as he made perfectly clear at the time, he viewed an alliance of liberal and conservative political elites, having a common interest in social stability—the American equivalent of a European government of national union—as the best response to the turmoil of the sixties. His decision was a political one, for which he must take political responsibility. There were other ways to be patriotic and to serve the public, even by standing and waiting.

If Moynihan's entry into the Nixon Administration was a political decision, which followed from a previously announced political strategy, it was also a *turning point*, which departed from that strategy in a crucial respect. Moynihan's ADA speech was addressed to liberals, and it assumed that Johnson would be reelected and "the national government will remain in the hands of the same kind of liberals who have been much in evidence for the last seven years." By May 1968, when he wrote his *Commentary* appeal for Robert Kennedy, Moynihan was no longer confident of liberal success at the polls, but he was no less a partisan of it. In other words, the liberal-conservative alliance he envisaged was one in which the conservatives would be the junior partners. Not only was the Nixon Administration cum Moynihan (as liberal) the extreme reverse of this situation, it was . . . well, a Nixon Administration. In May 1968, Moynihan had described the prospect of a conservative Republican Administration in distinctly unflattering terms, and it was clear he had Nixon in mind. Six months later he was in the ranks.

Hope is a virtue, not a frailty. Moynihan was gambling, and his gamble was for the best of ends. Hope, unfortunately, can degenerate into illusion, into self-deception; and that was the risk he ran. He had to answer others' questions about his service with Nixon, perhaps he had to answer his own; and he chose to reply by deflecting attention to "upper-middle-class liberals." "I decided to be disabused of their image of Nixon. . . . I'd already seen what they had done to me." This is curious reasoning indeed, as though Moynihan had to depend on the image of Nixon manufactured by some upper-middle-class liberal monopoly on information. Nixon, after all, had a public record, with which Moynihan, to judge from his negative comments of only a half-year earlier, was not unfamiliar. Yet attacking liberals suited Moynihan's newer political perceptions, redressed his old grievances, and gained him credibility with his new employers.

The problem of advising an Administration like Nixon's "as you really see it" was not simple—not if you wanted to retain effectiveness. The intellectual in opposition woos the voters; the intellectual in power woos his superiors. For the one, slogans; for the other, flattery. For both the same problem: how much varnish on the unvarnished truth? Consider the memo Moynihan addressed to Nixon, then still President-elect, in January 1969. Like the later "benign neglect" memo, its intentions were generally admirable. Its theme was the neoconservative one, "the erosion of the authority of the institutions of American society." It was a formulation on which he and the President could agree wholeheartedly, however they might diverge in specifying causes and remedies. Moynihan's recommend-ations, despite their note of social engineering, were decent and sound: (1) maintain the economy and combat recession; (2) "de-escalate the rhetoric of crisis about the internal state of the society in general"; (3) make the transformation of the "Negro lower class" a "clear national goal"; (4) prevent identification of the Presidency with the war in Vietnam; (5) "stress those things Americans share in common" rather than those which divide them. These are the solid kernel of what, in many respects, was a sycophantic document. It refers Nixon to "the logic of events, and your own sure sense of them"; compares him not so obliquely to Lincoln and Wilson; and contains the sneer at professors, millionaires, flower children, and Radcliffe girls who supposedly made up the mob that toppled Johnson.

Moynihan's objective was obviously to move the Nixon Administration in a direction that was not its natural inclination. The President's advisers, after all, included individuals like John Mitchell, who was alleged to have referred to demonstrating students being arrested in the streets of Washington as "Moynihan's people." He had to choose his formulations shrewdly, therefore, assimilating them as much as possible to the tendencies that were natural to the President and his Administration. Thus Moynihan's comments on the war, to which he had been opposed for some time, were strictly hard-nosed: the children of the middle class were against it because they might be drafted, their parents were against it because of taxes and inflation. "The war has not gone well, and increasingly in an almost primitive reaction—to which modern societies are as much exposed as any Stone Age clan—it has been judged that this is because the gods are against it." Moynihan was not about to risk his standing with the President-elect by suggesting that the moral issue, regardless of many citizens' motivations, might be anything more serious than a "primitive reaction."

Similarly he had to establish common ground by making the Admin-istration's enemies his own—a task to which perhaps he lent himself willingly. War protesters and the Left in general were reduced to caricature. "I have heard the head of SNCC state that we were in Vietnam 'for the rice supplies.' " (A year after Tet, there were surely more significant critics of the war than the head of SNCC, an organization not exactly flourishing in 1969, and more serious arguments than this one.)

However we may react to this, we should remember that these were not small stakes—to loosen the government from its attachment to the war, to steer it toward carrying forward rather than reversing the movement for Negro inclusion. Were a little tugging at the forelock and a few catty remarks about one's colleagues a fair price for bending Nixon's ear toward a decent program? Why not make the best argument one can, even if it means accepting the terms of one's allies (and employers) and trimming the truth a bit here and there? The good attorney plays on the prejudices of the jury. Did the causes of extricating the United States from Vietnam or assisting the urban lower class deserve any less?

At some point, of course, one ceases to play upon the prejudices of the political superior; one only confirms them. The intellectual becomes the courtier. Perhaps Moynihan's gamble was justified in 1969, but the returns were not long in arriving. Of his five recommendations the Administration made a full commitment to none, directly contravened several. It planned a recession and tolerated unemployment, though Moynihan had urged that "the single most important task is to maintain the rate of economic expansion." It wielded the "rhetoric of crisis" whenever an election approached. It did propose the Family Assistance Plan but never made the transformation of the Negro lower class "understood as a clear national goal." It chose to identify the Presidency with the war, with precisely the effect on the authority of government that Moynihan had warned against. It fostered divisiveness rather than unity whenever that promised political rewards. Moynihan wagered—and lost. And having lost, he did not quit clean. Instead, he blamed as much as possible on liberals, resigned with fulsome praise for Nixon, in effect supported him for reelection, and accepted an ambassadorship even as the second-term Nixon was demolishing the "Tory Democrat" image for good.

Moynihan had pointed out that many domestic programs had become a domestic Vietnam for liberals, who slogged on when they should have recognized the limits of their power and called it quits. The Nixon Administration, in those terms, was Moynihan's Vietnam. Here, perhaps, is the only explanation of Moynihan's blemish-free portrayal of Nixon, both in *The Politics of a Guaranteed Income* and the 1972 *Life* article. Moynihan, one can speculate, set out to construct a coherent persona for the President, one that weaved Nixon's impulses with Moynihan's, in hopes that the President would put on the mask Moynihan offered him. This was ghostwriting of a special sort—of a character, not a speech. It was also *hubris* of a special sort—of the intellectual. Politics could not be written like a novel. Moynihan sank into the quagmire; once committed, he could not admit he had been beaten. Even in 1972 he marched on.

Alienated from liberals by these events, Moynihan began to criticize liberalism in ever harsher terms. In *Maximum Feasible Misunderstanding* and *The Politics of a Guaranteed Income*, he reflected sourly on liberal motives; the subjective cast of his attack was demonstrated by the fact that many of his animadversions on social science and politics were as applicable to his own efforts as to those of his liberal antagonists. The extent to which his strong feelings had come to dominate his arguments could be seen in the gap between what both books announced as intention and what they actually did.

Maximum Feasible Misunderstanding was in principle a book only about the lack of clarity surrounding the community-action segment of the war on poverty and how this lack of clarity undermined community action and the poverty effort generally. *In principle* the book was not an overall judgment of community action (which would have required the establishment of criteria for "success" and "failure" as well as the kind of field work which several books attempted but Moynihan's did not), nor was it a postmortem on the Great Society's approach to poverty. To read it as such, Moynihan later protested, was an error—an error made by both favorable and unfavorable reviewers and even by the professor who wrote the foreword to the book! Clearly the fault was not that of the readers alone. Moynihan had insisted that his book was not concerned with the reality of community action but with the impression it made; by the same token, his readers were justified in attending not only to the thesis that, strictly speaking, the book argued but to the wider impression *it* made.

The Politics of a Guaranteed Income displayed the same dual personality. "There are no villains in this book," says the introduction. Yet Gus Tyler, an official of the International Ladies' Garment Workers Union and a shrewd political observer, quite accurately notes that Moynihan's "first motif" is that the Family Assistance Plan

> was killed by a coalition of people with mean motives: Liberal Democrats did not want to give a credit line to a Republican president. Southern Democrats did not want to emancipate their poor from economic exploitation or political intimidation. Conservatives did not want to pamper the undeserving poor. Social workers did not want to lose their pay or prestige. . . . Militant black mothers of the National Welfare Rights Organization (NWRO), the "aristocracy of welfare recipients," did not want to share their goodies with the less fortunate poor. The American Federation of State, County and Municipal Employees did not want to lose jurisdiction over numerous welfare bureaucrats. Even George McGovern was more interested in wooing blue-collar votes for his presidential ambitions than in caring for the politically apathetic poor.

The entire book is easily read as an indictment of liberals and a chronicle of villainy.

The Moynihan Style

The fact is that one cannot take the measure of Moynihan's thought without taking the measure of his prose style. He takes writing seriously. No other neoconservative, perhaps no other political writer in this period, can say as much by his manner. Moynihan, said Garry Wills, "writes a clumsy prose that almost begs to be misunderstood." I do not think this is right, although the repeated misunderstanding does demand explanation. Moynihan's is a formal, cadenced prose, at best genuinely witty and eloquent, at worst pretentious patter. Excepting his susceptibility to inflammatory formulations—and in fact almost all of these are found in documents not intended for public consumption—Moynihan has perfected a style superbly suited to the work of a professorial politician. Professorial, because he can make a case of considerable complexity, and make it lucidly and dramatically. (Wills was comparing Moynihan's prose unfavorably to Richard Goodwin's; yet when Goodwin had to go beyond the phrasemaking of writing speeches to the complicated argument of a book, he did not do as well as Moynihan.) Politician, because he can say a good deal more, or a good deal less, than what the printed word pins him to.

The elements of this style are several. First and perhaps most effectively, large and confident assertions, about political doctrines or the governing process or industrial society or the tendencies of the times, are combined with soft qualifications to account for the complexity of the facts and yet leave a striking impression that goes beyond them. Moynihan's article "The United States in Opposition," in which he warned that Third World nations were in the grip of the "British revolution," united, that is, by a redistributionist and anti-American legacy of Fabian socialism, exhibited his style at its most energetic. Aware of the many facts that collided with his thesis—Latin American jurists and generals, Arab oil sheiks, and Francophobe Marxists had *not* studied at the feet of Harold Laski—he forged an impression of Third World unity and threat by sheer style. Observe the movement in half of a single paragraph. Writing of these "heirs of the British revolution," Moynihan begins by conceding,

> British socialism is, was, and remains a highly moral creed. It is not a politics of revenge; it is too civil for that.

Already we have shifted slightly from "highly moral" to "civil." And do I detect the snickering hint that British socialism rejects revenge largely because revenge would be rude and ungentlemanly? Moynihan continues:

> But reparations? Yes: reparations. This idea was fundamental to the social hope of a movement which, it must ever be recalled, rested on the assumption that there existed vast stores of unethically accumulated wealth.

Another step from highly moral, but watch closely now:

> On the edges of the movement there were those who saw the future not just in terms of redistribution, but of something ominously close to looting.

Not central to the movement but "on the edges," not looting but "something ominously close to" it. Moynihan has placed his qualifiers—now he moves to his conclusion as though they did not exist:

> In any event, the past was by no means to be judged over and done with. There were scores to be settled.

From morality to priggery to foolishness to dangerousness! The passage begins with the admission that a highly moral British socialism was not "a politics of revenge"; it ends on "scores to be settled." The key words at the beginning are Latinate and restrained—"creed," "civil," "reparations." Those at the end are colloquial and emphatic—"looting," "scores." Moynihan has acknowledged the contradictory facts—for the record. His thought, however, flows right over them.

Others have noted an earlier passage in the same article as a similar masterpiece of manner over matter. Moynihan is describing two "concepts" which are part of the new nations' "imported political culture."

> The first is the belief—often, of course, justified—that they have been subject to economic exploitation, exactly as the working class is said in socialist theory to have been exploited under capitalism. The second is the belief—also, of course, often justified—that they have been subject to ethnic discrimination corresponding to class distinctions in industrial society. As with the belief in the right to independence, these concepts, which now seem wholly natural, rarely occur in nature. They are learned ideas, and they were learned mostly where they mostly originated, in the intellectual and political circles of Britain of the late 19th and 20th century.

This sent Pete Hamill into an untypically analytic mood. "Just what does Moynihan mean by all this?" he asked in *The Village Voice*.

> He mentions two beliefs held by Third World countries, and admits that they are "often, of course, justified." But he writes as if they are not justified at all. Does he mean that peasants in the colonies of the British Empire did not realize they were being exploited until they read about it in the *New Statesman*? If both beliefs are often "justified" by the facts, then how can Moynihan say that they "rarely occur in nature"? And does he actually mean that there are some ideas in the world that are *not* learned ideas? If so, where does one find them?

One can quibble further with Moynihan and Hamill about the problem of concepts occurring in nature, just as one could cut the discussion short with the truth of the matter, that Moynihan's point is a historical jumble. But it is the rhetorical element that concerns us now, and Hamill is right: Moynihan grants the reality of exploitation and discrimination with one hand, then reduces it with the other to the category of "learned ideas," learned, presumably, in some way other than the way in which all ideas are learned, and hence artificial. The point is not that Moynihan offers, in Hamill's words, "the old Outside Agitator theory raised to theological complexity," but that his style allows him to do it without taking responsibility for what he is saying.

A final example, this time for pure amusement. Moynihan is addressing the entering freshmen at Harvard in 1972. He has asked them to read Joseph Schumpeter's *Capitalism, Socialism, and Democracy*. The book, he says,

> is a work of analysis and passion on a level few can sustain; but it is more than that. It is the work of a man who has been around horses. I do not know this actually to have been true, but his stepfather is described in the *Encyclopedia of the Social Sciences* as a "high-ranking officer in the Austro-Hungarian Empire," and it ought to have been true. Schumpeter was not of the view that horses or riders are all alike. Dams counted, and sires counted, training and daring counted, resolution counted, and a tenth of a second could make all the difference in life. How to explain the beginnings of capitalism? A simple matter for Schumpeter: the "Supernormal intelligence and energy" of the early entrepreneurs brought success in nine cases out of ten. How to account for the appeal of socialism? Again, simple. Socialism, in scientific guise, formulated "with unsurpassed force that feeling of being thwarted and ill-treated which is the auto-therapeutic attitude of the unsuccessful many. . . ."
>
> (I would assume that many of you take exception to such views, and you have every right to do so. But if you think Schumpeter wholly wrong in such matters, let me offer you at the outset what could prove the best advice you will ever get at Harvard College. Stay away from race tracks.)

What, besides rococo charm, have we here? A Harvard professor, back from service with a conservative government, is telling a group of eighteen-year-olds that capitalism is the expression of the talented, socialism the revenge of the unsuccessful, not one of Schumpeter's most original or penetrating insights. That, of course, is the professor's privilege; other professors will undoubtedly tell the students the opposite. Nothing unusual so far. What is fascinating is how Moynihan makes the point without quite making it. All this rigmarole about horses, which Moynihan doesn't know "actually to have been true," but which he plunges on with anyhow. The quotes from Schumpeter are quickly followed by Moynihan's admission that his listeners may have objections, and justly so. He does not answer these objections, however; he only warns that "if you think Schumpeter *wholly* wrong" (another hedge), then stay away from race tracks. That is, although no evidence has yet been adduced, indeed the whole comparison between horsemanship and economic systems has been conjured out of thin air, only the student who is too foolish to spot the difference between a winner and a nag would doubt this account of capitalism and socialism. Illogical maybe, but deft.

There are several other twists to the Moynihan prose which allow him a slight distance between what he seems to be saying and what he explicitly takes responsibility for. He has a fondness for indirection. "This is no small matter." "This is no small achievement." "It would not be an exaggeration to argue . . ." "The concern . . . was hardly much in evidence." These formulations create a margin of ambiguity: if something is "no small matter," can we assume it is a "big matter"?

The note of resignation, bowing before the inevitability of the *fact*, also allows Moynihan to slip away from large assertions or harsh charges or prickly questions. "For the moment we have what we have." "Life will go on." "All, as I say, familiar enough, part of the game." Such phrases foreclose further discussion. Don't push me on that, nothing personal intended, what else can we expect?

"Now this sort of thing happens," Moynihan writes about Vietnam. "Nations lose wars. . . ." And he is off and running about the defeat of the foreign-policy elite and the elite's attempt to blame the war on the Catholic working class and the takeover of the Harvard ROTC building and how "shame was everywhere," to which fact Saul Bellow and Mr. Sammler are hauled in to testify, and then, just as one was about to sort out the connections, dong!—inevitability tolls again. "Time heals such hurts," says Moynihan solemnly, "time and the circulation of elites of which Pareto wrote." Wars happen and elites circulate, and if Moynihan is vilifying those who opposed this war, that too is but a sage observation on the eternal order of things.

How much of this is calculated, and how much is the natural—and lively—compromise between the pull of Moynihan's ardors and antipathies and the contrary tug of his awareness of unaccommodating facts? As always, it is difficult to tell. Certainly this ability to create an impression which goes beyond his assertions and to qualify his assertions without really amending them accounts for much of the controversial success as well as the confusion surrounding his writings. The narrative sections of *Maximum Feasible Misunderstanding*, for instance, picture hard-working and intelligent individuals (with proper names) making a number of "close calls" under the pressure of government deadlines. Suddenly, in the concluding part, an anonymous "good many men" are charged with doing "inexcusably sloppy work" and "play[ing] God with other people's lives." *The Politics of a Guaranteed Income* displays the same split personality. Were liberals responsible for the failure of the Family Assistance Plan? No. Moynihan says explicitly that this conclusion "misreads the event." Yet the book's introduction, in speaking of "a curious alliance of left and right" that defeated the measure, wastes ink only on the Left; and the book ends with a slap at intellectuals; and that is pretty much the story in between. It is difficult to choose one passage of this long and complicated text as illustrative of Moynihan's prose at work, but perhaps this will do:

> It was now a year since the president had made his proposal, and he did not, in truth, have much to show for it. It had produced deep misgivings within his Administration and his party; the most open-minded response from his opposition resembled that of Metternich at the Congress of Vienna, who on learning of the death of the Russian Ambassador is said to have asked, "What can have been his motive?" Still the tone with which he sought the support of the six senators was remarkably like that in which the previous summer he had talked to his own staff about his decision. Historians may come to regard this compartmentalization of issues as a mark of his presidency. This, together with a quality the British journalist Peregrine Worsthorne was to describe as immunity to hate. He had expected no credit, and he had got none. This was about his assessment of liberal response. Actually he had got a fair amount of praise from liberals but this had been balanced by about an equal amount of abuse. In any event, it didn't affect him much.

With his left hand, Moynihan notes the "deep misgivings" among Republicans, and with his right hand, he states that the "most open-minded response" from liberals was suspicion. The former group, however, is dropped from further consideration, even though almost all of the six senators whose meeting with Nixon was under discussion in this passage were basically conservative. (Comparing the liberal urge to "outbid" FAP as insufficiently generous with the conservative urge to "outbid" it as insufficiently stringent, Moynihan previously wrote: "While the left got more press, this tactic on the right was far the more devastating." The Left, however, gets the press in Moynihan's book as well.) The astounding remark about Nixon's "immunity to hate" is inserted as addendum to a "scholarly" generalization: "Historians may come to regard . . ." His right hand then makes the flat statement that Nixon expected no credit and received none, followed by the left hand's qualification that this was *Nixon's* assessment, followed by a little dialogue:
Left Hand: "Actually he had got a fair amount of praise from liberals . . ." (But hadn't their most open-minded response been suspicion only a few sentences before?)
Right Hand: ". . . balanced by about an equal amount of abuse." (So perhaps the President is correct, after all, in his assessment of having

received no credit? But do equal amounts of praise and abuse balance out to "no credit"? Why not be straightforward—the President had received *some* credit and indeed he received *some* abuse and, hardly being "immune to hate," he paid little attention to the former and burned at the latter?)

But the topic is quickly dismissed: "In any event, it didn't affect him much." So why bring it up? The passage is not important for the facts it juggles adroitly but for the impression it leaves—of querulous liberals and an imperturbable, long-suffering President.*

Moynihan has been taken to task more frequently for his scholarship than for his prose. In fact the same reality is at the root of the confusion— Moynihan's scholarship is that of the professorial *politician*. Thus he intersperses his arguments with bits of poetry and references to philosophers and cultural critics—as it happens, the same bits, the same references, used again and again. They are less the mark of the scholar's deep reading than the skillful essayist's literary conceits or even the politician's rhetorical embellishment. They are thrown out for effect, and accuracy is not of the first importance. Moynihan once began a pre-Watergate essay complaining that overly critical journalism was threatening the viability of Presidential government with a suspiciously elegant quotation from Harry S. Truman. Unfortunately the lines were from Thomas Jefferson, a trivial point, but also a hapless way to begin lecturing journalists on accuracy.

On the other hand, more serious charges of unscholarly inaccuracy have sometimes been made against Moynihan with no real understanding of his political aims. His neglect of qualifying data while preparing the Moynihan Report could be justified by the political nature of the document. It was "a case for national action," written for busy government officials, not researchers. Likewise there were good *political* reasons for leaning heavily on Stanley Elkins' theory about slavery and its devastating effect on the Negro life-style. Even at the time Moynihan wrote, this theory was highly controversial, and the conclusions drawn from it about the effects of slavery on black family structures have been discredited by scholars like Eugene Genovese and, most recently, Herbert Guttman. The place that this matter played in Moynihan's argument, however, was to emphasize that there were historical and social causes for contemporary black distress—and that responsibility for these problems could not be added to the burdens already laid on black shoulders.

---

* In 1978 Moynihan would write about Nixon in 1970: "I knew that his enemies had got to him, and that he would waste a good portion of his ascendancy hating those who hated him." This knowledge was evidently in eclipse when Moynihan wrote the above about Nixon's "immunity to hate."

Moynihan's text did not exclude other possible causes for the weakening of the black family, particularly those associated with twentieth-century urbanization; one could substitute any of the other theories without noticeably changing the conclusions he reached about male employment. Had he left the matter in a state of scholarly inconclusiveness, the danger of political misuse of the report would have been vastly increased, for which Moynihan, no doubt, would have been blamed.

Actually Moynihan displays a trait common among academics. The further he moves from his own professional area of urban studies, the more confidently he makes sweeping generalizations. He is obviously a quick study—a person of such productivity and so many roles would have to be—and he absorbs the "facts" he needs from all kinds of sources. In several essays he cites a book review by Robert Warshow on the role of the Communist Party in the thirties. In one essay he draws from it the assertion (which Warshow did not quite make) that "a huge proportion of American intellectuals were within the party orbit." In another, after citing no other authority but Warshow and the book Warshow was reviewing, Lionel Trilling's *The Middle of the Journey*, Moynihan states, "Stalinism brought the middle-class intellectual into American politics." One would not have to go far—to Daniel Bell's explication of "the growing myth that in the 1930s the Communists dominated the cultural life of America," to articles and books by Irving Howe, Daniel Aaron, and many others—to demonstrate that Moynihan's firm declarations are, to put it mildly, unnuanced. But debating the specific point is not as important as noting the way Moynihan resolves a complex issue, by quoting a single writer, an admittedly brilliant one but hardly the sole recognized authority.

In political philosophy as well as history, Moynihan is similarly limited in his scholarship—and knowing in his attitude. His 1976 essay for Nelson Rockefeller's Commission on Critical Choices shuffles categories like the "utilitarian ethic" and the "Freudian ethic" in a manner that may impress a Rockefeller but depress anyone familiar with the doctrines those terms refer to. The authorities Moynihan relies upon in many of his writings are those already congenial to his viewpoint; seldom does he confront, except by way of caricature, a serious opponent. His essay "On Universal Higher Education" contains citations from Nathan Glazer, Daniel Bell, Norman Podhoretz, Lionel Trilling, Irving Kristol, Robert Nisbet, Walter Z. Laqueur, Aaron Wildavsky, Paul Seabury, and a Nixon Presidential message composed in a prose that reads very much like . . . Daniel Patrick Moynihan! Here we are on the verge of a totally self-enclosed and self-validating world.

These observations on Moynihan's style and scholarship do not mean that his arguments are ordinarily without foundation. They do mean that this foundation is far more personal, more loosely joined to evidence, and more sensitive to shifts in the political climate than either the imposing character of Moynihan's writings or his credentials as a social scientist would suggest. Closely examined, Moynihan's critique of liberalism consists less of political science and more of personal disenchantment and political positioning. At odds with at least some liberals to begin with, and cornered by his own commitment to Nixon, Moynihan relaxed the creative tension of his mid-sixties neoconservatism and slipped into a critique carried along more by force of style than by attention to facts.

The same pattern can be traced, in different degrees, in the two remaining clusters of Moynihan's thought. Yet these deserve consideration in their own right.

Thinking About Black Americans

Moynihan rose to prominence on the strength or weakness or perhaps simple notoriety of his attempts to address the problems of black Americans. We might begin an inevitably simplified account of his ideas somewhat obliquely, with the observations Christopher Jencks made on the Moynihan Report: "Moynihan's analysis is in the conservative tradition. . . . The guiding assumption is that social pathology is caused less by basic defects in the social system than by defects in particular individuals and groups which prevent their adjusting to the system. The prescription is therefore to change the deviants, not the system."

Now that is not quite right. To get it right we must think in terms of two models. In one a group is kept out of the mainstream of economic and social life by obstacles almost totally outside itself. This is what Moynihan, with Nathan Glazer, calls the Jewish model. In contrast they propose an Irish model. Here the excluded group is a "displaced peasantry," lacking the skills for success in the new economic and social setting, and furthermore suffering from internal weaknesses resulting from past oppression. These "defects," to use Jencks's term, were caused by a social system but a *past* one. In a sense, this problem is one of "modernization." Yet that is not quite fair either. Just as the Irish met discrimination in America, Moynihan does not deny the obstacles to black progress which are within the present system rather than within the group as a result of the past system of enslavement and racial exclusion. Above all, the defect of the present system is its failure to provide employment for black males, thereby undermining an already weakened black family structure. In later writings Moynihan has no longer emphasized the psychological dynamics of matriarchy and male role models which were such a controversial aspect of the Moynihan Report, nor has he had to: with the overwhelming correlation between black poverty and female-headed households, everyone seems willing to accept, without psychological elaboration, the importance of keeping male wage earners from abandoning families.

So perhaps Moynihan's analysis is not properly "in the conservative tradition" after all? Still not accurate. Unfortunately, while pinpointing black male unemployment as the defect in the present system, he has never explored the reasons for that defect—except, of course, the Negro inheritance from the past. He does not dismiss "white racism," trade-union discrimination, and poor schooling altogether, but he considers them peripheral and counterproductive as objects of political action. Fundamental irrationalities in the economic system he does not consider at all.

One can say that Moynihan has held to the conclusion he reached at the end of the Moynihan Report:

> What then is [the] problem? We feel the answer is clear enough. Three centuries of injustice have brought about deep-seated structural distortions in the life of the Negro American. *At this point, the present tangle of pathology is capable of perpetuating itself without assistance from the white world.* [My emphasis.] The cycle can be broken only if these distortions are set right. . . . The object should be to strengthen the Negro family so as to enable it to raise and support its members as do other families. After that, how this group of Americans chooses to run its affairs, take advantage of its opportunities, or fail to do so, is none of the nation's business.

Thus in liberal fashion Moynihan has proposed various supplements to the job market—the acceptance of more blacks into the military, where they might obtain job training and a kind of father surrogate; an increase in postal-service jobs; family allowances and the income grants of the Family Assistance Plan. Only the last was a serious proposal. Secretary McNamara did institute a program, Project 100,000, which accepted previously disqualified, underprivileged youth, many of them black, into the military; there is little evidence that the program was a success, and Moynihan himself, though he had partially inspired it and though he has stressed the need for evaluation, never appears to have bothered with the matter further. The postal-service idea was always politically unlikely, more of a clever remark than a proposal. FAP, on the other hand, promised to be one of the major social innovations of recent decades. Its most widely discussed aim was to rationalize a disorganized, inequitable welfare system. But its real point, from Moynihan's perspective, was to strengthen the *still-intact* families of the working poor, especially among minorities. The resources for overcoming the interior obstacles to black success in America would be preserved and reinforced; the accumulation of further "defects" would be forestalled.

Such an analysis has definite implications for black politics. It would require that black leaders turn inward toward their own community, and that they exhibit a considerable degree of self-criticism while maintaining the pressure on the society at large which had opened up a new era of black gains in the sixties. It would have required an emphasis on "self-help"—Moynihan's observations on the black family's weakness elicited favorable comments in Black Muslim circles—but without the separatist ideology which lent some self-help movements a degree of militancy. In short, black leadership would have had to be both secure and sophisticated. In fact the black community had been set into turmoil by the civil rights movement; its leadership was new or changing in many cases and thrown on the defensive by the urban riots. Rainwater and Yancey pointed out, and Moynihan later acknowledged, that it was Watts, as much as anything, which did in the Moynihan Report. Watts exploded just as the report was emerging into the public consciousness; indeed the report was frequently presented, by officials as well as the media, as an explanation of the riots. This may have been done with good intentions: it was an alternative to the shift in image, from victim to aggressor, that threatened to accompany the shift from Selma to Watts. But black leaders were understandably unwilling to grant that outbreaks of ghetto violence were primarily due to the social "pathology" of their community. Though various black leaders were sympathetic to aspects of Moynihan's analysis, none of them could follow his implied prescription. Even Bayard Rustin, today a strong Moynihan supporter, could only insist in the sixties that the future of the Negro movement did "not lie along the line of making over millions of black personalities," but in organizing to alter the white-dominated economic system by using federal resources to rebuild slums and create employment.

Committed to a "realistic," interest-oriented understanding of the problems of group leaders, and perhaps unwilling to confront head-on people with a real constituency, Moynihan has frequently admitted the legitimacy of black leaders' concerns. Even the response of the National Welfare Rights Organization, so damaging to the Family Assistance Plan, made sense in terms of that group's membership and interests. But Moynihan still had a way of "saving the appearances." That was to displace the problems posed by blacks' inability or unwillingness to follow his prescribed course onto the account of white intellectuals, middle-class reformers, and the mass media. It was they who in "lust[ing] after the sensational and the exotic" or in protecting their own interests as professional do-gooders had fostered unreasonable militancy in the black community and undermined responsible leadership. They were, in effect, the traditional outside agitators, and rather effete, self-interested ones at that.

Apart from whether Moynihan's approach to these problems is "conservative" or not, what are its merits? The answer to that question depends largely on what one sees as the context of Moynihan's efforts. The context of the original Moynihan Report was that of the civil rights movement attempting to transfer its momentum from the South to the North, from questions of legal discrimination to those of social and economic inequality. Here Moynihan, though not Moynihan alone, pointed the way toward "the next and more profound stage of the battle for civil rights," seeking "not just freedom but opportunity—not just legal equity but human ability—not just equality as a right and a theory but equality as a fact and as a result." Moynihan's emphasis on the barriers to inclusion in the American mainstream that lay within the structures of the black community—what Kenneth Clark had called the "tangle of pathology"—was a simple recognition of facts which others, though again not all others, preferred to slide over out of fear of reinforcing racial stereotypes. His warnings about the danger of importing a style of political action appropriate to combating a system of Southern segregation into a Northern setting, where complicated bargaining between groups was both an opportunity and a necessity, were useful correctives to the moralism and naiveté of a good many public commentators. Moynihan was bringing unpleasant news, about problems within the black community and about the realities of urban politics. As usual, things did not go well for the messenger.

As one voice in a conversation, Moynihan made a lot of sense. But he left much unsaid. His unexamined premise, despite various qualifications, remained that the political and economic system was benevolent and rational. The source of today's problems was attributed to a regime of Southern segregation that was as good as dead; to the extent that "modern" institutions were responsible for the travail of black people, it was the ameliorative programs of recent generations, like welfare, that were to blame. The virus of racism would linger, but unless revived by lower-class black behavior it was doomed to disappear. The irrationalities of the job market, and the possibility that these might be structured along racial lines, were not considered. The economic and political obstacles to family income supplements or guaranteed employment—outside of those thrown up by "hyper-liberals"—were not fully acknowledged. The good will of the national government was taken for granted.

This outlook simply did not jibe with the experience of many black and liberal activists. The gains they had seen blacks make had been wrenched from recalcitrant political and economic institutions; and with troops in ghetto streets, with Johnson bending his tremendous energies toward a cruel war, with Nixon succeeding him, they were not about to turn the spotlight from the white to the black community in exchange for vague pledges and uncertain commitments to programs difficult to achieve in even the best of times. When representatives of the White House conference "To Fulfill These Rights" reported to President Johnson in the spring of 1966, the President devoted approximately four minutes to civil rights—*"and for 56 minutes the President harangued his council about Vietnam, the importance of the war, and the stupidity of domestic 'doves' and of foreign diplomats who run off to Hanoi and Washington trying to make peace through compromises."* Was this the surgeon on whose operating table the Negro family should be placed? Moynihan was right in insisting that the resistance of white Americans, especially working-class and ethnic Americans, to measures improving Negro status was a reality that had to be understood and not dismissed as primitive racism. But the reluctance of black leaders to agree with his formulations was also based on realities and not to be dismissed as the mischief spawned by liberal intellectual agitators. Racism there was, and is, and mischief too, but the analysis which ends there will not get beyond name-calling.

Which is pretty much what occurred. Another and not unrelated occurrence was a drift in Moynihan's own thinking about race and poverty. One shift was the politically shrewd one from a strategy of explicit commitment to the needs of Negro Americans, analyzed in terms of "family," to a strategy of enclosing black problems in those of low-income families generally. Another shift was the gradual abandonment of other levers of change; the Coleman Report persuaded Moynihan that education did not hold out the promise liberals had traditionally placed on it. Government pressure for the hiring of minorities appeared to him as moving toward rigid racial quotas, thereby threatening groups overrepresented in some areas, like the Jews, and politicizing previously private sectors of life. The failure of FAP, if one is to judge by some later remarks, may have convinced him that a guaranteed income is a political impossibility; and his current advocacy of welfare reform is limited to measures he has described in the past as stopgap. More and more, then, Moynihan seems to rely on the slow workings of the free market, accordingly hailing even the slenderest indications, no matter how slight, that blacks are being absorbed into the mainstream as past immigrant groups were. As his reaction has grown against the liberal tradition of social services, with which he identifies his antagonists, even the underlying psychology of Manchesterian ideology seems to appeal to him in greater measure. His comments—"boasts" would be a better way to describe them—about the stance he advocated for the Nixon Administration toward urban disorders, indeed the entire balance of his essay for the Commission on Critical Choices, sounded like a rehabilitation of Spencerian tough-mindedness toward the disciplining of the lower classes. During the New York Senatorial campaign, Moynihan positioned himself as representative of the New Deal tradition of federal activism. Against the old-style conservative James Buckley this was fair enough; indeed, it was inevitable. When pressed on programs, however—on full employment and national health insurance, for example—Moynihan gave himself lots of room to back up. The weight of representing New York's interests may alter his course once more; but unless it does, one can accurately describe Moynihan as drifting toward a theoretically rationalized acquiescence in "benign neglect," and not neglect of racially charged rhetoric only but of social-welfare measures of all sorts.

Whatever the limits of the earlier Moynihan analysis of race, poverty, and urban issues, it was a focused program that made demands on American society. The Family Assistance Plan, flaws and all, promised a degree of income and power redistribution remarkable for American legislation. A few individuals offered better alternatives to Moynihan's; Bayard Rustin, I believe, was one. But many offered much worse, and many offered what was, and could only be, talk. The shame was that so many, Moynihan included, finally turned to the defending and attacking of credentials and motives rather than compromising what could have been compromised, and living with the rest.

Taking On the World

If Moynihan's public reputation was based on his initiatives in the areas of race and poverty, his "breakthrough" as a political figure came in the area of foreign policy. And yet it is the area in which he is most unoriginal, most willing to restate, indeed eloquently insist upon, the validity of received opinion. There is no reason to believe that Moynihan ever held anything but the convictions of mainstream American liberalism about the Cold War. He served a political apprenticeship in the camp of Averell Harriman, a major influence on Cold War policy. He put in time at Freedom House, a bastion of Cold War liberalism. The Moynihan Report, early on, contained a characteristic warning about "the attraction of Chinese Communism" on the "far left" of the Negro American community.

By his own account, Moynihan "came late to opposition to the war" in Vietnam, "1966–67, thereabouts." A very strange opposition it turned out to be. Despite his hyper-articulateness, Moynihan made no major statement on Vietnam. On the contrary, the underlying premise of his thinking seems always to have been that very little could be done about the war. "President Johnson will almost certainly be elected in 1968 and . . . the war in Asia is likely to go on many years, too," he told the ADA National Board in 1967. In the same crucial speech he granted that Martin Luther King, Jr., and others were correct in saying, as he himself was to say, that the war had blocked domestic programs; "but they are wrong," he continued, "in their proposed solution: The government should get out of Vietnam." Washington would always give priority to foreign affairs and, presumably, this meant continuing the war despite urgent needs at home.

The strategy proposed in this speech, a liberal-conservative alliance of which his own service under Nixon became the prime example, rested on the assumption that Vietnam could be disregarded as a morally racking political issue in the country. It is hard to know whether Moynihan ever shared in the agony of many on the Left over the war. His remarks in the Phi Beta Kappa Oration of 1967 suggest he did, but that is all. Here is certainly one of the keys to his alienation from liberalism. From 1965 to 1972, the war preoccupied most liberals, seeping into their cells, stiffening their joints, charging their nerves. What was a central experience for others seems to have been for Moynihan a large hole. Perhaps he was overly impressed with his own parallel between overextension at home and overextension overseas. Both, perhaps, demanded reevaluation. But showering American citizens with remedial education and job-training programs of uncertain value was surely different from showering the people of another land with bombs and napalm. Moynihan urged Nixon to keep his distance from Vietnam but seemed content as long as matters were in the professional hands of Kissinger.

If the war stirred but small ripples in Moynihan's soul, the war resisters did not. Except for the Phi Beta Kappa Oration, they and their outrageous notions that a war like this implicated American society and institutions in some large sense—that the war was more than a blunder, was a crime, perhaps, and eroded the legitimacy of American government—became the objects of Moynihan's fierce disdain. In the end, he treated the "heresies of liberalism" the way that established churchmen usually treat heresies, seizing upon their most drastic versions to condemn the whole, taking for granted the realities against which they revolt. It is little surprise, then, that in the end of the war and the setback of American policy Moynihan could not recognize any vindication of the best of American principles, any release from a moral bondage, but only a collapse, a decline, a failure of nerve, a crisis of confidence.

He expressed his reaction to the post-Vietnam situation in a series of speeches and essays which are almost unsurpassed for the proportion of style to substance. Here Moynihan's style works overtime—posturing, prancing, brooding, puffing—to concoct a great drama without ever genuinely developing his few frail thoughts. These thoughts are (1) that liberal democracy is on the defensive, its influence at a low point in a decline which began in 1919; (2) that the cause of liberal democracy is the cause of the United States; (3) that a crucial factor in the current threat to liberal democracy, and one within our power to affect, is the crisis of confidence in America's cause among our leading elites; and (4) that we must counter this threat and this failure of the elites with a reaffirmation of America's role as the "party of liberty" in the world.

Each one of these points contains an amount of truth, but each also remains ambiguous. That ambiguity is not relieved in Moynihan's statements by an almost complete absence of the relevant facts; they contain virtually no reference to the specifics of diplomatic history, wars, treaties, falling or rising regimes, economic or military hegemony. There is no specification of the American elites in question, or documentation of their beliefs. Instead, Moynihan raises symbolic moments, quotations, and anecdotes from the corridors of international gatherings to the status of evidence for major shifts in world politics. What facts he does submit are questionable.

In "The United States in Opposition," the article reputedly linked to his appointment as Ambassador to the UN, he constructed something called the "British Revolution" to explain the present tensions between the United States and the Third World. The British Revolution consisted in the "fact" that by 1950 the "largest portion of the world's population lived in regimes" fashioned according to a preexisting, distinctive, coherent, uniform, and stable ideology, namely that of British Fabian socialism. This doctrine, promulgated through British civil servants and colonial elites educated at the London School of Economics, was characterized by a concern for the redistribution of wealth and a disdain for the problems of its production, by anti-Americanism, and by an acute sense of having been wronged and exploited by the Western powers. The ideological usefulness of Moynihan's construct was obvious. While avoiding the crude simplism that attributes all opposition to America to international Communist conspiracy, a simplism ill suited for the bright era of détente in any case, he produced an alternative international phenomenon unified and hostile enough to justify an aggressive American stance, a mild version of the Cold War crusade.

The ideological usefulness of the construct was clear; not so its factual base. His article was more than usually speckled with qualifications, but Moynihan was either saying what he was saying, or he was saying nothing at all. The whole thrust of his article was bound up with the words like "distinctive," "coherent," "uniform," "all," without which the case for "opposition" lost its bite. The qualifications could not eliminate difficulties like those listed by St. Clair Drake:

There must be gremlins in Professor Moynihan's computer, for it is simply not so that, by 1950, most of the people in the world lived under regimes "fashioned" by British Socialist thinking. At the time, at least a billion people were living under various kinds of Communist regimes and another half-billion were living in the United States, Japan, Indonesia, Brazil and Mexico, plus still more in Latin America and Asian-Oceanic areas who had not been even remotely influenced by British Socialist ideas. Only by the most generous stretching of the concept "under British influence" can one produce a figure of a billion people to match the non-British billion and a half. And of these, 115 million were in the "white" sector of the Commonwealth, which was by no means uniformly Socialist. . . .

If any such "coherent ideology" was actually spread throughout the Empire and Commonwealth by civil servants, the pattern certainly must have been broken in the Middle East among the 40 million people there who were "under British influence." Could anyone seriously contend that the bureaucracies of Ibn Saud and Hussein as well as those of Kuwait and the United Arab Emirates were suborned by Harold Laski? What of Aden and Somalia, Yemen and Bahrain? And asking us to believe, as he does, that Arab and African leaders who supported each other at the Lima Conference in 1971 did so because they "had all gone to the same schools" is asking a bit much.

The largest single bloc of Third World intellectuals influenced by Fabian socialism, was probably in the Indian subcontinent, with which Moynihan has had some contact, but one would have to stretch the term to include both Nehru and Gandhi under the same rubric. And Nepal and Bhutan were probably not affected at all by the Coles and Webbs, or by Cripps and Laski.

Only twelve of the thirty-nine *African* "new nations" were formerly British. The kings of Swaziland and Basutoland, before their countries became independent, were not under Fabian influence, although Bechuanaland (Botswana) did have close ties with British Labour through Seretse Khama. In most of the other nations, the leaders had working relations with individuals and groups in Labour Party circles, but to say that any of them had a "coherent" Fabian ideology is to reveal an ignorance of the situation that is inexcusable. The late Kwame Nkrumah, that favorite whipping boy of the American press, always referred to himself as a "Marxist Socialist and a nondenominational Christian," and treasured the memory of the eleven years he spent in the United States above the one spent at the London School of Economics. . . .

Many of the British African nationalist leaders studied in the United States, among them Banda of Malawi, Azikiwe of Nigeria, two of Kenya's cabinet members, and legislators everywhere. They had extensive circles of friends, white and black. Once in power, they continuously sought financial backing for industrialization projects and never rejected grants for improving managerial skills. Only some of them professed to be Socialist, but even those were aware that their progress depended upon increased productivity.

Of the African new nations, eighteen were formerly French. I dare say that Leopold Senghor, a French savant who was conversant with Marxism before he rejected it for his own variety of "humanistic socialism," would be amused by any suggestion that he was influenced by the Fabians. And to explain Fanon in terms of either British socialism or Second International social democracy is laughable. What then of Amilcar Cabral, whose keen mind led Guinea-Bissau to independence and left us an extensive body of theoretical literature? The following countries were neither British nor French in background: Zaire, Equatorial Guinea, Rwanda, Burundi, Somalia and Libya. Gadaffi's strictures against the United States certainly can't be blamed on British socialism.

Professor Drake's enumeration of names and places is not as exciting as Moynihan's grand. construct; it is, however, the reality. The "British Revolution" is international politics presented by Madison Avenue. But Moynihan can be no less cavalier with hard data than with big concepts. In the same article, for example, he contrasts Indian and Japanese economic performance by pointing out: "In the year of its independence, 1947, India produced 1.2 million tons of steel and Japan only 900,000 tons. A quarter-century later, in 1972, India produced 6.8 million tons and Japan 106.8." The Japanese statistics, he forgets, reflect an industrial base temporarily devastated by war; only a few years previously Japan had been producing 14 million tons of steel annually. In contrast to India, it had achieved the breakthrough in building an industrialized society decades earlier. By no means does this vindicate Indian economic planning; it only suggests what Moynihan might have learned from a raw recruit to international economics—that the entire comparison was dubious.

The title of an earlier essay asked, "Was Woodrow Wilson Right?" Evidently he was, but about what? We are left uncertain. The message of the essay is that America has a moral purpose in world politics, the defense and advancement of liberty and democratic principles. This is the "essential Wilson." It is not, of course, very helpful. What does it mean to defend and advance liberty and democracy in the world? Does it mean proclaiming principles? Building a model at home? Sending troops? Bribing officials? Preventing revolutions? Subverting left-wing governments? Aiding dictatorships, whether of the left or right? Upon whose definitions of liberty and democracy do we act? Moynihan is not unaware of these questions, but he writes as though they were not at the heart of the discussion. He expends three paragraphs on "a kind of corrupt Wilsonianism." Vietnam is mentioned once, in passing.

Having skirted all the questions that actually divide our political elites, Moynihan attacks them for an alleged inability to hold by Wilson's religious sense of patriotism, his belief in the duty to urge democracy in the world at large. To be sure, the attack is hopelessly vague. Does Moynihan refer to professorial opponents of the war in Vietnam or to a certain well-known professor who both prosecuted the war and advocated détente? Or both? All one knows is that the one body that Moynihan hails for keeping faith with Wilson is the official labor movement, which favored the war and opposed détente.

Take Moynihan's leading ideas one by one. No friend of democracy would want to belittle the power of anti-democratic forces throughout the world. But the fluctuations in the fortunes of liberal democracy, and the causes of these fluctuations, are much more complicated than the morality play Moynihan suggests. At one time, he speaks of the height of "influence" enjoyed by America and the liberal principles embodied by Wilson in 1919; on another occasion, he quotes Leo Strauss on the power of the West in 1914: Britain, Germany, and the United States could have had their way anywhere in the world. But, of course, this is something else: Germany was not a liberal democracy at home, nor was the British Empire overseas. Specific facts do not trouble Moynihan. The actual ups and downs of liberal democracy—the halting expansion of suffrage to women and minorities, the eclipse of parliamentarism by fascism, the postwar struggles, the latest developments in Portugal, Spain, and Greece—are not his concern. The general picture is simply one of decline.

There are hints of reasons—the rise of Communism, our own failures of commitment—but no serious explorations. Since it is the events in the ex-colonized nations, the darkening of the democratic flare held aloft by Wilson in 1919, that particularly provoke Moynihan, he might well have considered the working of the mandate system under the League of Nations, what one historian described as Wilson's attempt to sublimate traditional imperialism into a structure fusing American economic self-interest with liberal reformist ideals. Instead of such a complicated picture, Moynihan projects a drama very much like the slide shows sponsored by right-wing groups in the early sixties: a blank map of the world presents all nations as essentially "free," but in successive slides ever-increasing numbers of countries are lost to Communism until the tide of red creeps across Asia, Europe, Africa, and Latin America, surrounds the United States—and establishes beachheads first in Cambridge, then in New York, San Francisco, and Washington.

The same evasion of specifics afflicts Moynihan's identification of the United States as "the party of liberty." The very formulation is ambiguous. Does it mean that the moral purpose of the United States is to be "the party of liberty"—we *should* be the party of liberty—whether or not we always live up to that calling? Or is it a judgment of fact—that the United States has indeed been "the party of liberty"? In this case does it admit of nuance? Are we always the party of liberty? Sometimes? Frequently in one part of the globe but not in others? Or, finally, is this simply a matter of definition—the United States is identified with liberty, and whatever the United States does must be accepted as serving liberty? Moynihan starts with the first version, moves on to the second, concluding that though we have "done obscene things" (none specified), we are far and away a force in the world for liberty and human rights; and in practice he ends with the third, having refrained almost totally from criticism of *American* infringement of human rights overseas. The complicated questions of international economic relations are reduced by Moynihan to simple assertions: "I reject the proposition that . . . we are depriving other peoples of resources which rightfully belong to them." "The Third World must feed itself." "We repudiate the charge that we have exploited or plundered other countries, or that our own prosperity has ever rested on any such relationship. . . . We have been reasonably helpful and generous in our economic dealing with other countries."

Assertions like these have force only because they are put forward in rebuttal of exaggerated charges against the United States, "that the United States is the source of all the world's troubles." This brings us to Moynihan's third point, that there is among our leading elites, especially our intellectual elite, a collapse of faith in liberal democracy and a falling away from America's cause. Moynihan writes of Schumpeter's prediction that economic and political liberalism would be destroyed by an intellectual class it fostered and protected, and that the process is now far advanced. He writes of "the utter collapse of libertarian defenses in the second half of the twentieth century." He writes of American diplomacy toward the Third World that "three decades of habit and incentive have created patterns of appeasement so profound as to seem wholly normal." The evidence for such massive developments ought to be forthcoming. Such a crisis of elites should be readily documentable in editorials of national papers like *The New York Times* or *The Washington Post*, in journals like *Foreign Affairs* and *Foreign Policy*. "Patterns of appeasement so profound," like an "utter collapse of libertarian defenses," ought to be revealed in major events on the international scene. But Moynihan's evidence is nothing like that. He offers anecdotes about American tolerance of accusatory rhetoric in international meetings, or the hyperbolic statements of unidentified individuals.

It is true, as Moynihan puts it in a more moderate phrase, that "we have become uncertain about ourselves." In a nation of more than two hundred million, such uncertainty is sure to manifest itself in bizarre forms, from belligerent self-hatred to equally belligerent self-assertion. But the dimensions of that uncertainty among elites can be, and should be, noted carefully. Equally important is an inquiry into the sources of that uncertainty. Here, too, Moynihan swings wildly. Again, the outside agitator, now in intellectual form: American ideas have faded as foreign "waves of doctrine have broken on these shores." Communism dominated intellectual life in the thirties, according to Moynihan, and "when this influence began to move into the universities, as it did after World War II, resistance to it was disorganized and uncomprehending." But socialist ideas also "gained the widest currency." In addition there is what Moynihan describes as "the superior capacity of Marxist argument to induce guilt." (Social psychologists, unfortunately, have not reported on this phenomenon; literary evidence suggests that Marxist argument has mainly exhibited a superior capacity to induce boredom.) In short, Moynihan offers every explanation but the obvious one. The Vietnam War is the page torn out of Moynihan's argument. "Now this sort of thing happens. Nations lose wars. . . ." In Vietnam, America executed a policy that eventually seemed to contradict both our national interest and our moral purpose. We are uncertain, and we should be uncertain. If our responses to international events are slower, it is because we have reason to believe they were once too swift. What Moynihan calls a "failure of nerve" may be a calming of hyperactivity. Or indeed we may lapse into a state of torpor. But the process of reappraisal—what Moynihan recommended in the middle sixties—has been stimulated by genuine questions about our limitations and our disposition, not by Communism in the universities or the alleged disloyalty of intellectuals.

If the root of our present difficulties is nothing more substantial than ideological timidity, then the remedy is clearly ideological assertiveness. This is Moynihan's conclusion: not that the United States act differently but that we talk differently. In this there is an interesting contrast with Moynihan's earlier prescriptions for achieving racial justice and equality in the United States. The similarities between his analysis of that problem and his recent declarations, say, on the Third World have been noted. In both cases, the obstacles to progress were located largely within the emerging groups, inherited perhaps from past conditions—in the one instance, slavery and Jim Crow, in the other, colonialism and premodern cultures—rather than the present discriminatory structures of domestic or international economics. In both cases, the political leaders of the emerging groups have been seduced into unfortunate political stances by outside forces—in the one instance by the American liberal Left, in the other by Fabian socialism. Nevertheless, Moynihan's earlier analysis made *demands* on America—a massive effort centered on jobs, income maintenance, and urban reconstruction. His declarations on the Third World demand nothing of America—only that we have a better opinion of ourselves and say so frequently.

To Moynihan's four themes, I would counter another four:

1. Liberal democracy is threatened in the world. This is not a recent or extraordinary condition. It does not amount to a crisis of Western civilization, as Moynihan intimates, the collapse of the new Rome before the onslaught of nihilism at home and the politics of resentment and envy abroad. Throughout most of the world, liberal democratic institutions have never been firmly planted; they will continue to be difficult to create and defend. There will be victories—Portugal and Greece are recent examples—as well as setbacks. We should be vigilant but not demoralize ourselves with apocalyptic rhetoric.

2. The United States *should* be the "party of liberty" in the world. Unfortunately, as Richard H. Ullman wrote in *Foreign Policy*,

> it is now painfully obvious . . . that too often, despite the rhetoric underlying American policy, we did not attempt to use our influence to bring about democratic solutions, but instead deliberately lent our support to reactionary and repressive regimes if they were (in a phrase often used at the time) "with us in the struggle against Communism." . . . We often ignored the fact that some of our allies in the "free world" were as antithetical to ordinary notions of liberty as were any members of the Soviet camp. We tolerated abuses of our principles by our allies under the assumption that they were necessary to protect *embryonic* democracy—such as South Vietnam's or South Korea's. The details (e.g., meaningful elections) could be sorted out later.

The United States may be among the best of "less-than-perfect democracies," for which Moynihan is so proud to speak up. But given its power and wealth, its imperfections rest heavily upon many citizens of the globe, whose human rights we have helped snuff out. What Moynihan too easily calls a "corruption" of Wilsonian principles has also endangered rights at home, justifying the infringement of constitutional liberties in the name of national security. We have also defended liberty when our motives were less than noble, and crushed liberty when our motives were benign. All these realities cannot be put into a blender until they cancel one another out and produce a result which can be either condemned or defended unambiguously. They must be kept separately before us so that a given course of U.S. policy can be evaluated in its full complexity.

3. The post-Vietnam mood of uncertainty and reappraisal indicates, on balance, sanity rather than moral collapse. Neither the leading elites nor the mass of citizens have lost faith in democracy, become paralyzed by

Marxist-induced guilt, or been mesmerized by the fearful face of terrorism. They have become skeptical of the instruments of American policy, of its capacity for "fine tuning," of the truthfulness of official explanations, of the accountability of secret agencies and secretive statesmen. The danger in this attitude consists in the possibility that it will be indefinitely prolonged by the resistance to reform of the forces which have justly provoked it.

4. The reassertion of American moral purpose demands something more than self-congratulations and the criticism of other nations' very real failings. It demands that we live up to our principles. Ullman, for example, agrees with Moynihan "that the quality of political life in the United States is indeed affected by the quality of political life in other societies." But for him this has consequences: The United States should do more to assist the Third World economically, not steel itself against its claims. "Callousness toward misery abroad will eventually affect the way we lead our lives and deal with one another at home." The American government should consider the internally repressive policies of other nations in framing its relations with them, and "a central goal of American policy" should be the breaking of embraces with repressive regimes. The United States should rid its foreign policy of "vestiges of the democratic crusades of the 1950s and early 1960s." At the same time, "we should emphasize the inherent value of preserving nonauthoritarian governments which are protective of human rights and liberties"; this, as much or more than physical security, is the ground of our commitment to Western Europe, Japan, Canada, Israel, and other nations. "We should not confuse the maintenance of political democracy with the maintenance of a capitalist economic order," and we should recognize the impact abroad of the openness and accountability in our own political life. Such commitments, writes Ullman, are not stirring in the manner of John F. Kennedy's Inaugural Address, but "their implementation would require us to a much greater degree than we have done over the past three decades to make our practice fit our principles." *

* This account was already in galleys when Moynihan's latest elaboration of his theory about American foreign policy and the defense of democracy appeared. *A Dangerous Place,* his diary of service at the United Nations, pictures a world of three superpowers (Moynihan, Kissinger, and the Soviet Union) four minor powers (the Third World, the State Department, neoconservatism as represented by Podhoretz and Kristol, and *The New York Times)* and the relationships between them. The result is even more convoluted and elusive, yet finally little more complex or nuanced, than his previous statements. Along with the remarkable self-portrait of a highly combustible Moynihan, the book takes up several points, like the State Department's incapacity for the multilateral and quasi-parliamentary politics of the Third World and the role of ideology in international relations, that deserve extended treatment.

Moynihan once spoke similar language: "What is asked of us is honesty: and what that requires is a great deal more rigor in matching our performance to our standards." No more. Foreign policy is the area in which the decline of Moynihan's views is most apparent. For self-criticism, self-congratulations. For complexity, simple assertions. The scholar who once urged reappraisal and the dangers of ideology now derides doubts, broadcasts simplicities, and advocates an ideological offensive.

As Senator—and President?

There has been little in Daniel Patrick Moynihan's career as Senator that was not prefigured in his earlier work and opinions. Nonetheless, for the first year or so after his election, news reports liked to play on two apparently contradictory themes:

There was a new, subdued Moynihan who had abandoned public flair for quiet, competent, behind-the-scenes politicking on bread-and-butter issues. It was true that few freshman Senators had moved so deftly into the "club." Allying himself with Senate leaders Robert Byrd and Russell Long, Moynihan won a strategically important spot on the Senate Finance Committee. He doggedly monitored the funds that, following cabalistic formulas, flow to the federal government from New York State and back to New York from the federal government. Whenever the computers which alone understand these matters warned him of a danger or an opportunity, he set to work reformulating legislation and rallying support and winning for New York an edge that quickly ran into the hundreds of millions of dollars. In workmanlike fashion he pushed loans for New York City and protection for the garment industry and tuition tax credits for parents of parochial school students.

"Flamboyant" Pat Moynihan was back to his old tricks. After two quiet months in the Senate, he made his debut with an eloquent attack on Paul Warnke, the President's nominee for disarmament chief and SALT negotiator; *The New York Times* described the speech as a "zinger." Moynihan began to let his language rip as of old: the bureaucracy was "a pea-brained dinosaur"; a federal measure would "plunder" New York; a federal affirmative action plan in which the New York City school board agreed to counteract previous discrimination by reassigning teachers according to race recalled "the sorting out of human beings for the death camps," a comparison Moynihan later conceded was "a little intemperate." Witnesses from the White House and HEW found themselves

denounced by Moynihan at committee sessions, while Senators found themselves entertained by his florid interventions on the Senate floor.

But there is no contradiction between Moynihan's quiet competence and the method in his mayhem. He has always known how to pick and please his patrons. He has always known that the budget is the basic document of parliamentary government. And he has always possessed a shrewd sense of that Freudian rule of organizations, that structure is destiny. So he pays homage to Byrd and Long, jollies the other Senators, and saves his blasts for HEW and the White House. This, he is happy to explain, is what the Constitution intended Senators to do—balance the Presidency, prevent all power from settling in Washington, and stand guard over state interests.

Despite this concern for New York's fair share, Moynihan has not reversed his conservative skepticism about federal initiatives. The most telling case is his special interest, welfare. He first praised Carter's proposed welfare reform as "superbly crafted"; then (having encountered Administration opposition to a fiscal relief proposal of his own) discovered the reform to be "grievously disappointing," continuing nonetheless to berate liberal critics for their "ritual abuse" of Carter's bill. A year later Moynihan and Long introduced a welfare reform of their own that abandoned almost all of Moynihan's earlier concerns about regional disparities, the working poor, and fair and simple administration in favor of immediate fiscal relief to the states. The final step came in September of 1978. "Were we wrong about a guaranteed income!" Moynihan exclaimed. Examining the results of the guaranteed income experiments begun in the late 1960s, he now concluded "Seemingly it is calamitous. It increases family dissolution by some 70 percent, decreases work, etc." The new findings, in the view of many, were actually a good deal less conclusive than Moynihan suggested, with results reflecting well on guaranteed income schemes as well as negatively. But perhaps most significant was Moynihan's choice of platform to announce his loss of confidence in the one major social innovation he had championed almost to its realization: a letter to William F. Buckley, Jr.'s *National Review*. "And so you turn out to be right," he congratulated Buckley; "in addition," he lightheartedly added, "your recipe for apple soup works."

There remains a gap between Moynihan's New Deal image and his neoconservative reality. Of Moynihan's effort to enlist federal aid for the Northeast, Irving Kristol says, "Pat has to worry more about pleasing fifty-one percent of his party than about the quality of his arguments." If this is so, it will be an additional factor in pushing Moynihan toward the terrain he can hold with many old New Dealers—a strong anti-Soviet foreign policy. Almost all Moynihan's theoretical arguments since his election have dealt with international affairs. This, moreover, is "Presidential" stuff, and willingly or unwillingly Moynihan is in the Presidential competition.

Halfway through 1978, Morton Kondracke of the *New Republic* summed up the situation: "If there is not yet a Moynihan campaign, there is a Moynihan movement and a Moynihan logic." He added: "The Moynihan message, in short, is that America's great, but it lacks guts." Would a Moynihan presidency willy-nilly lock the United States into spiraling conflict with the Soviets, confrontation in the Middle East, and a possible alliance with white regimes in Africa? Kondracke feared it would. His fears would have been reinforced had he noted that (a) Moynihan thinks the United States "lost" the Cuban missile crisis, the supposed model of cool crisis-management; (b) Moynihan ascribes the "undoing" of Lyndon Johnson in Vietnam to his acceptance of the McNamara strategy of incremental pressure, which convinced the enemy that Johnson was "not a destructive man"; (c) Moynihan refers approvingly to the "very different message . . . Nixon sent to people . . . the possibility that he could, in fact, go crazy and do something incredible . . . that you had to treat him very carefully." Kondracke wished Moynihan a long and successful career in the Senate.

The Moynihan logic calls for a Presidential campaign to the right of Jimmy Carter on foreign policy and slightly to the left on domestic policy. More vigor, in any case, on both fronts. It also calls for the elimination of Ted Kennedy, who could pick up the pieces of a Carter collapse and preempt the labor movement support Moynihan would need. No surprise, then, that as Presidential season opened in 1979, Moynihan allies began dwelling on Chappaquidick.

But 1980 need only be a trial run. Moynihan is only fifty-two. Sooner or later he will be a contender. With his formidable intellect, his gift for language, his alternating fits of candor, flattery, and evasiveness, his ability to provoke enmity, and his own considerable capacity for bitter resentment and retaliation, Moynihan would be no common candidate but a figure more reminiscent of a Disraeli, a Clemenceau, a Lloyd George. Moynihan marching toward the Presidency is a prospect to entrance the dramatist. Whether the citizen ought to feel the same way is another question.

CHAPTER SEVEN

Daniel Bell,
Theoretician and Moralist

In 1938–39, a graduate student in sociology at Columbia University enrolled in a course on "Social Evolution." Summoned to discuss the topic of his term paper, the student was asked, "What do you specialize in?" Without self-consciousness or irony, the student replied, "I specialize in generalizations."

The student was Daniel Bell, then a precocious graduate of City College and its Alcove No. 1 of non-Communist socialists, today a professor of sociology at Harvard University. In the intervening years Bell has been the labor editor at *Fortune* magazine, a staff member of the Congress for Cultural Freedom, and a professor at Columbia University. He has also served as an editor of *The Public Interest* and a member of several important national commissions. Throughout all, he has retained his original vocation—to specialize in generalizations.

Bell's major works have been landmarks on the passing intellectual scene, each jutting out so as to define the landscape, each attracting a crowd of defenders and critics. *The End of Ideology*, published in 1960 and bearing the subtitle "On the Exhaustion of Political Ideas in the Fifties," clearly announced a new era: an era in which social reform would be accomplished by calculating, pragmatic steps; in which a thick membrane of skepticism would stand between utopian vision and practical politics. *The End of Ideology* became a *locus classicus* for the debate about pluralism and Cold War liberalism. Certainly its title, and the death sentence it sounded, made the book a lightning rod for radical criticism.

In the early sixties Bell turned from what had ended to what was coming: new technologies, "post-industrial society," and the year 2000. He served on the National Commission on Technology, Automation and Economic Progress, and he chaired a Commission on the Year 2000 for the American Academy of Arts and Sciences. Ideas which he floated during these years were finally brought together in a magnum opus, *The Coming of Post-Industrial Society*, in 1973. The book proposed a conceptual framework for analyzing a new type of social structure that Bell believed to be emerging, first of all in the United States. The growth of codified, theoretical knowledge is the key to its dynamism. The economy shifts from one that produces goods to one that provides services. A new technical and scientific elite emerges, riding the wave of "intellectual technology." Universities and research centers replace the corporation as the leading institution. Political problems center on the control and production of knowledge: on the direction of research; on the relationship between the technical-scientific elite and the political leadership; on the tension between growing professionalism and a demand for citizen participation; on access to education, especially higher education; on the conscious control of the economy—social choice and social planning—and the development of instruments to do this.

Post-industrial social structure was not without its shadows; but far more worrisome was the state of contemporary culture, analyzed three years later in *The Cultural Contradictions of Capitalism*. The radical individualism of bourgeois culture produced not only the discipline necessary for capitalism but—eventually—the sensual experimentation, adversary intent, and demonic release of avant-garde modernism and the self-seeking hedonism of the consuming masses. All of which leaves modern society without a set of meanings to ground the spirit of civic sacrifice needed to sustain a liberal polity burdened with increasing responsibilities.

In some respects, Bell's penchant for generalization has not served him well. It is not simply that these works have been the poles of controversy; that is to be expected. But they have been debated more as notable artifacts of passing cultural phases than as permanent contributions to social thought. *The End of Ideology* had barely appeared when first the civil rights movement and then the antiwar agitation returned passion to politics and raised anew basic questions about political mobilization and the renegotiation of "rules of the game." *The Coming of Post-Industrial Society* emerged only to have the oil boycott and energy crisis convey the impression that merely sustaining the industrial era was a more realistic concern than anticipating a transformed social structure. *The Cultural Contradictions of Capitalism* warned against psychedelic hedonism just as the nation seemed to be settling down from the cultural turbulence of the sixties. Bell is repeatedly caught announcing last week's cold snap as the approaching Ice Age.

This is a genuine defect in his work; he does *over*generalize, not only from current moods and developments but from current moods and developments *in the United States*. Still, the impression is heightened by several other factors. One is the ambiguity in his writings between description, definition, speculation, recommendation, and moral evaluation. When challenged on his supposed misjudgment of the "end of ideology," Bell can easily point to passages in which he suggested that "ideology" would persist; in fact, the message of his earlier book was less that it would not persist than that it should not: "If the end of ideology has any meaning, it is to ask for the end of rhetoric, and rhetoricians, of 'revolution.' . . ." Yet it is not difficult to match such passages with matter-of-fact statements that were soon belied by events: "the older 'counter-beliefs' have lost their intellectual force. . . . the ideological age has ended."

"Post-industrial society" is presented by Bell as an "analytical construct," an "ideal type," a "logical" pattern, a "scenario," an "as-if" or "fiction" against which future developments might be judged. Presumably, then, post-industrial society may never arrive—no more than a "pure market" or "rational, economic man." Concrete facts do not refute such a notion; they only prod us to explore the reasons why reality deviates from the model. Yet much of Bell's account and many of his claims read like a description of something that is already happening and will—barring, say, a major war—come to fruition.

Likewise, Bell sometimes presents post-industrial society as an additional analytical (or descriptive) framework alongside other frameworks— capitalism or socialism—or as one that cuts across these other models. ("As a social system, post-industrial society does not 'succeed' capitalism or socialism but, like bureaucratization, cuts across both.") Yet Bell also gives the impression that his framework is distinctly privileged; it reveals the central realities and problems in a comprehensive way no longer possible for other concepts, which are reduced to explaining peripheral matters. Thus "post-industrial" is at least implicitly claimed as *the* way of characterizing society, and in that respect does "succeed" other conceptions. "The social forms of managerial capitalism . . . are likely to remain for a long time. And yet the functional basis of the system is changing, and the lineaments of a new society are visible."

Perhaps these ambiguities can be resolved logically. At the level of rhetoric, they are undeniable: despite his caveats, Bell does put forward major claims of social change which the next round of political, economic, or cultural events have a way of undermining.

None of this is helped by Bell's methods of composition. Like most of the other neoconservatives he does not write books. He produces large thoughts which eventually fill books. Bell works out his ideas in conference papers and occasional articles over a period of years. Even when not published, these are often widely circulated and discussed—Bell's original 1962 paper on post-industrial society was said to be the most frequently quoted (and pirated) unpublished paper in sociology. In effect, the material assembled in *The Coming of Post-Industrial Society* had been debated for over a decade before the book's publication; the thesis had been popularized and vulgarized by less sophisticated writers. By 1973 not only had time crept up on it, but a band of critics were lying in wait. The fact that the final, assembled product did less to clarify or strengthen the argument than to repeat and elaborate it only added to the criticism and the sense of disappointment. Bell somehow managed to invite the suspicious scrutiny given a second novel without ever enjoying the eager and open welcome so often afforded a first.

None of this has kept Daniel Bell from being a major presence in American intellectual life. In 1970, Charles Kadushin's sociological search for "the most prestigious contemporary American intellectuals" found Bell among the leading ten (profiting from alphabetical order he was listed first). But Bell has enjoyed a presence somewhat different from the one he might prefer, or at least deserves. He has not, like most of the neoconservatives, enunciated a general social philosophy in the course of confronting particular contemporary problems; but instead made society as a whole the object of his analysis. He has dealt in Big Theory; dissatisfied with existing social thought, he has attempted an ambitious alternative. *The Coming of Post-Industrial Society* and *The Cultural Contradictions of Capitalism* propose a comprehensive framework of viewing the movement of contemporary society, buttressed by a dense, almost overwhelming, display of facts and interpretation ranging from art to economy, from automation to education.

In 1973, Bell listed the "several overlapping and divergent intellectual interests" that had occupied him for a decade: "the work on the post-industrial society, the development of social indicators, the interest in long-range social forecasting and the year 2000, an assessment of theories of social change and the idea of axial structures as a way of organizing the field of macro-sociology, and a large concern with what I have called the disjunction of culture and social structure." To these Bell has added in recent years a concern with the new information and communications technologies made possible by computers, miniaturization, and telecommunications and teleprocessing networks—this extends his earlier work on post-industrial society—and with the future of religion in modern culture—an extension of his work on the disjunction of culture and social structure.

A small literature has developed about even the most limited of these concerns, and obviously they cannot, and need not, be all addressed here. What will be addressed are those concerns of Bell's that bear on two narrower questions. In what sense can he be termed a neoconservative? And if it is fair to call him a neoconservative, in what ways does his own particular version of that outlook suggest neoconservatism's limitations and possibilities?

Why Neoconservative?

The first question is essential. To a large extent, Bell has been labeled a neoconservative because he runs with the neoconservatives. Kristol is an old friend, whom Bell repeatedly cites as such. His references to Kristol, with whom he founded *The Public Interest*, to Seymour Martin Lipset, a collaborator on several projects, to Samuel P. Huntington, a colleague at Harvard, to Herman Kahn, and to other neoconservatives almost always express agreement. If he takes exception to some of their views, the difference has not been such as to provoke him to public criticism. And yet it must be acknowledged that Bell adamantly refuses the neoconservative classification. The "designation is meaningless," he writes; it is a tag created by book reviewers and journalists to label work that otherwise resists labeling—a "new cultural criticism" that "seeks to transcend the lines of the present debates and to present the dilemmas of the society within a very different framework."

Bell is not at all evasive about what, if not a neoconservative, he actually is: "I would say, quite seriously, that I am a socialist in economics, a liberal in politics, and a conservative in culture."

What this means, first of all, is that Bell believes in the welfare state: a society's economic policy should "establish that 'social minimum' which would allow individuals to lead a life of self-respect" and should provide "work for those who seek it, a degree of adequate security against the hazards of the market, and adequate access to medical care and protection against the ravages of disease and illness." This is closer to "welfare liberalism" than to socialism: it says nothing about workers' control over their own output and the conditions of production; it says nothing about the tendency of market capitalism to transform human relations into "commodities." Bell does approach socialism in his belief that wealth should not "be convertible into undue privilege in realms where it is not relevant": he does not spell out the implications of this principle, but judging from the reference in his argument (an article by Michael Walzer in the socialist journal *Dissent*), such a limitation on the power of money might very well require major economic reforms.

As "a liberal in politics," Bell believes (1) that the individual and not the group must be the primary unit of a political system; (2) that beyond the point of a "social minimum," rewards and position in society should be determined by individual achievement, "the criterion of merit," rather than being inherited or prescribed or allocated by "numerical quota"; (3) that a distinction must be maintained between the public and the private realms, "so that not all behavior is politicized"; (4) that political power, barred from the private realm, should govern the public one according to the "rule of law which applies equally to all, and is therefore procedural: it does not specify outcomes between individuals."

By "a conservative in culture," Bell means that he respects tradition, believes "in reasoned judgments . . . about the qualities of a work of art," and regards "the principle of authority" as necessary in evaluating experience, art, and education.

Bell feels that many people might find this tripartite credo "puzzling." "They assume, in simple-minded fashion, that if one is a 'radical'—or a 'conservative'—in one realm, one is a 'radical'—or 'conservative'—in all others." Actually, Bell's three-level solution to the problem of labeling is quite appealing. It catches hold of the truth that all aspects of life are not so tightly linked as the politically doctrinaire would make them. Few reflective people have not experienced the irritation of having someone assume they must automatically be "for" A because they favor B. This can be silly enough in the political sphere alone—because you opposed sending arms and troops to Vietnam, you must (it is assumed) oppose sending arms and troops to the Middle East or to NATO. When totally different spheres are linked, the effect is absurd: thus if you are critical of capitalism, you must favor greater sexual permissiveness on TV, experimental novels, solar energy, anti-discrimination statutes for homosexuals and campaigns against cigarette smoking!*

As a shorthand formulation, Bell's socialist-in-economics, liberal-in-politics, and conservative-in-culture is attractive and useful—and quite probably shared by far more people than he suspects. At a deeper level it fails, or at least turns out to be only a starting point. The problem is that real issues do not pose themselves on these three separate levels. A

* Neoconservatives share the same weakness for monolithic labeling. They have been troubled, for example, by the fact that their *bête noire*, *The New York Review of Books*, has been consistently conservative in its literary and artistic judgments while ranging from liberal to radical in its politics. Their solution has been to imply that this represents either thoughtless inconsistency or bad faith: the editors are being hypocritical in one realm or another, e.g., their left-wing outlook is only a fashionable instrument of aristocratic elitism.

welfare measure or an educational reform may raise questions of the "social minimum," of forming policy in terms of groups, families or "quotas" rather than individuals, of considering "outcomes rather than merit," of the proper division between "public" and "private," of affecting cultural values like the work ethic or tradition and authority in intellectual matters. Proposals to provide employment or medical care or protection against disease often risk the expansion of government and hence the politicization of more behavior. Economic regulations redefine the line between public and private. So do those restrictions on advertising—or on televised sex or violence—which promise to protect people or respect cultural values. The expansion of civil liberties, and the corresponding breakdown of many formal or informal means of social control, doubtlessly protect the individual who deviates from group norms, but no less certainly undermine respect for tradition. Almost by definition, important social issues are the ones that mix realms and no longer allow one the luxury of being a socialist here, a liberal there, and yet a conservative over there. One is forced to balance and blend one's views, to decide which realm is more important in this instance, to reach a single conclusion. Nor can important social issues be isolated one from another. They may not form the single chain assumed in some ideologies; there is no "domino theory" of social questions dictating that a single conservative or socialist policy will make all policies turn up (or fall down) conservative or socialist. Nonetheless there are patterns. If one feels that the cultural ramifications of a measure are more important than its political or economic ramifications, this may only reflect the special character of that measure. It may, however, reflect—and the distinction is important—a judgment that *in general* the cultural realm is the one most in need of attention. It is this impossibility of keeping the economic, the political, and the cultural neatly separate, and the need to establish priorities and reach definite conclusions involving all of them together, that make a citizen not the socialist-liberal-conservative of Bell's formulation but a liberal with socialist and conservative sympathies, or a socialist whose socialism contains liberal and conservative elements, or a conservative whose conservatism embraces important aspects of liberalism and socialism.

Bell's tripartite statement of views is linked to his tripartite analysis of modern societies. This, he believes, is a novel contribution to social theory, an advance on both the "Hegelian-Marxist mode" and the "Durkheimian-Functionalist view" which in different ways insist on viewing society as a structurally interrelated whole, whether through the economic order or the reigning set of values. According to Bell, society is more usefully analyzed by dividing it into three realms—the social structure, the polity, and the culture. Each of these is "obedient to" or "organized on" a different "axial principle" and features an "axial structure" around which other institutions are "draped." Thus the axial principle of the social structure—that is, the economic-technological system—is functional rationality and efficiency; the axial principle of modern culture is self-realization.

This methodological approach probably deserves more attention from philosophers of social science or theoretically minded sociologists than it appears to have received. At times it seems eminently clear, if only because Bell repeats the schema again and again in the belief that his critics have missed the point. And yet there is a slight looseness about the language: to functional rationality and efficiency is sometimes added "bureaucratization" as the "structural principle" of the social structure, and "hierarchy" is then added to "bureaucratization." "Equality" and "representation," rather different notions to begin with, are yoked together as the axial principle of the modern polity and then extended to include the idea of "participation," which is said to run contrary to the social structure's principle of hierarchy and bureaucratization (does it necessarily?). Nor is the notion of "axial structures" entirely clear; Bell does not seem to apply it with the same consistency to every realm as he does "axial principles." And what exactly is an "axial principle"? Various metaphors come into play: the "obedience" of a realm to an axial principle; the "draping" of institutions around a principle or structure; an axial principle as indicating a "logic" or a "norm" or an "energizing principle." Axial principles and structures, Bell explains, are not meant to specify causation, which can only be done empirically, but to indicate centrality. But what, in fact, is their relationship to causation and to empirical facts? How could we, or Bell, reject one candidate for an axial principle in favor of another—or are all of them equal? If, against Bell's belief that the axial principle of modern polities is representation and equality, I should assert that the axial principle of modern polities is mobilization and oligarchy, what kinds of evidence would be adduced to support one or the other of us?

The ultimate value of Bell's methodology awaits the examination of these questions and no doubt more subtle ones as well. In Bell's eyes the advantage of his approach rests in the fact that it avoids two dangers: on the one hand, the monocausalism of, say, a vulgar Marxism that makes everything a reflection of economic relationships; on the other hand, the opposite extreme of positing all kinds of interrelationships without ever indicating which are more important or central (or axial). Bell certainly succeeds in emphasizing that none of his three realms determines the others; all proceed according to their different principles. Whether he is equally successful in indicating centrality is not so clear.

The problem is this: Bell resists the analysis of society as a whole (and therefore the necessity of a more integrated political stance) by not only proposing his scheme of three realms as useful sociologically but by insisting that in modern times these three realms are more and more divergent, their axial principles increasingly antagonistic. Yet the very notion of antagonism implies a unity within which it occurs. If the three realms simply existed side by side, each could go its separate way without tension. Not only is it obvious that the three realms are inextricably intertwined, *it is precisely their interrelationships that intensely concern Bell*. For all his analytical division of the three realms, he cannot get away from the notion of society as a whole; it crops up again and again in his prose, it is implied when it is not made explicit, it is the very object of his disquietude. If at one point Bell rejects the popular image of society as a "web" because it suggests a degree of social and cultural unity he believes no longer obtains, at another point he will declare that "society increasingly becomes a web of consciousness." The modern "disjunction of realms" is not for Bell simply a fact, it is a *problem*, and that implies an unstated norm of at least some unity among realms. In sum, Bell needs a theory of the relationship between realms as well as a theory of their divergences and of their separate axial principles. It need not be a simple theory of determination by one realm—that indeed would be a regression from his tripartite model—but it does need to specify somewhat the extent and the directions and the modes of interaction.

In fact, Bell has such a theory. It is incomplete. It is nowhere stated systematically. And therefore it can go unjustified and undefended. Yet it is this theory that allows us to say Bell is a neoconservative.

It has already been mentioned that for Bell the disjunction between realms is a problem, and this could also be said for the contradictions he uncovers within the different realms. It is the first thing to be noted: Bell's stance is an essentially cautionary one. He does not, like Marx, find in disjunctions and contradictions fruitful occasions and opportunities for moving history forward to a better state. It is true that Bell was once a "modernizer," optimistic about the potential of advanced industrial society and its technological base. That optimism extends through much of *The Coming of Post-Industrial Society*; but all along his own task seemed less the celebration of technological modernity, of which he was often accused, than the diagnosis of problems that would beset its arrival. As time passed, he saw these problems generated less by the survival of "premodern" pockets (the traditionalist impulse of right-wing radicalism, or the religious absolutism of left-wing ideologies) and more by the nature of modernity itself. Naturally he became more pessimistic and fearful. Bell's horizon is essentially one of danger, of potential decline and disruption.

Throughout the "Coda" attached to *The Coming of Post-Industrial Society*, throughout *The Cultural Contradictions of Capitalism*, the point of his analysis is not the discovery of means to a juster society or the removal of existing evils; it is the fending off of social and political instability, of "collapse," of "disintegration and revolution"; it is the restoration of legitimacy and the maintenance of constitutional institutions. At the beginning of *The Cultural Contradictions of Capitalism*, Bell invokes Nietzsche and Conrad and raises the specter of nihilism, terror, and madness as the fate of modern society. He then abandons this line of thinking as "apocalyptic" and says he prefers "a more complex and empirically testable sociological argument." But though Bell hews to a less dramatic, less cataclysmic view of social change, the specter of disintegration and nihilism is by no means exorcised. It looms over the portal of his analysis, an enlarged shadow of his own slightly more modulated fears.

With that shadow in mind, one can proceed to Bell's sketch of the relationships between his three realms. It is a rather blurry and uncertain sketch, with lines left uncompleted, with erasures and adjustments, with different versions overlaid and unresolved. At one point it does seem that Bell felt developments in the social structure—the decline of the family firm, the rise of the technical and professional employee, the impact of new science-based technologies, especially "intellectual technology"— were "decisive for social change." Yet Bell consistently maintained that the cockpit of modern society, the point of ultimate control, was the polity. He thereby rejected any economic or technological determinism and, despite charges to the contrary, any vision of rule by technocrats. The role of the political realm, he insisted, was in fact destined to grow larger and larger in the post-industrial era. At the same time, the relationship between the social structure and the polity was of a particular sort. Just as politicians would make the final decisions on issues that technicians had framed, so the polity would finally rule on an agenda of problems that were generated by the changing social structure. The reverse process—that the growth of technology and the shift in occupational patterns might be a response to governmental direction—is a logical corollary of ultimate political control; but Bell minimizes, without denying, this aspect of the relationship. When challenged by the criticism that his "coming of post-industrial society" was little but "government-directed war and space economy and big science in connection with that economy," Bell replied that the government war-and-space effort may use or accelerate the new post-industrialism, with its basis of theoretical knowledge, "but does not create it. It derives from underlying changes in the character of invention and innovation." To sum up the relationship: the social structure proposes, the polity disposes.

But that does not settle the matter either. Bell has always insisted on the ultimate importance of values: "the essential questions are those of values." Values are generated in each of the three realms—*different* values, of course, which is the crux of the problem. The axial principle of each realm—efficiency, equality, self-realization—is a sort of value, in addition to which Bell writes of the "ethos" of different realms and of society generally. (None of this is made clearer by his uncertain use of global terms like "society" or "social" when he may or may not mean "social structure" in its limited technical-economic sense.) "Any social system is ultimately defined by an ethos—the values enshrined in creeds, the justifications established for rewards, and the norms of behavior embodied in character structure." Just as the Protestant Ethic served for capitalism and socialist ideals for Soviet society, "the ethos of science is the emerging ethos of post-industrial society." Or again: "Ultimately the differences between social systems lie not in their social structures (the arrangements of reward and privilege around the organization of the economy) but in their ethos."

While Bell discusses values and ethos in connection with every realm, their primacy does in some ways order the realms themselves. It is precisely because "the essential questions are those of values" that the political realm finally controls the technical-economic one. The latter's "functional rationality and efficiency" may be values, but they are subordinate ones, relating to means rather than ends: "Only when men can decide what they want, can one move to the questions of how to do the jobs." The political realm is the arena for settling upon ends, through debate and the inevitable haggling that defeats all theories of rational decision-making and baffles the technocratic mind.

Yet if the centrality of values suggests the precedence of the political realm over the social structure, in Bell's recent writings it also indicates the precedence of the cultural realm over the political. Culture, after all, deals most directly with values, with the "moral ideas" that according to Bell "in the end" shape history "through human aspirations." Culture— once traditional religion and now its successor, secular modernism— legitimates social behavior, and forms the dominant character structure. It is true that the self-gratification and permissiveness of today's culture have their roots in the rugged individualism and repudiation of the past that marked the older bourgeois order, as well as in the hedonism of a mass-consumption society—hence the "cultural contradictions of *capitalism*." But much as Moynihan sees the problems of the underclass as having cut loose from the racial segregation and economic oppression that once caused them and taken on a life of their own, so too Bell sees the modern cultural impulse as having freed itself from its capitalist roots. "The relationship between a civilization's socio-economic structure and its culture is perhaps the most complicated of all problems for the sociologist. . . . Whatever the truth of these older arguments about the past, today culture has clearly become supreme." The techno-economic order "has been geared to producing the life-styles paraded by the culture. . . . The culture has taken the initiative. . . . There has been a significant reversal in the historical pattern of social change." It is also true that Bell still maintains that "it is the political order which has become the true control system of the society." But "control system" seems now to mean something like "proximate instrument of control." The ultimate force, shaping the political realm as well as the techno-economic one, is again the culture. The modernist idea of the avant-garde has assured "the primacy of culture in the fields of manners, morals, and, ultimately, *politics.*" (My emphasis.) Culture, says Bell in summation, "has been given a blank check, and its primacy in generating social change has been firmly acknowledged."

Not only does the culture prove to be immediately the most dynamic realm as well as ultimately the most decisive, it is also, in our time, the most troubled. "The lack of a rooted moral belief system is the cultural contradiction of the society, the deepest challenge to its survival." "The real problem of *modernity* is the problem of belief. To use an unfashionable term, it is a spiritual crisis. . . . a situation which brings us back to nihilism."

The reader who discovers in Bell not some even distribution of socialist, liberal, and conservative but a new kind of conservative is not therefore mistaken. Despite Bell's welfare sympathies and political liberalism, his perception of the economy and polity caught in the tow of a wildly unrestrained culture elevates his self-proclaimed cultural conservatism to a position of dominance.

Not only is Bell's first concern the destabilizing loss of legitimacy, authority, and moral restraint which he essentially ascribes to cultural forces, he holds with qualifications most of the other neoconservative tenets. The "adversary culture," of course, is the main object of his cultural criticism, and he has been developing a "new class" theory to go with it. *The Coming of Post-Industrial Society* takes up the "new class" at length, but it is in fact an older notion of the "new class," one emphasizing highly technical skills and arcane knowledge and posing the danger of technocracy rather than one emphasizing personal hedonism and unbounded appetite and posing the danger of cultural chaos. About this "knowledge class" Bell is reassuring: it is not as large as imagined, and its political loyalties will probably divide depending upon whether it functions in the public or private, profit or nonprofit sectors. Yet a different sort of "new class" emerges in the "Coda" Bell added to the book: the "new intellectual class" of neoconservative fears. It "dominates the media and the culture," is anti-bourgeois and anti-institutional, and sustains the triumphant "adversary culture." In *The Cultural Contradictions of Capitalism*, this group is labeled the "cultural mass" and consists "primarily of those persons in the knowledge and communications industries who, with their families, would number several million persons" and therefore forms "an audience large enough to sustain a world of cultural production on its own." Unfortunately, Bell defines this new entity and ascribes a character to it with none of the care and documentation he expended on the earlier "new class" of technical, professional, managerial, and scientific workers examined in *The Coming of Post-Industrial Society*.

Though Bell does not invoke the "new class" or "cultural mass" with either the frequency or the vehemence seen in other neoconservatives, there is no reason to believe he dissents from their views. About the "underclass" or its equivalents, however, he is significantly more circumspect. This may reflect only the fact that he has not focused on urban problems in the way many neoconservatives have; but it may also be one of his several important departures from neoconservatism. Throughout his writings there is not only an insistence on the inclusion of all disadvantaged groups in the society but the strong suggestion that the burden of effecting such inclusion falls upon the society at large. At the same time he shares neoconservatism's fear of the egalitarian impulse. His views on equality and a "just meritocracy" are nuanced; he doubts, for instance, that "today most of the disparate outcomes of status, income, and authority are justly earned." Yet the implicit task his analyses always set themselves is the limitation of egalitarianism rather than the overcoming of outstanding inequalities or even the achievement of his own "just meritocracy."

Like other neoconservatives, Bell is much concerned with "overload"; unlike them, he ranges farther in his search for causes: the end of the Cold War, demographic shifts, racial inequality, Vietnam, the disappearance of regional cultures, the domestic and world economic situations, and multinational corporations all play specific parts. But Bell's solution is part and parcel of neoconservatism: a generalized appeal for lowered expectations, a call for *limits*—to our use of resources, our international ambitions, our "tampering with biological nature," but above all to our appetites and wants, to the exploration of experience and the questioning of taboos, to utopian hopes and belief in radical change.

The tempering of expectations also demands a public philosophy that can establish equitable priorities. Like Kristol, Bell repeatedly announces the need for such a philosophy but takes only stabs at enunciating one. Like Kristol, Bell links the cultural predicament to the decline of religion, but much more straightforwardly than Kristol or other neoconservatives, he looks to a "return in Western society of some conception of religion" as the basis for a coherent and solid culture.

It should be clear that Daniel Bell is not unfairly enrolled among the neoconservatives. But his neoconservatism, like every individual expression of a political outlook, has its special traits. Bell's work is weakened by several strategic emphases and omissions, and these reflect on the limitations of neoconservatism generally. At the same time, in both style and theme Bell probably points neoconservatism toward its full potential as an intelligent, integral, American conservatism.

A Skewed Definition of Culture

Bell's first weakness is his definition of culture. He purports to steer halfway between the anthropological notion of culture as just about everything and Matthew Arnold's refined notion of the "pursuit of our total perfection by means of . . . the best which has been thought and said in the world." Within this vast middle ground, he proceeds by fiat and offers no real justifications for his further choices of focus. Citing Ernst Cassirer, Bell defines culture as "the realm of symbolic forms"—and then promptly narrows that to "the arena of *expressive symbolism*: those efforts, in painting, poetry, and fiction, or within the religious forms of litany, liturgy, and ritual, which seek to explore and express the meanings of human existence in some imaginative form." "I leave out here the question of cognitive modes, philosophy and science," he adds in a footnote, "which surely belong within the realm of culture." So much for the "scientific ethos" which was a pivotal concern of his earlier reflections on post-industrial society. In fact, Bell says nothing about contemporary religious forms either, which leaves painting, poetry, and fiction. But Bell narrows his concern again—to *modernist* painting, poetry, and fiction, giving a plausible but by no means unarguable interpretation of a constellation of works he has picked for the purposes of his theory.*

*There is a degree of circularity in all large-scale cultural interpretations: certain works provide the key models which are used to interpret (or eliminate as atypical) a wider body of art or literature. But the circularity becomes extreme when Bell recognizes that his characterization of 1960s novelists as "apocalyptic," asocial, and apolitical cannot contain "many prominent novelists of the decade—such as Updike, Salinger, Cheever, J.F. Powers, Styron, Roth, Malamud, and Baldwin" who "have busied themselves with the more traditional concerns of the novelists." He resolves this difficulty by eliminating these authors from consideration: "Given my own sociological reading of the apocalyptic temper of the times, I feel that the novelists I have chosen are the ones making the more distinctive statements about the sensibility of the decade."

This determined narrowing of "culture" to certain strands of modernism, and certain emphases within these strands, abruptly discards layers upon layers of complexity. As one reviewer commented:

> Bell talks as if a single-minded, ethereal culture (he rarely grounds sensibility in tangible strata) is all Baudelaire and not Bauhaus functionalism, all Heideggerean angst and not positivism. He excludes "cognitive modes" like science and philosophy which surely reveal tenaciously rational strains. He dismisses those who consider technocracy dominant and so disregards at least vigorous currents of behaviorism and structuralism. The drive for distinct patterns forces him to depreciate historical fluctuation. Even during the 1960s classical ballet flourished, but many of Bell's insights now seem especially dated in a period when "the fundamental conservatism of middle-class taste has regained its confidence," as Hilton Kramer puts it, and academic painting and Broadway revivals of the well-made play are prominent features of the cultural scene. Lastly, the lofty perspective of high culture neglects the profusion of everyday cultures which *are* crucial to the vigor of capitalism—from the ethnic to the evangelical, in Subdivision and Sunbelt, where they do not fret about Randall Jarrell.

Bell does not adhere to one of his own observations, that culture, in some respects, is cumulative and not supercessive: "Boulez does not replace Bach. The new music or the new painting or the new poetry becomes part of an enlarged repertoire of mankind, a permanent depository from which individuals can draw, in renewable fashion, to remold an aesthetic experience." This presents a problem for the critic who wishes to analyze a culture—in something like the anthropological sense or even in terms of Cassirer's "realm of symbolic forms"—on the basis of "culture"—in Bell's sense of the leading recent expressions in the arts and literature. The "avant-garde" may say something about the movement of a culture, but only when it is related both to the parallel experiencing, or reexperiencing, of the "permanent depository," and only when its passage into the arteries of mass culture is carefully noted. Not only did classical ballet flourish in the 1960s; but more people continue to see and read Shakespeare than Beckett (though they may begin to experience Shakespeare through the sensibility of Beckett). And even more people are reading gothic novels, or following the serializations of Victorian classics on public television, or being exposed to advertising that has absorbed the *fauves* and surrealism as well as *cinéma vérité*.

What is the effect of Bell's narrow focus and neglect of the complex relationships between modernism and the whole cultural "repertoire," on the one hand, and mass culture, on the other? First, he exaggerates the extremism of "high culture." Second, he eliminates much of the culture people actually live by, including religious traditions, popular ethical norms, folk knowledge, ethnic customs and codes, national ideals, the ethos of science, professions, or other occupational communities, and earlier, premodernist artistic and literary representations. Third, he ignores cultural tendencies which are not typified by modernist "irrationality" but may be no less problematic, e.g., the reduction of human activities and needs, in planning by business and government, to quantitative, "bottom line" calculations. Fourth, he minimizes the *current* role of the economy in producing, shaping, or limiting the society's culture: while "bourgeois society" and capitalism are given a historical responsibility for both modernism and mass hedonism, the present mechanisms by which hedonism is marketed and modernism packaged are screened by Bell's preoccupation with the more sensational expressions of the avant-garde.

A Complacent View of the Economy

The immoderation and autonomy that Bell ascribes to the cultural realm are built into his very definition of culture. The moderation and responsibility he appears to find in the economic realm seems no less a matter of definition. Bell is well aware of the plain reality: despite the growth of government and the nonprofit sector,

> the business corporation remains, for the while, the heart of the society. . . . Slightly more than 500 firms . . . account for 83 percent of all corporate assets; 200 firms . . . account for 66 percent of all industrial assets, while 87 firms . . . account for 46 percent. . . . Corporate power, clearly, is the predominant power in the society, and the problem is how to limit it.

The problem, however, seems to be resolved by the mere act of describing it. In a chapter of *The Coming of Post-Industrial Society*, Bell describes the corporation as standing between the "economizing mode" and the "sociologizing mode." The first of these involves the maximization of output through the market mechanism, and beyond that the general application of rational calculation as a *means* without concern for whatever ends might be attained. According to Bell, the economizing mode has transformed society; it animates modern industrialism and its characteristic organizational form, the corporation. Yet Bell is keenly aware of its limits: the many imponderables and "externalities," from friendship and work satisfaction to clean air and sunshine, that escape the economizing calculus and its definition of growth; the "imbalance between public goods and private goods" that results when the former are looked upon as subtractions from the latter; above all, the "atomistic view of society" on which the economizing mode is premised. The alternative is the sociologizing mode: "the effort to judge a society's needs in more conscious fashion and . . . to do so on the basis of some explicit conception of the 'public interest.' " This implies planning of some sort, which Bell discusses, along with new mechanisms for assessing the effect of technological or social innovations. Bell is confident that corporations are shifting from economizing to sociologizing, and he points toward their shift from single-minded pursuit of production and profit to greater concern for employees' job satisfaction, fringe benefits, minority employment, environmental quality, and good community relations. "All of this, historically, was inescapable," he concludes.

The argument seems naive and vague almost to the point of evasiveness. To begin with, it is naive to portray much of corporate concern for job satisfaction, fringe benefits, community relations, and so on as a shift toward sociologizing. In many cases, these "concessions" merely reflect a shrewder economizing, one that recognizes the effect of work-force morale and turnover and of public image on production and sales. In other cases, such changes have been won from corporations only by trade-union and government pressure. Bell, however, writes as though the process took place, and will continue to take place, of its own accord, without conflict and without the need to mobilize economic and political forces. He leans heavily on phrases like "inescapable," "we in America are moving," "long-run historical tendency." Indeed, the historical inevitability of it all allows him to remain personally undeclared about whether the shift from market to politics is really for the better. "No social or economic order has a writ of immortality, and the consumer-oriented free-enterprise society no longer satisfies the citizenry." (One wants to ask, says who? And should the citizenry be urged to change their minds?) "So it will have to change. . . ."

"The Subordination of the Corporation"—that is the chapter's title—will thus flow effortlessly from the wishes of the citizenry. Analysis can continue as though this remarkable transformation had as much as occurred. But it is not clear that the corporation has been at all "subordinated"; perhaps its vaunted "social responsibility" is only a step toward final "emancipation" from stockholders. Bell is not unaware of the danger:

> As a business institution, the "corporation" is the management and the board of directors, operating as trustees for members of the enterprise as a whole—not just stockholders, but workers and consumers too—and with due regard to the interests of society as a whole. But if this view is accepted, there is a significant logical corollary—that the constituencies which make up the corporation themselves have to be represented within the board of

corporate power. *Without that, there is no effective countervailing power to that of executive management.* More important, *without such representation, there would be a serious question about the "legitimacy" of managerial power.* [My emphasis.]

The question is indeed serious. But Bell, in a rare moment of unwillingness to board a topic, declares himself incompetent to evaluate various proposals to reform the governance of corporations—and he says nothing at all about the problems (or likelihood) of actually instituting even the most well-conceived scheme. Bell is satisfied to say that here is "a question to be explored," a problem that "is not going to go away." Once again, a central challenge to the theory of "subordination" is absorbed by acknowledging it and passing on.

The most grave difficulty, however, is one that numerous social analysts have raised: Why assume that the shift from market to politics will not bring the corporation's economizing to the political realm rather than the polity's sociologizing to the economic? Why assume that planning will be done in the "public interest" rather than in the corporation's interest? Given the size and concentration of corporate power that Bell himself cites, given the increasing ability of multinational corporations to evade any single nation's control, which Bell also recognizes, is it not as likely that "subordination" will be the other way around?

Joseph Featherstone has aptly described Bell's avoidance of these questions:

Though Bell does give us a stormy picture of strife in post-industrial society, and though that is in somber contrast to the placid future anticipated by "the end of ideology," there is still a corner of Bell's mind that recoils from conflict, longing for some automatic, apolitical means by which sociologizing values will tame the corporate order. . . . Somehow . . . the corporation will slide with effortless grace from the economizing to the sociologizing end of the spectrum.

Nowhere in the course of this agreeable fiction does Bell acknowledge that asserting a public interest over the corporations will require leverage against the corporation the political realm does not in fact now possess. . . . He offers no plausible explanation of how a public interest can prevail over private corporate interests. His notion of sociologizing contains communal values, but is empty of sources of power to achieve these noneconomic goals; his notions of politics are similarly devoid of thought *about* power. . . .

There is no doubt that politics will control more and more of our lives. The question is: who will control politics?

An Antiseptic Image of Politics

Featherstone points to the third major weakness of Bell's neoconservatism, his discreet withdrawal before questions of power. This weakness becomes more apparent in Bell's treatment of the political realm, which is curious, since the coming of the post-industrial society is in effect the coming of politicized society and the stability of the liberal political order is probably Bell's deepest concern. Yet, as Reinhard Bendix notes, half of *The Coming of Post-Industrial Society* is devoted to social trends, a fourth to the problems those trends will create, "but nothing of comparable length or substance to the outlines of the political structure." In Bendix's opinion, Bell "fails to deal with the topic he himself considers decisive: the politics of the post-industrial society."

It is not that Bell ignores political conflict; one of his gifts is an acute sensitivity to the many sources of such conflict. It is hardly too much to say that the political order of the future will be virtually overwhelmed by conflict—as the federal budget becomes the crucial arena for social planning and as social rights become defined in group as well as individual terms, a swarm of constituencies will push their demands. But the political realm where these conflicts will be worked out remains something of a blank. It is at most a civics-text creation, a neutral arbiter, where "politicians" who quite perfectly represent the wishes of the citizenry will resolve the almost innumerable problems brought before them. There is little hint that the political realm itself represents existing constellations of power, that "politicians" may themselves have interests or represent institutionalized power in other than textbook fashion, that the outcome of political bargaining may systematically reflect the dominant power of the wealthy or the organized rather than the "public interest" in some more democratic sense. It is preposterous, of course, to assume that Bell doesn't know all of this. But that is exactly how the matter seems to stand: *of course*, we know all that—boys will be boys, and politics will be politics—and so it has no particular bearing on Bell's theory and need not be mentioned. On one of the rare occasions when Bell alludes to the political power of social wealth and position—a reference to post-1945 America's "foreign policy establishment" and the connections of its members with the New York financial community—he is swift to insist that "it was not their *interests* that defined them as an elite, but their character and judgment." Bell's political realm is antiseptic and high-minded in a way that does not match the reality. It is besieged by competing groups, but is not itself a belligerent nor a consistent partisan of some groups over others.

This delicate retirement in the face of unequal political power vitiates one of Bell's more attractive notions. In view of the "overload" and the fiscal restraints now threatening the stability of what Bell terms the "public household," he advocates a rebirth of *civitas*, "that spontaneous willingness to obey the law, to respect the rights of others, to forgo the temptations of private enrichment at the expense of the public weal—in short, to honor the 'city' of which one is a member." *Civitas* is the emotional and moral bond that nourishes private compromise for public purpose. It implies therefore a "public philosophy" that "provides decision rules for the normative resolution of conflicting claims and a philosophical justification of the outcome." The public philosophy has to define the common good and adjudicate the claims of different groups. It must, for example, determine whether individual, family, ethnic group, voluntary body, or the state is the proper object of various policies and entitlements. It must balance liberty and equality, equity and efficiency. It must draw the line between "private" and "public" and thereby establish the limits of personal latitude and public regulation.

Like other neoconservatives, Bell does not actually propose a public philosophy but limits himself to thoughtful observations on the need for one and the problems that such a philosophy would face. The public philosophy is essentially an instrument of restraint in Bell's view—a way of equitably ordering the "no's" that must be said to contending forces in society. The idea is compelling. It is, in some manner, a resurrection of the "ideology" that Bell once buried, even to the point of fusing the theory of the public philosophy with the emotional bond of *civitas*. ("What gives ideology its force is its passion," Bell wrote, in criticism, in *The End of Ideology*.) But the refusal to acknowledge the unequal power already congealed in the political sphere makes it appear that the public philosophy is more likely a system of deference on the part of the have-nots than of restraint on the part of the haves. At best, Bell suggests that the restraining effect of *civitas* and the public philosophy ought to operate across the board, so that those who start ahead will remain ahead. (The one limit on this appears to be Bell's reiterated view that no one should be so unequal as to be effectively *excluded* from society.) At worst, Bell is suggesting that precisely those forces representing egalitarian demands, on behalf of the poor, the previously excluded, and the great number of lower and middle-income citizens, should shoulder the burden of restraint. His caveats appear aimed at those clamoring for a greater share of national wealth—obviously the established powers do not have to clamor.

He emphasizes the threat of equality to liberty and authority, and the problems of income redistribution. The "restraint of desire" that he endorses is not contrasted with oligarchic power or the aggrandizement of capitalist producers (as opposed to the mass of consumers); instead he says that such restraint is "uncongenial to a democratic ethos." The source of resistance that Bell anticipates to the public philosophy is revealed in a passage quoted from Walter Lippmann: "The public philosophy cannot be popular. For it aims to resist and to regulate those very desires and opinions which are most popular."

This is not to say that Bell's notion of *civitas* and the public philosophy could not be interpreted differently. Bell himself makes several references to "fairness" that could lead to a different coloration. By and large, however, there is no suggestion that his appeal for civic solidarity and sacrifice does not weigh equally, or even more heavily, on the graduates of Harlem's high schools and Cleveland's junior colleges than on Harvard's M.B.A.'s and elite lawyers. Mix Bell's assumption of a textbook democracy and a neutral political sphere with Lippmann's warning about opposing popularity, and *civitas* begins to resemble public acquiescence in an elite governance legitimated by the "public philosophy."

The Return of Religion

Thus far the weakness of Bell's neoconservatism. What of its strengths and its potential for future development? I believe these to be found in three areas: Bell's interest in religion; his attention, if not to corporate economic power, then to various other structural changes in American life; and finally his voracious, eclectic, and relatively nonpolemical style. All of these points, and especially the first and third, have been grist for the mills of Bell's critics. Yet what links the three, and makes them strengths rather than weaknesses, is the way in which they provide openings from the relatively closed world of neoconservatism, openings to a political horizon that is no less conservative but also richer, more complex, and more substantively affirmative.

"What holds one to reality, if one's secular system of meanings proves to be an illusion?" asks Bell, and then goes on to "risk an unfashionable answer—the return in Western society of some conception of religion." To call an assertion "unfashionable" is usually the intellectual's technique of self-congratulation; and a nostalgic longing for religion in fact runs through neoconservative writings. Yet Bell takes the idea beyond nostalgia; he predicts, and he recommends, a return to religion. Both

critics and sympathizers among his secular audience have largely preferred to neglect his concern, and religious readers have often been
plainly hostile.

This hostility is not difficult to explain. "Bell does not have an authentic
'feel' for religion," writes the theologian Gregory Baum. "Bell's treatment of religion suffers from a fault only too often found among
sociologists: total ignorance of theology." Bell's statements about religion
do bear out this charge: to date, they are rich in dramatic generalization
and colorful references but reveal little deep knowledge. This, however, is
less important than Baum's further complaint: Bell is interested in religion
mainly as a prop to the social order. "Bell thinks what we need to do as
the only solution of the cultural dilemma is to 're-establish that which is
sacred and that which is profane.' Religion is the answer to the present
contradictions. Religion alone can make the capitalist system work."
Aware of the sorry history of manipulating religion as the legitimating
ideology of threatened social orders, believers may thus be led to reject
Bell not out of indifference toward religion but solicitude for its integrity.

Bell, however, explicitly denies the view of religion that Baum
attributes to him. "I do not, *pace* Durkheim, see religion as a 'functional
necessity' for society and believe that without religion a society will
dissolve," he writes in his introduction to the paperback edition of *The
Cultural Contradictions of Capitalism*. "I do not believe in religion as a
patch for the unraveled seams of society. . . . Religions cannot be
manufactured. Worse, if they were, the results would be spurious and
soon vanish in the next whirl of fashion." *

Bell has also contrasted the societies that retain a sacred "space" with
the society that "is wholly absorbed into the economic engorgement of the
profane, as in a capitalism that treats nothing as sacred, but converts all
objects into commodities to be bought and sold to the highest bidders."

Despite these disclaimers, there is much in Bell's writing that supports
Baum's interpretation. In *The End of Ideology*, ideology was characterized as secular religion: it directed emotional energy and fear of
mortality into politics, whereas religion itself "symbolized, drained away,
dispersed emotional energy from the world onto the litany, the liturgy, the
sacraments, the edifices, the arts." Religion's function, though vital, was
essentially negative: it contained and defused the fanaticism, violence,

---

* Also: "Religion is not an ideology, or a regulative or integrative feature of
society—though in its institutional forms it has, at different times, functioned this
way. . . . Religions, unlike technologies or social policies, cannot be manufactured or designed. . . . The ground of religion is not regulative, a functional
property of society, serving as Marx or Durkheim argued, as a component of social
control or integration."

cruelty, frenzy, and mass emotion inherent to the human condition. In Bell's more recent writings, religion continues to appear in a context of fear—fear of social breakdown, mass libertinism, cultural anarchy. Religion is prized for its negative lessons and for the contrast between it and utopian hopes: "What remained valid in orthodox religion—its tough-minded view of human nature, its view of man as *homo duplex*, the creature of at once both murderous aggression and the search for harmony—is too bleak a view for the utopianism that has burnished modern culture." Religion is always linked with restraint—or at most the temporary release that makes restraint tolerable. Religion is never seen as the source of constructive upheaval or liberation. Bell does consider the possibility that religion may be a revolutionary force, tearing down established institutions, only to discard the idea with the exaggerated claim that today tradition and established institutions have no defenders in any case. To be revolutionary, therefore, a religion would have to be traditional.

There is a truth in Bell's view of religion, but one that remains confused and compacted with half-knowledge. To take one example, Bell stresses religion's role as guardian against the demonic. But, as Baum points out, biblical religion has never equated the demonic, as Bell does, with sensual hedonism. Certainly that was part of the story, but "in Christianity the face of the demonic is revealed in the struggle of the persecuted and crucified Jesus. What is disclosed here is that the enemies of human life are the powers and principalities operative in history, the mechanisms of power, the weight of imperial rule, the narrowness of law, the arbitrariness of the powerful, the blindness of religion whenever it becomes uncritical, and so forth."

Like Bell's "end of ideology," his "return of the sacred" is a mixture of the descriptive, the predictive, and the normative. As a description or prediction, his notion is either tautological, sheer *a priori* assumption, or unproved—depending on the specificity of his definition of religion. If religion is defined as whatever answers humankind gives to the existential questions posed by finitude, suffering, and death, then by definition religion will return. Indeed it can never be absent but merely must be uncovered in its various untraditional forms—national exaltation, utopianism, consumerism, and so on. If, on the other hand, religion is defined more specifically as involving transcendence, ritual, community, and code, then (a) its "return" may simply be asserted because religion "is a constitutive part of man's consciousness" in Weber's phrase, "as much a human universal as language"—or (b) it may be granted that while some responses to the existential questions of culture will inevitably be forthcoming, the degree to which these will recognize the transcendent, or "be woven into meanings that will extend over generational time and become embodied in new institutions," is as yet unknown. At different times, Bell adopts each of these positions.

But whether we assume that "religion" is always present in whatever our deepest response to existential questions, or whether we flatly assert or uncertainly anticipate its revival, the normative question is *what* religion do we want, what distinguishes the genuine faith from the false one—"who is God and who is the Devil." Is this to be determined by its compatibility with, or reinforcement of, the social order? Bell does not take that position. The criterion that clearly recommends religion to him, that he repeats in connection with it again and again, is "memory"—the "continuity of generations." This is obviously a conservative view, but nonetheless a legitimate one. Bell's problem now is to explore this conservative view in its full complexity, lest he be proposing an updated ancestor worship. In the Jewish and Christian traditions, at least, the "memory" which is ritualized, and to which fidelity is demanded, is often, perhaps paradoxically, the memory of decisive breaks in history—the exodus from slavery, God's covenant with his people, the establishment of a new covenant in Jesus' death and resurrection. The past does not simply bless the present; it may also judge it. Fidelity to the memory may demand repentance; true continuity may require an immediate discontinuity. If these are the themes in Bell's religious conservatism that he continues to pursue, he may find there some of the positive element that has thus far eluded the neoconservatives, a conservatism that is more than an accommodation with the *status quo*.

Bell's religious interest should be listed among his strengths because it has this potential. It promises to go beyond the nostalgia of other neoconservatives or the ritual invocation of religion as a negative counter to modernity and ideology. Liberalism and radicalism have generally abandoned the effort to explore the questions that have traditionally, and in my opinion most profoundly, been posed in religious language and symbol. While 90 percent of the American population retains at least some explicit commitment to religious belief or institutions, most of our cultural analysis and public philosophizing is done by the other 10 percent. That, too, might change if neoconservatism challenged them with an attention to religion that went beyond debating points.

Exuberance and Excellence

From Bell's religious interest to the second of his strengths is literally a step from the sacred to the mundane. Despite his ultimate concern with the "crisis of culture," far more than most neoconservatives Bell attends to other changes in the social structure. His essay "Unstable America," included in *The Cultural Contradictions of Capitalism*, and his contribution titled "The End of American Exceptionalism" to *The Public Interest*'s Bicentennial volume both survey such developments as population growth and the demographic shift from agricultural communities to cities; the emergence of a "national society" through the media, the political dominance of Washington, and the decline of regional cultures; the eclipse of distance within the nation and the diminishment of sheer space as well as unlimited abundance as ready safety valves for social tension; the impact of America's international hegemony and the uncertain future of an international economy shaped by transnational corporations. Specific events like the racial conflict of the sixties and the Vietnam War are also given their due. Though Bell may be unwilling to delineate any existing power structure behind such changes, his description is nonetheless full and multifaceted. One need not adhere to Bell's ideological outlook or his policy preferences to find in his work a rich mine of useful analyses and thoughtful "agendas" of social issues.

There is a connection between this latter fact and Bell's relatively nonpolemical style. This is not simply a matter of refraining from direct attacks on named individuals. Compared to other neoconservatives, Bell does not dwell heavily on the motives of those with opposing views, exposing the worms of envy, self-seeking, immaturity, or masochism behind their various commitments to reform. Bell can damn the "*culturati*" or casually call the supporters of George McGovern "extremists." But he refrains from the typical neoconservative psychologizing of adversaries. He seems more interested in overwhelming them with his facts than undermining them with innuendo, and this is surely a manner more open to intellectual give and take.

What is often counted by many a fault in Bell's style, his apparently uncontrollable impulse toward encyclopedic knowledge, is another safeguard against a narrow neoconservatism. More than one reviewer has frowned in annoyance at what sometimes seems like gratuitous display of slightly rarefied references. But Bell does not have to play the perpetual graduate student to establish his credentials. One senses, instead, a simple exuberance for connections and a drive to conquer the details of half a dozen disciplines, to learn from Henry Adams and Hegel as well as from Freud, Weber, Kenneth Arrow, and the latest OECD report on science policy. *The Coming of Post-Industrial Society* resembles a modern *Anatomy of Melancholy*, that fascinating compendium of baroque lore; all the digressions and footnotes that make Bell's text so trying to the reviewer make it a source of constant interest and provocation to the more casual reader. This sheer oversupply of intellectual spirits throws up a check to any sort of dogmatism. Bell may resolutely avoid the criticism of macro-business regularly articulated by left-wing social analysts; and yet he will not leave the disrupting power of the multinational corporations out of his picture. It is simply too fascinating.

Bell's style may also come closer than anything else to demonstrating how neoconservatism might overcome its split personality, how it might resolve the conflict between its commitment, on the one hand, to a reflective cast of mind and traditional values, and, on the other hand, to the calculating rationality and furious destructive energy of modern capitalism. Bell is no longer, if he ever was, infatuated with "modernity." The consciousness of its totalitarian potential burns at the core of all his reflections. Yet his descriptions of the triumphs of science, technology, and rational organization exude something akin to delight. He is, as always, the "specialist in generalizations." Yet his polymathic style seems to promise that immersion in the details of technological change and in the "hard facts" of social questions can protect against ideological extravagance. Certainly his style is itself a reproach to modern hedonism, an amassment and mobilization of data reminiscent of the great figures of Victorian social science. At the same time, in its swift summaries and catchy formulations, it exhibits the energetic packaging and marketing of the modern "knowledge industry."

Bell's is a brittle kind of brilliance. Like the society he analyzes it takes everything as raw material and processes it swiftly. It is fiercely competitive, sparing individuals but always conscious of opposing views, especially from the socialist Left, that must be countered. (Perhaps this is the Alcove No. 1 syndrome.) There is little serenity in this whirligig of information and ideas. Bell's mind is a fascinating place to visit but obviously it would be demanding to live there.

Implicit in this strenuous brilliance is a notion of excellence, probably the closest representation of the elusive neoconservative ideal of excellence we have so far seen. It is an excellence that does not look back to an unrealizable past but seeks discipline and even grandeur in the very press of modern capitalism, in its almost wild yet technically astonishing powers of innovation and adaptation. Despite his many warnings, Bell does not really offer any alternative but to ride the tiger of our fragmented and contradictory capitalism, to ride it, however, with an acute awareness of its fearful symmetry and constant recollection of the heritage that this ride endangers.

To those who advise another mount, this course appears blind and even oddly romantic. But then they are not conservatives, and would prefer other risks. Though Bell understandably bristles at terms like "moralist" which, even when not dismissive, ignore his theoretical aspirations as a social scientist, one reviewer's characterization of him as a "cautionary sage" is apt. Thus far his caution has been unduly addressed to the "culture" and neglectful of social and economic power, but that may be repaired. A party of neoconservative "cautionary sages" with Bell's scope, complexity, and open-endedness would be a valuable force in American political life.

CHAPTER EIGHT

Intellectuals, the Heart of the "New Class"

WHEN EDMUND BURKE sat down in 1790 to denounce those responsible for the French Revolution, still in its early and less fearful period, he turned at once to the intellectuals of his day, the French *philosophes* and their English admirers. "Literary caballers, and intriguing philosophers . . ." Burke wrote, "political theologians and theological politicians"; "petulant, assuming, shortsighted coxcombs of philosophy"; "cold hearts and muddy understandings."

Neoconservatism employs a different, though not very different, language; the animus is the same. If the times are out of joint, it is the intellectuals who have put them that way. When neoconservatives speak of the "new class," it is intellectuals who form the core of the class they conceive; other groups that have expanded enormously in recent years, and often through public programs—physicians and health-care providers, for example—are included in the "new class" only insofar as their roles and attitudes approach those of the intellectuals. When neoconservatives speak of the knowledge industry, it is the power of the intellectuals, and not, say, of the burgeoning data-processing sector, that they mean to emphasize.

Intellectuals and Counterintellectuals

The neoconservative critique of the intellectuals, though they may now link it to emergent phenomena like the "new class" and the knowledge industry, stands in a tradition almost two centuries old. Several years ago I attempted to describe that tradition, using the label "counterintellectual." The label is not a particularly happy one. It seems to be a characteristic of our negative era—the Age of the Prefix—that we describe things in terms of what they are not: "anti-," "post-," or "counter-." (In comparison, to be "neo-" is relatively positive.) Yet I sought a term that would distinguish this criticism of intellectuals from the garden variety of anti-intellectualism that then-Vice-President Agnew was trying to cultivate with his talk of "impudent snobs" and "nabobs of nihilism." The counterintellectual does not, like the anti-intellectual, scorn intellect; quite likely he purports to defend it. The counterintellectual does not deride sophistication and expertise; he is apt to insist on them. The counterintellectual does not launch his criticism from outside the intellectual community but from within it. Nor is his criticism simply a matter of the random internal feuds and unpatterned contentions that always beset intellectual circles; from Burke to de Tocqueville to Weber and Raymond Aron and others in our own day, there is a continuity of complaints and themes—recurrent bouts of civil war, in other words, along with the inevitable brawls and vendettas. Since the French Revolution, the intellectuals have never ceased to be shadowed by the counterintellectuals—the party of public thinkers that opposes the typical adversary role the intellectuals play in public life. The counterintellectuals warn against the intellectuals' politics in general and stand guard against its errors in particular.

In a sense, the term "intellectual" has always implied a politicization of the intellect, and almost always on the side of dissent and opposition. We see "intellectuals" when men from certain lines of activity join together on a public issue or when their products—paintings, writings, philosophies—themselves become public issues. Remove the heightened political context, as history does from time to time, and the category swiftly dissolves into its component parts of writers, professors, scientists, lawyers, artists, civil servants, and so on. As Richard Hofstadter insists, "The modern idea of the intellectuals as constituting a class, as a separate force, even the term *intellectual* itself, is identified with the idea of political and moral protest." It is this, precisely, that disturbs the counterintellectuals.

Burke, of course, wrote of "political Men of Letters," though he himself was one. It was not until a full century after his denunciation of the *philosophes* that the term "intellectual" emerged in its present meaning, though again the arena of dispute was France, a France gripped in the hysteria of the Dreyfus affair.

On January 13, 1898, Georges Clemenceau's journal *L'Aurore* published Zola's "J'Accuse." The following day a petition appeared: "The undersigned, protesting against the violation of legal procedures at the trial of 1894 and against the mysteries which have surrounded the Esterhazy affair, continue to demand a new trial." Below this simple declaration was a list of names: Zola himself, Anatole France, Marcel Proust, Léon Blum, and others from France's literary and scientific elites. Above the text was the headline: "Manifesto of the Intellectuals."

As a noun describing a certain social type, "intellectual" had occasionally been used before; but it was the political crisis that pumped blood into these syllables. Within a day of the manifesto's appearance, the literary critic Ferdinand Brunetière was heard denouncing the elitism implied by the new term; it was "one of the most absurd eccentricities of our time . . . that writers, scientists, professors, philologists, should be elevated to the rank of supermen." Brunetière's remarks were nothing compared to the savage attack by the novelist Maurice Barrès. He called the manifesto a "Who's Who of the Elite." "All these aristocrats of thought . . . who would be ashamed to think like ordinary Frenchmen." Barrès went on to compare "these self-styled intellectuals . . . these stunted geniuses, these poor poisoned intellects" to guinea pigs and lobotomized dogs which must be infected or mutilated for reasons of scientific progress. A few days later, Jean Psichari, dean of studies at the Ecole des Hautes Etudes and the son-in-law of Ernest Renan, sent an open letter to *Le Temps* asserting that "intellectuals" have the right to engage openly in political affairs.

The Dreyfus affair, then, which instructs us of the political circumstances surrounding the emergence of the new term, should also remind us that if the "intellectuals" were united, the intellectuals were not, and one of the things which divided them was precisely the public role which the new term designated.

To be sure, the two parties were primarily divided by the question of the captain's guilt or innocence and by all the issues of individual rights, justice, social stability, and national strength which the affair had accumulated; that is, they were divided along the ancient fault of Left/ Right. It is true that from Burke to today's neoconservatives, the counterintellectual critique has been advanced most often by those of conservative, or at least centrist, outlook. Yet Communists as well as conservatives have been profoundly suspicious of the rootless, undisciplined intellectual, always too insistent on personal "integrity" rather than organizational necessity. Even the left-wing criticism directed toward those intellectuals who serve power rather than maintain an independent and adversary posture—Noam Chomsky's assault on the "new mandarins," Christopher Lasch's accounts of the Progressive-era "radicals" and of the cultural Cold Warrior, for instance, or Ronald Steel's critique of "Green Beret intellectuals"—overlaps at certain points with the counterintellectual tradition, especially in its attribution to the intellectuals of a particular susceptibility to corruption by power. The relationship of the counterintellectual case to conservative politics should not be forgotten, but to some extent the case can be examined and evaluated independently and on its own merits. The counterintellectual case centers on a much-noted characteristic of the intellectuals, variously described as their independence; their distance from political power; their relative detachment from great class and institutional interests (except, add the counterintellectuals, from their own); their lack of attachment, even, to a professional or scholarly discipline. The intellectual takes pride in this independence. It allows him, he feels, to see what others do not; it qualifies him for his role as society's conscience. The intellectual is marginal; and it is this marginal position which Karl Mannheim hoped might permit intellectuals to transcend the limits of ideology. But for the counterintellectuals, this very independence is precisely what disqualifies writers, artists, professors, and clergymen from stepping out of these limited occupations and into the politically charged role of "intellectual."

Alexis de Tocqueville made the classic statement of the counterintellectuals' case in his analysis of the effect of the *philosophes* on the French Revolution:

> . . . living as they did, quite out of touch with practical politics, they lacked the experience which might have tempered their enthusiasms. Thus they completely failed to perceive the very real obstacles in the way of even the most praiseworthy reforms, and to gauge the perils involved in even the most salutary revolutions. . . . As a result, our literary men became much bolder in their speculations, more addicted to general ideas and systems, more contemptuous of the wisdom of the ages, and even more inclined to trust their individual reason. . . .
>
> Our revolutionaries had the same fondness for broad generalizations, cut-and-dried legislative systems, and a pedantic symmetry; the same contempt for hard facts; the same taste for reshaping institutions on novel, ingenious, original lines; the same desire to reconstruct the entire constitution according to the rules of logic and a preconceived system instead of trying to rectify its faulty parts. The result was nothing short of disastrous. . . .

Starting from the intellectual's distance from political power and practical life, the counterintellectual critique can move in a number of directions. It may stress the intellectual's incompetence and his capacity for inadvertent mischief: he bumbles onto the stage of history with florid speeches and pretentious manifestos; his own plans are ineffective but he may set into motion what he cannot, through lack of will or ingenuity, control. Or the critique may stress the intellectual's treacherousness, his elitism, and his authoritarian tendencies. The absence of power, poisoning him with resentment, renders him hungry for the taste of rule. In this case, he is no bumbler, but is immensely successful at noisily inflaming opinion or silently tunneling the bedrock of traditional values. He is an intriguer, not a dreamer; and for all his inexperience of power, a ruthless seeker of its substance.

The intellectual's detachment from power, then, renders him innocent in the ways of the world—or a Machiavellian. He lacks force of will; he is a fanatic. He is bloodless; he is bloody-minded. He is sentimental and humanitarian; he is cold and ruthless. He is soft. Or hard. In any case, he is rootless, volatile, and untrustworthy.

The trunk of the counterintellectual case swiftly branches into a number of themes. Burke catalogued many of them in explaining the causes of the French Revolution: "Along with the monied interest, a new description of men had grown up, with whom that interest soon formed a close and marked union; I mean the political Men of Letters. Men of Letters, fond of distinguishing themselves, are rarely averse to innovation." To compensate for the decline in "favours and emoluments," Burke went on, which had set in since the reign of Louis XIV, the Men of Letters caballed together, contriving to control public opinion and occupy "all the avenues to literary fame." They plotted the destruction of Christianity. Their "resources of intrigue" and "violent and malignant zeal" overcame "the desultory and faint persecution carried on against them." They

> pretended to a great zeal for the poor, and the lower orders, whilst in their satires they rendered hateful, by every exaggeration, the faults of courts, of nobility, and of priesthood. They became a sort of demagogues. They served as a link to unite, in favour of one object, obnoxious wealth to restless and desperate poverty.

Status anxiety, fascination with the exotic, monopoly of the media, baseless complaints of repression, elitism disguised as social concern, radical chic—for 180 years, counterintellectuals have elaborated the themes that Burke announced. But certain additions have been made to the canon. A major one dwells on the idea of secular religion. In an era when traditional religious beliefs are declining, the intellectual has inherited—or seized—the mantle of the theologians and preachers. He may supply the masses with secular dogma—ideology—to fill the place once occupied by traditional religion. He may bless or curse the rulers of society. Above all, the intellectual himself is most in need of this ersatz religion and apt, therefore, to outdo even his priestly predecessors in fanaticism, excommunication, and heresy hunting. This criticism may be informed with the sense that all religion is now anachronistic; simply by employing religious terminology in connection with intellectuals, it casts doubt on their modernity and good sense. Or the counterintellectual may warn that it is the *displacement* of hopes and longings from the realm of the sacred to that of the secular which makes them so explosive.

Other counterintellectual themes draw on the lore of psychology. A recurrent one is that the intellectuals suffer from a sort of masochism which drives them to provoke public retribution. Another theme is that of boredom: the intellectuals make trouble just so things will be a little less dull. A subtheme is sexual boredom, or even impotence. The intellectuals get their kicks by identifying with youth, revolutionaries, and purveyors of violence. Finally, the intellectuals are considered so unnaturally susceptible to attacks of guilt as to unhinge their judgment and produce self-destructive behavior.

In the twentieth century, the counterintellectual case has been made by writers as disparate as Charles Péguy, Harold Lasswell, and George Orwell, each, of course, in his own particular version. In the very influential *Capitalism, Socialism and Democracy*, Joseph Schumpeter devoted ten pages to a "Sociology of the Intellectuals"—as succinct and even sly an example of contemporary counterintellectualism as one could want. According to Schumpeter, the intellectual is a Frankenstein's monster created by modern capitalism. Having given him the printing press and a mass audience of the newly literate, it can neither control him (thanks to the freedom stemming from bourgeois *laissez-faire*) nor sufficiently reward him (the expansion of higher education creates an intellectual proletariat). The ungrateful monster, nursing his own anticapitalist resentment, penetrates the labor movement, political parties, and civil bureaucracies so as to unite all hostility to capitalism in a fatal challenge to the system. (The more realistic intellectuals, Irving Howe pointed out in 1954, "might have smiled a doubt as to their capacity to do *all that*.") Raymond Aron, admirer of de Tocqueville, has carried on the master's critique, most notably in *The Opium of the Intellectuals*. The secular-religion theme, reflected in Aron's title, was prominent in *The True Believer* by Eric Hoffer, whose popularized counterintellectualism seems to have teetered its way through a number of books toward old-fashioned anti-intellectualism.

Daniel Bell presented a sophisticated elaboration of the counterintellectual critique when, in *The End of Ideology*, he distinguished between "scholars" and "intellectuals":

> The scholar has a bounded field of knowledge, a tradition, and seeks to find his place in it, adding to the accumulated, tested knowledge of the past as to a mosaic. The scholar, qua scholar, is less involved with his "self." The intellectual begins with *his* experience, *his* individual perceptions of the world, *his* privileges and deprivations, and judges the world by these sensibilities.

Since business civilization refused intellectuals high status, according to Bell, they rejected it: "There was a 'built-in' compulsion for the free-floating intellectual to become political. The ideologies, therefore, which emerged from the nineteenth century had the force of the intellectuals behind them. They embarked upon what William James called the 'faith ladder.'. . .''

In a brief passage Bell thus blended the themes of unrequited ambition, status anxiety, unbalanced psyches, and secular religion into a description which he insists is not meant to be "invidious." However, since the ideologies with which the intellectuals are linked are now "exhausted," the intellectual is an anachronism, or perhaps a vestigial social organ, like the appendix, significant only because of an unfortunate tendency to become inflamed.

The Neoconservative Version

Denunciation and disparagement of intellectuals is pervasive in the literature of neoconservatism. At the beginning of the decade, Norman Podhoretz declared that "the state of consciousness within the intellectual community itself is in a parlous condition." Upon reflection he amended his characterization to "pathological"—and Arnold Beichman cites Podhoretz only to wonder "whether the phrase 'pathological condition' is too much of an understatement." Podhoretz's diagnosis of these diseased minds followed in the line of Barrès' reaction to the Dreyfusard intellectuals: "I think the pathology—it is a pathology of the spirit—derives precisely from the inability or the unwillingness of the intellectuals as a class to understand themselves as part of the common run of mankind. . . . The intellectuals have been trained to believe that they transcend the common destiny by virtue of the power of their minds. . . ."

Other examples illustrate not so much the pervasiveness of the counterintellectual case, which would be unnecessary, but the persistence of its individual themes.

Status anxiety: Zbigniew Brzezinski repeats the theory that today's political militants and their intellectual leaders "frequently come from those branches of learning which are most sensitive to the threat of social irrelevance. Their political activism is thus only a reaction to the more basic fear that the times are against them, that a new world is emerging without either their assistance or their leadership."

Monopoly of the media, fascination with the exotic, boredom: During the sixties, declare Daniel Moynihan and Nathan Glazer, the intellectuals effected a "surprising conquest of the mass media." Furthermore, "the intelligentsia, as it so often has, lusted after the sensational and the exotic. The hard work of politics and social change bored it."

When New York intellectuals turn to politics, write Irving Kristol and Paul Weaver, "their general purpose, in such cases, is to wreak as much mischief as possible so that American society will bore them a little less."

Baseless complaints of repression: As for intellectuals' talk of persecution, "one hears it wherever fashionable folk gather," states Walter Goodman. "Cocktail-party conversation in liberal circles starts from the understanding that those who are out to get us are well along in the process, and proceeds to further calamities." (Cocktail parties are to the neoconservatives what coffeehouses and salons were to Burke. Intellectuals are never heard to say anything except at cocktail parties, and then whatever they say is "fashionable.")

"One cannot escape the impression," concludes Andrew Greeley in an article criticizing the antiwar movement, "that some commentators are eagerly awaiting an 'era of repression' so that they can experience the same kind of 'subpoena envy' they experienced in the McCarthy era."

Elitism disguised as social concern, radical chic: Leopold Labedz denounces the "revolutionary Establishment of New York and London" which practices "alienation at fifty thousand dollars a year" and, "thrilled with revolutionary prospects, and displaying the characteristic *Salon-Maoismus*, contributes to the orgy of snobbery attendant upon the current Utopian wave."

Heirs of the priestly caste and propagators of secular dogmas: Looking at the Cholula pyramid, altar of Aztec sacrifices, Peter Berger contemplates "intellectuals in action." "Toltec priests succeeded Olmec priests, and were in turn followed by the Aztecs . . . worrying over Quetzalcoatl's feeding schedule. Then came the Spanish priests . . . and the fires of the Inquisition took over from the blood rites of the old gods. And today? . . . It is still the intellectuals who produce the theories of power.

The universities are the battlefields between the gods of *yanqui* evangelism . . . and those of the new faith of the left. . . ."

And writing of the hold of the "socialist myth" on intellectuals, Berger concludes, "Myths derive their power from those realms of the mind in which the gods used to dwell, and the gods have always been relentless."

Vicarious youth, compensation for failing sexual powers: Brzezinski analyzes "middle-aged admirers of the militants, who—though most often physically passive—outdid themselves in their efforts to drink again at the fountain of youth by vicarious identification with youth's exuberance."

Berger explains that "Intellectuals have always had the propensity to endow their libidinal emotions with philosophical significance, in sex as in politics, and in both areas one often suspects that the need for philosophy arises from an unfortunate combination of strong ambitions and weak capabilities."

The whole ball of wax: The radical professor, according to a portrait published in *Commentary*, "is a man who has wandered through life, never testing himself outside the university, never quite growing up. His emotional life is barren. He is envious, resentful. . . . His status is threatened. . . . He is an elitist at heart but represses this realization. . . . it pleases him to avenge his secret old elitist dream; he has helped rub the rabble in the faces of those privileged few still up there enjoying the power and the glory. . . . He cannot bear to be left out of a magic circle where power, glory, and virtue reside, if briefly; and in the rebellion . . . he is free to deny his own unmanly fraudulence. . . ."

Lewis Feuer provides an academic paper on "the evidence and sources of intellectuals' authoritarianism." He demonstrates this phenomenon by (a) remarking the "impressive tradition of philosophical Utopias" which all share "the same vision of the rule of the scientific intellectuals"; (b) citing the intellectuals' claim that "the pen is mightier than the sword" and Keynes's belief that the power of ideas exceeds that of vested interests; and (c) quoting several incriminating Chinese proverbs, such as "Without leaving his study, a Bachelor of Arts may understand the affairs of the empire." If this universal propensity were not bad enough, modern conditions "have bred in intellectuals a more acute authoritarianism." Intellectuals are frustrated because their thinking does not culminate in action, which "from the biological standpoint," Feuer informs us, is "a psychological anomaly." This frustration may be turned inward as self-aggression "in movements as diverse as monasticism and beatnikism." Or if "the desire for action is not subdued . . . the intellectual then tends to dictatorial, impatient, and ruthless modes of action."

Science marches on: "From a psychological standpoint . . . the intellectual can be said to have something about him of the feminine." And as

Feuer hauls out the image of "the bookish boy" treated by his rough companions as a "sissy" and, later, proving his manhood through bitter engagement in the struggle of ideas, the counterintellectual impulse reaches the border of self-parody.

The Problem of Evidence

In some instances, the counterintellectual critique represents a serious effort to understand the behavior of intellectuals by probing behind their own declarations and examining the social and material conditions in which they labor. Counterintellectuals, despite their hostility, have done a large measure of the intelligent theorizing about intellectuals. In its more casual expressions, counterintellectualism can be seen as a skeptical counter to intellectual pretensions, a teasing deprecation not demanding any hard evidence. Yet as the counterintellectual critique rises to the pitch and takes on the political significance it has in neoconservative polemics; as it creates and maintains a stereotype of an intellectual subversive of all traditional values, destructive in politics, sympathetic toward totalitarianism, and filled with loathing for his homeland and its citizens, then one is led to ask, amid the vast and confident assertions, "Is it true?"

The question, to begin with, is not easy to answer. Many of the counterintellectual assertions are hardly amenable to evidence. Charges of status anxiety, resentment, boredom, and elitism are flexible and often impossible to verify; one can manipulate them at will. If intellectuals look out for themselves, they are self-serving; if they try to put others' interests first, they are hypocrites. Counterintellectual "truths" can be turned inside out without the seams showing. If Daniel Bell asserts that intellectuals characteristically spin their abstractions out of their "self," making their personal experience the criterion for the world, Lionel Trilling asserts that "the characteristic error of the middle-class intellectual of modern times is his tendency to abstractness and absoluteness, his reluctance to connect idea with . . . personal fact." The professor who wrote on the *New York Times* Op-Ed page that "pessimism has always been intellectually fashionable" could just as well have written that "optimism has always been intellectually fashionable"—I doubt whether many readers would stop and wonder about the truth of the matter in either case. The operative word, in any case, is neither "pessimism" nor "optimism" but "fashionable." Since fashionableness is such a strong element in the intellectual stereotype, it matters little how you fill in the blank spaces.

Intellectuals do tend to abstractness and absoluteness. They do worry about their status, mistake their wishes for reality, suffer from middle-age malaise, etc., etc. But in comparison to whom? Politicians, generals, diplomats, bankers, and policemen have been known to exhibit these weaknesses as well. While the fault lines in intellectuals no doubt have their own special patterns, the divergences from those of other social "types" are probably far less dramatic, far more a matter of small degrees, than the usual generalizations allow. My own study of a cross section of left-wing French intellectuals and their debates on foreign policy in the 1930s suggested that for better or worse their politics resembled, rather than diverged wildly from, the politics of other milieus. Their "characteristic errors" turned out to be the characteristic errors of French politicians, military strategists, and businessmen, that is, of French society in general.

What does count for evidence in these discussions? Intellectuals, or what passes for them in these circumstances, are a fairly large and disparate group. It is not hard to string together examples to make a point. In one paragraph of a *Commentary* article on "The Intellectuals and the People," James Hitchcock quotes "a literary critic," "a white Catholic social worker," "a columnist for a liberal newspaper," "Margaret Mead," "a liberal book-reviewer," "a Yale professor," and "the historian A.J.P. Taylor." How are we to know which, if any, of these views are representative? "Radical social critics rejected almost unanimously the Moynihan thesis on black family life," says the same author. But who counts as "radical"? And since "liberal" social critics by no means rejected Moynihan unanimously, why should radicals rather than liberals stand in for the author's subject, "intellectuals"? When Peter Berger flatly declares, "Most American intellectuals have since Vietnam come to believe that the exercise of American power is immoral," how does he know? Or when he announces with certainty that "within the intellectual milieu . . . there is a broad, probably growing consensus . . . that the culture of the mass of American people ('Middle America') is inferior and pathological, and . . . that the political system of liberal democracy is a corrupt sham"?

Historical generalizations present the same problem. In his January 1969 memo to President-elect Nixon, Moynihan declared, "Since about 1840 the cultural elite in America have pretty generally rejected the values and activities of the larger society." But what does that mean? In point of fact, hardly any portion of America's cultural elite has rejected its society root-and-branch; most often, writers, intellectuals, scholars rejected *some* values and *some* activities (usually those connected with the urban, commercial forces remaking the nation) in the name of *other* American values and activities (usually the Jeffersonian myth of agrarian individualism and the universal application of the nation's founding principles); thus they were profoundly conservative.

A similar lack of distinction and nuance is present in most historical statements about the "adversary culture." Since the phrase originated with Lionel Trilling, Trilling's deserved authority is commonly invoked for its general use. This is not the place for a full-scale analysis of the concept's strengths and weaknesses as a device for interpreting modern intellectual history, though one can feel confident that Trilling, had he elaborated the notion, would have done so with far more subtlety than have most of the neoconservatives. The forms and degrees of opposition between intellectuals and the reigning values of their societies have been extremely various, shifting from nation to nation—nineteenth-century Britain, France, Germany, Russia, and America are all very different cases—and between writers, artists, and academics. In the hands of most neoconservatives, these crucial differences are ignored.

Seymour Martin Lipset is a leading example. A talented sociologist, Lipset writes "history" by assembling whatever quotations or examples support a preconceived thesis; by amalgamating distinct attitudes under vague headings of "opposition," "moralism," or "left"; and by disposing in subordinate clauses of the anomalies that nonetheless disturb his schema. As evidence of the longstanding adversary role of American historians, Lipset strings together, without evaluation of their political motivation or value as historical sources, complaints about intellectuals from John Adams, Thomas Jefferson (though the quotation actually has nothing to do with the issue at hand), Herbert Hoover, and Daniel Patrick Moynihan. In the latter instance, he quotes the very statement just noted from the memo to Nixon, so that a generalization in need of substantiation is now become, in a "scholarly" article, *evidence* of things asserted! Yet having granted that most intellectuals "challenge the system for not fulfilling the ideals implicit in the American Creed," Lipset faces a problem: "It may be argued, of course, that the 'leftist' orientation of American intellectuals is in fact largely liberal rather than radical. If so, then it is in harmony with the preponderant national tradition." A quick departure from logic, and the problem is solved: "While there can be little doubt that a majority of those involved in intellectually-linked occupations have been liberals or progressives rather than supporters of the extreme left [subordinate-clause strategy], it is also true that no other stratum in America has even approached intellectuals in their support of leftist, third party, socialist, and Communist activities, broadly defined." What Lipset has done is set up, first, a questionable opposition between *all* "leftist, third-party, socialist, and Communist activities"—i.e., Robert

La Follette, Eugene Debs, and Norman Thomas, as well as Earl Browder—and the "national tradition" and, then, an illogical and spurious identification of intellectuals with this amalgamated "extreme left"—i.e., if most intellectuals weren't Communists, still most Communists were intellectuals. Indeed, much of the material that follows traces the relationship between intellectuals and the Communist Party. Reality, however, keeps creeping in, and Lipset can only sustain his case by the constant slurring of "liberal *or* radical" and the lumping together of "left views" in his descriptions. He notes the fact that even the Communist Party's greatest success among intellectuals occurred during the Popular Front period when it called on them to *defend* their society against fascism, but he fails to see its significance for his unmovable thesis. He provides ample evidence that American intellectuals have often been at odds with their society; but the critical question has to do with the depth and breadth of this opposition, and his ideological *parti pris* is too crude to honor such distinctions, even when they loom up in his own account.

For the most part, then, the counterintellectual critique is a form of Higher Folklore. It consists of old bromides as well as enduring wisdom. It does not demand of its exponents, as they so often imagine, a stout streak of iconoclasm. On the contrary, the existence of a venerable counterintellectual tradition means that ideas can be picked, ready-to-wear, off the racks. Just as the left-wing intellectual has an abundant store of stock phrases and notions to tempt him from the hard work of thinking things through anew, the counterintellectual themes are similarly available in the dime stores of the mind. In truth, one doesn't really have to attend those cocktail parties; one can simply read other counterintellectual critics and grasp at a passing fact now and then to verify their clichés.

Two Empirical Studies

There is, however, *some* empirical evidence about the values and political attitudes of American intellectuals. Two major studies have appeared in recent years, and in many respects they are complementary. Both are by well-established social scientists. One focuses on "elite intellectuals," the other on the university and academic disciplines generally. The author of the former, Charles Kadushin, identifies himself as a liberal who shifted, in the course of his study, toward democratic socialism. The authors of the latter study, Everett Carll Ladd, Jr., and Seymour Martin Lipset, do not announce their politics but can be fairly identified, especially Lipset, as neoconservatives. Their study has the additional merit of summing up much other research.

Charles Kadushin's *The American Intellectual Elite* appeared in 1974. Kadushin's work represents a determined effort to escape the endless theorizing and subjective judgments of much of the literature about intellectuals; and it is not hard to find fault with the somewhat positivist, "bookkeeping" methods he consequently adopts. Let me sketch this methodology and state my own reservations before indicating why Kadushin's findings are in the final analysis helpful and summarizing what in fact he found.

Kadushin did not quit with the usual efforts, abstract or impressionistic, at defining an intellectual elite. Using two sets of judges (randomly selected editors, writers, and professors of English and the social sciences from leading academic departments), he first identified twenty-two "leading intellectual journals." The sample of "elite intellectuals" was drawn from the editors and contributors of these journals and from authors whose books were reviewed in them; the more often one wrote or was reviewed, the better one's chances of falling into the sample. Thus Kadushin located what he believed were the nation's leading intellectuals ("about 200"). With the help of a battery of interviewers and the perspicacity of the FBI, he then collected all the usual data about these intellectuals' age, occupation, religion, etc., and submitted them to an extensive grilling on their friends, their enemies, the books and newspapers they read, their contacts with government, the petitions they have signed, the organizations they have joined—and even, to a remarkable extent, on their ideas.

In addition, those interviewed were asked which intellectuals *they* considered most influential. The result is nothing less than a list: "The Seventy Most Prestigious Contemporary American Intellectuals."

The urge to poke fun at such explicitness is irresistible. There they are, names (though not addresses), with a top ten to boot, from Daniel Bell and Noam Chomsky (in alphabetical order) to Lionel Trilling and Edmund Wilson. The list dates from 1970, as Wilson's name and now Trilling's testify; but one imagines it being updated at regular intervals, if not under the auspices of the National Science Foundation, then perhaps by *The Guinness Book of World Records*. But despite the potential for party games and the reduction of intellectual life to a packet of baseball trading cards ("Hey, I've got two Saul Bellows—I'll trade you a Bellow for a Hans Morgenthau"), there is something to be said for the listing. Certainly we know what kind of people Kadushin is analyzing, as we do not when faced with generalizations about faceless guests at cocktail parties. A Daniel Bell, a John Kenneth Galbraith, and even an Arthur

Schlesinger, Jr., are fairly identifiable entities. My reservations about Kadushin's procedures do not focus on the list; indeed it is the explicitness of his "elite" that allows us to perceive the first of his study's weaknesses.

Two assumptions underlie Kadushin's method of identifying elite intellectuals: first, that intellectuals deal in "high-quality *general* ideas on questions of values and aesthetics" for a "fairly *general* audience" (my emphasis); and, second, that they can be selected by their peers through the "gatekeeping" of intellectually prestigious journals. In practice, that translates into an emphasis on literary criticism, on political and social commentary, and on a certain kind of cultural journalism. Science journals, and evidently other professional journals, were not included in the original search on what I believe is a mistaken assumption, that insofar as scientists and professionals like lawyers and doctors "wish to influence public policy on matters other than research grants, they generally make their views known outside their professional circles." (My impression is that these groups do express their wider views through professional vehicles, and leave the filtering process to others.) The bias is against the arts other than literature, against science, the "learned professions," and those whose influence does not depend on the written word. One reviewer noted that Kadushin's list included "hardly any novelists [there were half a dozen, but several were better known for their criticism], playwrights or poets, no judges or religious thinkers [Reinhold Niebuhr was on the list, and one might argue about Norman O. Brown!], no musicians, film-makers or artists, only one or two scientists, no lawyers, politicians, or physicians." That strikes me as a fair criticism, though it does not suggest an alternative procedure. What Kadushin's method needs is a "sensitivity test"; the initial steps like the selection of judges and the choice of periodicals should be altered, the process run through again, and the results compared.

My second reservation concerns the extensive pigeonholes Kadushin constructs to describe the complicated links between intellectuals and the range of convictions that they express. Thus there are five major "circles" of elite intellectuals. There were three major divisions of opinion on the Cold War—each subdivided into two further categories. On the war in Vietnam, there were those always opposed, those always in support, those who were early, middle, and late switchers. Switchers, in turn, were variously influenced by newspapers, journals, books, friends, or the general atmosphere; and their objections were pragmatic, ideological, or moralistic. Their other concerns were racial issues, domestic reform, the "culture crisis," and so on, and their contacts with government were direct, indirect, or deliberately limited. All these categories are correlated back and forth, till one expects certain chapters to end with a short quiz:

how many over-sixty Jewish Cold War "Stalwarts" (liberal-left version) who belong to the social science–literary circle and live in New York were pragmatic middle switchers on the war in Vietnam, had indirect government contacts, and ranked the "culture crisis" immediately after the war on their list of concerns? Kadushin has the answer, though no one else may have ever had the question. Whatever intellectuals are, they are not pigeons, and though such categorizing may be unavoidable, it often seems to do violence to the ideas being examined.

My third reservation has to do with Kadushin's reliance on interviews conducted in 1970, particularly when they concern changes of opinion on the war in Vietnam or racial issues that in some cases occurred several years earlier. The circumstances of a face-to-face interview might encourage a calmer, less outraged discussion of the war than the same scholar would have put in print or delivered at a campus rally. Then again, it might involve reading back into previous decisions a more intense feeling stirred by the protracted agitation. In any case, the expression of an intellectual community is somewhat different from the sum of its individual members' opinions; not everyone writes on everything. Kadushin, I must add in fairness, does supplement his interviews by establishing which books most influenced his elite intellectuals on Vietnam and then analyzing the contents of those works.

None of these reservations cancels the genuine usefulness of Kadushin's findings, particularly in the context of the neoconservatives' assertions. For whatever doubts one might have, for example, that Kadushin's intellectual elite is *the* intellectual elite, it is recognizably the same group that the neoconservatives have in mind. Whenever neoconservatives need to seize upon a symbol of the "enemy," it is *The New York Review of Books* they wave. And Kadushin's "Seventy Most Prestigious" includes the editors and most of the leading contributors (circa 1970) of *The New York Review. The New York Review of Books* was also overwhelmingly the most influential journal among Kadushin's sample.

As for the false precision of some of Kadushin's categories and the possible effects of interviewing, they simply require his reader to assume a generous margin of error in viewing his results. As it turns out, the results are not at all ambiguous.

What did Kadushin find? Very roughly speaking, his study tells us that in 1970, leading intellectuals were surprisingly evenly divided between academics and nonacademics, between New Yorkers and non–New Yorkers, between Jews and non–Jews. They are not young (two-thirds are over fifty; only 13 percent are under forty). Though writing is their forte, the term "literary intellectuals" is not completely accurate; about a fifth of them are social scientists. They are paid well (median family income was

$35,000 in 1969), though considerably less well than other sectors of the American elite. Many of them manage projects with significant budgets; in other words they "meet a payroll."

The elite intellectuals are unmistakably dissenters, but by no means revolutionaries. "The American intellectual elite," writes Kadushin, "is more liberal on any issue of public policy than the American public at large, more liberal than any other segment of the American elite. . . . But this is not to say that most of the intellectual elite are radical. They are not. . . . In 1970, less than half wanted to get out of Vietnam immediately, even though most intellectuals had strongly opposed the war since 1965, long before any other group in the population. And their opposition remained mainly on pragmatic grounds—the war did not work—rather than on ideological or even moral grounds." Most of them were opposed to Black Power, and an overwhelming majority were passionately hostile toward the New Left and the counterculture. By and large, they were wary of entangling alliances with men of power, though 30 percent had direct channels to government officials and another 25 percent had indirect channels or irregular contacts.

Let us review those findings more slowly.

On the war: The elite intellectuals were far ahead of the general public in concluding that the war was a mistake, yet even in 1970 they treated it largely as a *mistake*, grave and catastrophic no doubt, but not a crime. This situation may have changed after publication of *The Pentagon Papers,* but Kadushin's interviews were conducted, after all, two years after the Tet offensive and the McCarthy Presidential campaign and during the very period of the Cambodian invasion and Kent State. Still, almost 80 percent of the responding intellectuals opposed the war on "pragmatic" grounds—American power was limited and we could not win; there were more crucial foreign-policy objectives; the country was weakened by polarization over the war; domestic progress had been stymied. Forty percent cited "ideological" reasons—imperialism, philosophical pacifism, general anti-interventionism. And 20 percent offered "moral" reasons—immediate wrongs and atrocities, killing in *this* war (there were no absolute pacifists). This added up to over 100 percent "because some intellectuals offered several reasons. Indeed, almost everyone offered pragmatic reasons, so the distinguishing characteristic is whether or not some other kinds of reasons were also advanced." "The leading American intellectuals," concluded Kadushin, "are pragmatists, *not* moralists."

On America's problems generally: Kadushin compared his interviews with those conducted a year later of other American elites (business, labor, government officials, Congress, political-party leadership, voluntary associations, and mass-media leaders) and with public opinion polls.

"The great surprise is the extraordinary similarity among the intellectuals, the elite as a whole, and the general public in what they see as wrong with America."

Compared with other elites, the intellectuals were less concerned about the economy, which may have only reflected the different timing of the interviews, and more concerned about race relations, which seemed to be a significant divergence. On both issues, however, the intellectuals were aligned with the public at large. The intellectuals, almost all sectors of the elite, and the public all agreed in ranking "culture and values" as a major problem. One major difference between the intellectuals and the general public was their perception of "law and order" as an issue; but in this case, *every* sector of the elite, except Congress, also diverged from the public. (Intellectuals ranked "law and order" eighth in their priority of problems, just as did business and labor leaders.)

On ideology: Not only were most elite intellectuals "pragmatic" in their approach to Vietnam, even though Kadushin defined "ideological" reasons for opposing the war loosely. But when discussing all issues of special concern to them, most remained strikingly non-"ideological." Roughly a third of the interviewees expressing a personal involvement in issues of foreign policy or race placed that issue in a "larger picture, linked to other issues"; but very few invoked a specific theoretical explanation. About two-thirds saw domestic reform and cultural questions as part of a larger picture, but only half as many "invoked a theory."

> Then there is the alleged tendency of intellectuals always to invoke a theory as an explanation for whatever position they might take on any matter. This stereotype was not borne out in our conversations with leading intellectuals. Most, when they talked about social problems, did so in a fairly common-sensical manner. . . . No one talking about foreign policy did so from a theoretical point of view, but about one-third who spoke about domestic reform or the culture crisis did so. The theories invoked for domestic reform issues were mainly Marxian, while those in the realm of culture tended to be more general anthropological or social theories.

When not dealing with issues of most personal significance to them but in their opinion of great importance to the nation, Kadushin's sample was even less "ideological." "Less than 15 percent invoked any systematic theory, though radicals were somewhat more prone to this style." Forty percent of those interviewed did mention systems of belief like liberalism, Communism, and socialism, but evidently as reference points rather than explanatory "faiths."

> Ideology has traditionally been important currency among intellectual circles. Characteristically, intellectuals attack ideologies other than their

own with an even slightly greater frequency than they mention ideologies in a favorable context. More than half the sample attacked one ideology or another, with the New Left and radicals bearing the brunt of the attack.

On race: Confusion was the best way to sum up elite intellectuals' views of racial issues in 1970. Perhaps in keeping with that fact, Kadushin's data are not easy to interpret. About a third of his sample seemed to see the racial problem primarily in psychological terms, e.g., the "white racism" of the Kerner Report; about a third stressed social and economic structures; and the final third emphasized more immediate problems of political power and strategy. (The three orientations are obviously not exclusive but reflect differences in emphasis.) It is true that "militants" led the list of the books and authors that had influenced these intellectuals on race: Malcolm X, James Baldwin, and Eldridge Cleaver ranked one, two, three, with Daniel Patrick Moynihan and Martin Luther King together in the fourth position. Though Kadushin is not very precise on this point, about a third seemed sympathetic to black separatism; and "only a very few supported Black Power as expressed by the Panthers." The mood was baffled, pessimistic, and withdrawn rather than distinctly confident, militant, and assertive. "Very few intellectuals now have a clear idea of how to solve the race problem. . . . Their reaction is to back off. . . ."

On culture and values: Despite the widespread charges that the intellectual class is antinomian and nihilistic, the elite intellectuals in Kadushin's study proved to be as concerned about cultural norms and values as the public, or the other sectors of the elite—indeed, *more* concerned than labor leaders, political party officials, or Congress. The intellectuals talk about "alienation," the "culture crisis," and turmoil in the universities; other groups talk about "moral decay"; but Kadushin finds "the problem area is definitely the same."

> Intellectuals who were concerned with the culture crisis were by and large on the defensive, acting the role of establishment rather than vanguard. Instead of setting up new standards or presenting new ideas they tended to defend the old.

Those who talked about students and university problems were, not surprisingly, professors. Only one strongly approved the student rebellions, and even he admitted, "I'm still ambivalent. Sometimes I write out of one side of my ambivalence and sometimes out of the other and sometimes out of both." All the rest were opposed. They believed that "rationality was a main issue, and that the students were opposed to rationality. . . . Underlying the issue of rationality was one of work ethic." Of the intellectuals who spoke more broadly about the crisis of contemporary culture—and they were among the more prestigious individuals in Kadushin's sample—only six out of twenty-two favored the counterculture Even an ambivalent position toward youth and the counterculture was held by an equally small number. The rest were flatly opposed.

But of course one should not necessarily equate sympathy for student rebellion or the counterculture as necessarily antinomian or nihilist either: asked "What do you think man needs now?" one of the few individuals favoring the counterculture replied by ticking off the spiritual and corporal works of mercy.

On relationships with the government: Kadushin's findings do provide some support for the counterintellectual case in this area, though the Vietnam War and a Republican Administration in Washington might have a good deal to do with the results. Given the rather extensive contacts that seem to exist between elite intellectuals and government officials, the intellectuals nurse a rather refined sense of their isolation and a prickly wariness toward political power. Intellectuals are self-conscious about their role as critics and formulators of social ideals, but they are also "irresponsible" in holding that their first responsibility is to meet the critical standards of their intellectual peers. If they are sensitive about the "relevance" of their work, it is in a highly qualified way.

None of these divisions of opinion was particularly close; one could adjust for wide margins of error and still it would be true that (a) the elite intellectuals are to the left of the public (after all, in the spring of 1969, *94 percent* of a Gallup poll wanted administrators to take "a stronger stand" on student disorders and only 17 percent would even approve "a greater say" for students in university affairs); and (b) the intellectuals are anything but radical. One might almost argue with as much plausibility that the intellectual elite is a clerisy rather than an adversary culture. In fact, the truth is somewhere in between: these intellectuals do form an opposition—a very loyal opposition.

But perhaps elite intellectuals are, as elites often are, more moderate than the less established. Perhaps Kadushin's findings are colored, in some unclear way, by his own ideological commitments. Both these hypotheses collapse before the study of "professors and politics" by Everett Carll Ladd, Jr., and Seymour Martin Lipset. To begin with, the Carnegie Commission's Survey of Student and Faculty Opinion, which obtained responses from over 60,000 professors in 1969 and on which the Ladd and Lipset work is based, showed the professoriat *less* liberal than elite intellectuals on standard questions like withdrawal from Vietnam. But Ladd and Lipset's reanalysis of this data in *The Divided Academy* reinforces the Kadushin findings in many additional ways, despite the authors' rather different ideological perspective.

That perspective, expressed in their book's title, stresses conflict and the deviations of their subjects from the norm. Hypersensitive in the neoconservative fashion to the problems of stability or "equilibrium," Ladd and Lipset tend to a crude opposition between "authority" and all "criticism" or "social change." The article by Lipset criticized above is integrated into the book's first and last chapters, and many of the same objections hold against other parts of the book as well. The authors regularly lump "liberal" and "left" into a single category in analyzing data. (One reviewer called attention to "the distortions that are inevitably introduced by the imposition of a single spectrum. The implication . . . is that 'left' is 'liberal' only more so. . . .") Ladd and Lipset also highlight any notable support by professors of third-party or radical politics, even if the bulk of academics, like the bulk of the general population, remains untouched by these efforts. And their conclusion that "academics are distinguished by the intensely ideological character of their thinking" is based not on any questions about ideologies but on the fact that professors' replies to one set of questions correlate highly with their replies to other sets. That is one possible meaning for the protean notion of "intensely ideological," but it is not distinguishable from, say, "blandly conformist."

Other criticisms of Ladd and Lipset have to do with several rather interesting interpretations they adduce for academics' tendency toward a critical outlook and for the political differences between disciplines and between the more or less prestigious faculty. None of this is much to our point. The data they present are massively in support of the conclusion that academics, like elite intellectuals, are at most a very loyal opposition.

In 1968, 58 percent of professors voted for Hubert Humphrey, 38 percent for Nixon, 1 percent for Wallace, and 3 percent for other, presumably radical, candidates. Ladd and Lipset contrast these figures with the much more modest support of Humphrey by other groups; but the relevant contrast for our purposes is with the image of an "adversary culture": in 1968, Hubert Humphrey was hardly the darling of radicals. But was the Nixon vote largely an adversarial protest against Humphrey? In 1972, Nixon received *45* percent of the faculty vote against 56 percent for McGovern.

In 1969, busing for school integration was far more popular among professors than among the public, but it was still opposed by over half the professors surveyed.

Again, while more professors than other citizens approved the "emergence of radical student activism" in the late sixties, that approval was still a minority view: 58 percent of the faculty disapproved.

Of those who indicated knowledge of the 1968 Columbia University sit-ins and strikes, 64 percent approved the "aims" and 95 percent disapproved of the student militants' "methods."

Eight out of ten academics held that students disrupting a school's functioning should be expelled or suspended.

Large majorities of faculty opposed "relaxing" academic criteria in order to admit more minority students or to hire more minority faculty members.

In fact, the professoriat may be even more moderate in its views than the aggregated data in Ladd and Lipset's text suggests. The tables reveal, for example, that of the 43 percent approving the emergence of student radicalism in 1969, *only 3 percent* "unreservedly approve," with the remaining 40 percent approving "with reservations." Likewise, only 16 percent "unreservedly disapprove," while 42 percent "disapprove with reservations."

The Vietnam War was said to have "radicalized" faculty in regard to all institutions, and Ladd and Lipset are much taken with the unsurprising finding that "doves" do tend to be more liberal on various issues than "hawks." But even among "the most strongly antiwar faculty," 10 percent more *strongly agreed* that student disrupters should be suspended or expelled than *strongly disagreed*. (Counting in those having "reservations," 56 percent favored expulsion or suspension to 44 percent opposed.)

Again among the most antiwar academics, those favoring relaxed hiring standards to accommodate minorities were still a distinct minority (38 percent), and within this minority over two-thirds held "reservations." Not even militant doves could be called radically adversarial.

When faculty members were asked to characterize themselves politically as "left," "liberal," "middle-of-the-road," "moderately conservative," or "strongly conservative," 5 percent chose "left" while 41 percent chose "liberal."

Since liberalism had been the object of a scathing critique by radicals throughout the second half of the sixties, the loyalty of academics to this category and the relatively small number who chose the more radical option are striking. Indeed, when this response is compared to a five-point spectrum presented to the general public in a Gallup poll, the major difference is not in the farthest-left category (4 percent of the public called themselves "very liberal"); it is between the 40 percent "liberal" academics and the 16 percent of the public whose self-identification ("fairly liberal") occupied the same spot, to the left of "middle-of-the-road."

I limit myself to one more point from Ladd and Lipset. The Carnegie survey supplied data on job satisfaction as well as on pay, prestige, and publication. An earlier study by Paul F. Lazarsfeld and Wagner Thielens, Jr., reported academics' perception of how they appeared in the eyes of other citizens. None of this material confirmed the belief that intellectual dissent is caused by status anxiety. "*Uniformly, those who are the most satisfied show up as the most liberal and critical in political orientations.*" (Emphasis in original.) "We must question the broader thesis—that academics are led to a critical politics by a sense of being 'deprived' or 'cheated.' "

In the spring of 1975, Ladd and Lipset carried out another survey of professors, reporting the results in a series of articles in *The Chronicle of Higher Education*. Among the findings:

The great majority recognized that the underrepresentation of blacks on faculties was a serious problem, but refused to deviate from meritocratic principles to remedy it.

A great majority opposed any prohibition of controversial research on heredity and intelligence, with no differences between the "most liberal" and the "most conservative" on this point.

Eighteen percent of the faculty appeared to support radical revisions of economic institutions: stiff inheritance taxes, upper limits on incomes, nationalization of major industries. But only 3 percent of the professoriat "took the view in the spring of 1975 that the political system is failing badly . . . that 'meaningful change' is precluded by regular American political procedures, and that the use of violence to achieve political goals can be justified in the United States."

What was evident from the earlier study was now undeniable. Ladd and Lipset summarized their findings:

> American academics constitute the most politically liberal occupational group in the United States but [are] far from being a hotbed of radicalism. . . . They manifest values, expectations, orientations to government, moods, and concerns that broadly reflect those of the American public. . . . Most faculty liberals are far from supporting demands for basic changes in the society. . . . Most of them, like most of their fellow citizens, support the prevailing economic and political order.

Recasting the Neoconservative Case

It is not my intention to argue that the state of the intellectuals as revealed by Kadushin and Ladd and Lipset is either a good or bad thing. From the radical's perspective, it is certainly dismaying. But from any number of perspectives, it provokes speculation. Kadushin's portrait, for example, suggests that it was hardly the volatility but perhaps the exhaustion, if not of ideologies, then of ideologists, that was responsible for the mindlessness of so much radicalism in the late sixties. Passive and in disarray, the elite reacted to critical currents springing up elsewhere rather than providing critical leadership. A vacuum was created only to be filled by Yippies and apprentice desperadoes.

Still, we should not pretend that these studies tell us everything or even very much about intellectuals. Multiple-choice questionnaires and interviews even of several hours' duration are very crude investigative tools. What they do tell us is enough to raise more questions, the first of which is how to explain the gulf between these findings and the popular counter-intellectual image.

There is no clear answer. One might hazard a theory based on what we know about perception and particularly the tendency to reduce ambiguity. Intellectuals are sufficiently different from the rest of the population in political outlook that it may be simpler and more reassuring to cancel out the many similarities rather than keep them in mind. But perhaps it is simply the dramatic power of Burke's original portrait of the intellectual as eternal malcontent, incompetent but uncompromising, that has gripped our imagination so as to select out confirming evidence and ignore the rest. Kadushin notes that the intellectual elite itself shares this misconception of its own politics, consistently assuming that other intellectuals are farther to the left than they actually are. When Kadushin asked what authors his elite intellectuals recalled as influencing their views on Vietnam, most of the names turned out to be Southeast Asian or foreign-policy experts. Bernard Fall, David Halberstam, and Robert Shaplen headed the list—men who were hardly radical or uncompromising; strictly speaking, *critics* rather than *opponents* of the war. What was true for the public was surprisingly true for the intellectuals: "To have credence, an anti-Vietnam War position had to come from the ranks of those who were politically 'respectable.' " But it was also no less true of the intellectuals than of the public that they *perceived* the critique of the war in their own journals as more radical than it was. Kadushin believes this can be mainly accounted for by one fact: the replacement of Bernard Fall, killed in Vietnam, by Noam Chomsky as the most prominent writer on the war. Yet in terms of actual influence on the elite intellectuals, Chomsky rated only twelfth.

The more important question, at least for the present discussion of neoconservatism, is whether, in the face of the data Kadushin, Ladd and Lipset, and others have assembled, anything remains of the neoconservative case against the intellectuals, and of the larger and intimately intertwined case against the "adversary culture" and the "new class." I believe that something does remain, although it requires me somewhat presumptuously to reformulate the neoconservative argument.

If it cannot be maintained that the intellectuals were the source of the "infection," that they led the attack on culture and rejected the legitimacy of political institutions, then perhaps it can be maintained that they were insufficient bulwarks against these currents. Rather than argue that the intellectuals were intolerant of old values, neoconservatives must argue that they were insufficiently intolerant of the new ones. Kadushin discovered that the intellectual elite were not "originators of new moral ideas, but rather analysts, critics and disseminators." They were, he found, "gate-keepers." But the neoconservatives would have them be something more—sentries. If the image of an intellectual class relentlessly eroding the legitimacy of institutions is not to be dismissed as so much polemical vapor, then it must be recast as the demand that intellectuals positively mobilize in support of stability and authority, that they actively isolate and combat and discredit the minority of radical critics and the tiny fraction of true revolutionaries among them. This, of course, they failed to do.

This version of the neoconservative complaint, though it accords much better with our stock of facts, rests on an assumption and leads to further questions. The assumption is the old one that society is exceptionally brittle, that chaos is just below the surface. But this brittleness, this vulnerability to chaos, is not the work of the intellectuals. In the past, the stolidity and traditionalism of the populace balanced the irreverence and inquisitiveness of the intellectuals. But something has gone wrong, and that something cannot be attributed merely to a growth in the number of those exposed to what turns out to be a far from radical professoriat. Large segments of the populace have proved themselves unusually amenable to certain currents of cultural and political change, requiring, in neoconservative opinion, a reversal of the former relationship, with intellectuals not only abandoning an adversarial role, which in fact they barely exercised, but now positively supporting the established order. But what, if not the intellectuals, are the independent sources of this instability?

Neoconservatives cannot answer that question without casting a more critical eye on that established order, without examining more diligently the faultlines, of which they are well aware, in that liberal capitalist order they defend. The widespread distrust of institutions among all classes, the dissolution of religious values and the proliferation of cults offering swift access to personal integration and fulfillment, the anomie and hostility of many inner-city youth, the drift and hedonism of much popular culture, the abandonment of the vulnerable to bureaucratic dependency, the casual amorality of the business world, the retreat from civic con- sciousness and responsibility—these have causes that impinge more directly on great numbers of people than the "trickle-down" of modernist literature through introductory English courses and the alleged seduction of media executives.

Meanwhile, the neoconservative case against the intellectuals, like its case against the "new class," presents itself as a defense of democracy against a new elite. Stripped of its exaggerations and stereotypes, it emerges as a search for a check on democracy, a democracy neoconservatives cannot imagine as viable as long as they exclude the possibility of a more thoroughgoing transformation of American society.

CHAPTER NINE

Equality and Social Policy

ONE OF THE MORE perplexing aspects of neoconservatism is its apparent belief that America is in the grip of implacable egalitarianism. Nathan Glazer gloomily contemplates the "awesome potency" of "the revolution of equality . . . the most powerful social force in the modern world." It "not only expresses a demand for equality in political rights and in political power; it also represents a demand for equality in economic power, in social status, in authority in every sphere. . . . There is no point at which the equality revolution can come to an end." Martin Diamond writes of "a vast inflation of the idea of equality, a conversion of the idea of equal political liberty into an ideology of equality . . . a demand for equality in every aspect of human life."

"Everywhere, equality is the cry," declares Daniel Moynihan, meaning by "everywhere" the world outside our borders but soon indicating that the insidious enemy (British socialist notions) is within as well. Aaron Wildavsky wonders whether the society can withstand "the forces in favor of pushing public policy over the egalitarian precipice." Irving Kristol warns against those who "prize equality more than liberty," a point of view "especially popular in some circles—mainly academic ones—in the United States today." "The kind of liberal egalitarianism so casually popular today will, if it is permitted to gather momentum, surely destroy the liberal society."

Following a long and detailed discussion of "Meritocracy and Equality," Daniel Bell suddenly lets loose at something called "contemporary populism."

> Contemporary populism, in its desire for wholesale egalitarianism, insists in the end on complete levelling. . . . Its impulse is not justice but *ressentiment*. What the populists resent is not power . . . but authority—the authority represented in the superior competence of individuals. In the populist sociology, for example, the authority of doctors should be subject to the decisions of a community council, and that of professors to the entire collegiate body (which in the extreme versions includes the janitors).

No one has exercised himself more energetically on the topic than Robert Nisbet: "Equality has become more than a time-honored value. . . . It is by now tantamount to religion, carrying with it . . . the same kind of moral fervor and zeal, much the same sense of crusade against evil, and much the same measure of promise of redemption that have historically gone with religious movements." The end of this process, for Nisbet, will be nothing less than a "new despotism." Of all the "taking-off points of the new despotism in our time," what Nisbet calls the New Equality "has widest possible appeal, and . . . undoubtedly represents the greatest single threat to liberty and social initiative."

It is not easy, not at first glance anyway, to discern what has brought neoconservatives to this boil. They themselves observe with pleasure what radicals observe with distress, that a markedly greater equality of condition is by no means a popularly held ideal. Nor can it be said that equality of condition, insofar as income statistics measure it, has encroached noticeably in recent decades, if at all, upon our traditional disparities. Discrimination between races and sexes has certainly diminished, though the degree of change and its durability are matters of considerable debate. Yet this movement toward equality fits easily into the standing notions of equality of opportunity: minorities and women should have an equal chance of achieving the patterns of inequality existing among whites and males. Neoconservatives are quick to point out the traditional nature of this development and to attribute as little of it as possible to devices like affirmative action, reputed to depart from the old norms. With the exception of the intellectuals, writes Norman Podhoretz, "very little resentment exists anywhere else in this country over discrepancies of wealth and condition. . . . it would be hard to find anyone in this country who believes, or at least professes to believe, in equality of condition as a desirable social goal."

Is the problem, then, the intellectuals? To be sure, with the neoconservatives the problem is always the intellectuals. It is unlikely that neoconservatives will recognize that liberal intellectuals, like liberals generally and indeed the populace as a whole, have been concerned about *poverty* rather than equality, while even most radicals have extended this concern only to what they see as a necessary step for relieving poverty, the reduction of the political power of wealth. The banner of equality does fly over these campaigns, though remaining largely undefined, and drawing loosely upon both the American attachment to equality of opportunity and an elementary sense that it is not healthy for the bottom of a society to be deprived and the top to be overbearing. But even assuming what is manifestly not the case, that this extreme passion for equality fires the hearts of the intellectuals, why, with a citizenry so unreceptive and an economy so unbudging, should this be threatening?

Odder yet is that the supposedly perilous deviation in this march of equality can be traced to neoconservatives themselves. The critical document is the Moynihan Report, where the "demand for equality" received a rather extended discussion. "Liberty and Equality," wrote Moynihan,

> are the twin ideals of American democracy. But they are not the same thing. Nor, most importantly, are they equally attractive to all groups at any given time; nor yet are they always compatible, one with the other. . . .
>
> By and large, liberty has been the ideal with the higher social prestige in America . . . the middle class aspiration, par excellence. . . . Equality, on the other hand, has enjoyed tolerance more than acceptance. Yet it has roots deep in Western civilization and "is at least coeval with, if not prior to, liberty in the history of Western political thought."
>
> American democracy has not always been successful in maintaining a balance between these two ideals, and notably so where the Negro American is concerned. "Lincoln freed the slaves," but they were given liberty, not equality. It was therefore possible in the century that followed to deprive their descendants of much of their liberty as well.
>
> The ideal of equality does not ordain that all persons end up, as well as start out equal. . . . But the evolution of American politics, with the distinct persistence of ethnic and religious groups, has added a profoundly significant new dimension to that egalitarian ideal. It is increasingly demanded that the distribution of success and failure within one group be roughly comparable to that within other groups. It is not enough that all individuals start out on even terms, if the members of one group almost invariably end up well to the fore, and those of another far to the rear. This is what ethnic politics are all about in America, and in the main the Negro American demands are being put forth in this now traditional and established framework.
>
> Here a point of semantics must be grasped. The demand for Equality of Opportunity has been generally perceived by white Americans as a demand for liberty, a demand not to be excluded from the competitions of life—at the polling place, in the scholarship examinations, at the personnel office,

on the housing market. Liberty does, of course, demand that everyone be free to try his luck, or test his skill in such matters. But these opportunities do not necessarily produce equality: on the contrary, to the extent that winners imply losers, equality of opportunity almost insures inequality of results.

The point of semantics is that equality of opportunity now has a different meaning for Negroes than it has for whites. It is not (or at least no longer) a demand for liberty alone, but also for equality—in terms of group results. In Bayard Rustin's terms, "It is now concerned not merely with removing the barriers to full *opportunity* but with achieving the fact of *equality.*" By equality Rustin means a distribution of achievements among Negroes roughly comparable to that among whites.

As Nathan Glazer has put it, "The demand for economic equality is now not the demand for equal opportunities for the equally qualified: it is now the demand for equality of economic results. . . ."

. . . By and large, the programs that have been enacted in the first phase of the Negro revolution—Manpower Retraining, the Job Corps, Community Action, et al.—only make opportunities available. They cannot insure the outcome.

The principal challenge of the next phase of the Negro revolution is to make certain that equality of results will now follow. If we do not, there will be no social peace in the United States for generations.

Here Moynihan urged, and urged with a reference to "no social peace" that many neoconservatives would now denounce as an implicit threat, both the shifts in the meaning of equality that neoconservatism now finds so menacing: (1) the shift from equality of opportunity to equality of results; (2) the shift from equality between individuals to equality between groups.

Moynihan recognized that equality could both conflict with liberty and support it; he recognized that the emphasis on equality between groups was both a "new dimension" to the egalitarian ideal and a "now traditional" expression of American ethnic politics; he recognized that the emphasis on equality of results was both continuous with equality of opportunity and a divergence from it. His passage left a number of points ambiguous and unsettled, but it attempted to pay heed to different conceptions of American social ideals, rendering them neither starkly opposed nor perfectly harmonious. In this, it resembled most of the later cases for greater equality.

The same ambiguity was retained as Moynihan's argument made its way into Lyndon Johnson's June 4, 1965, Howard University commencement speech.

We seek not just freedom but opportunity—not just legal equity but human ability—not just equality as a right and a theory but equality as a fact and a result. For the task is to give twenty million Negroes the same chance as every other American . . . to pursue their individual happiness.

What developments made neoconservatives look upon the ambiguities of these formulations no longer as the inevitable concomitants of a difficult problem but as the intolerable basis of future disasters?

The next years were marked by an intense reexamination of the relationship between education and equality, a particularly tangled topic because the "result" of education, especially early education, is believed to determine "opportunity" for the rest of life, especially in a credential-conscious society. James S. Coleman and his collaborators completed their massive study *Equality of Educational Opportunity* in 1966; Moynihan then helped conduct a Harvard faculty seminar reanalyzing the data. At the end of the decade furious debates broke out over compensatory education programs like Head Start, over community control of inner-city schools, and over theories linking IQ differences and race. Ivan Illich popularized "de-schooling." And in 1972, the book *Inequality* by Christopher Jencks et al. seemed to tie all the debates together as it simultaneously rejected hereditarian theories of intelligence *and* liberal confidence in schooling as a remedy for inequality. Jencks called for a straightforward attempt to equalize income by government redistribution. As successful products of existing educational systems, as teachers and scholars within them, and as defenders, during the same years, of the liberal university's legitimacy against the criticism and sometimes disruption of the New Left, neoconservatives might easily have felt that "equality" was a key that had opened the door to the tiger and not to the beautiful lady. Furthermore, in 1972 leading neoconservatives were accused, along with the proponents of race-IQ links, of directing a "new assault on equality." Perhaps their critics, then, had partially determined the ground for future debate.

But behind most of the talk of the "revolution of equality," the "egalitarian precipice," "complete leveling," and the despotic "New Equality," one discovers two much more mundane issues: neoconservatism's disenchantment with the Great Society and its opposition to affirmative action. The Great Society and affirmative action are complex realities, not easily evaluated; but the difficulties of neither appear to justify these extreme fears.

Did the "Great Society" Fail?

Neoconservatism's attitude toward the Great Society is contradictory. In 1973, Nathan Glazer confessed he still found "it very hard to give summary judgments on the Great Society programs." At least he could say the effort "was clearly not a uniform failure," and found much good to report about the individual programs, even the more controversial ones like Community Action and Model Cities: "Most of the money . . . by the way, not very much . . . is providing useful social services." Yet the predominant neoconservative stance is one of critical dismissal: the Great Society was part of that "decade of rubbish"; it proved that the negative, unintended consequences of planned social intervention usually outweigh the positive, intended ones; it increased social conflict without relieving social ills; the burden of political commentary should be to oppose any movement toward similar programs rather than revive the spirit of that period. When pointing out that neoconservatism is "not at all hostile to the idea of a welfare state," Irving Kristol quickly notes its lack of sympathy for "the Great Society version of this welfare state." Having reckoned the results of the Great Society expenditures as "negligible," Norman Podhoretz even expressed surprise when challenged—"I had, I admit, thought that almost everyone agreed to the *fact* that the 'war on poverty' was a failure and that the only disagreements concerned the assignment of blame or responsibility."

> The Great Society's strategy of "throwing money at problems" was ill conceived and ineffectual, exaggerating the capacity of the government to change institutions and individuals.
> The nation was pushed too far, too fast, and was unable to afford or digest the overly ambitious agenda of the Great Society; its legacy was inflation, worker alienation, racial tension, and other lingering ills.

The words are President Nixon's, but the sentiments are equally neoconservatism's. Certainly neoconservatism *acquiesces* in the Nixon verdict, devoting much critical energy to the Great Society and its defenders but virtually none to its detractors. But the Nixon view is also explicitly affirmed by leading neoconservatives. In *The Politics of a Guaranteed Income,* Moynihan states:

A further argument which in retrospect may be adduced on behalf of the new conservatism is that diffusing social responsibility for social outcomes tends to retard the rise of social distrust when the promised or presumed outcome does not occur. The modern welfare state was getting into activities no one understood very well. It had not reached the point of picking every man a wife, but it was getting close enough to other such imponderables to find itself increasingly held to account for failures in areas where no government could reasonably promise success.

The conservative argument had heft. This became even more evident in the course of the 1960s as the Federal government undertook an unprecedented range of social initiatives designed to put an end to racial and ethnic discrimination, to poverty, and even also to unequal levels of achievement among groups variously defined by race, class, religion, national origin, and sex, primarily through the strategy of providing new, or "enriched," social services.

Did the government push too far and too fast in the sixties? Did it intrude pervasively in areas where it could not promise success? Did it undertake an unprecedented range of social initiatives? And was all this due to an extreme egalitarian impulse? Michael Harrington has replied to the Moynihan analysis. He points out that while the "human resources" portion of the federal budget did increase markedly in the years under discussion, more than 70 percent of that increase is accounted for by Medicare, Medicaid, Social Security, veterans' benefits, and aid to the blind, aged, and handicapped—in other words, by fairly traditional welfare-state programs with purposes that are widely accepted, though the precise design of some, like Medicare and Medicaid, can be challenged while that of another, Social Security, is due for an overhaul after decades of serving as the very model of an efficient program. The remaining 30 percent of the budget growth included increases for welfare, food stamps, housing subsidies, and student aid, a mix of programs of varying effectiveness but of no great novelty or intrusiveness. Only a small fraction of the new spending went to the controversial poverty programs like Community Action, Job Corps, and Legal Aid. As for the egalitarianism of this effort, Harrington acknowledges that "the sixties sometimes spoke—and rightly so—of national obligations to the victims of discrimination." But "it did not act radically on that premise." Neither in principle did the Kennedy-Johnson Administrations deviate from the established preference for favoring the private sector and respecting corporate wealth (direct creation of public-sector jobs, for example, was always upstaged by corporate tax relief or funding for private business to hire the hard-core unemployed); nor in practice did these Administrations set in motion any great degree of equalization.

A model expression of the neoconservative unhappiness over the Great Society is found in Aaron Wildavsky's article "Government and the People." The subject is "the manufacture of incompatible demands that impose burdens on government which no government can meet." The trouble began with the Great Society, which "wiped out the New Deal" and sowed confusion where once the bureaucracy and the citizenry had enjoyed clarity. The New Deal had served "the temporarily depressed but relatively stable lower and middle classes, people who were on the whole willing and able to work but who had been restrained by the economic situation. . . . It hardly mattered one way or the other what government did or did not do in their behalf." The Great Society, however, proposed to assist the *"severely* deprived" (Wildavsky's emphasis)—"those who actually needed not merely an opportunity but continuing long-term assistance . . . those whom Marx had called the lumpenproletariat." "Yet nobody," Wildavsky adds, "knew *how* to go about it." The result was that "an awful lot of money was invested without accomplishing very much."

Wildavsky goes on to develop his notion of "incompatible" demands, which turns out to depend heavily on his own highlighting of political rhetoric, his own choice of particular lines of policy for exhibition, and his own confusion of "incompatible" ("incapable of being held simultaneously") with "difficult" or "beyond present resources." To this "incompatibility" and the consequent frustration he ascribes virtually all our recent political ills, including our overextended foreign policy and Watergate.

How did American politicians, who could have expected to know better, get caught in such a blind alley? Once it was recognized that the War on Poverty, like the war in Vietnam, was bogged down, why didn't politicians call a halt? The answer is simple. They are Americans, and Americans are optimistic liberals. That is, "equality, no matter how abused or disused, has always been the prevailing American norm." The new social programs "came into the world bearing the banner of the liberal concept of equality." No one could oppose them "without appearing to be against equality or in favor of inequality. Individual politicians might have doubts, a few deviants might voice them, but there was too much guilt engendered by the rhetoric of equality to make collective action possible." America is being attacked at "its most vulnerable point . . . asked to make good on its most ancient and deeply-held beliefs, and it hovers between an inability to abandon its faith and an inability to make its faith manifest to the believers."

Should America abandon its belief in equality? Wildavsky does not quite say so. He does regret the absence of "an intellectually respectable conservative tradition." "A few pundits aside [neoconservatives?], there is not now, if there ever was, a social stratum able to support a conservative ethic against the forces in favor of pushing public policy over the egalitarian precipice."

In other words, only conservatives, who would temper the liberal American urge toward equality and dampen the boundless expectations the public holds of government, can rescue us from the present "crisis of confidence"—and possibly from worse. Wildavsky ends ominously. "Otherwise . . . government, seeing that the game is rigged, will respond once again by secretly attempting to change the rules."

Despite its series of confident assertions, Wildavsky's "historical" contrast between the New Deal and the Great Society is badly flawed. That the "clients of the New Deal" were only "temporarily depressed" and could hardly be affected by what government did in their behalf; that those of Great Society programs were "lumpenproletariat," unwilling or unable to work; that the latter were in need of "long-term assistance" while the former were not, are all inaccurate, and in some cases insulting, propositions. If one defines "clients" with hindsight—those whom the New Deal actually succeeded in aiding—then it is true that the beneficiaries were the better-off among the working and middle classes. But if one thinks of those whose problems the New Deal was supposed to alleviate—the one-third of a nation "ill-nourished, ill-clad, ill-housed" which Roosevelt evoked in 1937—then Wildavsky's sharp distinctions do not hold true. Many of those citizens, the victims of agricultural displacement, for example, were more than temporarily afflicted, in fact were in need of long-term assistance. So were the aged, for whom Social Security was initiated (and who were still a major element in the target population of the Great Society effort). Government action mattered a great deal, both the spotty humanitarian measures and the *unsuccessful* effort to get the nation back to work. It should be remembered that judged by the standards applied to the Great Society, the New Deal was even less successful. No more than in the 1960s did the government know precisely what to do; even more than in the 1960s did Roosevelt lurch from program to program. When the war began in 1940, there were still ten million Americans unemployed, one out of every four workers. A year earlier, looking at this situation, Harry Hopkins had declared that "we are socially bankrupt and politically unstable."

What the New Deal couldn't accomplish the war did; and what the war accomplished, America's dominance in the postwar world economy strengthened and spread. But what none of this could accomplish was left for the 1960s. In this sense, Wildavsky is right: the Great Society may have faced deeper problems. Not, however, because government was daring some radically new task, but because it was willing to take up again where it had previously failed.

That failure had little to do with a lumpenproletariat.* Millions who had been passed over by the economic advances of 1940–60 were family people (the overwhelming majority of poor children in 1963 were in families headed by males); or were aged (5.2 million of the poor in 1963); or were *fully* employed (the heads of two million poor families were working full-time in 1963, as were another half-million poor individuals); or were disabled or devastated by medical expenses.

Wildavsky's description of the egalitarian force of the Great Society also seems fanciful. The American egalitarian tradition is one of the few resources social programs can draw upon. But that politicians are so caught in the egalitarian tow, or so overwhelmed with the guilt it engenders, as to make such programs irresistible—is this a picture recognizable to anyone familiar with the workings of Congress; with the special circumstances, namely Kennedy's death and the Democratic sweep over Goldwater, that made the War on Poverty possible; with the political calculations that played a part in its inception and design; with the suspicion and opposition and worried monitoring it received despite the auspicious circumstances of its initiation; and with its swift demotion from favor once domestic turmoil and Asian commitments came to the fore? Wildavsky's vision of a few deviant critics bobbing helplessly in a swelling sea of egalitarianism would come as a surprise to many who were close to these programs.

The central issue, of course, remains the contention that "an awful lot of money was invested without accomplishing very much." One of the most recent and perhaps the most comprehensive effort to evaluate the evaluations and reach a general judgment on the Great Society is *The Promise of Greatness* by Sar A. Levitan and Robert Taggart. Having carefully reassessed the small library of data and analyses generated by the infant industry of evaluation, Levitan and Taggart announced that "the 1960s programs and policies and their continuation had a massive, overwhelmingly beneficial impact and that the weight of evidence convincingly supports this view." Though they, too, had been critical of Great Society programs, they now found that dismissing these endeavors as a

---

* Marx characterized this class in different ways: in *Capital*, he discusses in the same place paupers able to work, orphans and paupered children, and those unable to work—the "demoralized and ragged," the elderly, the disabled—as well as "vagabonds, criminals, and prostitutes" who compose the "dangerous classes." It is the latter group, however, who give the term its image; when Marx earlier spoke of "lumpenproletariat" in *Class Struggles in France 1848-1850,* he referred to a mass "strictly differentiated" from the workers, "a recruiting ground for thieves and criminals of all kinds . . . vagabonds, *gens sans feu et sans aveu,"* in short, rabble. This description may fit significant elements in America's ghettoes, but to apply it *grosso modo* to the vast numbers who were to be served by Great Society programs reveals a stereotyping that is more than a little disturbing.

failure had become a fad, indulged in by "discouraged liberals" and "disenchanted proponents" as well as by traditional conservatives. As a result, "the sweeping and erroneous conclusion that the Great Society failed, continues to hold sway over decision makers and the public, generating a timidity and negativism which has retarded needed and possible progress."

Levitan and Taggart agree with many other observers that the Great Society's inflated rhetoric made a later sense of failure inevitable: "We stand at the edge of the greatest era in the life of any nation," Lyndon Johnson declared in June 1964. Nonetheless the more specific goals were realistic; the social-welfare efforts were reasonably efficient; and the "negative spillover effects," though real, were frequently exaggerated.

It is worth noting that a special issue of *The Public Interest* devoted to "The Great Society: Lessons for the Future" had reached a cautious version of some of Levitan and Taggart's conclusions. The issue was not produced by the regular editors but sprang from a conference sponsored by the Ford Foundation, under the guidance of Eli Ginzberg and Robert M. Solow. Ginzberg and Solow seemed to chide—gently—those who were declaring the Great Society a failure, including "some people who would still probably describe themselves as liberals or even liberal Democrats." Like Levitan and Taggart, Ginzberg and Solow seemed to reject conclusively what might be called Kristol's Law of Unintended Consequences:

> There are sometimes unintended and unwanted side effects; and some public programs simply don't work or prove too costly. But there is nothing in the history of the 1960's to suggest that it is a law of nature that social legislation cannot deal effectively with social problems, or that state and local governments or private enterprise will always do better than the "Feds." We can find no support for such sweeping generalizations.

Most remarkable of all is that Aaron Wildavsky, in the article already cited, also grants that "fairly construed, the government's record on social policy during the last decade has been one of vigorous effort and some noteworthy if nevertheless defective accomplishments. . . . Steps have been taken in numerous areas to meet the needs of those who had previously been neglected." How does this jibe with his earlier statement that these programs ate up money without accomplishing much? How does it jibe with the notion that the problems the Great Society confronted are not merely resistant to solution but beyond it? The Great Society was neither so ambitious, nor so novel, nor so ineffective as to suggest that it represented any radically egalitarian departure from past social programs; and neoconservatism repeatedly concedes as much.

Ambiguities of Affirmative Action

There are some differences in the neoconservative case against affirmative action. Nathan Glazer, for example, states in his well-argued polemic *Affirmative Discrimination* that for him, "no consideration of principle—such as that merit should be rewarded, or that governmental programs should not discriminate on grounds of race or ethnic group—would stand in the way of a program of preferential hiring if it made some substantial progress in reducing the severe problems of the low-income black population and of the inner cities." At this point, in other words, Glazer holds to no absolute rejection of affirmative action but reaches a negative judgment on the basis of balancing various principles and factual assessments against one another. At other moments, and like other neoconservatives, Glazer writes of affirmative action and preferential hiring as an abandonment of "the first principle of a liberal society"—that public policy should take account of individual rights and welfare without consideration of group membership.

Many neoconservatives have declared themselves in favor of "genuine" affirmative action, that is, the attempt to search out qualified minority candidates for job openings, widening the pool of applicants as much as possible. But they have been militantly opposed to most of the steps devised to institutionalize and compel such an effort on a large scale—the gathering of racial information about job holders and applicants; the establishment of goals and timetables that, if not met, place the burden of proving a good-faith effort upon employers; a systematic skepticism toward job tests that disproportionately disqualify minority applicants; and the prescription of definite remedial measures (the hiring of a given number of minority candidates, the transfer or promotion of employees identified by race or sex) once discrimination has been found. When New York's school system, after a finding of discrimination, was required to assign new teachers by race, so that blacks and Hispanics would be represented throughout the city's schools and not disproportionately in certain neighborhoods, Daniel Moynihan compared the procedure to nothing less than Hitler's Nuremberg statutes.

Most neoconservatives base their rejection of affirmative action programs on at least several of the pillars of Glazer's argument:

1. In the mid-1960s the nation reached an effective consensus that

racial, religious, and ethnic distinctions had no place in the provision of public services, access to public facilities, public education, employment, and housing.

2. By the end of the sixties, discrimination was no longer a major obstacle to minority progress in employment, and minorities were in fact making considerable gains *before* affirmative action programs were instituted.

3. Lack of skills and ambition, cultural differences, and an understandable hesitance of whites do remain obstacles to black and Hispanic progress in employment, education, and housing; there is no very clear way to deal with these problems.

4. Affirmative-action programs promise no benefits for the inner-city poor who need assistance the most; instead, they boost segments of the minority population which are already rapidly improving their status.

5. Once caught up in the machinery of courts, federal commissions, and other enforcement agencies, affirmative action is transformed into a rigid, costly, and unjust exercise in which statistical compliance drives out any remaining concern for individual qualifications.

6. Affirmative-action programs, as they have evolved, threaten to make identification and distinctive treatment by racial (or social) category a pervasive and permanent aspect of American life, reversing the nation's traditional recognition of the individual's rights and abilities regardless of race, color, sex, or creed.

7. At least one form of educational affirmative action, busing, has proved to be educationally meaningless at the same time it has been politically and socially disruptive.

8. Affirmative action fuels the resentment of whites, especially "ethnics" and lower-to-middle-income groups, who feel that, after having had to "make it on their own," they are being forced to pay an undue proportion of the cost of preferential treatment, not only in taxes but in pressures on *their* schools, jobs, and neighborhoods.

To which one might add an argument advanced less by Glazer than by the black economist Thomas Sowell and several others:

9. While accomplishing few positive results, affirmative action undermines the efforts of successful minority-group members by creating a climate in which it will be assumed that their achievements do not reflect individual worth as much as special consideration.

There is no denying the force of these arguments, especially compared to the uncomplicated faith of the civil rights spokesman who declared, "Goals or quotas, it's really the same thing. Blacks and Hispanic Americans have been discriminated against. We've got to correct the imbalance, possibly at the expense of those who have profited from the system. We don't have enough black doctors, black lawyers, black principals. You have to take a slide rule to make sure all minorities are included. A change has to be made. If the pie is big enough, nobody will be hurt." This is straightforward but it is also oblivious to any of the immediate questions of justice or long-run problems of using racial classifications.

Another liberal position exists, and in fact is probably the dominant one. (How far liberals are from an aggressive unanimity on this topic can be seen in Ladd and Lipset's findings that an overwhelming proportion of the professoriat recognizes the need for greater minority representation in the university but is unwilling to respond by abandoning meritocratic standards.) It holds a contrasting set of premises.

1. Racial discrimination is still deeply embedded in American society, not only in overt prejudice but in inherited patterns of association, culture, and residence that work to perpetuate inequities even after racial prejudice has been eliminated.

2. The progress of blacks and other minorities in the last decade was facilitated by a happy economic situation and a vociferous civil rights movement; neither of these has maintained itself, and the continued economic gains of minorities have become correspondingly uncertain.

3. It is precisely the goal of a movement like that for civil rights in the sixties to institutionalize its demands so that they do not fade with the inevitable loss of the movement's momentum; one form of that institutionalization is government requirements for affirmative action.

4. The dangers of allowing bureaucracies to traffic in racial classifications are quite real; they can lead to absurdities and injustices; but it is possible to oversee this process and, allowing for trial and error, to establish distinctions that answer both the need to overcome a long-standing division in our society and the obligation to respect individual rights.

5. The resentment of whites should be attended to, but not by the abandonment of affirmative action and certainly not by misrepresentation or exaggeration of the advantages it grants minorities.

Both the neoconservative and the dominant liberal positions suffer from what Daniel C. Maguire has called "strategic naiveté." On the liberal part, this has to do with the potential of courts and bureaucratic agencies for implementing a policy requiring fine distinctions. As with the previous liberal illusions of a finely calibrated foreign policy, complete with brushfire wars and pinpoint bombing, or a "fine tuning" of the economy, the blind spot here may be a refusal to admit the inherent limitations of blunt instruments. Glazer, for example, provides an impressive account of legal and bureaucratic escalation and the hardening of flexible notions into rigid requirements.

Yet it is difficult to evaluate much of his evidence. Anecdotal material about affirmative action in the university (which incidentally leans heavily on the same examples and sources throughout the literature) may reflect a stubborn will to misunderstand or even sabotage the effort on the part of administrators as much as the dogmatism of enforcers. Glazer also gives but one side of the evidence. Thus readers are told that the lawyers on the Equal Employment Opportunity Commission increased from thirty to three hundred over several years. Apart from not clarifying that the big increase came when the EEOC was given *enforcement* powers and responsibility by Congress, he does not allude to the huge backlog of cases facing the commission—about 100,000 when he wrote his book.

The strategic naiveté of the neoconservatives is manifested in their optimism about the decline of discrimination in America. They vastly overestimate the degree to which meritocratic standards already operate in institutions like the university—and probably the degree to which they can or even should operate. Studies have documented the importance of personal associations, informal networks, and stereotypes of all sorts in hiring and selection procedures, no less so in the university than elsewhere. To some extent affirmative action has forced institutions to be *more* meritocratic by challenging these habitual practices, and this is no doubt a real source of the annoyance it has provoked. (Complying with affirmative action also suggests an admission that one is part of a generally discriminatory system; this may be particularly irksome to liberal academics. They know that the university has practiced little overt racial discrimination in recent years; but they are often loath to confront the discrimination against women that was blatant only a short time ago and is now often just below the surface.)

Just as the liberal case assumes a bureaucratic competence that may be illusory, the neoconservative case seems to be innocent of the reality of hiring or selecting among candidates for limited openings in a program of studies. Here one cannot avoid a huge element of subjective judgment; ironically it is the very instances where individual talents rather than interchangeable skills count—the professor of philosophy rather than the plumber—that present the most difficulty for definitions of "merit." It is much easier to reach a consensus on what constitutes a good plumber than on what constitutes a good professor of philosophy. In addition one cannot avoid a host of contextual factors, in which the "merit" of the individual is defined by subtle considerations beyond the candidate's control: the balance of skills, interests, or temperaments within a working group, the likelihood of congenial cooperation, the needs of a community which the program is meant to serve, or even the available options of competing candidates. It is true that race and sex are "givens," biological realities that individuals do not choose; but to weigh them in the balance when they serve to redress a wrong or achieve a valid social purpose is only to add them to numerous other "givens."

Neither proponents nor opponents of affirmative action often give much attention to the sloppy reality of selecting individuals for jobs or advancement.

A black assistant principal in an integrated New York school dies. At a parents' meeting, a white parent points out that for all her desire to see her children grow up in a racially mixed environment, they are developing a very negative attitude toward black males. "All they see are the drunkies hanging out by the Paragon Theater, the young men strung out on drugs, the teen-agers who threaten them. Mr. Richards was an important model for my kids—a hard-working, gentle, and friendly black man who also held a position of respect and authority." Black parents agree. Is the parents' association mistaken in pushing for a black replacement for Mr. Richards, if a qualified candidate is available?

Fifty young scholars apply for a single teaching position at an out-of-the-way college. The selection committee agrees that virtually all of them are qualified—indeed, "overqualified." They reduce the list to those who hold degrees from the top few graduate departments in that discipline, a process they recognize as rather arbitrary but at least indicative of some difference. The final choice appears almost totally arbitrary, but the chairman of the department (and of the committee), who is notorious for discriminating against women in the past, thinks he can please the dean by choosing a woman and "meeting HEW guidelines." He lets it be known that the position must be filled by a woman. Would a toss of a coin be more fair?

A program for advanced studies in a field bearing directly upon public policy offers several fellowships each year to encourage young researchers. The selection committee is painfully aware, from past mistakes, of the difficulty of awarding these fellowships, of the critical role of characteristics that were unforeseen despite the most careful examination of dossiers and intensive interviewing. There are no minority members and only a few women prominent in the field, though the perspective of both categories is extremely relevant to the kind of problems encountered. Even when inferior applications are received from minority members and women, special attention is given to them; sometimes extra cost is incurred so that these candidates can be interviewed, although white male applicants with original submissions of equal quality are not interviewed. In this case, none of these candidates initially submitting inferior dossiers happens to be chosen; but there is no question that the women and minority members among them have had a special chance to demonstrate their qualifications. Was the procedure unjustified?

These are real, though disguised, cases. Reasonable people could easily disagree on the proper course of action. The objection to weighing in race and sex (assuming that ascertainable qualifications remain the main standard of choice) is less that these are unachieved characteristics than that, as the courts put it, they are "suspect" categories, historically liable to abuse and only delegitimated as the basis for distinctions through long struggles. Does any reference to them now risk a thoroughgoing re-legitimation? How serious are the problems that would justify running such risk? Both liberals and neoconservatives can appeal to Edmund Burke's dictum: "Circumstances (which with some gentlemen pass for nothing) give in reality to every political principle its distinguishing color and discriminating effect. The circumstances are what render every civil and political scheme beneficial or noxious to mankind." None of these examples, furthermore, directly involves the fixed numbers that have proved so controversial—the percentage of entering medical-school classes set aside for minority applicants, the percentage of contracts a federal agency gives to minority firms, the precise formulas for school integration or minority employment ordered by courts. In one sense such numbers only represent the same murky problems raised to the institutional level; they can also be seen as the bureaucratic incarnation of what Moynihan called the "traditional and established framework" of ethnic politics, that is, the balanced ticket, the City Hall connection, the gerrymandered district. But precisely because they are institutional and bureaucratic, formal rather than informal, these schemes have a perilous aspect.

What is clear is not that neoconservatives are mistaken in their detailed criticism of affirmative action but that they are mistaken in interpreting this debate as a drastic revision of our notions of equality. Opinion in the courts, the administrative agencies, and the civil rights organizations continues to swing back and forth, to jiggle nervously around this or that issue. The point of equilibrium is far from established. Neoconservatism itself has had some hand in this swaying of opinion, but there have always been numerous countervailing impulses at work. The ambiguities and tensions in our ideals, especially as they are measured in the difficult task of redressing longstanding patterns of discrimination, seem to have been no more thrown over by most serious analysts of affirmative action than they were by Moynihan in 1965. Affirmative action, like the Great Society, represents an egalitarian thrust but one that remains tempered.

Neoconservative Fears

Little in the debate over affirmative action and less in the record of the Great Society suggests we are approaching the egalitarian precipice. It is the flickering light of neoconservative fears that has cast the Great Society and affirmative action and the rather moderate egalitarian impulse of recent years into outsized and ominous shadows. To those fears we should turn directly.

Equality versus liberty. A conspicuous sign of the passage from liberalism to neoconservatism has been the revival of the notion that preoccupied the nineteenth century, the conflict between equality and liberty. Not that an earlier liberalism denied the tension that could exist between equality and liberty, but it refused to harden this tension into an irreducible opposition and then place it at the center of political analysis. The premise of that opposition was either that liberty could be nurtured and protected only by an aristocracy or an establishment of independent wealth—this was the conservative belief—or that liberty was nothing but free and individual contract and therefore threatened by any exertion of government aimed at relieving the condition of those in need—this was the *laissez-faire* liberal or the Spencerian belief. In the 1950s it was the political Right in America that had inherited these discordant postures. When Daniel Bell took up the topic of equality in *The End of Ideology* it was to refute the anti-egalitarian and "aristocratic" criticism of mass society; and scarcely anyone addressed the apprehension that welfare-state measures were stifling American liberties—was this not the hoary complaint of anti-Roosevelt diehards? It would be difficult to imagine today's neoconservatives assenting in 1955, as they apparently did in 1975, to Daniel Moynihan's identification of the United States with the "liberty party" as against the "equality party." They would have squirmed at the opposition, confident that the United States was both.

The neoconservatives are not unaware that liberty in some measure assumes equality. One can have equality without liberty but not liberty without equality. To be free of others' power means, in some crucial respect, to be equal to them. Yet the problem for now, writes Daniel Bell, is "the contrast and not the conjunction" between liberty and equality.

The reason is the alleged transformation of equality of opportunity into equality of result or condition. That the two cannot be so precisely distinguished and that a healthy degree of the second as well as of the first is necessary for the flourishing of liberty are truths that the neoconservatives know because they are the commonplaces of political philosophy. Great inequalities of wealth are a danger to free government; and even short of such grave danger, the man who can wield a thousand times the political influence of another because he has made (or inherited) a fortune can reasonably be said to have limited the latter's liberty. The concern of egalitarians with great riches has been far less with the excessive consumption than with the excessive power they afford.

The relationship between equality of condition and liberty is also affected by the definition of liberty one has in mind. A purely "negative" liberty—the "right to be left alone," the absence of coercion by other people? Or some concept of "positive" liberty—a capacity for self-determination, the ability to share actively in political life and to exercise one's natural gifts? The compatibility or incompatibility of these notions is, of course, the subject of much political thought; but to the degree that one is concerned about positive as well as negative liberty, one will also be concerned about equality of condition. Neoconservatism, so far, has straddled this issue. Like the American liberal tradition generally, it values negative liberty as an absolute prerequisite, but it further advocates a reflective and self-disciplined personality that implies the ideal of positive liberty.

Neoconservatism has in fact been vague about the liberty it views itself defending against the onslaught of equality. Certainly it is the freedom from the racial categorization seen operating in affirmative action. It is freedom from government intervention into the university. But otherwise, is it primarily freedom from government regulation for large and small businesses? (Incidentally, it takes a stretch of terminology to attribute much of this regulation to egalitarian passion; preservation of the environment and protection of workers are natural expressions of government's concern for health, safety, and general welfare.) Neoconservatives have manifested small concern for the rights of dissent this side of the Iron Curtain. They excoriate the courts for extending the reach of government in busing and other questions of discrimination; but they have been lukewarm or negative toward legal efforts that limit government power, in areas like abortion, freedom of the press, school discipline, and the rights of prisoners, mental patients, and welfare recipients.

The opposition between liberty and equality, then, can be translated into several specifics. Negatively, it is a useful rhetorical gambit that portrays the advocates of equality as the enemies of freedom. Positively, it is a warning against the excesses of affirmative action; the championing of entrepreneurial freedom against government regulation; and the demand that well-established institutions, particularly those envisioned as providing social cohesion, be free to keep their own houses in order without government interference on the side of dissatisfied minorities.

Equality versus meritocracy. Neoconservatives are entirely correct in identifying one current of our time: the attack on professional authority and technical expertise. In 1967, Paul Goodman attempted to teach a graduate course on "Professionalism" at the New School for Social Research; his students utterly rejected the concept and the distinctions it implied. Yet this was not a phenomenon limited to angry students in the sixties or dropouts in the seventies; nor to the more subtle but equally radical analyses of Ivan Illich. It was reflected in the impatience of ordinary citizens with the medical profession and the consequent demand for patients' rights; in the complaints against the law profession and demands for greater access to legal assistance; in the flood of books and classes and self-help groups promising the possibility of becoming one's own doctor, lawyer, architect, auto mechanic, and (perhaps for native Americans) Indian chief. Neoconservatism sees in this mood a populist leveling, a resentment against "the authority represented in the superior competence of individuals." Again, the shift from equality of opportunity to equality of condition is said to be at fault. Equality of opportunity allows and encourages "every individual to better himself by means of his own exertions" and honors the distinctions based on those exertions. Equality of condition, on the other hand, rejects all such distinctions, in terms both of authority and of rewards. It rejects the meritocracy.

There are several ways in which this neoconservative explanation misses the mark. First, much of the hostility to professional authority and expertise does not express a rejection of "superior competence"; it expresses a disbelief, often backed with evidence, that the claimed competence is actually superior—or even competent. It is especially skeptical when the claim is based on some system of official credentials. Here the principle that superiority deserves special consideration is not at stake. The objection is directed toward this or that supposed instance of superiority—are the services provided by physicians or auto mechanics really ones most people couldn't provide for themselves or one another?—or toward the validity of the official tests of such claims—does a medical degree indicate a genuine skill at caring for the ill? Willingness to believe the evidence advanced against the competence of "experts" is no doubt affected by resentment at the special prerogatives that often accompany expert status; but the ground of the dispute is still the quality of the evidence rather than the principle of equality. Doubts about the credentialed expert—about "book-larnin' " and "know-it-alls"—have long coexisted in America with a respect for what was conceded to be "genuine," demonstrated talent.

Neoconservatives also exaggerate the attitude of those interested in greater equality of condition. Very few advocates of income redistribution have anything like leveling in mind; nor do critics of meritocracy object to any and all distinctions flowing from different talents or exertions—they object to the range of distinctions that *currently* flow from these things, and that, as we shall see, is a different matter.

Each faction in this debate entertains suspicions about the other. The neoconservatives suspect that the anti-meritocrats undervalue excellence and high cultural standards. An anti-meritocratic victory would relax the pressures for quality and blur the criteria by which quality is recognized. A sentimental refusal to admit differences in talent and character would squander resources on those that can benefit little from them and deprive those who can benefit greatly.

The anti-meritocrats, for their part, feel that talk of equality of opportunity and meritocracy is used to justify inequalities that have nothing to do with merit. "Most social systems need a lightning-conductor," wrote R.H. Tawney. "The formula which supplies it to our own is equality of opportunity." Tawney also outlined what he called the "Tadpole Philosophy":

> It is possible that intelligent tadpoles reconcile themselves to the inconveniences of their position, by reflecting that, though most of them will live and die as tadpoles and nothing more, the more fortunate of the species will one day shed their tails, distend their mouths and stomachs, hop nimbly on to dry land, and croak addresses to their former friends on the virtues by means of which tadpoles of character and capacity can rise to be frogs. This conception of society may be described, perhaps, as the Tadpole Philosophy, since the consolation which it offers for social evils consists in the statement that exceptional individuals can succeed in evading them. . . . Who has not encountered the argument that there is an educational "ladder" up which talent can climb. . . . As though opportunities for talent to rise could be equalized in a society where the circumstances surrounding it from birth are themselves unequal! . . . As though the noblest use of exceptional powers were to scramble to shore, undeterred by the thought of drowning companions.

Are not meritocratic theories, insofar as they suggest that present society is or is becoming stratified by merit, simply the croaking of the successful Tadpoles in celebration of their own frogginess? One well-known sociologist expressed his irritation at the neoconservatives' apparent satisfaction with the social order by saying that they "bring to mind an encounter with an old-time Chinese gentleman many years ago. When discussing the failures of the Chinese prerevolutionary regime, I happened to remark upon its unconscionably high infant mortality rate. 'The thing has been exaggerated,' he said, 'after all, *I* survived.' "

Whatever the truth behind these suspicions of motive and intention, there are at least three points of principled difference between the defenders of meritocracy and those who would increase equality of condition. The first two points can be illustrated by turning to John Rawls's *A Theory of Justice*.

Rawls has been a curious presence in this conflict. It is doubtful that the critics of meritocracy ever drew upon his work for their criticism, or even looked to it much for reinforcement after *A Theory of Justice* finally appeared in 1971. But the book was received among some neoconservatives with something approaching hysteria. Robert Nisbet reviewed it in *The Public Interest,* comparing Rawls to Rousseau and the eighteenth-century *philosophes* inhabiting Parisian salons (the consummate case of wickedness in Nisbet's mental world). To this thoroughly inept parallel, he added an almost willful misreading of Rawls's argument. Irving Kristol managed to link Rawls with New York City's financial problems. (The Securities and Exchange Commission, in calling numerous politicians and bankers on the carpet for their roles in New York's crises, somehow overlooked the Harvard philosopher.)

Nisbet, Kristol, Aaron Wildavsky, and Seymour Martin Lipset all take from Rawls not Rawls's theory in its complexity but what they assume that liberal egalitarians will make of him. Rawls's insistence, for example, on "the priority of liberty" is ignored or set aside, perhaps because it would be inconvenient to discover such sentiments in the egalitarian enemy. Daniel Bell and Charles Frankel add to the chorus making Rawls a monument of the "new" egalitarianism (it is worth pointing out that the nugget of Rawls's book was published in 1958, which means that not only can we say, with Wildavsky and Kristol, that Rawls is the after-the-fact rationalization of the new equality, he is also the before-the-fact anticipation of it); but Bell and Frankel are considerably more scrupulous and generous in their rendition of *A Theory of Justice*. Frankel's critique, published in *Commentary,* is temperate and engaging. He makes a number of points that are common to the philosophical criticism of Rawls's work: the problem of the abstract and detached character of its "pure theory"; the difficulty of identifying the "least well-off," whose condition is a touchstone in his scheme for judging the morality of inequalities; the potential of Rawls's theory for justifying any degree of inequality as long as some benefit, no matter how little, trickles down to the poor. (Most neoconservatives seem unaware that such aspects of Rawls's argument have left many politically active egalitarians quite chary of embracing it.) Frankel also cites Rousseau favorably, quotes Spinoza's statement that "if equality of conditions be once laid aside, liberty perishes," and entertains a most direct conception of the egalitarian ethic:

> It was a conviction that there are people of power and feeling hidden away in all sectors of society, and that life would be richer if they were found. It

was the suspicion that there is nothing like being on top to make a man a windbag, and that it does everybody a world of good to see him slip on a banana peel. It was the knowledge that the rich and powerful, not necessarily through malice but simply as a reflex of who they were and what they had, would have a natural tendency to try to form a closed club and keep others out.

When not appearing in *Commentary,* that is the sort of thing that provokes neoconservatives to quote de Tocqueville on envy and Max Scheler on *ressentiment.*

In the midst of the neoconservatives' flap over Rawls, two points emerge where his work clearly joins issue with the defenders of meritocracy. First, it is inequality of condition, not equality, that must be justified, that sits, so to speak, in the defendant's seat. Or at least this is true once the foundations of the argument are constructed and allowed. The defenders of a "just meritocracy" are not absolutely forced to brook at this point, for they allege to possess a principle, namely *merit,* that can in fact justify inequalities. But clearly neoconservatives do not like the change in climate this starting point implies: it threatens the meritocracy by constantly putting it on the defensive. To hold strictly to equality of opportunity as a value virtually assumes that inequality of condition results. A current condition of inequality may be due to the natural operation of equal opportunities as different individuals take advantages of these opportunities in different ways. Or it may not—it may be due to blocked chances, inherited privilege, and so on. But at the start one doesn't really know and presumably would not be led to investigate whether the connection really exists unless the inequalities were egregious. For the stability of the meritocracy, the latter, "neutral" starting point is obviously preferable.

The second point is far more crucial. Are the differences between individuals that a meritocracy would reward to be ascribed to individual responsibility or not? Neoconservatism indicates they are. Neoconservatives use language like "exertions," "efforts," and "achievements" in describing these differences. When Christopher Jencks found that variations in income between individuals could not be highly attributable to differences in family background, schooling, IQ, or some *a priori* notion of competence, he called the residual factor explaining success "luck." Daniel Patrick Moynihan replied, why not call it "pluck"? These are all active terms implying personal responsibility and moral worth. Rawls, on the other hand, speaks of the individual differences that are differentially rewarded by a meritocracy as "natural assets," "endowments," even the "natural lottery"—passive terms implying arbitrariness and moral neutrality. The conception of justice he seeks would not only nullify the "contingencies of social circumstance"—here the neoconservatives might agree, at least in theory—but also "the accidents of natural endowment."

Rawls describes, first, a "system of natural liberty" that would accept as just whatever distribution followed from a formal equality of opportunity in which legal barriers to talent are absent. He further describes a "liberal interpretation" of distributive justice that would not only require formal equality of opportunity but insist that class disadvantages should be mitigated so that the talented poor could in actuality take advantage of these open opportunities. But finally he writes:

> While the liberal conception seems clearly preferable to the system of natural liberty, intuitively it still appears defective. For one thing, even if it works to perfection in eliminating the influence of social contingencies, it still permits the distribution of wealth and income to be determined by the natural distribution of abilities and talents. Within the limits allowed by the background arrangements, distributive shares are decided by the outcome of the natural lottery; and this outcome is arbitrary from a moral perspective. There is no more reason to permit the distribution of income and wealth to be settled by the distribution of natural assets than by historical and social fortune. . . . The extent to which natural capacities develop and reach fruition is affected by all kinds of social conditions and class attitudes. Even the willingness to make an effort, to try, and so to be deserving in the ordinary sense is itself dependent upon happy family and social circumstances.

Rawls drives the point home later: "The assertion that a man deserves the superior character that enables him to make the effort to cultivate his abilities is equally problematic; for his character depends in large part upon fortunate family and social circumstances for which he can claim no credit."

This, says Frankel, is the "fundamental premise" of the new egalitarianism. It may hold true in some thoroughly abstract and ultimate sense but it is irrelevant to the real problems of human justice:

> If we look at matters from a less remote perspective, the man of twenty, in possession of a superior character that enables him to cultivate his abilities, can usually be shown to have done *something* to produce this character. Has there been no hard work, inner discipline, lacerating struggle with his soul? Is it all the throw of the dice?

Frankel's concern, and it is an underlying theme of neoconservatism, is easily appreciated: "a theory of justice which treats the individual as not an active participant in the determination of his fate, and which is guided by the model of life as a lottery, is unlikely to strengthen people's sense of personal responsibility."

But an uncharacteristic false note in Frankel's language points to a problem: he writes of the twenty-year-old's "lacerating struggle with his soul," and this touch of romantic agony alerts us to the possibility that Frankel protests too much. There is little evidence to suggest that students passing from elite colleges to Harvard or Yale medical school have been lacerating their souls in struggle any more, and quite possibly less, than the inner-city youth who resists hustling on the street for an honest job at a gas station. Nor is it clear that the inner discipline required by MIT and Harvard Business School is any more than that required to fulfill one's duties as parent and provider while working on an assembly line or at a supermarket. Some individuals struggle and work mightily; others nurture their talents with all the ease of breathing. But it is not hard work, discipline, and lacerating struggles with one's soul that the meritocracy singles out and rewards—except where these happen to coincide with natural talent, economic demand, and other factors having little to do with individual *moral* merit.

Nor has Frankel adequately responded to the point Rawls makes, and which most people know from their everyday observation—that capacities for hard work and discipline, initiative and ambition, are often enough either natural traits or the outcome of favorable family circumstances and early experiences. There is something in the cosmic viewpoint of a "natural lottery" and the passive image of "endowment" rather than "achievement" to which Frankel rightly objects; but the conclusion obtains, not that we should deny the truth in one or another characterization, but that we simply remain unable to determine the admixture of natural gifts and personal responsibility that constitute individual differences, and we must shape a social system in light of this unalterable limitation. In this regard, Rawls's "difference principle," which justifies inequalities of reward and opportunities as long as they eventually work to the benefit of the least advantaged, appears to be a respectable solution.

At this point Bell and Frankel, though they are among the most careful of Rawls's neoconservative critics, misrepresent him slightly. Frankel indirectly suggests that Rawls holds that "it is morally wrong for a society to notice, approve, or reward outstanding gifts, particularly when the individuals who have these gifts have played some part in developing them." Bell cites Rawls's belief that his theory covers the considerations stated by others under a "principle of redress":

> This is the principle that undeserved inequalities call for redress; and since the inequalities of birth and natural endowment are undeserved, these inequalities are to be somehow compensated for. . . . Society must give more attention to those with fewer native assets and to those born into the less favorable social position. . . . Greater resources might be spent on the

education of the less rather than the more intelligent, at least over a certain time of life. . . .

But Bell does not cite the qualifications in Rawls's following paragraph:

> Now the principle of redress has not to my knowledge been proposed as the sole criterion of justice. . . . It is plausible . . . only as a prima facie principle, one that is to be weighed in the balance with others.

Furthermore,

> the difference principle is *not* of course the principle of redress. It does not require society to try to even out handicaps as if all were expected to compete on a fair basis in the same race. But the difference principle would allocate resources in education, say, so as to improve the long-term expectation of the least favored. *If this end is attained by giving more attention to the better endowed, it is permissible; otherwise not.* [My emphasis.]

In other words, it is not at all wrong for society to reward outstanding gifts, as long as such unequal rewards promise to work for the eventual benefit of the less fortunate. This does, as Rawls says and Bell correctly emphasizes, represent "an agreement to regard the distribution of natural talents as a common asset and to share in the benefits of the distribution whatever it turns out to be. Those who have been favored by nature, whoever they are, may gain from their good fortune on terms that improve the situation of those who have lost out."

One may wish to qualify the single-minded stress on "nature" and "good fortune" but nevertheless find here a reasonable compromise that allows special treatment for special abilities and yet, in view of the impossibility of sorting out the effects of the "natural lottery" from those of personal responsibility, conditions such inequality on the benefit it does the least favored. Though Daniel Bell elaborates the difficulties of Rawls's position, his appeals for "a just meritocracy" finally seek justification in a very similar position: "a university has to be a meritocracy if the resources of the society . . . are to be spent *for 'mutual advantage,'* . . . the principle of meritocracy should . . . obtain in business and government as well. One wants entrepreneurs and innovators who can expand the amount of productive wealth *for society.* . . . Nor is this in contradiction with the fairness principle." (My emphasis.) In general, however, neoconservatism distrusts the Rawlsian compromise, preferring to encourage personal effort and responsibility by carrying on "as if" these were the essential elements of individual differences. This runs the risk of a new Calvinism in which the fact of success becomes itself the evidence that it was morally

deserved. But the alternative, apparently, is intolerable to neoconservatism: that inequalities, first, bear the burden of being justified and,
second, be justified by reference to their impact on the disadvantaged.

There is a third point at which the issue is joined between defenders of
meritocracy and their critics. It was most elegantly stated by Michael
Walzer in a response to Irving Kristol. Kristol had argued that (1) "human
talents and abilities . . . distribute themselves along a bell-shaped curve";
(2) "in all modern bourgeois societies, the distribution of income is also
along a bell-shaped curve"; and (3) "the political structure—the distribution of political power—follows along the same way." Kristol has some
difficulty fitting the Soviet Union into this pattern, but no matter: as
Walzer sums up the argument, "in the United States, nature is triumphant: we are perfectly bell-shaped." Kristol, to be sure, is wrong
about income distribution; but that is not Walzer's concern. He points to
another flaw: "It is a neat argument, but also a peculiar one, for there is
no reason to think that 'human talents and abilities' in fact distribute
themselves along a *single* curve."

> Consider the range and variety of human capacities: intelligence, physical
> strength, agility and grace, artistic creativity, mechanical skill, leadership,
> endurance, memory, psychological insight, the capacity for hard work—
> even, moral strength, sensitivity, the ability to express compassion. Let's
> assume that with respect to all these, most people (but different people in
> each case) cluster around the middle of whatever scale we can construct,
> with smaller numbers at the lower and higher ends. Which of these curves is
> actually echoed by the income bell? Which, if any, ought to be?

The problem, of course, is money. It, too, is distributed according to
the curve of the talent for making it (considerably modified by inheritance
and luck), and this, says Walzer, "might be morally plausible"—"People
who are able to make money ought to make money, in the same way that
people who are able to write books ought to write books. Every human
talent should be developed and expressed." But money, alas, is not its
own reward.

> In a capitalist world, money is the universal medium of exchange. . . .
> Political power, celebrity, admiration, leisure, works of art, baseball teams,
> legal advice, sexual pleasure, travel, education, medical care, rare books,
> sailboats—all these (and much more) are up for sale. The list is as endless as
> human desire and social invention. Now isn't it odd, and morally implausible
> and unsatisfying, that all these things should be distributed to people with a
> talent for making money? And even odder and more unsatisfying that they
> should be distributed (as they are) to people who have money, whether or
> not they made it, whether or not they possess any talent at all?

But Walzer is not simply campaigning against the rich.

> It would not be any better if we gave men money in direct proportion to their intelligence, their strength, or their moral rectitude. The resulting distributions would each, no doubt, reflect what Kristol calls "the tyranny of the bell-shaped curve," though it is worth noticing again that the populations in the lower, middle, and upper regions of each graph would be radically different. But whether it was the smart, the strong, or the righteous who enjoyed all the things that money can buy, the oddity would remain: why them? Why anybody? In fact, there is no single talent or combination of talents which plausibly entitles a man to every available social good. . . . Nor need there be a single distribution of all social goods, for different goods might well be distributed differently. Nor again need all the distributions follow this or that talent curve, for in the sharing of some social goods, talent does not seem a relevant consideration at all.

In short, concludes Walzer, "What egalitarianism requires is that many bells should ring. Different goods should be distributed to different people for different reasons." The neoconservatives assume that society must be stratified; that, after all, is the "-cracy" (-*kratia*, rule, power) in "meritocracy." Indeed Rawls resembles them insofar as he largely casts his theory in terms of a single axis of advantage/disadvantage. Against such views, Walzer is maintaining that if there be stratification, there should not be one but many. And one way of achieving such a situation is to limit the power of wealth and the sphere of money in society. There are many ways in which this could be done, of which but one is "a radical redistribution of wealth." The power of money in areas like medical care, the legal system and politics must be restricted; but "so long as money is convertible outside its sphere, it must be widely and more or less equally held so as to minimize its distorting effects upon legitimate distributive processes." Once again, Daniel Bell accedes to much of Walzer's argument; he had already written that in his version of the meritocracy "the question of justice arises" when those at the top (Walzer would question the necessity of *the* top) can convert their positions into large, discrepant material and social advantages over others." But again neoconservatism in general has ignored the point. The version of meritocracy it defends promises the fullest range of income, power, and privilege for those deemed talented, disciplined, and full of "pluck."

Equality versus legitimacy. Equality threatens liberty. Equality threatens meritocracy. And finally equality threatens American governmental power itself. Not only liberty but "authority" is declining, writes Nisbet, and equality is the culprit. Equality, writes Kristol, is only the latest expression of that subversive discontent with which intellectuals have gnawed at the legitimacy of government for two millennia. Central to the "democratic surge" which is rendering the United States ungovernable, according to Samuel P. Huntington's report for the Trilateral Commission, is "a reassertion of the primacy of equality." Perhaps Aaron Wildavsky states the neoconservative fear most clearly: America is being attacked at its most vulnerable point, its longstanding promise of equality.

Despite the acknowledged ability of America to honor equality in principle while denying it in practice, the force of the ideal strikes neoconservatives as almost irresistible—it is usually necessary (and apparently sufficient) to quote de Tocqueville on this point. But the force is simultaneously assumed to be more or less irrational—"passion," "obsession," and "impulse" come naturally to neoconservatives as descriptions of the egalitarian tendency. Equality propels the populace to desire what they cannot reasonably have, and to demand of government what it cannot practicably do. Envy and *ressentiment* are the hidden fuels of egalitarianism, although less so for the ordinary man than for the ambitious and factious "new class." But what appears worst of all is the effect of equality upon those in power and authority: it riddles them with guilt, it saps their determination to defend their patrimony. "There was too much guilt engendered by the rhetoric of equality," Wildavsky concludes, to permit resistance to the obviously foolhardy Great Society programs. "I would suggest that a liberal culture does indeed succeed in breeding aggression out of its privileged classes," pronounced Moynihan to Harvard alumni in 1976, "and that after a period in which this enriches the culture, it begins to deplete it."

Internationally, where the degree of inequality is so much greater and so much more visible, it follows that the situation is still more perilous. The United States and Western multinational corporations are faced with Third World claims drawing on our own rhetoric of equality. In neoconservatism's estimate, the result has been nothing less than "appeasement" on our part. In response, P. T. Bauer, a British economist, assured *Commentary*'s readers that twinges of guilt in regard to Third World poverty were groundless and—certainly for the sake of the impoverished as well as of ourselves—to be resisted. The acceptance of the allegation that the West was responsible for this poverty had provoked such guilt as to have "paralyzed Western diplomacy, both toward the Soviet bloc and toward the Third World, where the West has abased itself before groups of countries which have negligible resources and no real power." (Of course, Bauer held it a "delusion" to believe that his arguments against Western responsibility "could substantially influence the attitudes of those afflicted by a feeling of guilt. . . . Argument and evidence will not affect conduct and measures which are rooted in emotion. . . .")

Robert Moss, a British journalist favored by *Commentary*, made much the same argument in *The New York Times Magazine* under the title "Let's Look Out for No. 1!" On every side, complained Moss, "we are hectored" by those who "appeal to the guilty conscience of the well-fed with images of starving millions" and "lecture us on our moral obligation for the supposed crimes of colonialism and capitalist exploitation." Moss admits that this hectoring has not thus far accomplished very much, but "in the long run, can we ignore either the moral appeal or the threat?" He hopes so.

Bauer and Moss were enlarging the front opened up by Daniel Moynihan. Starting in 1975, Moynihan argued that the United States was besieged internationally by a new form of redistributionist socialism; in concentrating on the cruder dangers of Communism, we had failed to develop the ideological antibodies to this subtler threat. Later he merged the Communist and socialist challenge, and evoked "the superior capacity of Marxist argument to induce guilt." Liberal society was "torn by doubts" about its possibly insufficient generosity. Moynihan quoted Yeats, "Come fix upon me that accusing eye. I thirst for accusation," which also happened to be the lines quoted at the head of Bauer's article.

There is yet another reason why neoconservatism views equality as dangerous. Equality, in this view, is an aspiration that can never be assuaged. For Kristol, Nisbet, and to some degree Frankel, equality is but a surrogate issue for intellectuals, whose real aim is to solve the problem of evil, compensate for the loss of religious meaning, or destroy bourgeois society and extend their power through the state. For neoconservatives generally, equality is relentless in its demands because, in Nathan Glazer's words, "as it proceeds we become ever more sensitive to smaller and smaller degrees of inequality" as well as to new kinds of inequality. "The slogan of 'equality' in any society at all will continue to arouse passions and lead to discontent."

Daniel Bell agrees:

> As disparities have decreased . . . the expectations of equality have increased even faster, and people make more invidious comparisons . . . a phenomenon now commonly known as the "Tocqueville effect." The revolution of rising expectations is also the revolution of rising *ressentiment*. . . . The fascinating sociological puzzle is why . . . as inequality decreases, *ressentiment* increases.

Equality "in the highly limited sense Jefferson intended" is one thing, writes Nisbet.

> It is an entirely different matter when equality of economic and social condition becomes a god for the intellectual or politician. Expectations cannot do other than increase exponentially. Envy . . . quickly takes

command, and the lust for power with which to allay every fresh discontent, to assuage every social pain, and to gratify every fresh expectation soon becomes boundless.

It is not surprising that for Nisbet *equality* and *redistribution* are "code words" for revolution.

Among other neoconservatives perhaps only Kristol would go so far. Most view equality as a serious threat something this side of revolution. It is an attractive and, in America, honored ideal, all the more dangerous for that very reason. It must be kept in a tight harness. Equality before the law, forbidding rich and poor alike to steal bread and sleep under bridges, and equality of opportunity, offering every individual the equal chance at becoming unequal, must be sharply distinguished from equality of condition. The expectations of citizens must be curtailed and the confidence of elites maintained—or government will be overwhelmed and implode into tyranny. On both counts the moral claims of egalitarianism are baneful.

Neoconservatism declares that it favors the relief of poverty, international as well as domestic. Poverty, after all, is destabilizing as well as inherently degrading. With liberal interest in equality focused on problems of poverty, it would seem that, practically, a large field exists for common action; in some instances, like welfare reform, this may be the case. But neoconservatism's desire to abolish poverty is carefully hedged, and not to be confused with achieving equality. "I have no objection to a properly conducted assault on poverty," says Nisbet, and almost all neoconservatives say something similar. "But why seek to bring it within the rhetoric of the new equality?" The hedges are several.

To begin with, there is little to be done about much poverty—about the underclass at home and a good part of the developing world. Furthermore, neoconservatives (a) emphasize data leading to the conclusion that poverty in the United States or overseas is being steadily abolished, and (b) simultaneously stress the costs, human as well as economic, of doing this through planned redistribution. *"We have abolished poverty in New York City!"* insists Kristol. (His emphasis.) But isn't this the false triumph of "notoriously compassionate" politicians? Hasn't New York's high level of welfare benefits actually made things worse? "A visitor to the Greek islands, or to an Italian village, is impressed first of all not by the poverty of the people there—which is acute—but by their cheerfulness, their determination to make the best of things, their extraordinary ability to do so." For New York's poor, on the other hand, "it is not at all implausible to think that, had we been less generous in our welfare programs, these people would now be better off." In sum, because we must abide what cannot be helped and because government intervention is often worse than letting the economy take its course, it is all the more important that efforts to relieve poverty do not establish principles or practices likely to get out of hand. Anti-poverty measures must be carefully calculated so as not to tax our resources nor breed dissatisfaction nor hatch political turmoil. By elimination, what neoconservatism would welcome as a *"properly conducted* assault on poverty" appears to be an effort that is tightly managed from the top down, by an elite acting out of charity and something akin to *noblesse oblige.*

Preparing for Straitened Circumstances

How justified are neoconservative fears of equality? In the short run, they seem vastly inflated. It is a special kind of freedom that appears threatened by equality, and it is less equality than the modern web of interdependence that expands government action and regulation. Just as a considerable degree of equality—of condition as well as of opportunity— is the prerequisite for a flourishing liberty, it is also a prerequisite for the assumption of personal responsibility and the general recognition and reward of individual gifts. Equality may challenge the legitimacy of American institutions—but that largely depends on the capacity of those institutions to respond to the challenge.

Neoconservatives are pessimistic and resistant on the latter point, and that is why their fears have a significance for the long run. They sense a loss of room for maneuvering, a constriction of opportunities, a diminishment of flexibility, that will render even moderate abatements of inequality possible only on condition that we risk a major alteration in the social and economic structures. If the economic growth following World War II turns out to be the exception, and the straitened circumstances of recent years the rule, then the neoconservatives may well be right. We will be able to maintain the status quo only by keeping a tight cap on the claims of equality.

Why do neoconservatives expend so much energy attacking socialism as the embodiment of equality and state control, when in fact socialism is profoundly ambivalent on both these points ("from each according to his abilities, to each according to his needs" is, in many respects, an *in*-egalitarian formula), at least as much so as welfare-state liberalism? Though socialism is hardly a short-run contender for power in America, are neoconservatives, in effect, admitting that our ability to tinker with the present system has reached its limits, and the real choice is between a massive restructuring of society or the renunciation of egalitarianism altogether?

For those who would retain their commitment to greater equality, and even conceive of forms of socialism that respect and enhance liberty, responsibility, and individual merit, the neoconservative critique of egalitarianism nonetheless can be useful. There is a rote return to the existence of poverty, the concentration of wealth in America, the vast disparity between American and Third World consumption of food, energy, and nonrenewable materials, as though these inequalities, sometimes disputed, sometimes shockingly clear, of themselves resolved a host of economic, political, legal, and diplomatic issues. There does exist a vulgar materialism among reformers that is too willing to reduce all questions to a statistical sharing of the pie, that does throw up the facts of material inequalities as a screen before all the murkier and perhaps more trying questions of culture and spirit. It is possible to take to heart the neoconservative warning that indignation about inequality, as distinguished from stark poverty, may be a deflection from other issues, without accepting the implications, typically reductionist, that this is always the case, that the problems of inequality would no longer be posed once these other issues were openly confronted, and that the groping of egalitarians with more ultimate issues of social meaning or universal justice are immature or unworthy. The neoconservative attitude toward inequality and "merit" is even more vulnerable to charges of self-interest and no less concerned about finding a justification for an order of things they feel will always be unequal and hierarchical.

Of neoconservative fears about equality, it can also be said what John Stuart Mill wrote of de Tocqueville. Mill, of course, was a great admirer of *Democracy in America;* but reviewing de Tocqueville's volumes long before they had become, as they have for neoconservatism, a kind of sacred scripture, he offered a major criticism. De Tocqueville had "bound up in one abstract idea the whole of the tendencies of modern commercial society" and given the impression of ascribing "to equality of conditions" the range of effects—mobility, "want of deference," shallow culture, disregard of tradition, "habitual dissatisfaction," "the decay of authority," and "diminution of respect for traditional opinions"—that rather arise from modern economic progress itself. According to Mill, "Nearly all those moral and social influences" that de Tocqueville's second volume found operating in democratic, egalitarian America "are shown to be in full operation in aristocratic England." The reason was the spirit of commerce and industry as carried by the English middle class; it was, though Mill did not use the term, the spirit of a burgeoning capitalism. With few exceptions, the neoconservatives follow de Tocqueville's lead: they focus on the "passion for equality" and ascribe to it a host of dangers that a more comprehensive examination might find rooted in the very "tendencies of commercial civilization."

CHAPTER TEN

Democracy and Expertise

NEOCONSERVATISM REGULARLY RISES to the defense of democracy. "Democracy is indeed under attack, and increasingly the attack succeeds," warns Daniel Patrick Moynihan. The politics neoconservatism most opposes is attributed to the "elitism" of intellectuals, affluent suburbanites, or university students. Without going quite so far as to adopt President Nixon's "silent majority," neoconservatism celebrates what it represents as the commonsense moderation and attachment to traditional mores of the vast bulk of the population.

But there is something very qualified about the democracy neoconservatism defends. Its admiration for the people seems almost tactical; its fear of them quite profound and philosophically grounded. One minute Irving Kristol turns to the mass of people as the repository of good sense; the next he declares them a selfish and unrestrained "urban mob" and decadent to boot. "Populism" has consistently been a pejorative term in the neoconservative lexicon, and going back to the fifties these writers have worried about the populist threat to America's establishment. Moynihan links the danger to democracy with the decline of unquestioned authority and the post-Vietnam loss of confidence among America's elite. Daniel Bell, too, observes the passing of "an establishment which was confident of itself . . . [representing] a milieu for leadership—the Wall Street legal firms and investment companies." It has not been replaced, says Bell, and that is a loss. "A society has vitality if it has a strong establishment."

It is not surprising then to find Henry Fairlie echoing Moynihan: "The democratic idea is part of the public philosophy of America, and it is under attack . . . not just the capacity of democracy . . . in this or that respect; every political and intellectual and moral justification of it is being challenged"; except that Fairlie identifies the attack with neoconservatism. He refers to the case made by Irving Kristol (and stated even more authoritatively by Kristol's friend the late Martin Diamond) that exalts the "democracy" of the Founding Fathers, in particular the authors of *The Federalist,* and rejects its later transformation into a "democratic faith." To Fairlie, Kristol's views "are those of an elite, self-appointed, fashionable, and powerful." The Founding Fathers were not themselves democratic, but they planted a seed, particularly in the Declaration of Independence, which "had yet to grow." "Men such as Kristol would like to eradicate the whole of that further revolution . . . all history after 1787 is eliminated."

The strongest accusations of neoconservative rejection of democracy were reserved for the publication of an article on "The Democratic Distemper" by Samuel P. Huntington as the lead piece in the Bicentennial edition of *The Public Interest.* Huntington's article was a section of *The Crisis of Democracy,* a "Report on the Governability of Democracies to the Trilateral Commission," a document drawing special attention after the Trilateral Commission's director, Zbigniew Brzezinski, emerged as Jimmy Carter's foreign-policy adviser, and several other members of the commission (W. Michael Blumenthal, Richard N. Cooper, Walter F. Mondale, Henry D. Owen, Cyrus R. Vance, Paul C. Warnke, and Harold Brown—besides Carter himself) entered the Democratic Administration at a high level. Huntington argued that a "democratic surge" in the 1960s was rendering the United States "ungovernable"; and that, contrary to Al Smith's remark that "the only cure for the evils of democracy is more democracy," the appropriate cure today was less. "Some of the problems of governance in the United States today stem from an excess of democracy. . . . Needed, instead, is a greater degree of moderation in democracy." We have too much democracy for democracy's own good; we have to destroy a little in order to save it.

The Trilateral Commission's report made even some neoconservatives squirm; *Commentary* published a strong critique of it, which, though it did not mention Huntington's prominent appearance in *The Public Interest,* was still a noteworthy exception to the rule of no criticism within the ranks. Radicals of course were overjoyed: they saw the report as a candid confession that technocratic liberalism and democracy were incompatible. Yet it was not true that Huntington had repudiated democracy. Ostensibly he sought a "balance" in regard to it, and for the purpose of preserving it from its own inherent weaknesses. Should such language, as well as the protests from other neoconservatives, be dismissed as the compliment that vice pays to virtue, the necessary pussyfooting before the enshrined sentiment that Democracy is a Good Thing? But perhaps the shock over Huntington's words is equally hollow, the exploitation of conventional reactions to someone who has challenged a popular shibboleth?

What complicates the problem is that, just as Madison complained in *The Federalist* of the disparate governments that were all admitted to the title "republic," so the word "democracy" has come to have the loosest of meanings. Leave aside the contortions that give us "people's democracies" for Communist dictatorships. For the neoconservatives, democracy does not seem to mean much more than the Founding Fathers meant by a republic: a government deriving its powers ultimately from the consent of the people but exercising them through delegated representatives, operating within a constitutional framework that preserves the kind of liberties enumerated in the Bill of Rights. When Moynihan speaks of the decline of democracy it is the demise of this sort of government he has in mind. Yet democracy, in this sense, could coexist with a limited franchise, deference to aristocracy, extreme class differences, infrequent elections, and—most important for the modern situation—a passive citizenry marked by a low level of political consciousness. As long as liberty was not attenuated, neoconservatism would not be greatly dissatisfied with such a condition; indeed, Huntington proposes the United States achieve a greater "balance" in that direction. Governing, thought the Founding Fathers, was one of the great exercises of the human mind and character; but like other difficult tasks they thought it could only be carried out by superior individuals and certainly was not the regular business of the run of mankind. Others, however, see democracy in a different light. For them it means not merely consent and respect for liberty but active *participation*—and with participation *equality*. Good government is more than a system of protection against arbitrary interference with private and individual pursuits; it is also a system allowing and encouraging the exercise of individual citizenship and the expression of social solidarity.

Moynihan: Social Science & the Reform Elite

To understand neoconservatism's uneasy and qualified view of democracy, it is best to begin not with the controversial analysis of Huntington but with a vociferous defender of democracy like Moynihan. Since the mid-sixties Moynihan has made several major pronouncements on social reform and political change that are not only fascinating in themselves; in their consistencies as well as their contradictions, they reveal the limits of neoconservative confidence in democracy. The representative character of Moynihan's views is also suggested by the fact that the first of these statements was the lead article—lead manifesto, one might say—in the inaugural issue of *The Public Interest.*

Entitled "The Professionalism of Reform," this article was perhaps the last blast of the end-of-ideology trumpet. It described a new manner of reform evolving in "the profoundly new society developing in the United States," and offering "a profound promise of social sanity and stability." This technique had two characteristics. First, reform originated not, as in the past, from outsiders—the labor movement, the intellectuals, the poor or those dissatisfied with their conditions—but from within the ranks of government, from "officials whose responsibilities were to think about just such matters." These officials, often academics on leave, needed special skills, for the second characteristic of the new technique was that it "was based on essentially esoteric information"—income statistics, employment data, demographic trends, almost all of which is public, "but the art of interpreting it is, in a sense, private."

Three developments lay behind this new phenomenon. The first and most dramatic Moynihan called "the economic revolution":

> . . . in the area of economic policy there has occurred a genuine discontinuity, a true break with the past: Men are learning how to make an industrial economy work. . . . For two decades now . . . the industrial democracies of the world have been able to operate their economies on a high and steadily expanding level of production and employment. Nothing like it has ever happened before in history. It is perhaps the central fact of world politics today.

Since, to continue in the same vein of understatement, "the central political issue of most industrial nations over the past century and a half has been how to make an economy work," we were obviously moving into a new political era. All the more so, since the new situation was generating surplus revenues which the discovery of "fiscal drag" virtually forced government to disburse. To do this, it needed professionals. The task of "devising new and responsible programs for expending public funds in the public interest" would end up "in the hands of persons who make a profession of it." What this work entails "are less and less political decisions, more and more administrative ones . . . decisions that can be reached by consensus rather than conflict."

The reform of government is replaced by the administration of reform—it reminds one of Engels' prediction of a passage from the government of persons to the administration of things. But Moynihan's vision does not depend, as did Engels', on the extension of power to everyone in society. It rests on the emergence of an elite, a "reform elite."

The emergence of a reform elite was all the more natural, given the second development Moynihan pointed to, "the professionalization of the middle class." Higher education was transforming the middle class into professionals, a type marked by "independence of judgment, esoteric knowledge, and immunity to outside criticism." Moynihan's portrait of this type and its claim to "know better" was not particularly attractive, but he was willing to live with it: "as professionals in a professionalizing society, they are increasingly *entitled* to have their way. That is how the system works." (His emphasis.)

In fact, the power of professionals had just been demonstrated by the insistence on "maximum feasible participation" of the poor in community-action programs of the War on Poverty. "This is one of the most important and pioneering aspects of the entire anti-poverty program," wrote Moynihan, but it was brought about by social-welfare professionals and not by the poor, even though the professionals presented the program as a reassertion of the "indigenous nonprofessional."

Moynihan did not anticipate a reaction against professionalization, which he believed was part of a nearly perfect system of "careers open to talent." Indeed, America's success at recognizing ability and "drawing up talent from lower economic and social groups" may "deprive those groups of much of their natural leadership." Thus the poor and the minorities may be all the more dependent upon professionals, or at least retain their natural leaders only through a process whereby the latter become professionals dealing with the special problems of these groups.

Finally, the "professionalization of reform" was based on "the exponential growth of knowledge." The "industry of discovery" known in the physical sciences was emerging in the social sciences, based on a sophisticated system of social statistics and new techniques like simulation. Governments would be so finely attuned by surveys, simulation, and polls to the ways people believe and think that old-fashioned techniques of political agitation would be anachronistic; indeed the need to engage in such efforts would indicate that a cause is immature.

Did Moynihan see any perils in this extraordinary, technocratic vision? He did—very briefly. A "certain price" would be "a decline in the moral exhilaration of public affairs at the domestic level." A "considerable risk" was the combining of knowledge, resources, and skill into what Harold D. Lasswell called a "monocracy of power." But Moynihan devoted four sentences to the psychological "price," and one to the political "risk." His conclusion was upbeat: "The creation of a society that can put an end to the 'animal miseries' and stupid controversies that afflict most peoples would be an extraordinary achievement of the human spirit. . . . we may now turn to issues more demanding of human ingenuity."

Three years later, in *Maximum Feasible Misunderstanding,* Moynihan produced a chapter also titled "The Professionalization of Reform." Although there is no reference to the original article, he repeats its arguments—minus the original optimistic point. No talk now of a "profound promise of social sanity and stability" or an "extraordinary achievement of the human spirit." On the contrary. In the context of the argument of *Maximum Feasible Misunderstanding,* that the community-action programs were irresponsibly contrived by professionals enamored of dubious theory and promoting their own self-interest, the "professionalization of reform" becomes a somewhat sinister development. In 1970, Moynihan even humorously announced his "recantation"—his earlier analysis had been "hopelessly wrong."

What had happened? What led him to reverse his judgment? And had he, in fact, really reversed it? The natural place to seek answers is in the three initiatives which captured so much of Moynihan's attention—the Moynihan Report, the community-action programs, and the Family Assistance Plan—and in the three books which chronicled these initiatives, two of them by Moynihan himself and the third by friendly scholars for whom he was a prime informant.

All three of these initiatives, in Moynihan's view, were failures. In the case of the first and last, Moynihan's own proposals, responsibility for the failures rests with the opponents. In the case of the second, which was not Moynihan's proposal, responsibility rests with the proponents. In all cases, those responsible are associated with the class of professional reformers.

This is not the place to analyze each of these episodes separately nor to review the accounts given of them by Moynihan. That has been done by reviewers of *Maximum Feasible Misunderstanding* and *The Politics of a Guaranteed Income* as well as by Rainwater and Yancey and their reviewers. What is most striking about these three episodes is that—in sharp contrast to the impression one might get from Moynihan—they are all astonishingly similar.

Consider how Moynihan characterizes the community-action segment of the War on Poverty with its provision for "maximum feasible participation" of the poor:

1. It was conceived and promoted by white professionals with almost no input from minority representatives or the other groups it would largely affect.

2. It was an elite-initiated attempt to achieve massive political impact without a mass political base.

3. It was based on uncertain and incomplete social-science research.

4. It was so imprecisely defined and unclearly presented that misunderstanding about its intentions crippled it politically.

5. Its ultimate consequences were only dimly perceived and its potential political reverberations naively unanticipated.

Now allowing for the fact that the community-action programs actually operated while the Moynihan Report and FAP died on paper, the parallels between the three episodes are remarkable.

1. *Minimal involvement of blacks and other affected groups.* Black leaders had no part in the formulation of the Moynihan Report or even in the White House meetings which followed it in preparation for the conference "To Fulfill These Rights." This must be counted an important element in provoking black suspicion of the document. The Family Assistance Plan, Moynihan himself makes clear, "was planned by whites for blacks" and "was a quintessential example of the professionalization of reform."

2. *Elite effort without political base.* Though the Moynihan Report was intended, first of all, to mobilize elite opinion, it did seem to anticipate a broad movement built around the ideal of a strong family. For the Johnson Administration, however, the report, before proving too hot politically, was a means to "leap frog the movement"—get ahead of civil rights leaders and attach what had been a movement of outsiders to a new Administration agenda. In comparison, FAP was a clearer case of elite politics. Originating within at least one phalanx of reform professionals, it was sold by Moynihan and likeminded staff at the White House (a) to President Nixon and (b) to Wilbur Mills. There was no public pressure for a proposal like FAP and good grounds to suspect that the public might be hostile. In the event, the public was tolerant—give it a try, summed up the general attitude. But the fear that conservatives could turn FAP into a political liability kept Nixon from backing it straightforwardly. The public never was let in on the act, and Moynihan took this for granted. The message of *The Politics of a Guaranteed Income*, like Moynihan's comments on the Moynihan Report, is addressed to liberal elites. "Look," he is saying, "the country is pretty conservative. There's not much chance of changing that. But moments arise when fundamental change, packaged in conservative garb, can be put across swiftly and irrevocably—*if* liberal elites stick together and don't make political waves. In 1965 and 1970 liberals were unruly and blew their opportunities."

3. *Uncertain and incomplete research.* Though some of the research underlying the Moynihan Report had a perfectly good pedigree, E.

Franklin Frazier's work on the black family, it was obviously open to challenge. Even in 1965, Stanley M. Elkins' thesis about the impact of slavery on Negro Americans was highly controverted. Moynihan's colleagues in the government complained that he had ignored evidence contradicting the tenor of his report although it was made available to him. In the case of FAP, one of its major premises, that current welfare practices encouraged family breakup and a guaranteed income would reduce welfare dependency, was based on inconclusive findings. It seemed to make sense, but as Moynihan granted, "There was no evidence to suggest that a guaranteed income would have any immediate impact on dependency."

4. *Imprecise definition, unclear presentation.* One of the sad ironies in the debate over the Moynihan Report was that critics often offered *as alternative programs* precisely those economic and especially employment measures that Moynihan himself envisioned as the report's outcome. At the same time, critics feared the report might encourage psychiatric "messing about" with the black family—precisely the social-casework approach against which Moynihan, too, warned. Some of the fault was the critics', but some was the report's. It was ambiguous at several points: was the message that macroeconomic policy, such as providing full employment for black males, was *about* to lose its leverage on the problem of black family instability and dependence, and therefore had to be pressed all the more urgently? Or was the message that employment had *already* lost its link with dependence and therefore macroeconomics should give way to income maintenance or even psychiatric tutelage? Moynihan has ruled out the latter but is not consistent about whether the main upshot of the report was the need for employment opportunities, for income maintenance, or for both. Furthermore, the report appeared without recommendations. Whether that was justified in an internal document meant to define a problem without leaping hastily to urge programs, in public it created a "vacuum," as Herbert Gans wrote, that could "easily be filled by undesirable solutions, and the report's conclusions . . . conveniently misinterpreted."

The definition and presentation of FAP is yet another saga. According to Moynihan, FAP was presented as "simple, sensible, and relatively inexpensive." In fact, it was complicated, risky, and expensive—nothing less than "the most startling proposal to help poor persons ever made by a democratic government."

Was FAP a guaranteed income? Moynihan said yes, Nixon said no. Moynihan said that Nixon was justified in taking this line because Americans were irrationally prejudiced against the notion of a "guaranteed income." Besides, Moynihan and Nixon's "good" guaranteed income was not like the "bad" guaranteed income most people had in mind. Similarly for the question of a work requirement. Moynihan said there was no work requirement, the President said there was. Moynihan said that "it seemed fair to describe the very considerable work incentive . . . as a work requirement, and to hope it would be understood." To watch Moynihan exert his powers of argument in defense of this obfuscation is touching. But of course the President was not "understood," a fact which Moynihan blames on everyone but the President, and especially on liberals. It was their responsibility to see the "reality" behind Nixon's "workfare" rhetoric. But what was the reality? Richard P. Nathan, a principal actor in the formulation of FAP, has written that for

> liberals within the administration . . . Daniel P. Moynihan was one . . . the work requirement was a way to mollify possible opponents. . . . We know, however, that the President *did* take the *"work"* in *"Work*fare" very seriously. . . . The press and the public saw FAP as a victory for liberals within the Administration and read into it advocacy by the President of a guaranteed minimum income. They were wrong.

Whatever the reality, what Moynihan daintily terms "a tension between symbol and substance" was fatal politically.

Unfortunately, the imprecision in FAP extended to substance as well. Its sponsors had done their homework but never quite finished, and conservatives on the Senate Finance Committee caught them out. The key to FAP was its promise to provide an incentive to work and a disincentive to dependency. Thus an increase in earned income did not lose the recipient an equal sum in FAP benefits. *But* when other benefits contingent on income level were taken into account—Medicaid, public housing, food stamps, etc.—then the supposed incentive to work under FAP shrank drastically or disappeared altogether. The situation was no different under current welfare arrangements, to be sure; but FAP had been presented as something better. When its sponsors were caught unprepared to answer questions on this point, the bill was doomed.

5. *Uncertain consequences, unanticipated political impact.* The Moynihan Report, lacking programmatic recommendations, made no pretense to charting consequences. Although its author was aware of the misuse to which the report's data might be put by racists, he naively underestimated the explosiveness of the illegitimacy aspect, overestimated the power of "family" to allay controversy, and allowed the report to become public knowledge in the worst possible manner.

Of FAP, Moynihan has written that there was not "evidence of any kind as to *what* effects a guaranteed income would have." As for political reverberations, conservative White House critics of FAP had warned

Nixon that the measure might only alienate friends, without placating enemies. Moynihan himself was conscious that welfare militants would not find FAP in their own interests, and that Democratic liberals might hesitate to enlist in a campaign their enemy of two decades was waging (from a safe distance) under the banner of "workfare." Nonetheless, he seemed unduly dismayed when some of these forces actually behaved as Moynihan's standards of interest politics said they would. And this dismay contributed to the unreadiness of FAP's sponsors for the truly devastating attack—which came from the Right. "This was in part a personal reaction," writes Moynihan, in a revealing passage,

> by men who felt they had done something large and expansive, and who too easily became defensive and hurt when it was charged [by liberals] that their work was mean and repressive. . . . By contrast, conservatives who regarded the legislation as profligate and near demented had no power to wound, and so it was possible to overlook their power to destroy.

One could add other similarities between the Moynihan Report, the community-action programs, and FAP. Despite his fondness for broad assertions, Moynihan resolutely compartmentalizes these controversies from much of the real context of American politics. Thus he only briefly alludes to the war in Vietnam, and then more in terms of its impact on liberal opponents than on the government. Yet Rainwater and Yancey effectively argue that the escalation of the war, at the very moment of the controversy over the Moynihan Report, foreclosed any massive federal initiatives to assist the black community; if all that came out of the report were arguments over whether the problem was actually within the black community itself, that was not terribly inconvenient for a beleaguered White House.

Much the same can be said about community action. With a war-imposed limit on funds, the poor could enjoy "maximum feasible participation" in poverty programs—but there was not much substantial to participate in, certainly not the major job program that had been urged earlier but would have required another $2-10 billion.

Finally, FAP sponsors were pleading for liberal support at a time when the Nixon Administration was expanding the war to Cambodia and letting unemployment rolls rise by two million. FAP always rested on a good deal of trust: we'll iron out the defects later if only the principle can be established now, went the argument, employing the analogy of periodic improvements in Social Security. But liberals had some good grounds for being distrustful about that "later," especially since the President, in both his policies and his preachments, did not seem even to recognize the guaranteed-income principle.

What is the point of these comparisons? Not that the three initiatives were unworthy. Quite the contrary. Despite their flaws, they were all valuable efforts. The point is simply that Moynihan's criticisms of the one program hold for his own efforts as well. What then is the decisive difference between them? Surely more than Moynihan's role in the controversies.

Ultimately, the explanation for Moynihan's different judgments on similar events does turn on the issue of "professionalization of reform," but in a manner almost opposite to what might be assumed from the impression Moynihan gives. The problem is not the professionalization itself but the fact that some professional reformers, in the case of community-action programs, betrayed their own cause and made life more difficult for other professional reformers, e.g., Moynihan and the social scientists he addressed in *The Public Interest*. In urging "maximum feasible participation," perhaps these reformers were Machiavellian, as Moynihan implies. Or perhaps they were quixotic, as he also implies. Or perhaps they were simply Jeffersonian—or perhaps they were all three. In any case, they tried to open up the process of elite decision-making to greater citizen participation, mucking up the well-laid schemes of the other professionals with the less predictable play of group interest and emotion. This is what Moynihan ultimately objects to. It is not the professionalization of reform but its *de*professionalization that distresses him; not the pretensions of professionals (the *real* professionals are people like himself) but the interference of unprofessional professionals and of rank amateurs (that is, the insufficiently cautious).

For all his intellectual agility, there is no sign that Moynihan has ever grappled with any other vision of sane politics except the one dominating political science when he came to maturity. In that vision, elite representatives of different interest groups, united by a wide consensus on the shape of the social order and the "rules of the game," bargain with one another for marginal advantages. "One way to look at American democracy," Moynihan has even advised, "is to see it *as not so much a democracy,* but rather a society with an unprecedentedly large and varied assortment of elites. *The people are asked which elite will govern them for which purposes."* (My emphasis.)

But this "troublesome question of elites," as Moynihan calls it, is also exacerbated by the role of social science, so large a factor in the "professionalization of reform" and in the three specific reform initiatives that Moynihan observed. Again and again, he has insisted, the political facts of life were altered by a series of social-science studies appearing in the mid-sixties—James S. Coleman's findings on education being the prime example. These studies strongly contradicted commonsense assumptions; several times Moynihan quotes Jay W. Forrester's dictum that "with a high degree of confidence we can say that the intuitive solutions to the problems of complex social systems will be wrong most of the time." Coleman's data, for example, were not only "counterintuitive," they were "almost impenetrable to the layman." One could go further.

> The methodology of most social science is now quite beyond the comprehension of non-social scientists. In particular, it is beyond the ken of the lawyer class that tends to wield the levers of power in American government. Thus a priestly role of interpreting the mysteries is gradually emerging. And with it the anticlericalism of priest-ridden societies.

The social scientists, in short, were as essential as ever, however much the society (and Moynihan) had come to distrust them. They had in fact a new assignment. The elites had shown themselves unwilling to contain their competition for power within the accepted bounds; they had "summoned up, or at very least been altogether willing to make use of, terribly destructive forces within our society." Social science, or so Moynihan asserted, should oppose this. It should

> keep the process of competition between elites from being abused to the point of trifling with the stability of society. . . . Social scientists have an extraordinary potential for ring-keeping, for maintaining, that is, certain standards of conflict, and for detecting derelictions from such standards. . . . Let us face it, no one else can afford to be honest about these things. *Only a very special and dedicated cadre—itself an elite of sorts—can hope to keep the other elites of the country from tearing the country apart.* [My emphasis.]

Moynihan offered several guidelines for this "very special and dedicated cadre." (1) Since social science's ability to say, with authority, what won't work has far outstripped any capacity for predicting or designing what will, the new elite should insist on the lack of evidence supporting new policy proposals rather than concoct any of its own. (2) The dedicated cadre should increase its "objectivity" by recruiting to its ranks more persons from the "nonintellectual classes" and more conservatives, as well as women and minorities. (3) "We need to break the Marxist spell which . . . has now returned to our campus in a vulgarized but appallingly virulent form." (4) "Most of all we need a sense that our mission involves the maintenance of social stability as well as the facilitating of social change. . . . The abyss is real and is near at hand."

There is no reason to suppose that Moynihan, at least in his up-from-the-streets persona, does not genuinely *feel* as democratic as Walt Whitman. There is no reason to believe him insincere in his indignation at elite social scientists, elite journalists, and elite intellectuals. But when he turns to practical measures, it is not really elitism to which he objects but the wrong elitism. It is not the extension of democratic participation that concerns him—quite the contrary—but the improvement of the elites. In five years the task of reform professionals changed from ushering in a new era of political history to saving society from the abyss; but at the very moment of "recanting" his earlier statement, Moynihan concluded that "the professionalization of reform will continue." Instead of being the activist coaches and players, the reform professionals would now be the conservative rule-makers and referees.

Kristol: "New Men" vs. "New Class"

What is true for Moynihan is even more true for Irving Kristol, whose skeptical view of political democracy is disguised by his admiration of marketplace democracy and whose low estimate of the populace's capacity for political participation is matched by his high estimate of the people's saving inertia. Like Moynihan, Kristol is ready in denunciation of "elite" intellectuals; other elites, like businessmen, diplomats, and military leaders, are treated quite gently. But even among intellectuals, Kristol makes an exception for Moynihan's "reform elite." Writing on "The Troublesome Intellectuals" in the heady days of the second issue of *The Public Interest,* Kristol made clear that not all of them were troublesome. His description of the " 'new men' in government" could not have been more flattering.

> They are not—as is sometimes said—*merely* hired professionals. To begin with, they are not dependent on government for their livelihood, since practically all of them are on loan, as it were, from the academic community, to which they will eventually return. More important, their very standing and reputation in their professions is fixed by their colleagues in the academic community, not by their superiors in government. And lastly, it should be said that, for the most part, they are genuinely cultivated men, interested in the arts and in the life of the mind.

The "new class," unlike these "new men," can never be described by Kristol without mention of its ambition, arrogance, and "elitism." Yet surprisingly, Kristol assumes that this "elite" too must be granted its place: "The 'new class' is here, it is firmly established in its own societal sectors, and it is not going to go away." Like Matthew Arnold contemplating the arrival in power of Britain's middle and working classes,

Kristol proposes a strategy of education, conversion, and cooption. Luckily the members of the "new class" are "not doctrinaire socialists . . . even if they sometimes look like it." They share in the popular distrust of big government, and if they cannot be won over to "free enterprise," they may be convinced of the need to maintain a sizable private sector to safeguard individual liberty.

> They have long wanted their "place in the sun," they are in the process of seizing and consolidating it—and now they have to be assimilated into the system. . . .
>
> A good part of this process of assimilation will be the education of this "new class" in the actualities of business and economics—*not* their conversion to "free enterprise"—so that they can exercise their power responsibly. It will be an immense educational task, in which the business community can play an important role.

Later Kristol gave business some further advice on this educational task. The occasion was Henry Ford's resignation from the board of the Ford Foundation, and the immediate concern was corporate philanthropy's role in shaping a public climate favorable to capitalism.

> One preliminary step . . . would be to decide *not* to give money to support those activities of the New Class which are inimical to corporate survival.
>
> A more positive step, of course, would be for corporations to give support to those elements of the New Class—and they exist, if not in large numbers—which do believe in the preservation of a strong private sector. . . .
>
> "How can we identify such people and discriminate intelligently among them?" corporate executives always inquire plaintively. Well, if you decide to go exploring for oil, you find a competent geologist. Similarly, if you wish to make productive investments in the intellectual and educational worlds, you find competent intellectuals and scholars—"dissident" members as it were, of the New Class—to offer guidance.

Kristol stopped short of giving his address and telephone number. If this was rather blatant promotion for neoconservatives, it was purchased with the admission that they, too, were part of the "new class," though to be sure a "dissident" part. Previously Kristol had accused the "new class" intellectuals of being undemocratic because they allegedly did not advance their anti-capitalist spirit "by elevating and refining the preferences of all those ordinary people."

> That, supposedly, is the liberal democratic way. But it is so much easier to mobilize the active layers of public opinion behind such issues as environ-

mentalism, ecology, consumer protection, and economic planning, to give the government bureaucracy the power to regulate and coerce, and eventually to "politicize" the economic decision-making process.

In fact the "new class" has made considerable efforts to enlarge "the active layers of public opinion" and reach the "ordinary people," always to neoconservatism's distress. But it is very hard in any case to distinguish between the undemocratic "new class" strategy that Kristol describes and the one that, in practice as well as in his own recommendations, neoconservatism has pursued—to mobilize elite opinion and to influence the government bureaucracy. If there is any difference between Kristol's and Moynihan's views of the "reform elite," it is Kristol's emphasis, suggested by his sympathetic interest in censorship, on the tutorial function, the active monitoring and shaping of cultural institutions so that the bourgeois ethos, even without its religious base, and the conservative ideal of excellence, yet to be formulated, may prevail.

Huntington: Democracy vs. Government

This brings us, finally, to the Trilateral Commission's "Report on the Governability of Democracies," published under the title *The Crisis of Democracy*. The commission itself, funded by David Rockefeller and linked with the Carter Administration, was a godsend to anyone needing a visible example of elite organization. Even its name had a ring of Pythagorean mystery, a hint of post-industrial Masonry. But the report went further. Its analysis was remarkably candid; its recommendations ("Arenas for Action") were ominously vague. No wonder that the report was greeted with alarm by liberals, given an embarrassed cold shoulder by some neoconservatives, and welcomed by radicals as an unusual revelation of ruling-class outlook.

The candor *is* remarkable. Citing the remark of Al Smith that "the only cure for the evils of democracy is more democracy"—a formulation easy on American sensibilities, since it acknowledges difficulties but reaffirms a national ideal—Samuel P. Huntington, who wrote the report's section on the United States, straightforwardly disagrees.

> Applying that cure at the present time could well be adding fuel to the flames. Instead, some of the problems of governance in the United States today stem from an excess of democracy. . . . Needed, instead, is a greater degree of moderation in democracy.

Huntington's account of the "deal" that elected Presidents must make with the Establishment—business primarily, but key Congressmen and military leaders as well—is, for all its tact, a brutal contradiction of textbook democracy:

> Once he is elected president, the president's electoral coalition has, in a sense, served its purpose. The day after his election the size of his majority is almost—if not entirely—irrelevant. . . . What counts then is his ability to mobilize support from the leaders of the key institutions in society and government . . . key people in Congress, the executive branch, and the private establishment. The governing coalition need have little relation to the electoral coalition.
>
> For twenty years after World War II presidents operated with the cooperation of a series of informal governing coalitions. Truman made a point of bringing a substantial number of nonpartisan soldiers, Republican bankers, and Wall Street lawyers into his administration. He went to the existing sources of power in the country to get the help he needed in ruling the country. Eisenhower in part inherited this coalition and was in part almost its creation. . . . Kennedy attempted to recreate a somewhat similar structure of alliances. Johnson was acutely aware of the need to maintain effective working relations with the Eastern establishment and other key groups in the private sector. . . .

Despite this candor, Huntington's thesis is somewhat circuitous. He argues that (1) a "democratic surge" in the late 1950s and early 1960s brought about (2) "a substantial increase in governmental activity" and (3) "a substantial decrease in governmental authority" and that the consequence is (4) a "democratic distemper" which should be relieved by (5) "a more balanced existence" for democracy in terms of public expectations, egalitarianism, citizen involvement, and opposition to government authority—or more precisely, *reduced* expectations, egalitarianism, involvement, and opposition.

At first glance, it may not seem that this argument deserves to be called circuitous. That the tempo of political life picked up during the sixties and early seventies—indeed became frenzied at times—is undisputed. So too is the decline in governmental authority at the end of that period. Between the one and the other the connections have been drawn by many observers. The heightening of black consciousness which began with the Supreme Court school-desegregation decision, the Montgomery bus boycott, Little Rock, and other incidents, and which finally issued into the sit-ins, the freedom rides, and the March on Washington, was the most unalloyed example of "democratic surge." One immediate consequence, however, was the stimulation of militant opposition to Washington on the part of whites in the South and elsewhere. After 1964 the assertiveness of the civil rights movements combined with the apparently intractable and demoralizing conditions of urban ghettoes to ignite in a series of "long hot summers" and a flare of black separatism. Racial suspicion flitted like summer lightning around all the Great Society programs, and no matter what the resolution the federal government was apt to be blamed for the tensions. The civil rights movement had given birth to a growing radicalism on campuses; but except for an unusual instance like Berkeley, confrontation on campuses was a development of the second half of the decade. The next phase of polarization and challenge to authority was indeed the result of expanded government activity—but not activity that was mandated by the "democratic surge." It was the war in Vietnam, an elite policy, that both soured the Great Society programs and interacted with the race issue to make the challenge to authority a general one. The pursuit of the war, the growing evidence that democratic norms were regularly flouted in that pursuit, and the recognition of widespread institutional acquiescence in this apparently destructive and willful foreign policy provoked questions about the legitimacy of leadership in business, universities, and the military as well as in government. The disorder produced by this conflict itself sapped confidence in governing institutions, while the orderly processes of dissenting politics seemed to be regularly baffled by violence and illegality—from the assassinations of Martin Luther King and Robert Kennedy and the "police riot" at the 1968 Democratic Convention to the deeds, sometimes violent or deadly, of terrorists and undercover operatives, the various show trials and finally Watergate. No wonder that by the mid-seventies, polls reported that citizens no longer trusted government as much, had lost confidence in other institutions and professions, increasingly felt that government was run for a "few big interests," and that what ordinary people thought "doesn't count much anymore."

In these events, Huntington admits, we have the most straightforward explanation of the "democratic surge" and its effects:

> The most specific, immediate, and in a sense "rational" causes of the democratic surge could conceivably be the specific policy problems confronting the United States government in the 1960s and 1970s and its inability to deal effectively with those problems. Vietnam, race relations, Watergate, and stagflation: these could naturally lead to increased polarization over policy, higher levels of political participation (and protest), and reduced confidence in governmental institutions and leaders.

Unfortunately, for Huntington's purposes this will not do. Only by minimizing the part of the specific outstanding issues and the actual performance of political leadership can he characterize the difficulties of recent years as *inherent* to democracy itself, discovering in this way an "excess" of it and concluding that we need less. On this point the Trilateral Commission report is thankfully clear: at the heart of its worry are what the introduction sees as the dangers of "the inherent workings of the democratic process itself," or the fact that, as the conclusion states, "Quite apart from the substantive policy issues confronting democratic government, many specific problems have arisen which seem to be an intrinsic part of the functioning of democracy itself." To ascribe too much to the nature of the "substantive policy issues," especially if one major issue involved the denial of full citizenship to American blacks and all the festering consequences of that restriction on equality and democracy, or to point up the failures of governing elites, especially in the case of a foreign policy shot through with deception, would raise the possibility that Al Smith might have been right after all.

Instead, while granting that specific issues and certain government policies did have "some impact," Huntington insists that "a far-from-perfect fit exists between the perceived inability of the government to deal effectively with these policy problems and the various attitudinal and behavioral manifestations of the democratic surge." Exhibit One is the fact that black opposition to U.S. involvement in Vietnam ran far ahead of white opposition by 1967 and yet blacks expressed a more favorable view of government until Nixon came to power in 1969. Furthermore, polarization and increasing distrust of government appear to have begun before the agitation over Vietnam.

Neither of these facts is difficult to explain if one takes seriously the distinctions between black and white reactions to events and the deep divisions over racial issues among whites. Thus black opposition to the Vietnam War, though widespread, may simply not have been enough to cancel the effects of an Administration that had visibly identified itself with the cause of racial equality. (Polls are extremely poor instruments for measuring *intensity* of beliefs.) On the other hand, the civil rights movement and Great Society programs had already stirred hostility toward government among the whites who opposed them as well as disappointment among those who thought the government had not moved decisively enough. Huntington seems to assume that distrust of government is a "left" phenomenon, when in fact it was (and is) both a "left" and "right" phenomenon, often coming in succeeding or overlapping waves.

If the "rational" explanation of the decline in authority is said to fit the data in a "far-from-perfect" manner, Huntington's own thesis displays an even further-from-perfect fit. The notion of the "democratic surge" encompasses a number of realities: greater participation in political campaigns, white-collar unionization in public and private bureaucracies, greater attention to equality in intellectual and political circles, and "marches, demonstrations, protest movements, and 'cause' organizations." This "increased participation" in and of itself leads to polarization, followed by distrust and political disenchantment.

Yet the data Huntington provides do not support his conclusion. For one thing, increased participation was not an across-the-board reality. Voting, for example, "which had increased during the 1940s and 1950s, declined during the 1960s, reaching lows of 55.6 percent in the 1972 presidential election and of 38 percent in the 1974 midterm election." The greatest increase in participation in political campaigns took place during the *1950s* and reached a peak in 1960, then declined somewhat in 1962, fluctuated in 1964 and 1968, peaked again in 1970, and then dropped back somewhat in 1972. Yet Huntington's evidence for polarization—an "index of ideological consistency"—shows that this did not correspond to the period of greatest increase in participation but occurred in 1960–64, which were the years of the civil rights movement. Huntington's effort to trace the cause of greater campaign activity points finally to increased black political participation—and we have seen that this group retained its confidence in government longer than did whites. He cites the work of Sidney Verba and Norman H. Nie showing that higher rates of political participation and ideological consistency resulted from the fact that "the political events of the last decade, and the crisis atmosphere which has attended them, have caused citizens to perceive politics as increasingly central to their lives." Again, this conclusion appears to back the "rational" explanation as much or more than the case for an excess of democracy. So does another finding Huntington notes, that confidence in state and local government had declined much less than confidence in federal government; that, in fact, substantial majorities even favored an increase in state and local power. Yet state and local governments had been responsible for the larger portion of increased government spending in this period. Why was disappointment in government for so long not registered at these levels—except that it was the federal government which was seen to bear major responsibility for action on first the race issue and the war, and later the economy and Watergate?

Detached from events and issues and the specific shortcomings of governing institutions, Huntington's "democratic surge" naturally becomes an almost primal force. It compounds elements as different as the unionization of police forces, the draft resistance of antiwar militants, and the campaign for an Equal Rights Amendment. It amalgamates activities that challenged existing authority in widely differing degrees, some that proposed alternative patterns of authority and discipline as well as those simply reacting negatively to the expansion or abuse of established authority. In its "essence," writes Huntington, "the democratic surge of the 1960s was a general challenge to existing systems of authority, public and private . . . in the family, the university, business, public and private associations, politics, the governmental bureaucracy, and the military service." How the challenge to authority became so generalized is not explained; that is simply the nature of the beast. The "democratic surge" becomes the all-purpose explanation rather than what needs to be explained.

At one level, of course, Huntington is merely saying that when "democratic, liberal, and egalitarian values" are taken seriously in a society he frankly describes as significantly undemocratic, illiberal, and unequal, trouble ensues. During certain periods the "democratic and egalitarian values of the American creed are reaffirmed," and this "intensity of belief . . . leads to the challenging of established authority and to major efforts to change government structures to accord more fully with those values." Is this bad? Is the ensuing trouble worth it? Or should we agree with the writer who summarized the above statement of the "problem" with the observation: "Democracy, in short, starts to work."

If confidence in government has declined, or the belief spread that government serves "big interests," is that unfortunate? Or is it merely an accurate recognition of reality on the part of the citizenry? If it is bad, at what point does it become so? And why? Because it injures democracy by fostering withdrawal from political life, greater "apathy and noninvolvement"? (It is precisely such "apathy and noninvolvement" that Huntington would welcome as required for "the effective operation of a democratic political system.") Or is it bad because it inhibits the government's ability to "impose" sacrifices for foreign-policy reasons or " 'hard' decisions" for domestic economic reasons?

The pursuit of these questions brings into sharp relief the assumptions of the Trilateral Commission's report, assumptions which, not surprisingly, are more important than empirical data in determining its conclusions. The first of these is that "government" and "democracy" stand in opposition to each other. In effect, an "excess" of democracy means a deficit in governability. But since the authors have no independent standard for determining how much democracy is an "excess," that dictum, in practice, is reversed: A deficit in governability means an excess of democracy. By definition. The possibility that a deficit in governability might imply an insufficiency in democracy is effectively eliminated.

Huntington does write that democracy is "one way of constituting authority," qualifying this as "only one way" and insisting that the arenas where democratic authority is appropriate are "limited." His working assumption, however, is that "authority" and "government" are at odds with "democracy," and must be "balanced." Thus democracy is not a way of constituting or realizing government; it is a *check* on government. This is what makes it natural for him to characterize the "democratic surge" simply as a *challenge* to authority and to associate every challenge to authority with the "democratic surge."

The second assumption at work here is that "government" means *management,* the successful accomplishment of technical tasks posed by the economic and international order. A well-governed society is an efficiently managed one. And a third, and crucial, assumption is that "government" is (and should be) a largely independent managing force, somehow floating above society and performing its work in a technically competent, professional manner. Democracy is a legitimate check or influence on this independent governing body—as long as the "balance" is maintained so that government can do its job efficiently. Thus Huntington regrets that democracy renders difficult "the imposition of 'hard' decisions imposing constraints on any major economic group" and that democratic restraints on central leadership make the government subservient to "special interests." This contrasts with the common impression that central governments unconstrained by democracy, while less inhibited in making economic decisions adverse to large numbers of people, are very often subservient to, if not identified with, "special interests," including that of the governing class itself.

Authority, for Huntington, should be tempered by democracy, but largely constituted by rank, status, possibly wealth (he certainly does not object to the role of wealth in the "governing coalition" and seems surprised at the objections to it raised in the 1960s), and—above all—managerial skill. "In many situations the claims of expertise, seniority, experience, and special talents may override the claims of democracy."

So we return, once more, to government by an elite of experts. This is the ideological burden of the Trilateral Commission's report, in particular its section on the United States. Leadership, which was once successfully exercised by a "governing coalition" of financial and industrial executives, Congressional barons, labor leaders, the military, and the Presidency, can now be restored with the help of the intelligence and direction of experts—provided that a sufficient deference to such authority can be nurtured. The sometimes platitudinous, sometimes ominous recommendations of the report—for economic planning, centralization of Congressional power, "restoring a balance between government and media," restructuring of higher education to fit limited job opportunities, and so on—should be read in that light. A number of members of the Trilateral Commission itself seemed disturbed by the call for less democracy, the minimization of government's poor performance, the hint of restraints on freedom of the press, and the leaning toward a technocratic elite. Without naming the report itself, Ralf Dahrendorf warned against

> the belief that the very progress which these democracies made possible for a large number of citizens must now be undone because it feels uncomfortable for some . . . the belief that a little more unemployment, a little less education, a little more deliberate discipline, and a little less freedom of expression would make the world a better place, in which it is possible to govern effectively.

And from neoconservative quarters, one critic, although he was worried about the report's illiberal tendencies (possible restrictions on private choice) rather than its undemocratic ones (limits on citizen participation), noted its "distinctly *dirigiste*" ambitions.

Democracy in a "Libertarian, Negative Sense"

How far from democracy could the Trilateral strand of neoconservatism lead us? A hint may be found in some much earlier remarks by Zbigniew Brzezinski, the Trilateral Commission's director and co-author of a book with Huntington. In 1965, participating in the work of the Commission on the Year 2000, sponsored by the American Academy of Arts and Sciences, Brzezinski spoke of "the generalized danger of the political system increasingly becoming a conservative instrumentality . . . in relation to social change." This was the case, he said, because the government "generates essentially post-crisis management institutions" when we need "pre-crisis management institutions." To create the latter, "we will have to increasingly separate the political system from society and begin to conceive of the two as separate entities." If this jargon was more than a little opaque, Brzezinski helped somewhat by providing an example: "In some respects France under de Gaulle is a relevant model. French society, which still remains libertarian, democratic, and pluralistic, is being separated from the political system, which is increasingly technical in orientation and self-contained." Several other participants seemed unhappy with this position, and the following, abbreviated dialogue took place between Brzezinski and Daniel Bell:

> DANIEL BELL: Do you think such a system is democratic?
> ZBIGNIEW BRZEZINSKI: The political system is not democratic, but the society remains so. . . .

DANIEL BELL: In what sense do you mean that the society is democratic?

ZBIGNIEW BRZEZINSKI: In a libertarian, negative sense; democratic not in terms of exercising fundamental choices concerning policy-making, but in the sense of maintaining certain areas of autonomy for individual self-expression.

Perhaps Brzezinski has become more chastened (and more democratic?) in his views since then. At that time he was convinced that the areas "where innovation in recent years has been most effective" and "most imaginative" were "in technology, in defense, in foreign policy on a broad level, in developing foreign programs—in areas of public policy that are the least susceptible to domestic pressure." He also found that the "most imaginative domestic institution, the one which comes closest to what I would call a pre-crisis management institution, is the Supreme Court . . . one of the least 'democratic' institutions in the Federal Government." What is interesting to note is that whether the problem is a conservative government resistant to "pre-crisis management" and innovation (Brzezinski's view in 1965) or an overactive government pressured to innovate and expand rapidly (Huntington's view in 1975), the cure is always the same: a contraction of democracy.

That at least one voice has been raised in a neoconservative forum against this *dirigisme* we have already seen. But if that voice protested the Trilateral Commission's ambitions to save democracy from itself, the writer's own view of democracy is hardly more expansive. "Democracy," Elie Kedourie writes, ". . . is a form of government in which authority to rule is deemed to be derived from the governed." The idea that "democracy, 'participation,' and egalitarianism necessarily go together . . . is the cant of the age." Democracy "entails nothing about participation, which relates to the way in which government is carried on; and it does not imply that the members of a democratic polity are, or ought to be, equal." This is certainly a remarkable definition, which gladly abandons most of the characteristics that, from Aristotle to yesterday's dictionary, have denoted democracy; Kedourie would make democracy indistinguishable from any form of government—absolute monarchy, oligarchy of wealth, military dictatorship—that happens to be sanctioned by the governed or, to use his even more pliable language, "deemed to be derived" from them. The Trilateral Commission, however, had in mind something more: "regular elections, party competition, freedom of speech and assembly." About this "usage that is now quite prevalent" the author seems a bit vexed; but his "puzzlement is, if anything, increased" when he discovers the Trilaterals also under the impression that a narrow concentration of wealth and learning would not be conducive to democracy.

Such a misapprehension! "All the world knows that 18th- or 19th-century England, in which wealth and learning were concentrated in the hands of a few, had regular elections, party competition, and freedom of speech and assembly."

It is not the report's doubts about democracy that disturb this critic but its lack of doubts about central government; not its proposed contraction of participation but its assumed contraction of the private sphere "in which citizens may pursue and realize their own various, spontaneous, self-chosen purposes" (presumably with whatever concentration of wealth and learning happens to be the case); not its contradiction of Al Smith's dictum but its neglect of the lesson that "governments can do very little" and that the attempt to do more "may in fact make them fit to do even less."

Plainly this critique of the Trilateral Commission's report sticks very closely to neoconservative—and not very democratic—assumptions. By noting that the report's conception of democracy can be encompassed within the kind of constitutional, libertarian, but elitist governments that ruled 18th- and 19th-century England, it does however clarify the debate. There appears to be very little in the way of *principled* objection that neoconservatism might make to those restricted governments. Of course, neoconservatives are not interested in turning back the clock; it is a part of conservative wisdom that one makes concessions to the spirit of the age. But their internal differences center on what new elites—an alliance of "improving" corporate executives and academic brain-trusters, for instance—might take the part played by patricians and rising middle-class leaders in industrializing England; and on what effect the makeup of a new establishment will have on the expansion and efficiency of government.

One would have to fly in the face of all political philosophy to deny that democracy, like every form of government, has its intrinsic problems. How do we resolve the issue between the Greek ideal of self-realization by active participation in the life of the *polis* and the modern liberal ideal of self-realization in a private sphere protected from government intervention? How much of life, in other words, should be politicized? What *are* the capacities of ordinary citizens, potential as well as current, for conducting public affairs, and what is the proper part of technical expertise? What are the limits that size and cultural pluralism place on a modern democracy like the United States? It is hard to explore these questions sincerely, so heavy is the fog of orthodoxy, both the orthodoxy of our minimally democratic practice, spelled out in the theories of pluralist elitism, and the orthodoxy of our highly democratic sentiments, professed, either in hope, compensation, or mystification, on most public occasions. These questions, moreover, are never closed; they need to be reexplored within the changing contexts of new technologies, new economic relationships, and new perspectives, optimistic or pessimistic, on human psychology and social organization.

Neoconservatives might contribute to this exploration. Thus far, and for understandable reasons, they have not. Irving Kristol's admiration of the Founding Fathers may be ahistorical and incomplete, but his reminder that the Founding Fathers always thought democracy "problematical" is salutary: even if the authors of *The Federalist* feared democracy, their fear may have bespoken a greater respect for it than does our current complacency. Yet Kristol is quick to take cover in populist sentiments if this should be polemically profitable, and so are most of the other neoconservatives. Moynihan professes and practices an elite reform strategy but denounces the same strategy in others. If neoconservatism mounted a profound and frank argument for its fear of democracy, its skepticism about wider participation, its conviction of the necessity of hierarchy and a strong establishment, it might contribute to our public understanding. But it would probably not contribute to its own popularity. The easier course is to honor democracy while arguing for its restriction: elitism as the last, best hope of democracy.

CHAPTER ELEVEN

Conclusion: The War for the "New Class"

THERE HAS BEEN no shortage of theories "explaining" neoconservatism, that is, searching behind its expressed ideas for personal motivations, group interests, and contending social forces. Most of these explanations barely deserve the name "theory," put forward as they are in casual justification or condemnation of the movement. Most of them contain at least a germ of truth, however, and some have been thoughtfully formulated.

We-Remained-Faithful

The first theory is the neoconservatives' own. Neoconservatism is nothing but the continuation of liberalism, slightly adjusted to changing circumstances. Whatever motivated liberals traditionally, whatever social forces they represented, explains neoconservatism as well. Neoconservatives have remained constant in their principles while the political spectrum shifted to the left in the 1960s. Even Irving Kristol suggests that the apparent conservatism of neoconservatism is mostly a matter of this shift in others' beliefs. "Is neoconservatism the right label for this constellation of attitudes? I don't mind it—but then, if the political spectrum moved rightward, and we should become 'neo-liberal' tomorrow, I could accept that too. As a matter of fact, I wouldn't be too surprised if just that happened." Others, like Midge Decter, insist adamantly that what passes nowadays for liberalism is reactionary and that those who have come to be called neoconservative should not let their "enemies and would-be usurpers of our revolution [the belief in individual rights and an open society] . . . abscond with its good name."

In one sense, this explanation is no explanation at all, but simply shifts the need for explanation elsewhere. It is the abandonment of true liberalism by others, and not the constancy of the neoconservatives, that demands explanation—which the neoconservatives are hardly reticent about providing. This shift of attention avoids too much. Most obviously it avoids the questions why, even with a Nixon in the White House, with the New Left long since fragmented and the counterculture tamed, with the campuses quiet and America "cooled," the neoconservatives continued training their fire on the Left, raking over the federal initiatives in the areas of poverty, environmental protection, and equal rights, and growing in admiration of the "market"; why they did not return to traditional liberal concerns about concentrations of economic power; why, indeed, they grew even more militant in calling for national self-assertion and the identification of virtue with the United States.

Yet the "we-remained-faithful" explanation, or nonexplanation, does underline some important truths. In stressing continuity, it does remind us of the strong conservatism that in fact marked postwar American liberalism—and, behind that, of the conservatism embedded in liberalism from its seventeenth-century origins. Godfrey Hodgson devotes a brilliant chapter of his brilliant history, *America in Our Time,* to "The Ideology of the Liberal Consensus." He notes that by the 1950s "a strong hybrid, liberal conservatism, blanketed the scene . . . from Americans for Democratic Action—which lay at the leftward frontiers of respectability and yet remained safely committed to anti-communism and free enter-prise—as far into the board rooms of Wall Street and manufacturing industry as there could be found a realistic willingness to accept the existence of labor unions, the rights of minorities, and some role in economic life for the federal government." The Left, according to Hodgson, had virtually ceased to exist—eclipsed by the liberals.

To draw a distinction between the Left and the liberals may sound sectarian or obscure. It is not. . . . What I mean by the "Left" is any broad, organized political force holding as a principle the need for far-reaching social and institutional change and consistently upholding the interests of the disadvantaged against the most powerful groups in the society. The liberals were never such a force.

What I mean by the liberals is those who subscribed to the ideology I have described: the ideology that held that American capitalism was a revolutionary force for social change, that economic growth was supremely good because it obviated the need for redistribution and social conflict, that class had no place in American politics. Not only are those not the ideas of the Left; at the theoretical level, they provide a sophisticated rationale for avoiding fundamental change. In practice, the liberals were almost always more concerned about distinguishing themselves from the Left than about distinguishing themselves from conservatives.

Hodgson, at least in these passages, may understate the extent to which fierce opposition from unreconstructed businessmen and conspiracy-minded right-wingers could convince the liberals that they were a bold vanguard rather than defenders of the *status quo;* and he may understate the lingering attention some of them paid to the role of class. But about the issue of fundamental change he is surely right. Liberals did not contemplate it. And when their optimistic consensus about capitalism and growth and the disappearance of social conflict collapsed, these liberals turned not to the left but back to the even more conservative elements of classical liberalism, the beliefs that human needs cannot be defined or circumscribed, that the drive for more power and possessions is insatiable and always about to go wildly out of control, and therefore that self-aggrandizement can only be limited by painful constraints.

Return-of-the-Repressed

There is a family resemblance between the "we-remained-faithful" theory of neoconservatism and what might be termed the "return-of-the-repressed" theories: all of them look back to earlier decades—the 1950s, the 1940s, even the 1930s. Oddly enough, the notion that the sixties' squabbles among political intellectuals marked the "return of the repressed" also started with the neoconservatives themselves, who applied the idea to their adversaries. A long attack on *The New York Review of Books,* appearing in the November 1970 *Commentary,* ended by suggesting that the *Review's* radicalism was a "rekindling of long-buried sentiments." In the face of Vietnam, individuals whose radical origins and instincts had been repressed in the Cold War era could now—as Susan Sontag said of herself—exclaim "imperialism!" with an easy heart. It was natural enough, however, to apply the same theory across the board: what about the intellectuals who had invested so much in the anti-Communist struggles of the 1930s, 1940s, and 1950s and then found themselves

threatened by the antiwar movement and the new legitimacy which
radicalism gained in the 1960s? Weren't they relieved at the opportunity
to shed the ambiguities of their personal histories and now call out "anti-
American!" and "Stalinist!" as wholeheartedly as in the old days?

Thus for many observers, today's neoconservatism is but the latest stage
in the battle anti-Stalinists fought with Stalinists before and after World
War II, or the continuation of the division between *"hard* anti-Communists" and *"soft* anti-Communists" that Norman Podhoretz recalls so
succinctly in *Making It.* Perhaps ideology is only secondary at this point,
the intellectual surface on deep layers of animosity and distrust.

Ideology gets even less consideration in the "marketing" theories of
neoconservatism. Briefly, these are all variations on the idea that *The New
York Review of Books* stole *Commentary*'s radical thunder; so Podhoretz
had to differentiate his product and "reposition" his journal.

Whether portraying neoconservatism as psychological return and release, as an intellectuals' version of the Hatfields and the McCoys, or as a
struggle for turf and attention, each of these theories must ignore half a
dozen discordant facts. Moreover, these explanations are essentially
petty. No doubt, the personal and the petty play a significant part in what
passes for large, theoretical disputes; but to reduce neoconservatism to
these elements belies a rather desperate wish to deflect its impact.

Defending Hard-Won Privilege

At first glance, the same pettiness could be charged against the many
representations of the neoconservatives as a newly established group
fiercely defending its hard-won privileges. Referring back to the controversy about the CIA and "Cold War liberals," Midge Decter derides "a
general Left theory that Bell and the rest were the grubby sons of
immigrants who were bought off by fat jobs, status, and money." Yet
changes in power and position must surely have something to do with
changes in the neoconservatives' political perspectives, and complaints
about such correlations come strangely from quarters that have so
assiduously detected "radical chic" or the unholy taint of wealth, either
ambitious or guilt-laden, behind most left-wing politics. A document like
Norman Podhoretz's *Making It,* after all, tugs at the reader's coat sleeve
with the message that money, success, and upward mobility swell the
literary man's soul no less than the furniture manufacturer's, and by no
means for the worse. If the neoconservatives are more sensitive about the

occupation of university buildings than of lunch counters, if neoconservatives defend meritocratic principles with a vigor they do not show (as yet) for opposing high taxes on estates, is it unreasonable to find here a protectiveness about the social ladders they themselves have climbed and found reliable? And if, when they contemplate the possibility of overextending government, they weigh the risks to legitimacy and good order more heavily than the immediate effects of cutbacks in services, mightn't this reflect their present place in society and the particular pains that do, and do not, impinge on them most directly?

One can almost assume such relationships *a priori*. But what then? The problem is illustrated by Lewis Coser's complaint about neoconservatism's "infuriating complacency," the spirit of "I'm all right, Jack" that, according to him, "permeates the writings of our new Panglossians."

> Most of these men belonged to the Left camp not so very long ago. . . .
> They were young men eagerly making their way onto the intellectual scene
> . . . and acutely sensitive to the shortcomings of the social and political
> order. They have now made it, and having made it they are concerned with
> the maintenance of an order that has been good to them. But gratitude,
> though an estimable private virtue, too often degenerates into smugness
> when extended to public institutions.

Yet Coser proceeds to criticize Irving Kristol's blatant "reductionism" of egalitarian ideas and aspirations to "self-interested ideology." The usefulness of linking political outlook with social interest clearly depends on its being done in an inquiring, nonreductionist spirit.

Fear of Anti-Semitism

Another explanation of neoconservatism is equally, perhaps even more, open to misinterpretation but nonetheless serious. It turns on the prominence of Jewish intellectuals among neoconservative writers and the lesson they learned from the Holocaust. Isidore Silver has stated the case in a level and careful manner. Surveying the writings of neoconservatives through the 1950s as well as the 1960s, he notes:

> The answer, if there is any one answer, I believe, cannot be found in the
> realm of ideology or principle. Although psychohistorical explanations have
> substantial built-in limitations, it is apparent that the development of
> neoconservatism in the last twenty years has consisted of a reaction to one

major trauma—the fear of anti-Semitism. Since, of course, not all Jewish intellectuals are neoconservatives nor are all neoconservatives Jewish, a conventional disclaimer of universality should and must be entered. Despite the caveats, however, there can be little doubt that the Holocaust constituted the seminal event not only for European Jewry but for many American Jews not far removed from their East European or German heritages.

Silver recalls the argument of Hannah Arendt's *Origins of Totalitarianism*.

Her recapitulation of the status of the Jew in Europe concluded that he was protected by strong national states and endangered by Populist movements (such as Pan-Germanism and Pan-Slavism) that swept through Europe in the late 19th century. The idea that an elite, a conservative elite, rooted in privilege, protected the Jew, while "the people" in nationalistic (or, more accurately, "tribalistic") movements constituted the "enemy," was central to her sweeping vision of the growth of both totalitarianism and anti-Semitism. The great failure of modern times was the inability of the ruling elites in France, Germany and the Slavic countries to retain their own legitimacy in the face of a wave of social and political convulsion.

Arendt's thesis, said Silver, struck home

to a group of Jews who were brilliant, poor, faced with discrimination even in academia and who had fought their way into positions of importance and influence. Preservation of hard-won privilege was a matter not just of comfort but of survival. Institutional barriers, such as academic tenure, to potentially explosive outbursts of irrationality were necessary. America was certainly not free of anti-Semitism; even the best colleges in the 1940s had their quotas for Jews. The neoconservatives' sense of always being besieged, even as they commanded the heights of academic power and social respect, can be explained only by an apocalyptic vision.

Silver's explanation has distinct limitations. The stress on Arendt's thesis puts his explanation more in "the realm of ideology" than he at first supposes. In addition, some leading neoconservatives were severe critics of Arendt, although Silver could have pointed out that in the 1950s Arendt's was only one of a family of popular theories emphasizing the danger of the "masses" and the role of elites as bulwarks against totalitarianism. Moreover, he does not really explain why neoconservatism, or the Arendt world view, appealed to some and not others—"not all Jewish intellectuals are neoconservatives nor are all neoconservatives Jewish." What he does bring into high relief is one deep and unifying source of neoconservatism and of the powerful personal and moral claims it makes. The fear of anti-Semitism, an anti-Semitism associated with the "people" rather than with elites, persists. The convulsive politics of the 1960s may have long faded, but the threat to Israel and the shadow of quotas have taken their place.

An Ideology for Policy Professionals

Though there is something to be learned, and also to be avoided, in each of these theories, the most substantial explanation of neoconservatism is the one that sees it as the ideology of a new caste of experts, variously described as technocrats, "new men," "new mandarins," and so on. Irving Kristol, as we have seen, referred to the "permanent brain trust":

> The men who commute regularly to Washington, who help draw up programs for reorganizing the bureaucracy, who evaluate proposed weapons systems, who figure out ways to improve our cities and assist our poor, who analyze the course of economic growth, who reckon the cost and effectiveness of foreign aid programs, who dream up new approaches to such old social programs as the mental health of the aged, etc., etc.

In his 1965 article "The Professionalization of Reform," Daniel Moynihan attributed the War on Poverty simply to "officials whose responsibilities were to think about just such matters." He added: "These men now exist, they are well paid, have competent staffs, and have access to the President." Moynihan was speaking for, and to, the constituency of *The Public Interest,* the future neoconservatives; and one appropriate term for the group is obviously "reform professionals." Yet "stability professionals" might do equally well, since their interest in reform is less than evident at the moment and always stemmed largely from their agreement with Burke's dictum "A state without the means of some change is without the means of its conservation." Perhaps "policy professionals" is the most neutral and suitable description, as long as the larger political and ideological purposes suggested by "reform" and "stability" are kept in mind. This group has far broader interests than devising federal standards for this or that, doing technical calculations of tax rates or employment possibilities, or overseeing government programs in the field.

Concern with this emergent group, in any case, is not new. The increasing incorporation of American intellectuals into the decision-making apparatus of government and industry provoked uneasy and sometimes angry discussions throughout the 1950s and early 1960s. Numerous critics of the "end of ideology" had perceived in that outlook precisely the necessary ideological lubricant for this assimilation of intellectuals. Though friendly toward the editors of *The Public Interest*, Norman Podhoretz originally portrayed that venture in essentially those terms in *Making It*. Others, less friendly, were more specific:

> *The Public Interest* represents those scholar-consultants who, in Daniel Moynihan's apt description in the magazine's first issue, constitute a vanguard of "professional reformers." . . . Like the Calvinist stewards of New England, the architects of *The Public Interest* administer to client America from the highest motives.
>
> But the angle of vision is constricted. Most of the contributors have failed to note the promotion of professionalism as, perhaps, the major interest of *The Public Interest*. Witness the long and growing list of public movements castigated by *The Public Interest*. . . . The magazine rejected, even excoriated, major socio-political movements which embody the theme of expanded public participation. Could it be that the editors see this approach as a negation of their own arrogated status as the sole source of institutional reform?

Daniel Bell denied that his *Coming of the Post-Industrial Society* was the technocratic rationale some critics accused it of being, but the book did provide a framework for understanding the central role of "new elites based on skill . . . the technical and professional intelligentsia."

The apotheosis of the policy professionals actually was left to Theodore H. White and *Life* magazine. In June 1967, White offered the readers of *Life* a three-part pageant on what he called "The Action Intellectuals." "This is the story of a new power-system in American life," White announced, the story of

> the new priesthood, unique to this country and this time, of American action-intellectuals.
>
> In the past decade this brotherhood of scholars has become the most provocative and propelling influence on all American government and politics. Their ideas are the drive-wheels of the Great Society: shaping our defenses, guiding our foreign policy, redesigning our cities, reorganizing our schools, deciding what our dollar is worth. . . . For such intellectuals now is a Golden Age, and America is the place. Never have ideas been sought more hungrily or tested against reality more quickly. From White House to city hall, scholars stalk the corridors of American power.

White went on in this breathless style. He counted professors in the cabinet ("drawn . . . from the brotherhood of learning"). He described the flow of ideas ("task forces . . . ceaselessly scout the campuses"; action-intellectuals "throw a bridge" across the "gulf" between government and "primary producers of really good ideas"; the White House serves as "a transmission belt, packaging and processing scholars' ideas to be sold to Congress as programs"). He contemplated the historic changes that make all this necessary ("Man must find his way across the buckling landscape of the changing world"; "Americans have left behind the historic era of scarcity"; "Today the Politics of Distribution is being replaced by the Politics of Innovation—abundance invites us to the Age of Experiment").

For pedigree White traced his action-intellectuals back to the Founding Fathers, but the story really began with Roosevelt's brain trust, and continued with the wartime work of James Bryant Conant and Vannevar Bush at the Office of Scientific Research and Development, the research and analysis team at the Office of Strategic Services that selected targets for the Eighth Air Force's heavy bombers, the 1950s analyses of strategic defense policy, and finally Kennedy's Camelot. At first hard scientists, then economists, and most recently social scientists had entered the new priesthood. White touched base with land-grant universities like Michigan ("brokerage houses of ideas"), with the Ford Foundation ("world's largest investor in new ideas"), the Rand Corporation (" 'We have bred,' says its new president, Henry Rowen . . . 'a new generation of people with a new kind of problem-solving skill' "), and of course the Harvard-MIT complex in Cambridge ("power center . . . remarkable energy cluster . . . seedbed of the new elite").

The action-intellectuals stood in contrast to two other types: First "the classic—or pure—intellectual" who feels "outrage or despair as he looks down from the ivory tower on the man-in-action and scolds the hypocrisy or compromise which action forces on dreams." Second, "the alienated intellectuals of what is called 'The New Left,' " guilty of "wild and rumbling rhetoric" and about whose ideas "there is very little new . . . except for the sour and hopeless quality of their talk." These two contrasts do spur White to pose some of the problems raised by the role of his heroes. "The action-intellectuals worry about the contradictory tugs of pure contemplation and contaminating involvement. . . . Do social scientists yet know enough to guide us to the very different world we must live in tomorrow? Do they offer wisdom as well as knowledge?"

It is the social scientists—that is, the policy professionals—who particularly worried White. He mentioned their failure in urban renewal, their unpreparedness for ghetto riots, their new uncertainties about centralized power in Washington. He foresaw the need to define the scholar's role in government more precisely. But all of this was presented sympathetically, softly, indeed through the eyes of the policy professionals themselves: "the best of them stand at the dawn of a self-doubt unknown to earlier generations of scholars who preceded them to Washington." The portrait, one feels, needed a few shadows for both drama and credibility. This was, after all, 1967.

Despite the air of boyish wonderment—*Tom Swift and His Action-Intellectuals*—White's series celebrated a genuinely important development. Kristol put it more soberly: "It has always been assumed that as the United States became a more highly organized national society, as its economy became more managerial, its power more imperial, and its populace more sophisticated, the intellectuals would move inexorably closer to the seats of authority—would, perhaps, even be incorporated en masse into a kind of 'power elite.' " Indeed even White's tone was revealing; the accompaniment was overrich with 101 strings, but the tune was substantially the same as that of Moynihan's confident manifesto on "The Professionalization of Reform." The heady romance of power was by no means a creation of White's; certainly he had absorbed much of it—quite willingly, to be sure—from his subjects.

Unfortunately White was two years late. His celebration of the rise of action-intellectuals, like so many public celebrations, came at the very moment when they were threatened with decline. By 1967 Moynihan was turning his back on the earlier confidence and, at least momentarily, holding his liberal colleagues up to the judgment of the New Left (itself already well embarked on decline). The causes of the action-intellectuals' difficulties were suggested in White's concluding pages. But far more emphatically, though unconsciously, they were revealed in his choice of military metaphors: the action-intellectuals established "beachheads of scholarship"; they provided "platoons of front-line operators" backed up by "the support elements of great scholarship"; most astonishingly, they

> have transformed the ivory tower. For them, it is a forward observation post on the urgent front of the future—and they feel it is their duty to call down the heavy artillery of government, now, on the targets they alone can see moving in the distance.

The question of Vietnam is skirted in White's articles. Yet Tet was six months away. The metaphor had become a literal statement; the ivory tower was transformed into a forward observation post; the heavy artillery of government was indeed heavy artillery; the targets were real people;

and all that scholarly discipline, expertise, professionalism, and practical experience ("We have bred a new generation of people with a new kind of problem-solving skill") only seemed to magnify a subservience to doctrine and a cruel absolutism that had supposedly been left behind with "ideology."

The war was a grave blow for the policy professionals. It divided them and discredited them. In the universities it brought them under attack, and in Washington it brought to power an administration that threatened their status. Both their bases were crumbling. Their morality was challenged as well as their competency. The war's drain on economic and political reserves dealt a death blow to their social programs, ruling out the possibility of correcting false starts. The civil rights movement had bestowed an aura of moral authority on all kinds of challenges to the *status quo,* cultural as well as political; the war precluded any possibility of containing those challenges within the framework of the policy profession- als' expertise and authority.

Neoconservatism was the most profound response to this situation. In some ways, it mapped an orderly retreat for the policy professionals. Too much had been promised in the mid-sixties, and certainly much less could be delivered now. This was to accept a measure of self-criticism, but then much of the blame for this disjunction between demands and realistic possibilities was deflected onto politicians, the "people," or the culture. The specific causes of turmoil in the sixties were traced to larger movements, indeed swallowed up in them: the rise of the "new class," the expansion of egalitarianism, the crisis of authority. In this perspective, the difficulties of policy professionals—and their need for a more supportive atmosphere—was understandable. At the same time, they took their distance from Washington, which, between social programs and the war, had aroused antagonism across the political spectrum. They discovered the virtues of the provinces and the high-powered business elements that Nixon tried to represent. Above all, they strove to discredit their discreditors, carrying the fight to the morals and motives not only of violent protesters, or of practitioners of civil disobedience, but of virtually all who diverged from their own style of professional, managerial politics.

But how does this square with neoconservatism's conspicuous hostility to "social engineers," politicized intellectuals, rootless reformers, and the "new class" which has been created by the need for educated experts and bureaucrats? How can neoconservatism profess such hostility while itself expressing the interests and perspectives of a caste of policy professionals? Why should Irving Kristol, as we have seen, exempt these " 'new men' in government" from his animadversions on "The Troublesome Intellec- tuals," assuring his readers that they are not "hired professionals" but "genuinely cultivated men, interested in the arts and in the life of the mind"? A glimpse at the history of social thought may help, and a closer look at the "new class" and its relation to the "new men" will help even more.

Philosophes *Versus Policy Professionals*

Historically, the reform professionals are successors to Burke, Saint-Simon, Comte, de Tocqueville, and the other members of the "sociological tradition" who consciously opposed their work to that of the Enlightenment's *philosophes*. The great figures of nineteenth-century social thought, as Robert A. Nisbet has pointed out, "wrote as though the Jacobins were looking over their shoulders." For most of them, the French Revolution—and behind it, the *philosophes*—were essentially destructive. Destruction may in some respects have been necessary—here opinions differed—but it had certainly gone too far, and it should certainly yield to a period of *construction*. Where the *philosophes*, given over to abstraction, ambition, and ideology, had bungled, these new students of society would put matters on a sounder, perhaps even a "scientific," basis. In this opposition to the *philosophes* arose a distinctive "sociology of the intellectual," to cite Nisbet again, "that was to persist from Comte to the present day." In effect, this was the counterintellectual tradition, carried on by the neoconservatives and by Nisbet himself with his ferocious attacks on Rawls and egalitarian intellectuals as *salon* revolutionaries. Most importantly, this tradition rooted itself in certain disciplines—sociology, economics, and political science—as they emerged in the modern university. It is precisely these disciplines from which the policy professionals largely come and which have achieved a special status in recent years. When the American Academy of Arts and Sciences established a Commission on the Year 2000, Robert L. Heilbroner noted that three-quarters of its members were from the social or natural sciences: "economists, sociologists, political scientists, psychologists, physicists, and the like. Gone are the sooth-sayers, the clergymen, the philosophers, and all but two historians . . . no artists or writers, no politicians or soldiers, no architects or engineers, no businessmen or students." The commission was chaired by Daniel Bell.

In the nineteenth century, Comte could fume that "any man who can hold a pen may aspire to the spiritual regulation of society . . . whatever may be his qualification"—and yet propose to establish a veritable priesthood of intellectuals at the pinnacle of society. The latter, it should be understood, would be qualified. In our time, Moynihan can attack the presumption of other elites, especially those that have been engaged in social reform, and yet call on an elite cadre of social scientists to preserve stability by "maintaining . . . standards of conflict" in society and "detecting derelictions from such standards." And why? "Let us face it, no one else can afford to be honest about these things." Moynihan's notion is far more moderate than Comte's and far more acceptable to a democratic ethos, but the resemblance subsists. Because they share a common tradition of contrasting their allegedly stabilizing, constructive, sound, and scientific outlook with the destabilizing, fantastical, and uninformed social schemes of the *philosophes* (Seymour Martin Lipset once bluntly spoke of "the shift away from ideology towards sociology"), they can denounce political intellectuals without including themselves in the denunciation. Their complaints are in fact the complaints about "quacks" by those who consider themselves the true professionals, based in learned disciplines that claim to have a more effective grasp on society's problems. To this might be added a residue of the Marxist-Leninist formation of a number of neoconservatives, a formation that, at one and the same time, idealized the "masses," posited an intellectual vanguard that understood the masses' real interests (though the masses did not), and derided the bourgeois reformers who substituted sentiment and vague aspirations for an unblinkered, "scientific" analysis of society.

Reenter the "New Class"

If neoconservatism is the ideology of the policy professionals, it is also linked to the rise of the "new class." The link is not at all the purely negative one that the neoconservative polemic on the "new class" suggests. Assuming that the "new class" is something more than a term of opprobrium for those holding uncongenial opinions, that it is indeed the serious development in social structure that many observers, outside as well as within the ranks of neoconservatism, think it is, then the " 'new men' in government" are obviously key members of it. They are academics and intellectuals—at the very heart of the "new class." They are prominent operators in the "knowledge industry"—in the universities, the think tanks, publishing, and journalism—and they, as Kristol puts it, "commute regularly to Washington." Neoconservative remarks about the "new class" frequently boomerang. When Moynihan wrote that the upper reaches of Washington journalism "constitute one of the most important and enduring *social* elites of the city," someone checked the Social

Register and found only Joseph Alsop—and Daniel Patrick Moynihan.
(This does not mean, however, that Washington journalists, in their way,
do not constitute an important elite.) Of Moynihan it was also noted that,
though he was sensitive to New York's Democratic "Regulars," displaced
by "Reformers" in the early sixties,

> he cast his lot with the winners. His description of "Reformers," written in
> 1961—aggressive, mobile, successful in private life and appointive politics,
> lacking roots in the neighborhoods—applies to Moynihan himself more than
> it does to many of the heroes of reform. . . . Moynihan is wisely sensitive to
> the bureaucratic self-interest of the "social service" and "poverty" cadres
> because he is part of the class, part of the elite of "policy planners" that was
> a major legacy of the New Frontier.

The same can be said of most neoconservatives, and now and then a
neoconservative like Kristol will own up to membership in the "new
class."

Neoconservatives are right in the attention they pay this new segment of
the population. They are wrong in holding that the "new class" is
essentially radical or adversarial in its politics. Not even the professoriat is
actually adversarial; and as far as anyone knows, the "new class" as a
whole is tugged in several different directions politically. Its political
allegiance is as yet undetermined—and that is exactly where neoconservatism emerges in its full social significance.

The "new class" is not, however, a *tabula rasa*. Despite the polemics,
exaggeration, and confusion surrounding the term, those who use it agree
on certain characteristics. First, the "new class" derives its power from
two very different sources: from, on the one hand, "expertise"—technical
knowledge and skills, often of a fairly advanced sort—and, on the other
hand, from "position"—posts in large, complex organizations that both
depend on the expertise of the "new class" and provide the necessary
conditions for its exercise. Second, the "new class" acquires its advanced
expertise and achieves its positions, at least to begin with, through higher
education and the credentials thereby earned.

From these two very general characteristics, it is a relatively small
speculative step to postulating several other things about the "new class."
Hostile and sympathetic observers alike note that the "new class" assumes
that a good measure of independence and authority ought to accompany
its technological capacities; indeed, some such independence and authority is often necessary for it to carry out its technical assignments
effectively. Over against this, however, the "new class" encounters the
constraints of the large and frequently hierarchical organizations where it
operates. A basic tension is introduced into its existence. Unlike the

classical proletarian, denuded of everything but his raw labor power, the "new class" member contains in his person—even in his personality—a considerable investment; he is walking, talking, thinking "human capital." Unlike the skilled craftsman of old, he commonly possesses knowledge and skills that have the aura of the future rather than the past—another claim to authority in a future-oriented society. Further unlike the skilled craftsman or even the solo professional—that individual lawyer or physician of happy, though somewhat foggy, memory—the "new class" member depends on an organizational complex for his bag of tools and for the opportunity to exercise his talents; even the traditional professionals are absorbed into large law firms, or attached to hospitals, or employed by corporations, or linked with universities, and put into everyday intercourse with the government. If some "new class" members, the star professors or management whiz kids, for example, have the wherewithal to move easily from one organization to another, once there they are still immersed in the life of the organization, with all its rival strands of authority and inner conflicts. Obviously the "new class" not only experiences a significant degree of conflict between its proclivities for independent and self-directed action and the necessity of bending to corporate or bureaucratic constraints; it also undergoes an everyday training in a kind of politics. That is part of what Daniel Bell means when he says that where industrial society involved a "game against nature," post-industrial society involves a "game between persons."

With different emphases, radical and neoconservative commentators have pushed this analysis further. Some radicals have endowed the "new class" with "revolutionary potential." Scientists, engineers, technicians, and intellectuals, in this view, are being "proletarianized," forced to work under hierarchical control, their efforts fragmented and specialized and subject to the distorting rule of profit. As a "new working class," or at least as natural allies of ordinary working people, this group in society is likely to press for far-reaching changes, to rebel against corporate capitalism, and to support democratic, egalitarian, and ultimately socialist measures. Many neoconservatives appear no less ready to endow the "new class" with "revolutionary potential," though they look on that fact fearfully and portray it more in terms of an ambitious elite grasping for power rather than of human capacities frustrated by outmoded institutions. The "new class" may indeed institute far-reaching changes, even ostensibly democratic and egalitarian ones, though the neoconservatives consider these mere camouflage for elitist intentions, a facade behind which the "new class" can wield its finely honed political skills and enforce its cultural ideals.

In fact, the "new class" is much less "revolutionary" than either of these views allows. The "new class" enjoys a large measure of privilege, which dampens its enthusiasm for any really radical changes. It also suffers from the right amount of insecurity, especially about passing its privileges on to its children, to prevent it from frontally challenging the "system." There will be no risk-taking with young Jessica's or Jason's chances at entering professional school: the nervousness of the "new class" about education is almost comic, and yet reasonable in view of the crucial role for the "new class" of credentialed knowledge.

If the stereotypical "new class" life-style, centered on "self-fulfillment," often by way of a kind of experimental hedonism, is subversive of stable social norms, it is equally subversive of any concerted challenge to those norms. The "new class" concern with personality sinks easily into a narcissism denounced by social reformers, who see in it the fact that personality, too, is part of the "human capital" on which depends the place of the "new class" in the economy and social structure. Furthermore, the identification of many "new class" members with technical skills or professional roles, achieved through protracted effort, renders them extremely impatient with social change that entails extensive disruption of their own work life. Finally, much of the "new class" is by tradition or social interest linked to a conservative outlook. Dissatisfaction with the *status quo* may express itself in the practice of *pro bono publico* or poverty law, but most young lawyers also absorb the moderate habits and conservative traditions of the legal profession. A few young physicians may agitate for radical health-care reforms, but the burgeoning health-care sector—the literal representation of Moynihan's "therapeutic class"—generally falls into line behind its established medical and corporate leadership. Engineers and researchers working in tight harness with business interests consistently express moderate to conservative political views. And much of the "new class" in the public sector—for example, in the multimillion-dollar network of "think tanks" and research centers, in numerous foundation divisions, academic departments, and government agencies—has always been aligned with the policy professionals, whose neoconservative offensive has been warmly welcomed in these quarters.

In short, the "new class" is neither a traditionally conservative privileged group nor an adversarial element seething with frustration, ambition, or revolt. It is restless, dissatisfied, and critical; it is also doing quite well for itself and has a large stake in the way things are. Its political future remains undetermined.

That is why another trait of the "new class" becomes so important. Educated and articulate, often detached from local communities, traditional religion, and ethnic outlooks, loosed from the wear of manual labor, the regimentation of routine jobs, or the solidarity of shared danger and collective work, the "new class" is relatively sensitive to questions of legitimacy. More than others, the "new class" is apt to pursue public issues back to the basic "fit" that must exist between a society's central values and symbols and its social and political institutions; it is this "fit" that sustains the loyalty of citizens to the existing order. If an "accountable" government is caught out lying, it is not enough to repeat the folk wisdom of the humble, that governments always lie. The "new class" wants a reason. The contradiction between the proclaimed good intentions of authority and its actual performance is more than a disappointment; it, too, demands an explanation. Failures are not shrugged off; frequent failures indicate a systemic problem. Violence and physical pain having been strikingly reduced in the lives of the "new class," it is easily unsettled by exposure to institutions that employ the former or remain unmoved by the latter. Whether due to its training in mental work or its escape from the everyday routines that so reinforce social reality for much of the population, the "new class" quickly registers the incoherencies or inconsistencies of governmental or institutional policy. And ready access to a range of information sources, without the censoring and interpreting screens of inherited beliefs, opens the "new class" to a shower of conflicting images and reports, all of them putting pressure on standing justifications for authority and demanding constant reassessment, revision, and reassertion in that sphere of ideas and symbols that legitimates social institutions. Relative to other segments of society, the "new class" is thin-skinned about legitimacy, high-strung, liable to a "case of the nerves."

If America's social, political, and economic institutions could be trusted to function smoothly, this "new class" skittishness would not matter. If, as both the neoconservatives and other social critics believe, we are entering an "age of limits" in which these institutions will be overburdened or transformed, the "new class" sensitivity to issues of legitimacy could become critical. "If one cannot count on these people," says Irving Kristol of roughly this group, "to provide political, social, and moral stability—if they do not have a good opinion of our society—how long, one wonders, can that stability and good opinion survive?"

So neoconservatism's solicitude for the state of culture and belief turns out to be tactically sound. Culture may not be the seething caldron that threatens to boil over and drown our steady political and economic life with its disruptive forces; but if in fact our political and economic institutions are overtasked and insecure, susceptible to surprise failures, maybe even combustible, then the culture had better be kept at a low simmer.

What the "new class" needs, quite simply, is ideology—a large and coherent set of principles and symbols that will ground and guide its politics. From the neoconservative viewpoint, this ideology must integrate the restless "new class" firmly into "the system." And one of the tasks of the policy professional—this distinguishes him from the mere technician—is to be an expert in providing such ideology. Neoconservatives can be very direct about offering their services—Moynihan warning that America has to promote the same kind of expertise in knowing and combating socialism as it did in the struggle against Communism, Kristol advising business leaders that it had better hire dissident members of the "new class" to direct pro-business forces in the "war of ideas."

The Third World Comes Home

One might think this a curious assignment for the former proponents of the "end of ideology." In fact, their current ideological role was foreshadowed in that earlier literature. In "The End of Ideology?"—the concluding essay of *Political Man* (1959)—Seymour Martin Lipset distinguished sharply between the decline of ideological politics in Western nations and the "need for intense political controversy and ideology" in the underdeveloped world. This need arose because basic political issues remained unsettled in developing nations, because the economic dislocations of modernization bred resentment and forced "the democratic leftist leader to find a scapegoat," and because only an alternative ideological mobilization could prevent the masses from being lost to Communism. "The Leftist intellectual, the trade-union leader, and the socialist politician in the West" have to understand this situation. They "have an important role to play in this political struggle" against Communism. They cannot "demand that such leaders [radicals or socialists in developing nations] adapt their politics to Western images of responsible behavior." Instead, "Western leaders must communicate and work with non-Communist revolutionaries in the Orient and Africa at the same time that they accept the fact that serious ideological controversies have ended at home."

Obviously there is something dangerously condescending about this view. Condescending insofar as it tolerates ideology not simply as a cultural response to unresolved and fundamental political divisions but as a demagogic response to an allegedly greater need for scapegoating and mass indoctrination in the poor nations. Dangerous insofar as it approaches a doctrine of "two truths," one for the knowing Westerners and perhaps the more sophisticated non-Western leaders, the other for "the masses who need the hope implicit in revolutionary chiliastic doctrine." Here is the justification for those ventures in manipulation that joined leftist intellectuals and trade unionists with the Central Intelligence Agency.

But the relevance of Lipset's argument to the "new class" and today's America is simply that, in an unexpected way, the Third World has come home. The strategy that formerly could be relegated to the non-Western nations turns out to be pertinent here and now. Modernization has not done away with ideology but thrown up a "new class" particularly sensitive to it. In the developing nations, according to Lipset, social and economic turmoil required "our allies" to wield ideological politics against the wrong kind of revolutionaries. Today, social and economic uncertainties make it necessary for the policy professional to wage an ideological offensive for the "hearts and minds" of the "new class." Fortunately, the "new class" is no less exigent and fickle in its attitude toward the legitimacy of most social, political, and economic countercurrents. Even the members of the "new class" love old-fashioned individual liberty and distrust big government, says Kristol with relief. "It is our good fortune that they are not doctrinaire socialists."

By emphasizing the inconsistencies, moral failures, or unexpected consequences of such countercurrents, neoconservatism can at least achieve a stasis and perhaps justify the management of change by the policy professionals. Then, too, the "new class" can be reminded of the advantages it currently enjoys, or of the fears it has, for example, that its children might be excluded from the critical places in higher education. It can be persuaded that its own security flows naturally from first principles upholding the present social arrangements. The pride of the "new class" in its own technical skills is honored by the very style of the neoconservative policy professionals. And "new class" nervousness about social inequities is explained and soothed by the theories of the meritocracy and the underclass. Even the exaggerated characterizations of "new class" ambition or lack of morals become a weapon in this ideological combat, undermining the confidence of the "new class" in its critical impulses: it had better prove itself responsible and not like *that*.

In sum, the ideological offensive of neoconservatism has two purposes. One, fairly conscious, is to bind the "new class" to the institutions of liberal capitalism, thus assuring that system's stability and survival. The second, less conscious, is to ensure the leadership of the policy professionals in the "new class" and their influential position near the pinnacles of power.

Virtues and Vices

It would be mistaken to evaluate neoconservatism completely in terms of the social forces that help explain its origins or that suggest its political uses. It would be a logical error, obviously. The origins of a set of ideas or the political interests of their adherents may illuminate but do not determine whether the ideas themselves are true or false, enriching or impoverishing. It would also be an intellectual error of a more general sort. For neoconservatism may provide valuable insights quite apart from its sources or its political functions. Those out of sympathy with either the one or the other may still be able to accept and profit by many of its criticisms and concerns. At the same time, neoconservatism may prove dangerous in ways that have little or nothing to do with the intentions of its intellectual sponsors.

The great virtue of neoconservatism is the serious attention it pays to the moral culture that is a fundament of our political and economic life. There is barely a serious school of liberal or even Marxist thought that holds humans to be economically determined and values, culture, and beliefs the mere reflection of socioeconomic forces. And yet in practice liberals, radicals, and socialists concentrate on questions of economic deprivation or physical pain rather than of meaning or moral capacity. They do not deny the importance of culture and values; but when they would act upon them, they almost inevitably propose to enter the chain of causes at the point of providing material support or physical well-being. Otherwise, the Left, broadly speaking, has been primarily concerned with culture by way of removing constraints—commercial pressures, government censorship, insufficient funding, traditional taboos, established conventions. The New Left did criticize liberalism in the sixties for its rendering of politics as procedure and its presentation of social science as value-free. Irving Kristol and the New Left were thus agreed on the necessity of "republican virtue" (though the New Left, unlike Kristol, would not rally to the "bourgeois ethic"). But the New Left's concern dissolved into assorted dogmatisms on the one hand, and into the cultural *laissez-faire* of "do your own thing" on the other. It was left to neoconservatism, sworn enemy of the New Left, to be the serious force reminding us that the capacity of self-government and self-direction is not a given which simply emerges once restraints are removed. It is an active power that must be fostered, nourished, and sustained; that requires supporting communities, disciplined thinking and speech, self-restraint, and accepted conventions. In a number of ways neoconservatism is not itself faithful to this insight, even contradicts it; but it has put the moral culture of society on the public agenda and no doubt will keep it there.

The second virtue of neoconservatism is its rejection of sentimentality. By sentimentality I mean the immediate emotional response that renders a reality all of a piece and "obvious." When sentimentality governs our responses to the world's ills, it clings to the visible or physical evils at hand and tends to ignore the less apparent, more diffuse, and distant dangers. It leaps to solutions and short-circuits reflection. Neoconservatism has countered this sentimentality by forcing back the discussion of many political issues to first principles and by its delight in exposing unintended consequences of well-meant measures. There is a good bit of sentimentality in neoconservatism; there is even a sentimentality of anti-sentimentality—a reflexive granting of credibility to whatever, through irony, paradox, or complexity, appears to resist the pull of sympathy, and an equally automatic suspicion of whatever appears untutored or unguarded in its registration of experience. And there is also the tendency toward that hard-headed constriction of feeling that Dickens, in *Hard Times,* fixed in the very name as well as character of Gradgrind. Nonetheless, the neoconservative presence in public controversy has certainly reduced the likelihood that the "obvious" will escape questioning. Is money what the poor need? Or better schools the solution to illiteracy? Does poverty breed crime? Should more people vote? Or campaign spending be limited? Is equality desirable? To some people, the very posing of such questions is an annoyance and a diversion. To those, however, who believe that the unexamined proposal is not worth pursuing, the neoconservative attitude appears salutary.

The third virtue of neoconservatism is related to the second: the thoroughgoing criticisms that it has made of liberal or radical programs and premises. This is less an attitude, like its anti-sentimentality, than a self-assigned agenda. Neoconservatism has taken pride in frontally challenging the excesses of the New Left and the counterculture; more important—because those excesses were probably self-liquidating and already on the wane when neoconservatism set to work—have been the detailed and often technically superior critiques of mainstream liberal notions. Despite the polemical overkill that too frequently mars such critiques, they provide a much more factually informed and sophisticated debating partner for liberal or left-wing thought than has traditional American conservatism, in any of its rugged individualist, agrarian aristocrat, or super-nationalist manifestations.

To every virtue a vice. The outstanding weaknesses of neoconservatism have already been amply suggested: its formulation of an outlook largely in negative terms; its lack of internal criticism; its unwillingness to direct attention to socioeconomic structures and to the existing economic powers; its exaggeration of the adversarial forces in society; its lack of serious respect for its adversaries. If neoconservatism is to construct a convincing defense of an outlook emphasizing a stoic rationality, public restraint, and the maintenance of an ethic of achievement and excellence, it will have to confront the extent to which such an ideal challenges contemporary capitalism. If it is to defend freedom in a bureaucratic age, it will have to understand freedom in a richer sense than anti-Communism and a derived anti-statism. If it is to defend high culture and intellectual rigor, it will need to celebrate the enlarging and life-giving force of superior work and not merely issue self-satisfying strictures on the inferior or fashionable.

Neoconservatism began as an antibody on the left. Many of its leading figures originally conceived of it that way and perhaps still do: it was a reaction to what they considered the destabilizing and excessive developments of the sixties, and when these had been quelled, it would once again be indistinguishable from mainstream liberalism. Its own excesses, or at least its somewhat narrow focus of attention on one set of adversaries, would be balanced by the native strengths of the liberalism of which it was part. That, of course, has not turned out to be the case. Neoconservatism is now an independent force. To return to the biological analogy, antibodies which overreact can destroy the organism. The great danger posed by and to neoconservatism is that it will become nothing more than the legitimating and lubricating ideology of an oligarchic America where essential decisions are made by corporate elites, where great inequalities are rationalized by straitened circumstances and a system of meritocratic hierarchy, and where democracy becomes an occasional, ritualistic gesture. Whether neoconservatism will end by playing this sinister and unhappy role, or whether it will end as a permanent, creative, and constructive element in American politics, is only partially in the hands of neoconservatives themselves. It will also be determined by the vigor, intelligence, and dedication of their critics and opponents.

Notes

Chapter One

p. 2 "All about us . . .": Daniel P. Moynihan, "Introduction" to Nathan Glazer and Irving Kristol, eds., *The American Commonwealth—1976* (New York: Basic Books, 1976), p. 6. This volume originally appeared as the special Bicentennial issue of *The Public Interest*. Moynihan on "Correcting course . . .": *New York Times,* May 28, 1976, Op-Ed page, A-25.

p. 3 Peter Berger's views: Peter Berger, "Ideologies, Myths, Moralities," in Irving Kristol and Paul H. Weaver, eds., *The Americans: 1976* (Lexington, Mass.: Lexington Books, 1976), pp. 347, 354. This book is Vol. 2 in the series "Critical Choices of Americans" organized and funded by Nelson A. Rockefeller.

p. 3 Wolin on liberalism: Sheldon S. Wolin, *Politics and Vision* (Boston: Little, Brown, 1960), pp. 293–94.

p. 4 *Newsweek: Newsweek,* November 7, 1977, p. 34.

p. 5 Kadushin on most prestigious intellectuals: Charles Kadushin, *The American Intellectual Elite* (Boston: Little, Brown, 1974), pp. 30–31.

p. 5 De Tocqueville: Quoted in Kristol and Weaver, *The Americans,* p. xviii.

p. 6 Memo to Nixon: [Patrick J. Buchanan] " 'The Ship of Integration is Going Down,' " *Harper's,* June 1972, pp. 66–67.

p. 6 Change in China reviewers: Roger Hilsman, *To Move a Nation* (Garden City, N.Y.: Doubleday, 1967), pp. 297–98.

p. 9 Neoconservative summary to Nixon: reported in Daniel P. Moynihan, *The Politics of a Guaranteed Annual Income* (New York: Random House, 1973), pp. 77–78.

p. 9 Drew on Jackson dinner: *New Yorker,* May 31, 1976, pp. 86–87.

p. 13 $100,000 from Rockefeller: "Rockefeller to Keep 4 of His Top Aides," *New York Times,* December 13, 1973, pp. 1, 56.

p. 13   Payment for "new class" study: personal communication from a contributor.

p. 13   Trilling on liberalism's need for conservative adversaries: Lionel Trilling, *The Liberal Imagination* (Garden City, N.Y.: Doubleday Anchor Books, 1954), pp. 5–6.

p. 14   Mill's remarks: "Coleridge," originally in the *London and Westminster Review,* March 1840.

p. 14   Epstein: In Lewis A. Coser and Irving Howe, eds., *The New Conservatives* (New York: Quadrangle, 1974), pp. 9, 10, 11.

p. 16   Viereck's 1954 essay: "The Revolt Against the Elite" in Daniel Bell, ed., *The Radical Right* (Garden City, N.Y.: Doubleday Anchor Books, 1964); quotes from pp. 176–77.

p. 16   Viereck's 1962 essay: "The Philosophical 'New Conservatism,' " ibid.; quotes on pp. 187, 188, 199, 200.

p. 17   Wolin: Sheldon S. Wolin, "The New Conservatives," *New York Review of Books,* February 5, 1976, pp. 6, 8.

p. 20   *Time* on Moynihan: "A Fighting Irishman at the U.N.," *Time,* January 26, 1976, p. 26.

p. 21   *Commentary* on counterculture sports: W.J. Bennet, "In Defense of Sports," *Commentary,* February 1976, pp. 68–70.

p. 21   *Commentary* on *Ragtime:* Hilton Kramer, *Commentary,* October 1975, p. 76.

p. 21   *Public Interest*'s essays: "What Is the Public Interest?" *Public Interest,* Fall 1965, p. 4.

p. 22   Newsweeklies: For example, "Is America Turning Right?" *Newsweek,* November 7, 1977, pp. 34–44.

p. 22   "Great Society liberalism . . .": Patrick J. Buchanan, *New York Daily News,* May 14, 1978.

p. 22   Personal vendetta between Podhoretz and Epstein: Merle Miller, "Why Jason and Norman Aren't Talking," *New York Times Magazine,* March 29, 1972.

p. 22   Frances FitzGerald's attack: Frances FitzGerald, "The Warrior Intellectuals," *Harper's.* May 1976, p. 45.

p. 23   Orde Coombs, "The Retreat of the Liberal Sages," *New York Times,* May 17, 1976, Op-Ed page, p. 29.

p. 24   Mill: "Coleridge."

Chapter Two

p. 25   Initial issue: Daniel Bell and Irving Kristol, "What Is the Public Interest?" *Public Interest,* Fall 1965, p. 4.

p. 26   Kazin on socialist atmosphere: Alfred Kazin, *Starting Out in the Thirties* (Boston: Little, Brown Atlantic Monthly Press Book, 1965), p. 4.

p. 27   Kazin on Granville Hicks: ibid., p. 146.

p. 29   Bell: Daniel Bell, *The End of Ideology* (New York: Free Press, 1962), p. 311.

p. 29   Podhoretz on "hard anti-Communism": Norman Podhoretz, *Making It* (New York: Random House, 1967), pp. 289–90.

p. 30   Complaint against McCarthy as amateur: see Christopher Lasch's comments on Sidney Hook in Christopher Lasch, *The Agony of the American Left* (New York: Alfred A. Knopf, 1969), pp. 83–86. Kristol, Cohen, and Glazer on McCarthy: besides the original articles in *Commentary*, see comment by Irving Howe in "This Age of Conformity," originally in *Partisan Review* in 1954, reprinted in Howe, *Steady Work* (New York: Harcourt, Brace & World Harvest Book, 1966), pp. 328–29; and "The New York Intellectuals," originally in *Commentary*, reprinted in Howe, *The Decline of the New* (New York: Harcourt, Brace & World, 1970), pp. 233–34. Also Lasch, *Agony*, p. 85.

p. 30   Podhoretz: *Making It*, p. 291.

p. 30   Podhoretz change of mind: Norman Podhoretz, "Making the World Safe for Communism," *Commentary*, April 1976, p. 32. Earlier view: *Making It*, p. 292. Glazer review: Nathan Glazer, "An Answer to Lillian Hellman," *Commentary*, June 1976, p. 36.

p. 31   CIA connection: Lasch, *Agony*, pp. 63–114. This section of Lasch's book, "The Cultural Cold War: a Short History of the Congress for Cultural Freedom," originally appeared in *The Nation*. In 1967 I researched an article, never published, on CIA support of *Encounter* magazine and interviewed many of the editors and writers in *Encounter*'s circle. Various apologies can be found in "Liberal Anti-Communism Revisited: a Symposium," *Commentary*, September 1967, pp. 31–79.

p. 34   Rogin: Michael Paul Rogin, *The Intellectuals and McCarthy* (Cambridge, Mass.: MIT Press, 1967), p. 282.

p. 36   Characteristics of moralism: Daniel Bell, ed., *The Radical Right* (Garden City, N.Y.: Doubleday Anchor Book, 1964), pp. 18, 24, 61–64, 71–72, 317.

p. 36   Bell on moralism: ibid., p. 64, Lipset on moralism: ibid., p. 317.

p. 36   Burke and Lipset: see Seymour Martin Lipset, "The Paradox of American Politics," in Nathan Glazer and Irving Kristol, eds., *The American Commonwealth—1976* (New York: Basic Books, 1976), p. 143; compare with Edmund Burke, *Speech on Conciliation with the Colonies,* ed. Jeffrey Hart (Chicago: Henry Regnery Gateway Edition, 1964), p. 64 and *passim*.

p. 37   Hawthorne's warning: quoted by Arthur M. Schlesinger, Jr., in an essay on Richard Hofstadter, in Marcus Cunliffe and Robin W. Winks, eds., *Pastmasters* (New York: Harper & Row, 1969), p. 299.

p. 37   Rogin on neglect of conservative moralism: *Intellectuals and McCarthy,* p. 266.

p. 37   "New framework" of "status politics": Bell, *Radical Right,* pp. 84–85, 308–09.

p. 38   Schlesinger on Bell's and Hofstadter's status approach: in Cunliffe and Winks, *Pastmasters,* pp. 311–12.

p. 39   Status theory not applied to New Deal: ibid., p. 308.

p. 39   Rogin on role of status anxieties: *Intellectuals and McCarthy,* pp. 246–47.

p. 40   Summary by Haber: in Chaim I. Waxman, *The End of Ideology Debate* (New York: Funk & Wagnalls, 1968), pp. 182–83.

p. 41   "Fundamental political problems . . .": Seymour Martin Lipset,

Political Man (Garden City, N.Y.: Doubleday Anchor Book, 1963), p. 442.

p. 41 Kirkpatrick: Jeane Kirkpatrick, "Why the New Right Lost," *Commentary,* February 1977, p. 39.

p. 42 Kennedy's messages: quoted in Waxman, *End of Ideology Debate,* pp. 225–26.

p. 42 Bell on "the faith ladder": Daniel Bell, *The End of Ideology* (New York: Free Press, 1962), p. 402.

p. 42 "A prior commitment . . .": *Public Interest,* Fall 1965, p. 4.

p. 43 Lippmann's definition: ibid., p. 5.

p. 43 Moynihan: "The Professionalization of Reform," in ibid.; passage quoted, p. 12.

p. 43 Podhoretz' objection: *Making It,* p. 316.

p. 44 Moynihan on *The Public Interest:* "Introduction," Glazer and Kristol, *American Commonwealth,* p. 6.

p. 45 Glazer's concluding sentence: "On Being Deradicalized," *Commentary,* October 1970, p. 80.

p. 46 Programmatic sentence dropped: see Nathan Glazer, *Remembering the Answers* (New York: Basic Books, 1970).

p. 46 Howe on Glazer's earlier unaccountable minimization of McCarthy: *Steady Work,* p. 329.

p. 46 Bell on lack of enemy: *End of Ideology,* p. 301.

p. 47 Radical denunciation of Panther violence: Julius Lester in *Liberation,* cited in Peter Steinfels, "The Cooling of the Intellectuals," *Commonweal,* May 21, 1971, p. 257.

p. 48 "A most improbable conservative": *Wall Street Journal,* November 10, 1970.

p. 48 *National Review*'s imprimatur: *National Review,* March 9, 1971, pp. 249–50.

Chapter Three

p. 51 Kristol on neoconservatism: Irving Kristol, "What Is a Neo-Conservative?" *Newsweek,* January 19, 1976, p. 87.

p. 54 Moynihan: Daniel P. Moynihan, *The Politics of a Guaranteed Annual Income* (New York: Random House, 1973), p. 79.

p. 54 Trilateral Commission: Michael Crozier, Samuel P. Huntington, and Joji Watanuki, *The Crisis of Democracy: A Report on the Governability of Democracies to the Trilateral Commission* (New York: New York University Press, 1975), pp. 161, 2.

p. 54 Wildavsky: Aaron Wildavsky, "Government and the People," *Commentary,* August 1973, p. 25.

p. 55 Wilson on conditions in sixties: James Q. Wilson, *Thinking About Crime* (New York: Basic Books, 1975), pp. 4–5, 7.

p. 56 Wildavsky: "Government and the People," p. 25.

p. 56 Hofstadter: Richard Hofstadter, "Two Cultures: Adversary and/or Responsible," *Public Interest,* Winter 1976, p. 74.

p. 57 University growth and legitimating power: Everett Carll Ladd, Jr., and

Seymour Martin Lipset, *The Divided Academy* (New York: McGraw-Hill, 1975), pp. 1–2.

p. 57 Novak: Michael Novak, "Make Room for Family Democrats," *Washington Star,* August 29, 1976.

p. 58 Bell: Daniel Bell, *The Coming of the Post-Industrial Society* (New York: Basic Books, 1973), pp. 212 ff.

p. 58 Trilateral report: Crozier, Huntington, and Watanuki, *Crisis of Democracy,* p. 8.

p. 59 Huntington on "Welfare Shift": ibid., pp. 65–74.

p. 59 Wildavsky: "Government and the People," p. 27.

p. 63 Alfred Marshall: ibid., p. 29.

p. 64 Moynihan on market: *Politics of a Guaranteed Annual Income,* p. 53.

p. 66 Moynihan repeating Forrester: ibid., p. 239; Daniel P. Moynihan, *Coping* (New York: Random House, 1973), p. 24.

p. 66 Characteristic line: Elie Kedourie, "Is Democracy Doomed?" *Commentary,* November 1976, p. 43.

p. 66 Bell on establishment: "Creating a Genuine National Society," *Current,* Sept. 1976; excerpts from an interview with Daniel Bell originally published in *U.S. News and World Report,* July 5, 1976.

p. 67 Moynihan: Daniel P. Moynihan, "Waging Ideological Conflict," *Center Magazine,* March–April 1976, p. 8.

p. 69 Trilateral Commission: Crozier, Huntington, and Watanuki, *Crisis of Democracy,* "Introductory Note."

p. 69 Kristol: Irving Kristol, *On the Democratic Idea in America* (New York: Harper & Row Torchbook, 1972), p. 87.

Chapter Four

p. 71 Howe on New York intellectual style: "The New York Intellectuals," in Irving Howe, *The Decline of the New* (New York: Harcourt, Brace & World, 1970), pp. 240–42.

p. 72 "Taut with a pressure . . .": ibid.

p. 73 Moynihan: Daniel P. Moynihan, "Was Woodrow Wilson Right?" *Commentary,* May 1974, pp. 30–31.

p. 74 David Riesman: *Time,* January 26, 1976, p. 34. For the two speeches see Daniel P. Moynihan, *Coping* (New York: Random House, 1973), pp. 116–33 ("Nirvana Now") and pp. 420–30 (" 'Peace' ").

p. 74 Banfield: Quoted by Joseph Epstein, "The New Conservatives: Intellectuals in Retreat," in Lewis A. Coser and Irving Howe, eds., *The New Conservatives* (New York: Quadrangle, 1974), p. 18.

p. 74 Drucker's reversals and misstatements: see James Henry, "How Pension Fund Socialism Didn't Come to America," *Working Papers,* Winter 1977, pp. 78–87.

p. 75 Howe on *tournament: The Decline of the New,* p. 241.

p. 75 Nineteenth-century *Saturday Review:* John Gross, *The Rise and Fall of the Man of Letters* (New York: Macmillan, 1969), pp. 63–64.

p. 76 Uphold the values . . .: Glazer, "On Being Deradicalized"; Dennis H.

Wrong, "The Case of *The New York Review,*" *Commentary,* November 1970, pp. 49–63.

p. 76 *New York Review* and "next Stalin": Martin Mayer in *Esquire,* May 1971, quoted by Philip Nobile, *Intellectual Skywriting* (New York: Charterhouse, 1974), p. 5.

p. 76 Kissinger's diplomacy as immoral: *Commentary,* July 1976, p. 3.

p. 76 On "anti-Americanism": see Peter Steinfels, "The Cooling of the Intellectuals," *Commonweal,* May 21, 1971, p. 260.

p. 77 Moynihan on treachery: "Crisis of Democracy a Challenge to 'Educated Class,' Says Moynihan," *Harvard Today,* Summer 1976, p. 6.

p. 77 Glazer on Wills: Nathan Glazer, "An Answer to Lillian Hellman," *Commentary,* June 1976, p. 39; for a critique of Wills, see Irving Howe, "Lillian Hellman and the McCarthy Years," *Dissent,* Fall 1976, pp. 378–82.

p. 77 Phillips on New Critics: Norman Podhoretz, *Making It* (New York: Random House, 1967), p. 151.

p. 78 Review of *Blind Ambition:* James Q. Wilson, *Commentary,* February 1977, pp. 67–68.

p. 78 Welfare rolls, desegregation, and Moynihan: Frederick Doolittle, Frank Levy, and Michael Wiseman, "The Mirage of Welfare Reform," *Public Interest,* Spring 1977, pp. 65–66, 75–76; David L. Kirp, "School Desegregation and the Limits of Legalism," ibid., p. 108; Daniel P. Moynihan, interview, *Playboy,* March 1977, pp. 74, 76, and "A Country in Need of Praise," *Saturday Review,* September 11, 1973, pp. 20–21.

p. 78 On Cheever and Wolfe: John Romano, "Redemption According to Cheever," *Commentary,* May 1977, pp. 66–69; Dorothy Rabinowitz, "Satire and Beyond," ibid., pp. 76–77.

Chapter Five

p. 81 A matter deserving of explanation: Nathan Glazer, *Remembering the Answers* (New York: Basic Books, 1970), p. 3.

p. 81 Kristol asserts: Irving Kristol, *On the Democratic Idea in America* (New York: Harper & Row Torchbook, 1972), p. ix.

p. 81 Discomfort with liberalism or conservatism: ibid., p. viii.

p. 81 "The more I think about . . .": Irving Kristol in "What Is a Liberal—Who Is a Conservative? A Symposium," *Commentary,* September 1976, p. 74.

p. 81 On Alcove No. 1: Irving Kristol, "Memoirs of a Trotskyist," *New York Times Magazine,* January 23, 1977, pp. 42–43, 50–51, 54–57.

p. 82 "The honor I most prized . . .": ibid., p. 43.

p. 82 Handed in card to Howe: See the exchange between Kristol and Howe over "The New York Intellectuals," *Commentary,* January 1969, p. 14.

p. 82 Recalls "issuing protests . . .": ibid.

p. 82 Harrington's interpretation: Originally published in *Dissent,* quoted in Irving Howe, *The Decline of the New* (New York: Harcourt, Brace & World, 1970), p. 233.

p. 83   Lasch: Christopher Lasch, *The Agony of the American Left* (New York: Alfred A. Knopf, 1969), pp. 78–98.

p. 83   Initial editorial: *Encounter,* October 1953. Kristol wrote the editorial, according to Stephen Spender, *The Thirties and After* (New York: Random House, 1978), p. 127.

p. 84   Braden: Thomas W. Braden, "I'm Glad the CIA Is 'Immoral,' " *Saturday Evening Post,* May 20, 1967, p. 10.

p. 84   "Gentle interventions": Irving Kristol, "Memoirs of a Cold Warrior," *New York Times Magazine,* February 11, 1968, p. 90.

p. 85   Braden on credibility of front: "I'm Glad," p. 10.

p. 85   While saying that his lawyer warned: in an interview I had with Kristol in 1967. This account is based on 1966–67 stories in the American and British press, my own survey of *Encounter*'s contents during its early years, and my interviews with its editors and contributors.

p. 85   Good reasons not to take them seriously: Kristol, "Memoirs of a Cold Warrior," pp. 24, 90 and ff.

p. 86   "I was a member . . .": Diana Trilling, *We Must March My Darlings* (New York: Harcourt Brace Jovanovich Harvest/HBJ Book, 1978), pp. 60–61.

p. 87   Kristol on Humphrey and Nixon: Irving Kristol, "Why I Am for Humphrey," *New Republic,* June 8, 1968, p. 21.

p. 88   A front page story: John M. Naughton, "U.S. to Tighten Surveillance of Radicals," *New York Times,* April 12, 1970, pp. 1, 69 ff.

p. 88   Agnew praising Kristol: in Philip Nobile, *Intellectual Skywriting* (New York: Charterhouse, 1974), p. 5.

p. 88   "Basic principles of riot control": Kristol, *On the Democratic Idea,* pp. 123–24. Originally in *New York Times Magazine,* December 8, 1968.

p. 89   "Just say nothing": Israel Shenker, "Many Academics Regret Supporting President in Newspaper Ads," *New York Times,* September 5, 1973.

p. 89   Even a report: Evans and Novak column, November 19, 1972, quoted by Nobile, *Intellectual Skywriting,* p. 5.

p. 89   "For all the world . . .": Yosal Rogat, "I'm All Right, Dick," *New York Review of Books,* September 21, 1972, p. 6.

p. 89   Dinner at the White House: "Nixon Hails Reader's Digest on Jubilee," and "Singer Protests War at a Nixon Dinner for Digest Editors," *New York Times,* January 29, 1972, p. 26.

p. 90   Common theme: Kristol, *On the Democratic Idea,* p. vii.

p. 90   "historic watershed . . . prevailing traditions": ibid., pp. 22–24.

p. 91   One essay: "The Shaking of the Foundations," ibid., pp. 25–30.

p. 91   Another essay: "Urban Civilization and Its Discontents," ibid., pp. 1–21.

p. 91   Yet another essay: "American Historians and the Democratic Idea," ibid., pp. 48–67; quote on p. 53.

p. 91   Elsewhere Kristol expresses concern: ibid., p. 14.

p. 92   Social scientists: ibid., pp. 41–42.

p. 92   Replacement: ibid., p. 56.

p. 92   "Jacksonian-egalitarian-populist . . .": ibid., p. 59.

p. 92   Revolution in American thought: ibid., pp. 56–59.

p. 92   "To see something . . .": ibid., p. 26.

p. 92   The causes "are so obvious . . .": ibid., p. 11.

p. 92   Americans who defend capitalism: Irving Kristol, "On Conservatism and Capitalism," *Wall Street Journal,* September 11, 1975. This essay is reprinted in Irving Kristol, *Two Cheers for Capitalism* (New York: Basic Books, 1978), p. 136.

p. 93   Performance and legitimacy: Irving Kristol, "Who Stands for the Corporation?" *Think,* May–June 1975, p. 10; *On the Democratic Idea,* pp. 99–100.

p. 93   What critics really want: Kristol, *On the Democratic Idea,* pp. 80–91; Irving Kristol, "Capitalism, Socialism, and Nihilism," *Public Interest,* Spring 1973, pp. 7–9, in *Two Cheers,* pp. 61-62.

p. 93   "A secular society . . ."; "Capitalism, Socialism, and Nihilism," p. 10, in *Two Cheers,* p. 63.

p. 93   "Under capitalism . . .": "Capitalism, Socialism, and Nihilism," p. 11, in *Two Cheers,* p. 65.

p. 94   Artists and intellectuals: Irving Kristol, "About Equality," *Commentary,* November 1972, p. 43, in *Two Cheers,* p. 178.

p. 94   "As conceived . . . by intellectuals": "About Equality," p. 44, in *Two Cheers,* p. 178.

p. 94   "Likely to move 'Right' . . .": "About Equality," p. 44, in *Two Cheers,* p. 179.

p. 94   "A connection . . .": "Capitalism, Socialism, and Nihilism," p. 11, in *Two Cheers,* p. 65.

p. 94   Not only free but just: *On the Democratic Idea,* pp. 96–97.

p. 94   "Accumulated moral capital . . .": "Capitalism, Socialism, and Nihilism," p. 11, in *Two Cheers,* p. 65–66.

p. 94   "Bureaucratization . . .": "About Equality," p. 45, in *Two Cheers,* p. 181.

p. 94   "A legitimating idea": "Who Stands for the Corporation," p. 10.

p. 94   "Faceless and nameless . . .": "About Equality," p. 45, in *Two Cheers,* p. 181.

p. 95   The "new class": Irving Kristol, "On Corporate Capitalism in America," in Nathan Glazer and Irving Kristol, eds., *The American Commonwealth—1976* (New York: Basic Books, 1976), p. 134, in *Two Cheers,* p. 15.

p. 95   "The simple truth . . .": "About Equality," p. 43, in *Two Cheers,* p. 177.

p. 95   "New class" assault: "On Corporate Capitalism," pp. 135, 141, in *Two Cheers,* pp. 16–17, 23–24.

p. 95   "Practically defenseless": "On Corporate Capitalism," p. 137, in *Two Cheers,* p. 18.

p. 95   "An utterly defenseless institution . . .": "Who Stands for the Corporation," p. 11.

p. 96   Kristol on "idealism": Irving Kristol, "Notes on the Spirit of '76," *Wall Street Journal,* April 23, 1976.

p. 96   "The law insists . . .": Irving Kristol, "On Conservatism and Capitalism," *Wall Street Journal,* Sept. 11, 1975, in *Two Cheers,* p. 138.

p. 96   Solicitousness toward businessmen: Irving Kristol, "Ethics and the Corporation," *Wall Street Journal,* April 16, 1975, in *Two Cheers,* pp. 78–83.

p. 97   Antitrust lawyers: "Corporate Capitalism in America," p. 129, in *Two Cheers,* pp. 9–10.

p. 97   "These same people . . .": "Corporate Capitalism in America," pp. 134–35, in *Two Cheers,* p. 16.

p. 97   "Not motivated . . .": "About Equality," p. 43, in *Two Cheers,* p. 177.

p. 98   First small shoots of New Left: Irving Kristol, "Teaching In, Speaking Out: Letter from New York," *Encounter,* August 1965, p. 68.

p. 98   "All of them have contacts . . .": ibid., p. 69.

p. 98   Explanation of antiwar agitation: Irving Kristol, "American Intellectuals and Foreign Policy," originally in *Foreign Affairs* (July 1967), reprinted in *On the Democratic Idea;* quotes from pp. 70, ibid., 69, 85, 86, 88.

p. 99   The "ideological essay": Daniel Bell and Irving Kristol, "What Is the Public Interest?" *Public Interest,* Fall 1965, p. 4.

p. 99   "Unanticipated consequences . . .": *On the Democratic Idea,* p. ix.

p. 99   "The history . . .": ibid., p. 15.

p. 100   "Today drug-taking . . .": ibid., p. 20.

p. 100   "What is called . . .": ibid., p. 26.

p. 100   "All the codes . . .": ibid., p. 38.

p. 100   "Religion begins . . .": *Commentary,* September 1976, p. 4.

p. 100   "The Founding Fathers . . .": "On Corporate Capitalism," p. 125, in *Two Cheers,* p. 3.

p. 100   "The Left in Europe . . .": "On Corporate Capitalism," p. 132, in *Two Cheers,* p. 12.

p. 100   "The members of this 'new class' . . .": "On Corporate Capitalism," p. 135, in *Two Cheers,* p. 16.

p. 100   Joseph Epstein: in Lewis A. Coser and Irving Howe, eds., *The New Conservatives* (New York: Quadrangle, 1974), pp. 22–23.

p. 100   "Obviously, socialism . . .": "On Corporate Capitalism," p. 132, in *Two Cheers,* p. 13.

p. 100   "The plain truth . . .": *On the Democratic Idea,* p. 91.

p. 100   "The simple truth . . .": "About Equality," p. 43, in *Two Cheers,* p. 177.

p. 100   "The proposition . . .": *On the Democratic Idea,* p. 86.

p. 100   "A demonstrable fact . . .": "About Equality," p. 46, in *Two Cheers,* p. 184.

p. 101   *Forbes* article: Mentioned by Yosal Rogat, "I'm All Right, Dick," *New York Review of Books,* May 21, 1972, p. 6.

p. 101   On New York crisis: Irving Kristol, "New York Is a State of Mind," *Wall Street Journal,* December 10, 1975.

p. 101   On welfare: ibid.

p. 101   On Great Society illusions: Irving Kristol, "The Conservative Prospect," *Wall Street Journal,* June 13, 1975.

p. 101   On busing: ibid.

p. 101   On trade unions: Irving Kristol, "The Economic Consequence of Carter," *Wall Street Journal,* December 22, 1976.

p. 101   On medical care: Irving Kristol, "The Republican Future," *Wall Street Journal*, May 14, 1976, in *Two Cheers*, p. 127.

p. 101   "Few serious studies . . .": *On the Democratic Idea*, p. 101.

p. 101   On pornography: ibid., p. 39.

p. 101   But one reference: ibid., p. 18.

p. 102   Old movies: ibid., pp. 10–11.

p. 102   Butler on parishioners: Samuel Butler, *The Way of All Flesh* (Baltimore: Penguin Books, 1971), p. 94.

p. 102   "Pre-modern political philosophy . . .": *On the Democratic Idea*, p. 106.

p. 102   Empty belief: "Capitalism, Socialism, and Nihilism," pp. 13–15, in *Two Cheers*, pp. 63–69.

p. 103   An exception for the market place: *On the Democratic Idea*, pp. vii–viii.

p. 103   Disputes capitalist justification: "Capitalism, Socialism, and Nihilism," pp. 11, 13, 15, in *Two Cheers*, pp. 65–69.

p. 103   Inherent to liberal society: Irving Kristol, "What Is 'Social Justice?' " *Wall Street Journal*, April 12, 1976, in *Two Cheers*, p. 192.

p. 103   On the mob: *On the Democratic Idea*, p. 16.

p. 103   On lack of moderation: ibid., pp. 26–27.

p. 103   On decadence: Irving Kristol, "Of Decadence and Tennis Flannels," *Wall Street Journal*, September 21, 1976, in *Two Cheers*, pp. 250–54.

p. 103   Hails the common man: "About Equality," passim, in *Two Cheers*, pp. 171–87; also Irving Kristol, "Thoughts on Equality and Egalitarians," in Colin D. Campbell, ed., *Income Redistribution* (Washington, D.C.: American Enterprise Institute, 1977), pp. 25–42.

p. 103   Intellectuals' conviction: "About Equality," p. 44, in *Two Cheers*, pp. 178–79.

p. 104   "Silly liberal chatter": "What Is a Liberal—Who Is a Conservative?" p. 74.

p. 104   Urban civilization, drugs, and Pogo: *On the Democratic Idea*, pp. 19–21.

p. 104   "Death of God": ibid., p. 30; and "About Equality," p. 47, in *Two Cheers*, p. 187.

p. 104   "The long trek . . .": *On the Democratic Idea*, p. 106.

p. 104   Founding fathers' philosophy: ibid., p. 66.

p. 104   Democracy and slavery: ibid., p. 2.

p. 104   Period of transformation: ibid., p. 56.

p. 104   Tasks of conservatism: "On Conservatism and Capitalism," in *Two Cheers*, p. 140; and Irving Kristol, "The Conservative Report," *Wall Street Journal*, June 13, 1975.

p. 105   "Major intellectual question": *Two Cheers*, p. xi.

p. 105   What counts is "feeling" free: *On the Democratic Idea*, pp. 98, 102.

p. 105   "Influence of Christianity . . .": "About Equality," p. 42, in *Two Cheers*, pp. 174–75.

p. 106   Good welfare state: "The Republican Future," in *Two Cheers*, pp. 126–27.

p. 106   "Conservative reformer": *On the Democratic Idea,* p. ix.

p. 106   Models: ibid., p. 105.

p. 106   Proposals for corporate reform: "Who Stands for the Corporation," p. 11; interview in *Forbes,* May 15, 1974, pp. 74–75.

p. 106   Pornography and republican morality: *On the Democratic Idea,* pp. 40–47.

p. 106   Bribery and post-Watergate morality: Irving Kristol, "Post-Watergate Morality: Too Good for Our Good?" *New York Times Magazine,* November 14, 1976, pp. 35, 50 ff.

p. 106   One reviewer: Rogat, pp. 6–8.

p. 107   Importance of political ideas: *On the Democratic Idea,* pp. 64–65.

Chapter Six

p. 108   Opening session: Lee Rainwater and William L. Yancey, *The Moynihan Report and the Politics of Controversy* (Cambridge, Mass.: MIT Press, 1967), p. 248.

p. 109   "A combination . . .": Quoted in St. Clair Drake, "Moynihan and the Third World," *Nation,* July 5, 1975, p. 9.

p. 110   A man "happiest . . .": "A Fighting Irishman at the U.N.," *Time,* January 26, 1976, p. 34.

p. 110   Rainwater and Yancey on Moynihan's style: *Moynihan Report,* pp. 160–61, 144.

p. 111   "Central event . . .": Daniel P. Moynihan, "The Case for a Family Policy," *America,* September 18, 1966, reprinted in Rainwater and Yancey, *Moynihan Report,* p. 385, and in Daniel P. Moynihan, *Coping* (New York: Random House, 1973), p. 69.

p. 111   With the death of Kennedy: Daniel P. Moynihan, *Maximum Feasible Misunderstanding* (New York: Free Press, Paperback Edition, 1970), p. vi.

p. 111   "The judgment of Kenneth Boulding . . .": Moynihan, *Coping,* p. 179.

p. 111   "First heresies . . .": Moynihan, *Coping,* p. 117.

p. 111   1967 AFDC amendments: ibid., p. 134.

p. 111   Lyndon Johnson: Daniel Patrick Moynihan, "A Memorandum to the President-Elect, January 3, 1969," in Murray Friedman, ed., *Overcoming Middle Class Rage* (Philadelphia: Westminster Press, 1971), p. 188.

p. 112   No less than five profiles: *New York Times Magazine,* July 31, 1966; November 2, 1969; March 31, 1974; December 7, 1975, January 7, 1979.

p. 112   *Time:* July 28, 1967; January 26, 1976.

p. 112   Hamill: Pete Hamill, "What Makes Pat Moynihan Run On?" *Village Voice,* February 16, 1976, p. 20.

p. 112   Crouse: Timothy Crouse, "Ruling Class Hero," *Rolling Stone,* August 12, 1976, pp. 45–46.

p. 114   Closest high-school friend: ibid., p. 46.

p. 114   Rainwater and Yancey: *Moynihan Report,* p. 22.

p. 114   "That lady . . .": Crouse, "Ruling Class Hero," p. 50.

p. 114 Early on: Daniel P. Moynihan, " 'Bosses' and 'Reformers,' " *Commentary,* May 1961, reprinted in *Coping,* p. 65.

p. 115 "Nearly everybody . . .": Crouse, "Ruling Class Hero," p. 46.

p. 115 Banfield: Edward C. Banfield, "The Politics of Pat Moynihan—II," *New Leader,* May 28, 1973, p. 12.

p. 116 Moynihan on Johnson: Daniel P. Moynihan, "The Democrats, Kennedy & the Murder of Dr. King," *Commentary,* May 1968, p. 15; "A Memorandum," in Friedman, *Middle Class Rage,* p. 188.

p. 116 Imagery like that of Nixon memo: Moynihan, *Maximum Feasible Misunderstanding,* pp. 148, 190.

p. 116 *Life* article: Daniel P. Moynihan, "How the President Sees His Second Term," *Life,* September 1, 1972, pp. 26–29.

p. 117 Addendum: Moynihan, *Coping,* p. 50.

p. 119 Wicker's praise: Tom Wicker, "Who Crushed Nixon's Revolution?" *New York Review of Books,* March 22, 1973, p. 9.

p. 121 One of first essays: Moynihan, " 'Bosses' and 'Reformers,' " in *Coping,* pp. 53–68.

p. 121 "Nirvana Now": In Moynihan, *Coping;* quotes from pp. 132–33, 117, 120–22, 128–29, 132, 133.

p. 125 Different in 1975: Daniel P. Moynihan, "Presenting the American Case," *American Scholar,* Autumn 1975, pp. 576–77.

p. 125 ADA plea: Daniel P. Moynihan. "The Politics of Stability," *New Leader,* October 9, 1967, in *Coping,* pp. 185–94.

p. 126 Clear to him in 1968: Moynihan, *Coping,* p. 46.

p. 127 May 1968 article: "Democrats, Kennedy & the Murder of Dr. King."

p. 129 After death of Robert Kennedy: Moynihan, *Maximum Feasible Misunderstanding,* p. vi.

p. 130 Impressed by businessmen: *New York Times Magazine,* November 2, 1968.

p. 130 "Reaction of the liberal left . . .": Daniel P. Moynihan, "The President & the Negro: The Moment Lost," *Commentary,* February 1967, p. 42.

p. 130 Reactions to Moynihan Report: Rainwater and Yancey, *Moynihan Report,* passim.

p. 131 "High technical sophistication . . .": ibid., p. 187.

p. 131 "An inspirational novel . . .": *New York Times Magazine,* July 31, 1966, p. 5.

p. 131 "When the only President . . .": *New York Times Magazine,* November 2, 1969.

p. 132 Assumed Johnson's reelection: Moynihan, *Coping,* p. 187.

p. 132 By May 1968: Moynihan, "Democrats, Kennedy & the Murder of Dr. King," pp. 20, 26, 28.

p. 132 Unflattering terms: ibid., p. 20.

p. 132 Deflecting attention: *New York Times Magazine,* November 2, 1969.

p. 132 Memo to Nixon: In Friedman, *Overcoming Middle Class Rage,* pp. 181–93.

p. 135 Moynihan later protested: "Introduction to the Paperback Edition," *Maximum Feasible Misunderstanding,* p. xi.

p. 135   The impression it made: ibid., p. xxxvi.

p. 135   "No villains . . .": Daniel P. Moynihan, *The Politics of a Guaranteed Income* (New York: Random House, 1973), p. 14.

p. 135   Tyler: Gus Tyler, "The Politics of Pat Moynihan," *New Leader,* April 2, 1973, reprinted in Lewis A. Coser and Irving Howe, eds., *The New Conservatives* (New York: Quadrangle, 1974), pp. 181–82.

p. 135   Wills: Garry Wills, *Nixon Agonistes* (New York: New American Library Signet Book, 1971), p. 474.

p. 136   "British socialism . . .": Daniel P. Moynihan, "The United States in Opposition," *Commentary,* March 1975, p. 34.

p. 137   "The first is the belief . . .": ibid.

p. 137   "Just what does Moynihan mean . . .": Hamill, "What Makes Pat Moynihan Run On?" p. 22.

p. 138   "Outside Agitator theory . . .": ibid.

p. 138   Moynihan on Schumpeter: In *Coping,* pp. 407–08.

p. 139   "This sort of thing happens": Daniel P. Moynihan, "Waging Ideological Conflict," *Center Magazine* 10 (March–April 1976): 8.

p. 139   In the concluding part: Moynihan, *Maximum Feasible Misunderstanding,* p. 168.

p. 140   "Misreads the event": Moynihan, *Politics of a Guaranteed Income,* p. 534.

p. 140   "Curious alliance . . .": ibid., p. 16.

p. 140   "It was now a year . . .": ibid., p. 522.

p. 140   Moynihan previously wrote: ibid., p. 460.

p. 141   Moynihan in 1978, on Nixon's hating: Daniel Patrick Moynihan, *A Dangerous Place,* (Boston: Little, Brown Atlantic Monthly Press, 1978), p. 8.

p. 141   A pre-Watergate essay: Moynihan, *Coping,* p. 314. This originally appeared in *Commentary,* March 1971.

p. 141   Neglect of qualifying data: Rainwater and Yancey, *Moynihan Report,* pp. 180–84.

p. 142   "A huge proportion . . .": Moynihan, "The American Case," p. 516.

p. 142   Moynihan states: *Coping,* p. 415.

p. 142   Daniel Bell: Daniel Bell, ed., *The Radical Right* (Garden City, N.Y.: Doubleday Anchor Book, 1964), pp. 65–66.

p. 142   Essay for Rockefeller: Daniel P. Moynihan, "Social Policy: From the Utilitarian Ethic to the Therapeutic Ethic," in Irving Kristol and Paul H. Weaver, *The Americans, 1976* (Lexington, Mass.: Lexington Books, 1976), pp. 25–50.

p. 142   "On Universal Higher Education": Moynihan, *Coping,* pp. 289–301.

p. 143   Jencks: Originally in *New York Review,* October 14, 1965, quoted in Rainwater and Yancey, *Moynihan Report,* p. 443.

p. 144   The conclusion he reached: [Daniel P. Moynihan], *The Negro Family: The Case for National Action* (Washington, D.C.: Office of Policy Planning and Research, U.S. Department of Labor, 1965), p. 48. Also in Rainwater and Yancey, *Moynihan Report.*

p. 144   Project 100,000: Paul Starr, *The Discarded Army, The Nader Report on Vietnam Veterans and the Veterans Administration* (New York: Charterhouse, 1973), pp. 184–97.

308

THE NEOCONSERVATIVES

p. 145   Rustin: Bayard Rustin, "Why Don't Negroes . . ." *America,* June 4, 1966, reprinted in Rainwater and Yancey, *Moynihan Report;* see pp. 421–26.

p. 145   Even NWRO response made sense: Moynihan, *Politics of a Guaranteed Income,* pp. 334–35.

p. 145   "Lusting after . . .": Nathan Glazer and Daniel P. Moynihan, *Beyond the Melting Pot,* 2nd ed. (Cambridge, Mass.: MIT Press, 1970), p. xvi.

p. 146   "The next . . .": Lyndon B. Johnson, Address at Howard University, June 4, 1964, drafted by Richard N. Goodwin and influenced, to an extent difficult to determine, by Moynihan and his then-unpublished report.

p. 147   "For 56 minutes . . .": Rainwater and Yancey, *Moynihan Report,* pp. 283–84. Italics in the original.

p. 150   "British Revolution": Moynihan, "United States in Opposition," pp. 31–36.

p. 151   Drake: St. Clair Drake, "Moynihan and the Third World," *Nation,* July 5, 1975, pp. 11–12.

p. 152   Indian and Japanese steel: Moynihan, "United States in Opposition," p. 40.

p. 152   Earlier essay: Daniel P. Moynihan, "Was Woodrow Wilson Right?" *Commentary,* May 1974, pp. 25–31.

p. 153   Quotes Strauss: Moynihan, "Waging Ideological Conflict," p. 10.

p. 153   What one historian: N. Gordon Levin, Jr., *Woodrow Wilson and World Politics* (New York: Oxford paperback, 1970), pp. 221–37.

p. 153   "Party of liberty": Moynihan, "Waging Ideological Conflict," p. 10; "United States in Opposition," p. 43; Moynihan campaign advertisement, "Here's Where Pat Moynihan Stands," *New York Times,* September 1, 1976, p. 13; and Daniel P. Moynihan, "America's Crisis of Confidence," *Current,* December 1975, p. 8.

p. 154   "Obscene things": "Here's Where Pat Moynihan Stands."

p. 154   Complicated economic questions: ibid., Moynihan, "United States in Opposition," p. 43, and "America's Crisis of Confidence," p. 8.

p. 154   Exaggerated charges: "Here's Where Pat Moynihan Stands."

p. 154   Process is far advanced: "Crisis of Democracy a Challenge to 'Educated Class,' Says Moynihan," *Harvard Today,* Summer 1976, p. 7.

p. 154   "Utter collapse . . .": Moynihan, "American Case," p. 578.

p. 154   "Patterns of appeasement . . .": Moynihan, "United States in Opposition," p. 43.

p. 155   Foreign doctrine: Moynihan, "American Case," p. 576.

p. 155   Communist and socialist ideas: ibid., pp. 576–77.

p. 155   Capacity to induce guilt: Moynihan, "Waging Ideological Conflict," p. 8.

p. 156   Ullman: Richard H. Ullman, "Washington versus Wilson," *Foreign Policy,* Winter 1975–76, pp. 107–08.

p. 157   Ullman agrees, but: ibid., pp. 120–24.

p. 157   Moynihan's latest elaboration: Daniel Patrick Moynihan, *A Dangerous Place* (Boston: Little, Brown Atlantic Monthly Press Book, 1978).

p. 158   Moynihan once spoke: Moynihan, *Coping,* p. 132.

p. 158   Bread-and-butter issues: Nick Thimmesch, "Pat Moynihan's Surprising

First 100 Days in the Senate," *New York,* April 11, 1977, pp. 41–46; Michael Daly, "The Senator from Benign Neglect," *Village Voice,* October 31, 1977, pp. 11–14.

p. 158   A "zinger": Edward C. Burks, "Moynihan: How He Won His Senate Spurs," *New York Times,* April 5, 1977, p. 35.

p. 158   "Pea-brained dinosaur": Edward C. Burks, "Moynihan's Flamboyance and Quick Wit Draw Attention to Washington Freshman," *New York Times,* November 7, 1977, p. 37.

p. 158   "Plunder": ibid., p. 54.

p. 158   "Sorting out of human beings . . .": ibid. and, earlier, Edward C. Burks, "Moynihan Decries Plan to Assign New York City Teachers by Race," *New York Times,* September 24, 1977.

p. 158   "Little intemperate": Burks, "Moynihan's Flamboyance," p. 54.

p. 159   Moynihan on welfare: Daly, "Senator from Benign Neglect"; Edward C. Burks, "Senate Panel Backs Welfare Fund Rise," *New York Times,* July 29, 1977; *New York Times,* October 3, 1977, p. 11; Edward C. Burks, "New York City in Line for New Relief Aid," *New York Times,* November 2, 1977; and Gordon L. Weil, *The Welfare Debate of 1978* (White Plains, New York: The Institute for Socioeconomic Studies, 1978), passim.

p. 159   "Ritual abuse": "The Wiley Controversy," *New Republic,* January 14, 1978, p. 38.

p. 159   Moynihan-Long bill: Senate Budget Committee, "Analysis of S. 3505, State and Local Welfare Reform and Fiscal Relief Act of 1978," mimeo, September 25, 1978.

p. 159   "Were we wrong. . . !": *National Review,* September 29, 1978, pp. 1196–97.

p. 159   A good deal less conclusive: Henry Aaron, "Statement Before the Subcommittee on Public Assistance of the Senate Finance Committee, November 17, 1978," Department of Health, Education, and Welfare.

p. 159   Kristol: Geoffrey Norman, "The Godfather of Neoconservatism (and His Family)," *Esquire,* February 13, 1979, p. 41.

p. 159   Theoretical arguments: Daniel P. Moynihan, "The Politics of Human Rights," *Commentary,* August 1977, pp. 19–26; "Is There a Crisis of Spirit in the West? A Conversation with Dr. Henry A. Kissinger & Senator Daniel P. Moynihan," *Public Opinion* 1 (May/June 1978), 3–8, 58–59.

p. 160   Kondracke: Morton Kondracke, "The Moynihan Movement," *New Republic,* July 22, 1978, pp. 10–13.

Chapter Seven

p. 161   "Specialize in generalizations": Daniel Bell, "The Return of the Sacred: The Argument on the Future of Religion," *British Journal of Sociology,* December 1977.

p. 161   Major works: Daniel Bell, *The End of Ideology* (New York: Free Press paperback, 1965), originally published 1960; *The Coming of the Post-Industrial Society* (New York: Basic Books, 1973); *The Cultural Contradictions of Capitalism* (New York: Basic Books, 1976).

p. 163   "If the end of ideology has any meaning . . .": Bell, *End of Ideology*, p. 40.

p. 163   "Ideological age has ended": ibid., pp. 402–03.

p. 163   "As a social system . . .": Bell, *Post-Industrial Society*, p. 483.

p. 163   "The social forms . . .": ibid., p. 372 and see following pages.

p. 164   Bell among the leading ten: Charles Kadushin, *The American Intellectual Elite* (Boston: Little, Brown, 1974), p. 30.

p. 164   Overlapping interests: Bell, *Post-Industrial Society*, p. xii.

p. 165   "Designation is meaningless": Bell, *Cultural Contradictions* (New York: Basic Books Harper Colophon Book, 1978), "Foreword: 1978" to the paperback edition, p. xi.

p. 165   "Socialist in economics . . .": ibid.

p. 165   Society's economic policy: ibid., pp. xii–xiii.

p. 165   "Convertible into undue privilege . . .": ibid., p. xiv.

p. 165   Reference to Walzer: ibid., p. 260.

p. 166   "Liberal in politics": ibid., pp. xiv–xv.

p. 166   "Conservative in culture": ibid., p. xv.

p. 166   "They assume . . .": ibid., pp. xi–xii.

p. 167   An advance on both: Bell has contrasted his own position with the Marxist or functionalist ones in many places; these phrases come from *Transaction/Society,* May–June 1974, p. 23.

p. 169   Society as a "web": Bell, *Cultural Contradictions*, pp. 9, 149.

p. 170   Nietzsche, Conrad, and Bell's preferred argument: Bell, *Cultural Contradictions*, pp. 3–7.

p. 170   At one point: Daniel Bell, "The Post-Industrial Society: The Evolution of an Idea," *Survey*, Spring 1971, pp. 165–67.

p. 170   When challenged: "Review Symposium," *Contemporary Sociology*, 3 (March 1974), pp. 102, 108.

p. 171   "Essential questions . . .": Bell, *Post-Industrial Society*, p. 337.

p. 171   "Ethos of science . . .": ibid., p. 386.

p. 171   "Ultimately the differences . . .": ibid., p. 481.

p. 171   "Only when men . . .": ibid., p. 337.

p. 171   The political realm is the arena: ibid., pp. 365–67.

p. 171   "Moral ideas": ibid., p. 433.

p. 171   Culture and dominant behavior and character: Bell, "Foreword: 1978," *Cultural Contradictions*, pp. xvi, xxiv, and passim.

p. 171   "The relationship . . .": ibid., p. 33.

p. 172   "Culture has taken the initiative . . .": ibid., p. xxv.

p. 172   Bell still maintains: ibid., p. xxx; in the 1976 hardbound edition, p. xi.

p. 172   "The primacy of culture . . .": ibid., p. 34.

p. 172   "A blank check . . .": ibid., p. 35.

p. 172   "Lack of a rooted moral belief . . .": Bell, *Post-Industrial Society*, p. 480.

p. 172   "Real problem of *modernity* . . .": Bell, *Cultural Contradictions*, p. 28.

p. 172   Different sort of "new class": Bell, *Post-Industrial Society*, pp. 478–79.

p. 173   "Cultural mass": Bell, *Cultural Contradictions*, p. 20, footnote 21; also p. 34.

p. 173   Burden of inclusion: Daniel Bell, "The End of American Exceptionalism," in Nathan Glazer and Irving Kristol, eds., *The American Commonwealth—1976* (New York: Basic Books, 1976), p. 223; *Post-Industrial Society*, pp. 366–67; the discussion of racial conflict, *Cultural Contradictions*, pp. 183–86.

p. 173   Doubts about "disparate outcomes": Bell, *Cultural Contradictions*, p. 264.

p. 173   "Overload": The term can be found, among other places, in ibid., p. 235.

p. 173   Limits: See the conclusion of Bell, "Foreword: 1978," p. xxix, and *Cultural Contradictions*, pp. 281–82.

p. 174   Return of religion: ibid., p. 29.

p. 174   Arnold's refined notion: Matthew Arnold, *Culture and Anarchy* (Cambridge: Cambridge University Press, 1971), p. 6; Bell, *Cultural Contradictions*, p. 12.

p. 174   Bell on culture: *Cultural Contradictions*, p. 12.

p. 174   Circularity of Bell's interpretation of culture: ibid., p. 137, footnote.

p. 175   One reviewer: Jonathan Rieder, "Review Symposium," *Contemporary Sociology*, 6 (July 1977), 414.

p. 175   Culture is cumulative: Bell, *Cultural Contradictions*, p. 13.

p. 176   Bell on corporation's power: *Post-Industrial Society*, pp. 269–70.

p. 176   Limits of economizing mode: ibid., pp. 279–83.

p. 177   The sociologizing mode: ibid., p. 283.

p. 177   "Inescapable" shift: ibid., p. 289.

p. 177   "No social or economic order . . .": ibid., p. 298.

p. 177   "As a business institution . . .": ibid., p. 296.

p. 178   Multinationals' power: ibid., p. 484–85; Bell, *Cultural Contradictions*, pp. 207–08.

p. 178   Featherstone on Bell: Joseph Featherstone, "A Failure of Political Imagination," *New Republic*, September 15, 1973, pp. 26–27.

p. 179   Bendix on Bell: Reinhard Bendix, "Review Symposium," *Contemporary Sociology*, 3 (March 1974), p. 101.

p. 179   Reference to foreign-policy establishment: Bell, *Cultural Contradictions*, p. 201.

p. 180   *Civitas:* ibid., p. 245.

p. 180   "Public philosophy": ibid., p. 252.

p. 180   Role of "public philosophy": ibid., pp. 256–77.

p. 180   "What gives ideology . . .": Bell, *End of Ideology*, p. 400.

p. 181   "Uncongenial . . .": Bell, *Cultural Contradictions*, p. 252.

p. 181   Lippmann: quoted in ibid., p. 279.

p. 181   "Unfashionable answer . . .": ibid., p. 29.

p. 182   Baum on Bell: Gregory Baum, *The Ecumenist* 14 (May–June 1976).

p. 182   Bell denies: Bell, "Foreword: 1978," p. xxviii.

p. 182   "Religion is not an ideology . . .": Bell, "The Return of the Sacred."

p. 182   "Capitalism that treats nothing as sacred . . .": ibid.

p. 182   Religion itself: Bell, *End of Ideology*, p. 400.

p. 182   Religion's negative function: ibid., p. 401.

p. 183   Religion versus utopia: Bell, *Cultural Contradictions*, p. 167.

p. 183   Baum on demonic: *The Ecumenist,* May–June 1976.

p. 183   Different positions on "return" of religion: Bell, *Cultural Contradictions,* p. 169; and conclusion of "The Return of the Sacred."

p. 184   "Who is God . . .": Bell, *Cultural Contradictions,* p. 169.

p. 185   On extremists: ibid., p. 248.

Chapter Eight

p. 188   Burke: Edmund Burke, *Reflections on the Revolution in France* (Garden City, N.Y.: Doubleday Dolphin Book, 1961), pp. 22, 64, 90.

p. 189   Hofstadter: Richard Hofstadter, *Anti-intellectualism in American Life* (New York: Random House Vintage Book, 1965), p. 38.

p. 190   Origins of "intellectual": See Louis Bodin, *Les Intellectuels* (Paris: Presses Universitaires de France, 1963), pp. 6–7; Joseph Reinach, *Histoire de l'affaire Dreyfus,* vol. 3: *La Crise* (Paris: Librairie Charpentier et Fasquelle, 1903), pp. 245–47; Victor Brombert, *The Intellectual Hero: Studies in the French Novel, 1880–1955* (Philadelphia and New York: J. B. Lippincott, 1961), pp. 23–24 ff.

p. 191   Chomsky, Lasch, Steel: Noam Chomsky, *American Power and the New Mandarins* (New York: Pantheon, 1969); Christopher Lasch, *The Agony of the American Left* (New York: Alfred A. Knopf, 1969), and Christopher Lasch, *The New Radicalism in America: the Intellectual as a Social Type* (New York: Alfred A. Knopf, 1965); Ronald Steel, *Imperialists and Other Heroes* (New York: Random House, 1971), especially pp. 350–55, and various essays in *New York Review of Books.*

p. 191   Transcend ideology: Karl Mannheim: *Ideology and Utopia* (New York: Harcourt, Brace & World Harvest Book, n.d.; original English edition, 1936), pp. 11–12, 155–64.

p. 191   De Tocqueville: Alexis de Tocqueville, *The Old Regime and the French Revolution* (Garden City, N.Y.: Doubleday Anchor Book, 1955), pp. 138–47.

p. 192   Burke: *Reflections,* pp. 124–26.

p. 193   Howe: Irving Howe, "This Age of Conformity," *Partisan Review* 21 (January–February 1954): 7, reprinted in Howe, *Steady Work* (New York: Harcourt, Brace & World Harvest Book, 1966), p. 315.

p. 194   "Scholars" and "intellectuals": Daniel Bell, *The End of Ideology* (New York: Free Press paperback, 1965), p. 402.

p. 194   "Parlous," "pathological" or what?: See *Freedom at Issue,* July–August 1971, p. 4.

p. 195   Brzezinski: Zbigniew Brzezinski, *Between Two Ages* (New York: Viking, 1970), p. 108.

p. 195   Glazer and Moynihan: Nathan Glazer and Daniel P. Moynihan, "Introduction to the Second Edition," *Beyond the Melting Pot* (Cambridge, Mass.: MIT Press, 1970), p. xvi.

p. 195   Kristol and Weaver: Irving Kristol and Paul Weaver, "Who Knows New York?" *Public Interest,* Summer 1969, p. 56.

p. 195   Goodman: Walter Goodman, "The Question of Repression," *Commentary,* August 1970, p. 23.

p. 195   Greeley: Andrew N. Greeley, "Turning Off 'The People,' " *New Republic,* June 27, 1970, p. 16.

p. 195   Labedz: Leopold Labedz, "Students and Revolution," *Survey* (July 1968), pp. 25–26. Quoted in Brzezinski, *Between Two Ages,* p. 99.

p. 195   Berger: Peter L. Berger, *Pyramids of Sacrifice* (Garden City, N.Y.: Doubleday Anchor Book, 1976), pp. 4–5; and "The Socialist Myth," *Public Interest,* Summer 1976, p. 16.

p. 196   "Middle-aged admirers . . .": Brzezinski, *Between Two Ages,* p. 98.

p. 196   "Libidinal emotions": Berger, *Pyramids,* p. 77.

p. 196   Radical professor: Dorothy Rabinowitz, "The Radicalized Professor: A Portrait." *Commentary,* July 1970, pp. 62–64.

p. 196   Feuer: Lewis S. Feuer, *Marx and the Intellectuals* (Garden City, N.Y.: Doubleday Anchor Book, 1969), pp. 58–63.

p. 197   Trilling: Lionel Trilling, "Introduction" to George Orwell, *Homage to Catalonia* (New York: Harcourt, Brace & World Harvest Book, n.d.), pp. xv–xvii.

p. 197   The professor: F. M. Esfandiary, "An End to the Cries of Despair," *New York Times,* July 3, 1971, p. 25.

p. 198   My own study: Peter Steinfels, "French Left-Wing Intellectuals and Foreign Policy: The Ligue des Droits de l'Homme, 1933–1939," unpublished doctoral dissertation (Columbia University, 1976).

p. 198   In one paragraph: James Hitchcock, "The Intellectuals and the People," *Commentary,* March 1973, p. 65.

p. 198   "Most American intellectuals . . .": Peter L. Berger, "The Greening of American Foreign Policy," *Commentary,* March 1976, p. 24.

p. 198   "Within the intellectual milieu . . .": Berger, "The Socialist Myth," p. 4.

p. 198   "Since about 1840 . . .": Daniel P. Moynihan, "A Memorandum to the President-Elect," in Murray Friedman, ed., *Overcoming Middle-Class Rage* (Philadelphia: Westminster Press, 1971), p. 109.

p. 199   Lipset: Seymour Martin Lipset and Richard B. Dobson, "The Intellectual as Critic and Rebel," *Daedalus,* Summer 1972, pp. 138–44. See the commentaries that follow by Jill Conway and Martin E. Malia.

p. 201   Kadushin: Charles Kadushin, *The American Intellectual Elite* (Boston: Little, Brown, 1974).

p. 201   The list: ibid., pp. 30–31.

p. 202   Two assumptions: ibid., pp. 7, 14–15.

p. 202   Mistaken assumption: ibid., pp. 7, 16, 21; and Charles Kadushin, Julie Hoover, and Monique Tichy, "How and Where to Find the Intellectual Elite in the United States," *Public Opinion Quarterly* 35 (Spring 1971): 1–18.

p. 202   One reviewer: Paul Starr, *New York Times Book Review,* September 15, 1974, p. 6.

p. 204   "The American intellectual elite . . .": Kadushin, *Elite,* pp. 27–28.

p. 204   On the war: ibid., pp. 162–75.

p. 204   On problems generally: ibid., pp. 226, 227, 229.

p. 205   "The great surprise . . .": ibid., p. 223.

p. 205   On ideology: ibid., pp. 251, 248, 232, 233.

p. 206   On race: ibid., pp. 268–70, 266, 272, 273.

p. 206   On culture and values: ibid., pp. 226, 228, 276, 278, 279, 282, 285–86.

p. 207   On relations with government: ibid., p. 300 and throughout chapter.

p. 207   Reanalysis of this data: Everett Carll Ladd, Jr., and Seymour Martin Lipset, *The Divided Academy: Professors and Politics* (New York: McGraw-Hill, 1975).

p. 208   Reviewer called attention: Walter P. Metzger, *Science*, January 23, 1976, p. 280.

p. 208   "Intensely ideological character . . .": Ladd and Lipset, *Academy*, p. 46.

p. 208   In 1968: On p. 29 of *The Divided Academy*, Ladd and Lipset mistakenly lump the Wallace vote and presumably radical votes as "4 percent for *left* third-party candidates" (my emphasis). On p. 62, Table 11, they correctly divide the Wallace vote and the left third-party vote, but here Humphrey is given 59 percent and Nixon 37. The figures I have used come from their monograph *Academics, Politics, and the 1972 Election* (Washington, D.C.: American Enterprise Institute, 1973), p. 13, Table 1.

p. 208   1972 Nixon vote: Ladd and Lipset, *1972 Election*, p. 68, Table 7.

p. 208   Busing: Ladd and Lipset, *Academy*, p. 33.

p. 208   Radical student activism: ibid., p. 34.

p. 208   Columbia sit-ins: ibid., p. 35.

p. 209   Professoriat may be even more moderate: ibid., pp. 48–49, Table 7, and text, pp. 47, 50.

p. 209   Self-characterization: ibid., p. 26.

p. 210   Lack of status anxiety: ibid., pp. 83–86.

p. 210   1975 survey: This series ran in *The Chronicle of Higher Education* from September 15, 1975, to May 31, 1976. The items on racial equality and meritocracy appeared March 1, 1976; on banning possibly harmful research, March 15, 1976; on economic and political institutions as well as summary statement, October 20, 1975.

p. 211   Intellectuals share misperception: Kadushin, *Elite*, pp. 191–92.

p. 212   Not "originators . . .": ibid., p. 353.

p. 212   In the past: A common theme of Kristol as well as Hitchcock, "The Intellectuals and the People," esp. p. 69.

Chapter Nine

p. 214   Glazer: Nathan Glazer, "The Limits of Social Policy," *Commentary*, September 1971, p. 52.

p. 214   Diamond: Martin Diamond, "The Declaration and the Constitution: Liberty, Democracy, and the Founders," in Nathan Glazer and Irving Kristol, eds., *The American Commonwealth—1976* (New York: Basic Books, 1976), p. 55.

p. 214   Moynihan: Daniel P. Moynihan, "Presenting the American Case," *American Scholar* 44 (Autumn 1975): 572, 577–78.

p. 214   Wildavsky: Aaron Wildavsky, "Government and the People," *Commentary*, August 1973, p. 32.

p. 214   Kristol: Irving Kristol, "Thoughts on Equality and Egalitarianism," in Colin D. Campbell, *Income Redistribution* (Washington, D.C.: American Enterprise Institute, 1977), pp. 41–42.

p. 215   Bell: Daniel Bell, *The Coming of the Post-Industrial Society* (New York: Basic Books, 1973), p. 453. Originally in "On Meritocracy and Equality," *Public Interest*, Fall 1972, p. 65.

p. 215   Nisbet: Robert Nisbet, "Where Do We Go from Here?" in Campbell, *Income Redistribution*, p. 182, and "The New Despotism," *Commentary*, July 1975, p. 32.

p. 215   Podhoretz: Norman Podhoretz, "The Intellectuals and the Pursuit of Happiness," *Commentary*, February 1973, p. 7.

p. 216   "Liberty and Equality . . .": [Daniel P. Moynihan], *The Negro Family: The Case for National Action* (Washington, D.C.: Office of Planning and Research, United States Department of Labor, 1965), pp. 2–3. The quotation about the priority of equality in Western thought comes from Robert Harris, *The Quest for Equality* (Baton Rouge: Louisiana State University Press, 1960), p. 4. The phrase about Lincoln is not identified.

p. 217   Howard University speech: Quoted in Lee Rainwater and William L. Yancey, *The Moynihan Report and the Politics of Controversy* (Cambridge, Mass.: MIT Press, 1967), p. 24.

p. 218   "Assault on equality": The subject of an entire issue of *Social Policy*, May–June 1972.

p. 219   Glazer on Great Society: Nathan Glazer, "Nixon, the Great Society, and the Future of Social Policy: A Symposium," *Commentary*, May 1973, pp. 34–35.

p. 219   Kristol: Irving Kristol, "What Is a Neo-conservative?" *Newsweek*, January 19, 1976, p. 87.

p. 219   Podhoretz: Norman Podhoretz, *Commentary*, November 1972, p. 38; see preceding correspondence and Podhoretz's column, *Commentary*, July 1972.

p. 219   Moynihan: Daniel P. Moynihan, *The Politics of a Guaranteed Annual Income* (New York: Random House, 1973), p. 53.

p. 220   Harrington: Michael Harrington, "The Welfare State and Its Neoconservative Critics," in Lewis A. Coser and Irving Howe, *The New Conservatives* (New York: Quadrangle, 1974).

p. 221   A model expression: Wildavsky, "Government and the People," passim.

p. 222   Harry Hopkins: Quoted in Godfrey Hodgson, *America in Our Time* (Garden City, N.Y.: Doubleday, 1976), p. 49.

p. 223   Marx on lumpenproletariat: Karl Marx, *Capital* (New York: Modern Library, n.d.), vol. 1, pp. 706–07; *The Class Struggles in France 1848–1850* (New York: International Publishers, 1964), p. 50.

p. 223   Levitan and Taggart: Sar A. Levitan and Robert Taggart, *The Promise of Greatness* (Cambridge, Mass.: Harvard University Press, 1976), pp. vii, viii, 4–9.

p. 224   Ginzberg and Solow: Eli Ginzberg and Robert M. Solow, "An Introduction to This Special Issue" and "Some Lessons of the 1960's," *Public Interest*, Winter 1974, pp. 8, 212.

316   THE NEOCONSERVATIVES

p. 224 "Fairly construed . . .": Wildavsky, "Government and the People," p. 28.

p. 225 Glazer's differing views: Nathan Glazer, *Affirmative Discrimination: Ethnic Inequality and Public Policy* (New York: Basic Books, 1975), pp. 73, 220–21.

p. 225 Comparison to Nuremberg statutes: *New York Times*, September 24, 1977, p. 9.

p. 226 Civil rights spokesman: *New York Times*, June 18, 1977, pp. 1, 3.

p. 227 "Strategic naiveté": Daniel C. Maguire, "Quotas: Unequal but Fair," *Commonweal*, October 14, 1977, p. 648.

p. 228 Glazer on EEOC: *Affirmative Discrimination*, p. 38; editorial, "The Equal Employment Mess," *New York Times*, February 12, 1977, p. 20.

p. 231 Bell: Daniel Bell, *The End of Ideology* (New York: Free Press paperback, 1965), pp. 28–30.

p. 231 "Liberty party" versus "equality party": Daniel P. Moynihan, "The United States in Opposition," *Commentary*, March 1975, p. 44.

p. 231 "The contrast . . .": Daniel Bell, *The Cultural Contradictions of Capitalism* (New York: Basic Books, 1976), p. 260.

p. 233 Students reject "professionalism": Paul Goodman, *New Reformation: Notes of a Neolithic Conservative* (New York: Random House Vintage Book, 1971), p. 47.

p. 233 Resentment against authority: Daniel Bell, *Post-Industrial Society*, p. 453; originally in "On Meritocracy and Equality," p. 65.

p. 233 Allows and encourages: Podhoretz, "The Intellectuals," p. 7.

p. 234 Very few advocates . . .: For example, Herbert J. Gans, *More Equality* (New York: Random House Vintage Book, 1974), pp. xi–xii, Ch. 3 and 8.

p. 234 Tawney: R. H. Tawney, *Equality* (New York: Capricorn Books, 1962; originally published in 1931, revised edition, 1951), pp. 106, 108–09.

p. 234 Neoconservatives' apparent satisfaction: Lewis A. Coser, "Introduction," Coser and Howe, *New Conservatives*, p. 5.

p. 235 Almost willful misreading: Robert Nisbet, *Public Interest*, Spring 1974, pp. 103–20.

p. 235 Kristol on Rawls: *Wall Street Journal,* December 10, 1975.

p. 235 Wildavsky and Lipset: Wildavsky, "Government and the People," p. 32; Lipset in *Chronicle of Higher Education*, March 1, 1976, p. 12.

p. 235 Frankel: Charles Frankel, "The New Egalitarianism and the Old," *Commentary*, September 1973, pp. 60–61.

p. 236 Jencks: Christopher Jencks et al., *Inequality* (New York: Basic Books, 1972), pp. 213–28.

p. 236 "Contingencies . . . accidents . . .": John Rawls, *A Theory of Justice* (Cambridge, Mass.: Harvard University Press, 1971), p. 15.

p. 237 "While the liberal conception . . .": ibid., pp. 73–74.

p. 237 "The assertion . . .": ibid., p. 104.

p. 237 "Fundamental premise": Frankel, "New Egalitarianism," p. 58.

p. 237 Frankel's concern: ibid., p. 59.

p. 238 Frankel indirectly suggests: ibid.

p. 238   Bell cites: "On Meritocracy," p. 57; *Post-Industrial Society,* p. 443.

p. 238   "This is the principle . . .": Rawls, *A Theory of Justice,* pp. 100–01.

p. 239   Rawls's following paragraph: ibid., p. 101.

p. 239   "An agreement to regard . . .": ibid.

p. 239   A very similar position: Bell, "On Meritocracy," p. 66; *Post-Industrial Society,* p. 454.

p. 240   Kristol had argued: "On Equality," *Commentary,* November 1972, p. 46; *Two Cheers for Capitalism* (New York: Basic Books, 1978), p. 185.

p. 240   Walzer: Michael Walzer, "In Defense of Equality," in Coser and Howe, *The New Conservatives,* pp. 108, 109–10, 117.

p. 241   Bell: *Cultural Contradictions,* p. 268; "On Meritocracy," p. 67, and *Post-Industrial Society,* p. 454.

p. 241   Central to the "democratic surge": Michael J. Crozier, Samuel P. Huntington, and Joji Watanuki, *The Crisis of Democracy* (New York: New York University Press, 1975), p. 62.

p. 242   Wildavsky: "Government and the People," p. 32.

p. 242   "Too much guilt . . .": ibid.

p. 242   Moynihan: "Crisis of Democracy a Challenge to 'Educated Class,' Says Moynihan," *Harvard Today,* Summer 1976, p. 7.

p. 242   Guilt toward poverty abroad groundless: P. T. Bauer, "Western Guilt & Third World Poverty," *Commentary,* January 1976, pp. 31, 38.

p. 242   Moss: Robert Moss, " 'Let's Look Out for No. 1!' " *New York Times Magazine,* May 1, 1977, p. 31.

p. 243   Moynihan, Marxism, and guilt: Daniel P. Moynihan, "Waging Ideological Conflict," *Center Magazine* 9 (March–April 1976): 8; also "The United States in Opposition," *Commentary,* March 1975, and "Presenting the American Case," *American Scholar* 44 (Autumn 1975).

p. 243   Equality is surrogate issue: Frankel, "The New Egalitarianism and the Old," p. 59; Kristol, "About Equality," p. 47, and "Taxes, Poverty, and Equality," *Public Interest,* Fall 1974, p. 28, in *Two Cheers for Capitalism,* pp. 186–87, 224; Nisbet in Campbell, *Income Redistribution,* passim.

p. 243   Equality is relentless . . .: Glazer, "The Limits of Social Policy," p. 53.

p. 243   Bell: "On Meritocracy and Equality," p. 64, in *Post-Industrial Society,* p. 451.

p. 243   Nisbet: in Campbell, *Income Redistribution,* p. 182. Code words: ibid., pp. 182, 189.

p. 244   "I have no objection . . .": ibid., p. 223.

p. 244   "We have abolished poverty . . .": Kristol, in Campbell, *Income Redistribution,* pp. 36–37.

p. 246   Mill on de Tocqueville: John Stuart Mill, Gertrude Himmelfarb, ed., in *Essays on Politics and Culture* (Garden City, N.Y.: Doubleday Anchor Book, 1963), pp. 257, 262. Originally published in *Edinburgh Review,* 1840.

Chapter Ten

p. 248   Democracy under attack: Daniel P. Moynihan, "America's Crisis of Confidence," *Current,* December 1975, p. 5, reprinted from *New Leader,* October 27, 1975, pp. 10–13.

p. 248   Decline of unquestioned authority: Daniel P. Moynihan, "Waging Ideological Conflict," *Center Magazine* 9 (March–April 1976): 8.

p. 248   Bell: Daniel Bell, "Creating a Genuine National Society," *Current,* September 1976, pp. 18–19, reprinted from *U.S. News & World Report,* July 5, 1976.

p. 249   Fairlie: Henry Fairlie, *The Spoiled Child of the Western World* (Garden City, N.Y.: Doubleday, 1976), p. 274.

p. 249   "Men such as Kristol . . .": ibid., pp. 274–75.

p. 249   "An excess of democracy . . .": Michael Crozier, Samuel P. Huntington, and Joji Watanuki, *The Crisis of Democracy* (New York: New York University Press, 1975), p. 113.

p. 250   Madison on "republic": *The Federalist,* No. 39.

p. 251   Moynihan on reform: Daniel P. Moynihan, "The Professionalization of Reform," *Public Interest,* Fall 1965, pp. 6–16.

p. 253   Three years later: Daniel P. Moynihan, *Maximum Feasible Misunderstanding* (New York: Free Press Paperback, 1970), pp. 21–37.

p. 253   Moynihan's "recantation": Daniel P. Moynihan, *Coping* (New York: Random House, 1973), pp. 260–61.

p. 254   Black leaders had no part: Lee Rainwater and William L. Yancey, *The Moynihan Report and the Politics of Controversy* (Cambridge, Mass.: MIT Press, 1967), pp. 16, 33–34, and passim.

p. 254   "Planned by whites for blacks": Daniel P. Moynihan, *The Politics of a Guaranteed Income* (New York: Random House, 1973), p. 167.

p. 254   "Quintessential example . . .": ibid., p. 238.

p. 255   "There was no evidence . . .": ibid., p. 549.

p. 255   Is not consistent: ibid., pp. 111, 328.

p. 255   Gans: Reprinted in Rainwater and Yancey, *The Moynihan Report,* p. 449.

p. 255   According to Moynihan: *Guaranteed Income,* pp. 216–17.

p. 256   "It seemed fair . . .": ibid., p. 220.

p. 256   Nathan: Richard P. Nathan, "Workfare/Welfare," *New Republic,* February 24, 1973, p. 19.

p. 256   Moynihan daintily terms: *Guaranteed Income,* p. 220.

p. 256   Sponsors caught unprepared: ibid., pp. 457–81.

p. 256   No evidence for FAP: ibid., p. 548.

p. 257   "This was in part . . .": ibid., p. 458.

p. 258   "One way to look at American democracy . . .": Moynihan, *Coping,* p. 268.

p. 258   Forrester's dictum: Moynihan, *Guaranteed Income,* p. 239.

p. 259   Coleman's data: Moynihan, *Coping,* p. 266.

p. 259   Social science beyond lay comprehension: ibid.

p. 259   Elites and destructive forces: ibid., p. 269.

p. 259   "Keep the process of competition . . .": ibid.

p. 259   Guidelines: ibid., pp. 266–67, 270–71; also Daniel P. Moynihan, "Social Science—the Public Disenchantment: A Symposium," *American Scholar* 45 (Autumn 1976): 347–48.

p. 260   Moynihan concluded: *Coping,* p. 267.

p. 260   Kristol on "new men": Irving Kristol, "The Troublesome Intellectuals," *Public Interest,* Winter 1966, pp. 5–6.

p. 261   Educating the "new class": Irving Kristol, "On Corporate Philanthropy," *Wall Street Journal,* March 21, 1977, reprinted in Irving Kristol, *Two Cheers for Capitalism* (New York: Basic Books, 1978), pp. 141–45.

p. 261   Previously Kristol had accused: Irving Kristol, "Business and the 'New Class,' " *Wall Street Journal,* May 19, 1975, reprinted in *Two Cheers,* pp. 25–31.

p. 262   Huntington straightforwardly disagrees: Crozier, Huntington, and Watanuki, *Crisis of Democracy,* p. 113.

p. 263   Presidents and establishments: ibid., pp. 96–97.

p. 264   Most straightforward explanation: ibid., p. 107.

p. 265   Thankfully clear: ibid., pp. 8, 161.

p. 265   "Far-from-perfect fit . . .": ibid., p. 107.

p. 266   Voting "which had increased . . .": ibid., p. 60.

p. 266   Polarization did not correspond: ibid., pp. 76–77.

p. 266   Verba and Nie: Quoted in ibid., p. 112.

p. 266   Favor state and local power: ibid., p. 101.

p. 267   "A general challenge . . .": ibid., p. 75.

p. 267   "Democratic, liberal, and egalitarian values": ibid., p. 112.

p. 267   "Democracy . . . starts to work": Alan Wolfe, *The Limits of Legitimacy* (New York: Free Press, 1977), p. 328.

p. 267   Apathy welcomed: ibid., p. 114.

p. 267   Government's ability to "impose" decisions: ibid., pp. 104–05.

p. 267   Limits on democratic authority: ibid., pp. 113–14.

p. 268   "Imposition of 'hard' decisions . . .": ibid., p. 104.

p. 268   "Claims of expertise . . .": ibid., p. 113.

p. 268   Members themselves disturbed: ibid., pp. 196–97.

p. 269   Dahrendorf: ibid., p. 194.

p. 269   *"Dirigiste"* ambitions: Elie Kedourie, "Is Democracy Doomed?" *Commentary,* November 1976, p. 42.

p. 269   Brzezinski in 1965: in "Toward the Year 2000: Work in Progress," *Daedalus* 96 (Summer 1967): 670, 686–87.

p. 270   Most effective and imaginative government: ibid., p. 689.

p. 270   Kedourie's definition of democracy: "Is Democracy Doomed?" pp. 41, 42.

p. 271   "All the world knows . . .": ibid., p. 41.

Chapter Eleven

p. 273   Kristol: Irving Kristol, "What Is a Neo-conservative?" *Newsweek,* January 19, 1976, p. 87.

p. 274   Decter: Midge Decter, "What Is a Liberal—Who Is a Conservative?" *Commentary,* September 1976, pp. 50–51.

p. 274   Hodgson: Godfrey Hodgson, *America in Our Time* (Garden City, N.Y.: Doubleday, 1976), pp. 73, 89–90.

p. 275   A long attack: Dennis Wrong, "The Case of *The New York Review,*" *Commentary,* November 1970.

p. 276   Midge Decter derides: in Philip Nobile, *Intellectual Skywriting* (New York: Charterhouse, 1974), p. 142.

p. 277   Coser: Lewis A. Coser, "Introduction," in Lewis A. Coser and Irving Howe, eds., *The New Conservatives* (New York: Quadrangle, 1974), pp. 4–5.

p. 277   Criticizes Kristol's "reductionism": ibid., p. 5.

p. 277   Silver: Isidore Silver, "What Flows from Neoconservatism," *Nation,* July 9, 1977, pp. 49–50.

p. 279   "Permanent brain trust": Irving Kristol, *On the Democratic Idea in America* (New York: Harper & Row Torchbook, 1973), p. 35.

p. 279   Moynihan: Daniel P. Moynihan, "The Professionalization of Reform," *Public Interest,* Fall 1965, p. 9.

p. 280   Podhoretz: Norman Podhoretz, *Making It* (New York: Random House, 1967), pp. 315–16.

p. 280   Others, less friendly: Maurice R. Berube and Marilyn Gittell, "In Whose Interest Is 'The Public Interest'?" *Social Policy,* May–June 1970, pp. 5–6.

p. 280   "Story of a new power-system . . .": Theodore H. White, "The Action Intellectuals," *Life,* June 9, 1967, p. 44. This series ran in the issues of June 9, June 16, and June 23, 1967.

p. 281   "Man must find his way . . .": ibid., June 9, pp. 57–58.

p. 281   "Americans have left behind . . .": ibid., June 23, p. 77.

p. 281   "Classic—or pure—intellectual": ibid., June 9, p. 57.

p. 281   Wisdom and social scientists: ibid., June 23.

p. 282   Kristol: *On the Democratic Idea,* p. 84.

p. 282   Military metaphors: White, "The Action Intellectuals," June 9, pp. 57, 70.

p. 283   Kristol: Irving Kristol, "The Troublesome Intellectuals," *Public Interest,* Winter 1966, pp. 5–6.

p. 284   Nisbet: Robert A. Nisbet, *The Sociological Tradition* (New York: Basic Books, 1966), pp. 32–33 and passim.

p. 284   "Sociology of the intellectual": ibid., p. 118.

p. 284   Heilbroner: Robert L. Heilbroner, *New York Review of Books,* September 26, 1968, p. 53.

p. 284   Comte: Quoted in Nisbet, *Sociological Tradition,* pp. 118–19.

p. 285   Moynihan: Daniel P. Moynihan, *Coping* (New York: Random House, 1973), p. 269.

p. 285   "From ideology towards sociology": Seymour Martin Lipset, *Political Man* (Garden City, N.Y.: Doubleday Anchor Book, 1963), p. 453.

p. 286   Moynihan as "Reformer": Wilson Carey McWilliams, *New York Times Book Review*, January 27, 1974, pp. 3–4.

p. 289   Kristol: Irving Kristol, *Two Cheers for Capitalism* (New York: Basic Books, 1978), p. 37.

p. 290   Integrating "new class" into system: ibid., p. 30.

p. 290   Lipset: *Political Man*, pp. 454–55.

p. 291   "Not doctrinaire socialists": Kristol, *Two Cheers*, p. 30.

Index

328

About the Author

Peter Steinfels is Executive Editor of *Commonweal.* Born in Chicago in 1941, he graduated from Loyola University and received a Ph.D. in European history from Columbia. Before returning to *Commonweal,* where he was on the editorial staff in the 1960s, he was Associate for the Humanities at the Institute of Society, Ethics and the Life Sciences and, with Margaret O'Brien Steinfels, edited *The Hastings Center Report,* a bimonthly journal dealing with ethical issues in science and medicine. He has contributed to several books, is co-editor of *Death Inside Out,* a collection of philosophical and historical essays on dying, and has written articles and reviews for *Dissent, The New Republic, The Nation,* the *New York Times Book Review, New American Review,* and numerous other journals.

About the Author

279 - Best expl. for idiocracy — its idealism)
       policy intellectuals — these recaps
       victim lives — actually "new class)
       intellects — cotes to keep etiquette)
       guilty attack privileges (develops us)

It is a war waged for the 'new class' & won it t
stakes you — libel prem endeavor
new class vulnerable, jitters, feel guardian) legitimes serious
                                              (287)

92 - Desire plausible advertising —